GUIDE TO REFERENCE IN BUSINESS AND ECONOMICS

STEVEN W. SOWARDS and
ELISABETH LEONARD, Editors

AN IMPRINT OF THE
AMERICAN LIBRARY ASSOCIATION
CHICAGO • 2014

Printed in the United States of America

18 17 16 15 14   5 4 3 2 1

Extensive effort has gone into ensuring the reliability of the information in this book; however, the publisher makes no warranty, express or implied, with respect to the material contained herein.

ISBNs: 978-0-8389-1234-8 (paper); 978-0-8389-9634-8 (PDF); 978-0-8389-9635-5 (ePub); 978-0-8389-9636-2 (Kindle). For more information on digital formats, visit the ALA Store at alastore.ala.org and select eEditions.

Library of Congress Cataloging-in-Publication Data
Guide to reference in business and economics / Steven W. Sowards and Elisabeth Leonard, editors.
    pages   cm
   Includes bibliographical references and index.
   1. Business—Bibliography. 2. Business—Reference books—Bibliography. 3. Business—Computer network resources. 4. Economics—Bibliography. 5. Economics—Reference books—Bibliography. 6. Economics—Computer network resources. 7. Business libraries. 8. Economics libraries. I. Sowards, Steven W. II. Leonard, Elisabeth.
   Z7164.C81G85 2014
   [HF1008]
   016.33—dc23   2014022113

Cover design by Alejandra Diaz. Image © everything possible / Shutterstock, Inc.

Text design in the Berkeley and Helvetica typefaces. Composition by Scribe Inc.

♾ This paper meets the requirements of ANSI/NISO Z39.48-1992 (Permanence of Paper).

GUIDE TO REFERENCE IN BUSINESS AND ECONOMICS

CONTENTS

CONTRIBUTORS

Elisabeth Leonard, formerly Associate Dean of Library Services at Western Carolina University, served as the primary Contributor for the Economics and Business section of the online *Guide* from 2006 to 2012. This 2014 edition builds on her extensive work in selection, organization, explanation, and writing, which supported the 2008 launch of the online *Guide*.

Steven W. Sowards, Associate Director for Collections at the Michigan State University Libraries and the *Guide*'s Division Editor for the Social Sciences since 2005, reviewed and updated entries for this print format edition.

INTRODUCTION

This volume is a tool for librarians and library staff who are selecting economics and business titles for library collections, or answering business questions at the reference desk; LIS students learning about core tools in these areas; and library users seeking the best resources. The potential audience among library users includes not only students and academic researchers, but also professional and business persons, and individuals educating themselves about investments, mortgages, or the functioning of a global 21st-century economy.

The content is based on the Economics and Business portion of ALA's online *Guide to Reference* (www.guidetoreference.org), a database that descends from volumes in the long-running series *Guide to Reference* books edited in turn by Alice Kroeger, Isadore Mudge, Constance Winchell, Eugene Sheehy, and Robert Balay, beginning in 1902 and concluding in a print format with the 11th edition of 1996. The online version became available in 2008 under the direction of Robert Kieft. The move to an online *Guide* reflected the transformation of reference services because of the World Wide Web and digital publishing. A database format offers the potential for continuous editing and revision of the *Guide*, by recording changes in URLs for online tools, publisher acquisition of titles or imprints, and the release of updated editions of older titles, as well as addition of new works. The database format also makes it possible to publish segments in print or e-book format, and to incorporate user participation through online feedback.

The *Guide to Reference* is selective: the Business and Economics section presents more than 800 individual entries, chosen for potential value. Entries offer summary bibliographic information, a descriptive annotation, an ISBN for printed works, and a URL pointing directly to online content if possible, or if not, leading to the publisher's website. In the table of contents, entries are grouped under major headings, such as "General works" or "Company information." Each section includes more specific categories: some such as "Dictionaries" or "Internet resources" reflect format, while others such as "Motor vehicles" or "Biotechnology" reflect economic or industrial sectors. Titles may be assigned to more than one section; in such cases, the entry is repeated in full to allow easy browsing and comparison to other resources, without the trouble of following cross-references. Examples include *International historical statistics: Africa, Asia & Oceania, 1750–2005* with statistics from multiple geographic regions, and the *Hoovers* online site or *IBISWorld United States* with reports covering multiple companies and industry sectors. An index of titles supports known-item searching, and includes titles and alternative titles noted in the annotations.

Much has happened in business reference publishing since 2008. First, the trend toward online access accelerated: materials budget expenditures in libraries serving graduate business schools, in particular, now are weighted heavily toward online tools that offer 24/7 remote access, multiple simultaneous users, and interactive features. Second, the growth of websites and other digital tools made a number of publications obsolete, especially traditional directories and bibliographies. Third, the financial crisis of 2008 and the resulting recession put a number of publications out of business as budgets and sales contracted. Some well-known resources ceased, including government publications. For example, the *Statistical Abstract of the United States* was the victim of congressional budget-cutting, only to be revived by a publisher. Entries remain in the *Guide* for many ceased titles: long back-runs with potentially useful information are still found on library shelves, and it may be helpful for selectors and acquisitions staff to realize that no future editions will appear for some well-known titles, such as the *Rand McNally Commercial Atlas and Marketing Guide*.

Volatility in publishing makes it hard to stay current with business reference resources. Publishers buy and sell publications, sometimes change product names, or may publish unlike content under similar titles. Annotations in the *Guide* may record both old and new names, so that a search in the index under either title will lead to the current entry. An example is *Passport GMID*, still recognized by many librarians under its earlier name as *Euromonitor*. URLs often change because of sale of a product to another publisher or reorganization of server addresses. URLs were checked during preparation of this volume, but further changes are inevitable: in most cases, searching in the online *Guide to Reference* or on the Web by product title and publisher name will lead to a current URL.

This updated *Guide* offers expanded coverage for topics of recent interest. New or enriched content covers the financial crisis of 2008 and the resulting recession, unions and human resources, real estate and mortgages, consumer information, Islamic economics, entrepreneurship, and trade with the three largest trading partners of the United States (Canada, China, and Mexico).

The reference tools for business and economics are extensive and complex. In addition to the usual array of publication types—dictionaries, indexes, statistical compilations, and others—this literature reflects geographical regions (such as North America or Asia), functional activities that take place in all businesses (such as human resources or accounting), and specialized information tools that serve specific industry sectors (such as transportation or retail). These factors are recognized in the design of chapters and sections. A few comments may help readers anticipate the kind of information to be found in various parts of the *Guide*.

"Dictionaries," "Encyclopedias," and "Guides and handbooks" are related tools, but publications are assigned in this *Guide* along the following lines. Dictionaries offer concise definitions of key words, terms, and phrases, extending at times to brief identification of organizations, places, or individuals. Encyclopedias provide a summary of knowledge at greater depth and with more detail, surveying what is known about a larger or smaller subject area. Guides and handbooks offer advice to readers, either about methodology and techniques employed to investigate a topic, or to indicate the current state of research findings and cutting-edge lines of scholarly investigation and publication. For more about these kinds of tools in the social sciences including economics, see the lively article by Alan Sica on "Encyclopedias, Handbooks, and Dictionaries" in the *International Encyclopedia of the Social and Behavioral Sciences* 7 (2001): 4497–4504.

Entries for "Organizations and associations" are most often the homepages of nonprofits, trade associations, and other advocacy groups, or in some cases government agencies. The ease of publishing on the World Wide Web allows sharing of position papers, policy statements, membership directories, and statistical reports. Prior to the Web, it was not easy for groups to publish and disseminate these publications, or for libraries to collect them: at best, scattered works might have been available as ephemera in vertical files at a few libraries. Now, these texts are simple to locate and use. Issue-oriented content may be partisan and intended to influence the public, the press, and the government, but is helpful to document policy debates, while readers are no longer confined to the secondary literature. This wide-open online market for ideas can be confusing, but also can put at our fingertips the perspectives of underrepresented groups. Some content on these websites typically is available to all viewers, but other content will be limited to organization members or paying subscribers. Even if libraries do not offer access to the full content, library visitors can be made aware of options to pursue at their own discretion.

Access to "Statistics" sources has notably improved in the online environment. Numerical content from both commercial vendors and government agencies benefits from digital publication of time series and spreadsheets, often available at no cost and with sophisticated capabilities to download and manipulate files. The migration of government publications to Web versions puts much more information in view, often in the form of statistics or statistic-laden reports.

Directories

The ability to look up current contact information on the Web has eliminated the market for some directories, but a select group of enhanced directories remains. These survivors include works in both print and online formats that dig deep into companies and organizations to offer extended lists of executives, members or officers; others that gather together related listings for comparative purposes (for example, lists of all banks serving a particular city); and others that allow interactive searching. To some extent, these tools overlap with marketing databases. Complete content or advanced features may be limited to paying subscribers.

Periodicals

No attempt is made to identify all potentially useful periodicals: indexing services will point to relevant contents. Selected core magazines and journals are noted as sources for book reviews, news reports, and articles about trends—current or historical: an example is the *Economist* weekly. Other kinds of serials such as annuals generally are not noted here as periodicals, but instead assigned to categories on the basis of function such as providing statistics. Also listed here are major aggregators, from which many libraries receive full text of business and trade magazines.

Most newly published reference works and a growing portion of the backlist from major U.S. publishers now are available in both print and digital formats. The *Guide* makes an effort to note when works are "available as e-books" or "available in online format" without trying to specify the source. Access may be direct from the publisher, or through various aggregators or platforms such as ebrary, EBL, or EBSCO. In this *Guide*, the descriptive and bibliographic information for books tends to reflect the print format version. Given the trend to digital publishing, it may make more sense in some future edition of the *Guide* to note instead older works that are *not* yet available as e-books.

Given that so many resources are available in digital format, what does the *Guide* mean by an "Internet resource?" While there are exceptions, most entries with this classification are born-digital Web sites that have no print counterpart. Some provide interactive capabilities that go beyond any print tool, such as statistical or bibliographic databases that can be searched or sorted, and perhaps exported or downloaded. Other Internet resources are portals that gather together extensive sets of links to other websites.

This *Guide* makes no systematic attempt to indicate which sources are free and which require payments or membership fees, and no attempt at all to indicate prices, which change over time and may vary as a function of library size. Obviously, traditional print format works exist under a purchase model, as do nearly all subscription journals and many databases. If a library does not subscribe to or own certain content, library staff can assist users to identify other libraries where the information may be available. It is worth noting that nearly all publications and websites of the U.S. government are free of copyright and openly available to all users. An increasing number of international documents are also free on the Web, including statistical databases and recent years of major reports that appear as printable PDFs. Examples include the United Nations source *UNdata*, and *Africa Development Indicators* from the World Bank.

This volume does not advise readers about techniques and strategies for choosing among resources, either to answer reference questions, or to work up analyses of business cases or reports for company research. For that kind of guidance, readers can turn to the many available guides, ranging from classic works such as *Business Information Sources* by Lorna Daniells (University of California Press, 1993) to newer publications that address the impact of the Internet, digital publishing, and social media, such as *Making Sense of Business Reference* by Celia Ross (American Library Association, 2013). Works of this kind are collected as "Advice for librarians" in the chapter on General Works.

Acknowledgments: For this print format snapshot, all records in the Economics and Business section of the online *Guide to Reference* were reviewed and updated if appropriate during late 2013 and early 2014. More than one hundred new entries have been added since the 2011 publication of an earlier print version, the *ALA Guide to Economics & Business Reference*. The *Guide* has always been a cumulative effort, beginning with the first edition in 1902, continuing to the 11th print format edition in 1996, and migrating to the 2008 online version edited by Robert Kieft. In addition to Elisabeth Leonard, I wish to acknowledge contributors to the economics and business sections of earlier print editions: Ben C. Driver, Frank Gibson, Diane K. Goon, Rita W. Moss, and Bessie M. Carrington. For this 2014 print edition, I also am indebted to Erica Coe (University of Washington–Tacoma), Breezy Silver (Michigan State University), Laura Leavitt (Michigan State University), and Celia Ross (University of Michigan–Ann Arbor) for advice and suggestions. Denise Beaubien Bennett (University of Florida) as General Editor and James Hennelly as Managing Editor at ALA Digital Reference have kept the project on course and on time. At the same time, responsibility for errors and omissions remains mine alone.

Steven W. Sowards
Division Editor for Economics and Business, *Guide to Reference*

General Works

Advice for Librarians

1   Academic business library directors.
http://www.abld.org/. ABLD. Stanford,
Calif.: ABLD. 1987–

Home page of ABLD, an organization made up of the
directors of the fifty largest academic business libraries in the U.S. and Canada. Contact information
for the major business libraries, bylaws, record of
annual conference sites and dates. Links to an online
guide to rankings of business schools, maintained by
librarians at Wake Forest University.

**2   The basic business library: core
resources and services. 5th ed.** Eric J.
Forte, Michael R. Oppenheim. Santa
Barbara, Calif.: Libraries Unlimited, 2012.
xi, 227 p. ISBN 9781598846119
016.0276/9   Z675.B8

Reference resources are presented in the context of
essays on topics such as core collections, investment
sources, start-ups, government information, and
marketing research. Tips and advice for working with
library users. Updated since the 4th edition of 2002,
to reflect the growing importance of online tools in
the last decade.

**3   Best of the best business websites
(free resources): Reference and
User Services Association (RUSA).**
http://www.ala.org/rusa/sections/
brass/brassprotools/bestofthebestbus/
bestbestbusiness. ALA Business Reference
and Services Section (BRASS). Chicago:
American Library Association. 2000–
016   Z675

Portal with links to free websites in the areas of
accounting and taxation, advertising and marketing,
American corporations, banking, business ethics,
economics, electronic commerce, financial markets
and investments, general management, hospitality,
human resource management and labor relations,
insurance, international business, MIS and knowledge management, real estate, and small business.
Displayed on a LibGuides platform, and maintained
by librarian volunteers.

4   BEOnline. http://www.loc.gov/rr/
business/beonline/. Library of Congress
Business Reference Services. Washington:
Library of Congress. 1996
025.06   HF54.52.U5

Provides business-related online sources selected
by staff of the Library of Congress. Listed by title or
subject, with links. Includes web sites maintained by
state and federal government agencies, trade organizations, scholarly associations, universities, libraries, private companies, think tanks, publishers, and
international organizations. More than 100 subject
categories, including career assistance, companies,
entrepreneurship, government agencies, grants,
investing, statistics and trade unions.

5   Best practices for corporate libraries.
Sigrid Kelsey, Marjorie J. Porter. Santa
Barbara, Calif.: Libraries Unlimited, 2011.
xiii, 337 p., ill. ISBN 9781598847376
025.1/9769   Z675.C778; B47

Not a management manual, but a collection of 16
essays and case studies, grouped under the headings: Services and facilities; Communication and
networking; Management; Marketing and demon-
strating value; Change management and reorganization; and Current state of libraries. Specific topics
include: the pre-computer-age history of the corporate library; intellectual property and information
sharing; outsourcing; and assessment. Brief glossary
of business terms.

**6   Business information: How to find it,
how to use it. 2nd ed.** Michael R. Lavin.
Phoenix: Oryx Press, 1992. xi, 499 p., ill.
ISBN 9780897745567
650.072   HF5356

Along with Daniells' *Business Information Sources*
(7), one of the classic and still relevant guides for
librarians. Combines descriptions of major business
publications and databases, with detailed coverage
of major business research areas. Discusses forms
of business information, including experts, reference works, reports, periodicals, directories, and
news sources; common topics of business reference, including corporate finances, sources for both
public and private companies, investment analysis,
and general economic statistics; and specialized
sources dealing with marketing, accounting, taxation and legal matters. Title and subject indexes. A
3rd ed. appeared in 2002, but is not widely held in
libraries.

**7   Business information sources. 3rd
ed.** Lorna M. Daniells. Berkeley, Calif.:
University of California Press, 1993. xix,
725 p. ISBN 9780520081802
016.33   HF5351

One of the classic guides to business information,
and still useful for advice on business research (also
see Lavin's Business Information: How to find it, how
to use it (6)). Identifies core reference resources such
as handbooks, bibliographies, indexes, dictionaries,
directories, statistical sources, periodicals and online
tools; discusses approaches to finding frequently
needed information such as economic trends, U.S.

and world statistics, company and industry information, and investment analysis; and lists tools serving specialized areas such as finance and banking,
management, or marketing. Subject index. Author/
title index.

**8   Encyclopedia of business information
sources.** Paul Wasserman, Verne
Thompson, Virgil Burton III, Gale
Research Company. Detroit: Gale
Research, 1970– ISSN 0071-0210
016.33   HF5351

Annual, since 1997. Comprehensive source for
print and electronic sources. Arranged alphabetically
by topic such as "beverage industry" or "bonds."
Entries then list tools by type: these include indexes, databases, yearbooks, directories, handbooks,
periodicals, sources of numerical data, and relevant
institutions and associations. Provides contact information and pricing, and brief descriptions in some
cases. Edited by different hands over time. 2013
marked the 30th ed. Available as an e-book.

**9   How to find business information: a
guide for business people, investors,
and researchers.** Lucy Heckman. Santa
Barbara, Calif.: Praeger, 2011. vi, 208 p.,
map ISBN 9780313362804
016.65   HD30.4

Introduction to published and online resources for
basic research in areas such as industry and company information, stocks and bonds, commodities,
banking, insurance, entrepreneurship, marketing,
accounting, taxation, and real estate. The introduction discusses major library-oriented publications.
Appendixes list acronyms and business libraries,
government agencies, and stock exchanges. Index of
authors, publication titles and agencies. Available as
an e-book.

**10   International business information:
how to find it, how to use it. 2nd ed.**
Ruth A. Pagell, Michael Halperin.
New York; Chicago: AMACOM;
Glenlake, 1999. xvii, 445 p., ill.
ISBN 9781573560504
016.33   HF54.5

"Describes key international business publications
and databases, and provides the subject background
needed to understand them."— *Pref.* While dated,

many of the resources are still applicable. Most sources are English-language directories, yearbooks, reports, and electronic files that describe companies, industries, markets, and international transactions. Extensively illustrated with examples and tables. Appendixes, title and subject index.

11   Journal of business and finance librarianship. New York: Taylor & Francis, 1990–. ill. ISSN 0896-3568
027.6905   Z675.B8

Quarterly journal. Articles are peer reviewed. Occasional theme issues. Publishes reviews of books, databases, and Web sites, written by librarians for librarians. "The immediate focus of the journal is practice-oriented articles, but it also provides an outlet for new empirical studies on business librarianship and business information. Aside from articles, this journal offers valuable statistical and meeting reports, literature and media reviews, Web site reviews, and interviews." —*About*. Available as an e-journal.

12   Making sense of business reference: a guide for librarians and research professionals. Celia Ross. Chicago: American Library Association, 2013. xiii, 186 pages ISBN 9780838910849
025.5/27665   Z711.6.B87

Provides name, URL and description for more than 250 business reference resources. The overwhelming majority are web-based tools, some freely available (such as U. S. government sites) but most requiring fee payment and authenticated access. Covers sources of economic data and scholarly articles, and research about companies, industries, investment, marketing and advertising, small business and international business. Aimed at reference desk librarians, and supported by practical tips and analysis of sample questions. Index.

13   Managing library employees: a how-to-do-it manual. Mary J. Stanley. New York: Neal-Schuman Publ., 2008. xi, 247 p. ISBN 9781555706289
023/.9   Z682.S76

Intended as "a basic orientation in human resources management for librarians"—*Pref.* Covers federal laws; recruitment and selection of staff; training, retention, and professional development;

compensation and benefits; performance appraisal; problem employees; conflict resolution and discipline; communication; technology in human resources management; and change management. Includes sample forms, checklists, and bibliographic references. More specialized works on employee relations include *Managing student assistants: a how-to-do-it manual for librarians* by Sweetman and *Managing library volunteers*, Second edition by Driggers and Dumas.

14   Research on Main Street: using the Web to find local business and market information. Marcy Phelps. Medford, N.J.: CyberAge Books, 2011. xxiii, 254 p. ISBN 9780910965880
025.06/3386   HF54.56

Intended for students, researchers or librarians seeking information about local businesses in the United States. Introduces websites (mostly free) that provide information in five categories: demographics, economics, companies, people, and issues. Suggested sources include government websites, local news media, local organizations, social media, and plain footwork such as interviews. Appendix of sample questions and answers. Index. Available as an e-book.

15   Strauss's handbook of business information: a guide for librarians, students, and researchers. 3rd ed ed. Rita W. Moss, David G. Ernsthausen. Santa Barbara, Calif.: Libraries Unlimited, 2012. xix, 399 p., ill. ISBN 9781598848076
016.33   HF1010

Excellent introduction to basic business concepts and publications, updated in this edition to include more Web-based and digital resources. Begins with an overview of print and electronic reference tools, then discusses sources for company information, industry information, government information, statistics, marketing, accounting and taxation, credit and banking, investments, stocks, bonds and other fixed-income securities, mutual funds and investment companies, futures and options, insurance, and real estate. Appendices cover acronyms and abbreviations; Federal government departments and agencies; business information from state governments; key economic indicators; selected free web sites; and sources of business case studies. Bibliography. Index.

16   Using the financial and business literature. Thomas P. Slavens. New York: Marcel Dekker, 2004. xiv, 655 p. ISBN 9780824753184

016.33   HG173

Lists resources that assist with general business, company, industry, and marketing research. Pt. 1 covers electronic resources and pt. 2 covers print resources. Each section is arranged alphabetically by topic, which range from disciplines like accounting, to subjects like African Americans in business. Entries cover publisher information, URLs (where relevant), and general content of the resource. Available as an e-book.

Guides and Handbooks

17   AMA handbook of business writing: the ultimate guide to style, grammar, punctuation, usage, construction, and formatting. Kevin Wilson, Jennifer Wauson, American Management Association. New York: American Management Association, 2010. xxvii, 637 p. ISBN 9780814415894

808/.06665   HF5726

Concise entries to assist with a wide range of writing needs. Longer entries use bullet points for clarity. Section 1: The writing process: advice about research, writing and revising a draft, and documenting sources. Section 2: The business writer's alphabetical reference: tips for dealing with abbreviations, capitalization, commas, numbers, paragraphing, and grammatical problems. Section 3: Sample business documents: examples for 50 commonly used texts, such as annual reports, job descriptions, and trip reports. Detailed table of contents; index.

18   The Blackwell guide to business ethics. Norman E. Bowie. Malden, Mass.: Blackwell, 2002. x, 363 p., ill. ISBN 9780631221227

174.4   HF5387

Signed essays on ethics in contexts such as corporate governance, sales and marketing, accounting, human resources, the environment, and information technology, citing publications and research findings. Index. Available as an e-book.

19   Business ethics for dummies. Norman E. Bowie, Meg Schneider. Hoboken, N.J.: Wiley, 2011. xx, 360 p., ill. ISBN 9780470600337

174.4   HF5387

Accessible essays on topics such as conflicts of interest, marketing and deceptive practices, publicity, consumer privacy, corporate espionage, lobbying and PACs, levels of executive compensation, and "green" business opportunities. Bowie is professor emeritus at the Univ. of Minnesota. Index. Available as an e-book.

20   Business ratios and formulas: a comprehensive guide. 3rd ed. Steven M. Bragg. Hoboken, N.J.: Wiley, 2012. xvii, 355 p., ill. ISBN 9781118169964

650.01/513   HF5691

Covers some 250 operational criteria available to managers: these are numerical analytical tools useful for founding or running a business. Definitions for ratios and formulas that look at asset utilization, operating performance, cash flow, liquidity, capital structure, return on investment, market performance, finance and accounting matters, engineering of parts and products, human resources, logistics and supply chain, production, and sales and marketing. Measures are explained, with illustrative examples. "Cautions" explain when another measure would be better suited, as well as how a measure can be misunderstood. Appendix lists all measures. Glossary of terms in finance and accounting. Designed for managers, but useful for anyone who must calculate and understand business ratios. Available as an e-book.

21   Codes of professional responsibility: Ethics standards in business, health, and law. 4th ed. Rena A. Gorlin. Washington: Bureau of National Affairs, 1999. xvii, 1149 p. ISBN 1570181489

174   BJ1725.C57

Collects some 60 codes of ethics or similar documents ("statements of principles," "ethical guidelines," etc.) of North American organizations within the three domains listed in the subtitle. Construing these domains broadly, it embraces, e.g., professions such as engineering, computing, and journalism under "business," and mental health and social work under "health." Also includes directory of U.S. and worldwide organizations and programs concerned with professional responsibility and an extensive guide to information resources including periodicals, reference works, and web sites. Indexes of issues, professions, and organizations. Serving a similar function for the U.K., *Professional codes of conduct in the United Kingdom*, 2nd ed. by Harris, presents an even broader range of codes, numbering around 200 reproduced in full plus summary descriptions of some 300 more.

An extensive web-based collection, "Codes of Ethics Online," is among the resources offered at the Center for the Study of Ethics in the Profession at IIT website (http://ethics.iit.edu/), which also provides links to other ethics centers and the catalog of CSEP's extensive library—a virtual bibliography of the field of professional ethics.

22 The Economist numbers guide: the essentials of business numeracy.
6th ed. Richard Stutely. London: Profile Books Ltd., 2013. vii, 256 p., ill.
ISBN 9781846689031
650/.01/513   HF5691
Introduction to numerical methods and quantitative techniques used in mathematics, statistics, business, accounting, and economics. Explains methods of analyzing and solving problems in finance, and the use of numbers in business forecasting and decision-making. Uses charts, graphs, tables, figures and examples to explain in layman's terms. Appendix is a dictionary of relevant terms, with cross-references to the main section. Index.

23 Economists' mathematical manual.
4th ed. Knut Sydsæter, Arne Strøm, Peter Berck. Berlin: Springer, 2005. 225 p., ill.
ISBN 3540260889
330.0151   HB135.B467
Mathematical formulas, results, and theorems commonly used in economics. Coverage includes game theory and statistical concepts and distributions. Useful for any student or researcher in economics.

24 Guide to economic indicators. 4th ed.
Norman Frumkin. Armonk, N.Y.: M.E. Sharpe, 2006. xx, 283 p., ill.
ISBN 0765616467
330.9730021   HC103
Completely updated, with over 60 economic indicators. Entries have definitions, availability,

methodology, accuracy, relevance, and recent trends for each indicator. Covers topics such as earnings, balance of trade, CPI and PPI, GDP, mortgages and home sales, and interest rates. This edition added indicators for unemployment, housing, and energy. Available as an e-book.

25 Handbook of the economics of giving, altruism and reciprocity.
Serge-Christophe Kolm, J. Mercier Ythier. Amsterdam, The Netherlands; London: Elsevier, 2006–. 2 v. (xxv, 1588, 28 p.), ill.
ISBN 9780444506979
330   HB523
Giving (termed "nonmarket voluntary transfers") is examined from economic and societal perspectives in this careful handbook. Historical foundations of the field are presented, as well as perspectives on giving from various disciplines. The second volume provides a comprehensive set of applications for family giving, and charity and charitable institutions. International aid is considered, as is the welfare state. Includes bibliographical references and indexes. Available as an e-book.

26 Handbooks in economics. North-Holland Pub. Co. Amsterdam, The Netherlands; New York: Elsevier, 1981–. ill. ISSN 0169-7218
030   HC21
Surveys of recent literature in economics, written by scholars in the field. Each handbook focuses on a different topic. Titles in this growing series to date include: *Handbook of agricultural economics, Handbook of computational economics, Handbook of defense economics, Handbook of development economics, Handbook of econometrics, Handbook of the economics of finance, Handbook of environmental economics, Handbook of game theory with economic applications, Handbook of health economics, Handbook of income distribution, Handbook of industrial organization, Handbook of international economics, Handbook of labor economics, Handbook of macroeconomics, Handbook of mathematical economics, Handbook of monetary economics, Handbook of natural resource and energy economics, Handbook of population and family economics, Handbook of public economics, Handbook of regional and urban economics,* and *Handbook of social choice and welfare.* Available as e-books.

27 Mathematical formulas for economists. 4th ed. Bernd Luderer, Volker Nollau, Klaus Vetters. Heidelberg, [Germany]; New York: Springer, 2010. x, 198 p., ill. ISBN 9783642040788

330.0151   HB135

Defines formulas and differential equations used in economics, finance, and accounting, including definitions for the notations used in formulas. Gives basic formulas, as well as alternate formulas. Assumes some prior knowledge. Enlarged from the 3rd edition of 2007 "to include methods of rank statistics and the analysis of variance (ANOVA) and covariance." Bibliography. Index. Available as an e-book.

28 The Oxford handbook of business ethics. George G. Brenkert, Tom L. Beauchamp. Oxford; New York: Oxford University Press, 2010. xii, 733 p., ill. ISBN 9780195307955

174.4   HF5387

Twenty-four signed essays on topics such as corporate responsibility, fairness in salaries and benefits, civil rights, globalization and multiculturalism, deceptive practices, whistleblowers, conflicts of interest and insider trading, privacy, intellectual property, lobbying, product safety, and the environment. Index.

29 Success by the numbers: statistics for business development. Ryan Womack, Reference and User Services Association (RUSA). Chicago: American Library Association; Reference and User Services Association, 2005. vii, 59 p., ill. ISBN 9780838983270

016.33   HF54.56

A guide to U.S. statistical resources, with information on how the data is gathered, as well as where to find it. Based on a 2004 BRASS program. Chapters on: Federal business statistics and the 2002 economic census; Finding Florida statistical resources and data; Demographics and marketing; Economic forecasts; Industry statistics; Financial statistics; Labor, employment, and wages statistics; and Trade statistics. State and national sources are provided and sources are both free and fee-based.

30 21st century economics: a reference handbook. Rhona C. Free. Thousand Oaks, Calif.: SAGE, 2010. 2 v. (xxvi, 1000 p.), ill. ISBN 9781412961424

330   HB171

Ninety-two chapters by academics summarize concepts in contemporary economics. Intended for university readers, without the intense mathematics of some economic writing. Includes an overview history of economic thought, econometrics, supply and demand, labor markets, game theory as a tool in economics, public finance, macroeconomic models, the balance of trade, East Asian economies, economics of aging, gambling, economics of crime, and feminist economics. Index.

Indexes; Abstract Journals

31 ABI/Inform global. http://www.il.proquest.com/products_pq/descriptions/abi_inform_global.shtml. ProQuest. Ann Arbor, Mich.: ProQuest. 1971–

HF54.7.A25

ABI/Inform, an early and important entrant in the bibliographic database marketplace, has expanded coverage and changed platforms over the years: access today of course is via the Web. Indexing and abstracting of business periodicals, some economics periodicals, as well as other periodicals related to business. Periodical coverage extends back as far as 1923 in some cases. Sold in several versions: extent of content varies with price.

ABI/Inform global covers more than 3,700 publications, with more than 2,600 available in full text. Includes 18,000 business-related dissertations, some 5,000 business case studies, the *Wall Street Journal* since 1984, and *EIU ViewsWire*.

ABI/Inform complete includes more than 6,000 periodicals, 30,000 business-related dissertations, the *Economist* and *Wall Street Journal*, 100,000 working papers from sources like OECD, and analysis of industries, markets and countries.

ABI/Inform research covers over 1,800 journals, with more than 1,200 available in full text.

ABI/Inform dateline offers some 280 periodicals, with more than 230 available in full text. These include journals, newspapers, trade magazines and regional sources.

A comparable and competing product is Business source elite (34).

32 **Abstracts of working papers in economics: The official journal of the AWPE database.** Cambridge University Press. New York: Cambridge University Press, 1986–2004 ISSN 0951-0079

330.05   HB1

Indexes and abstracts of over 100 working paper series from universities and research organizations. Each issue covers about 550 working papers. Entries are alphabetical by author and include abstracts, bibliographic information, web links, and contact information for obtaining the paper. Includes indexes for series, keywords, issuing institution, and permuted titles. Formerly available through EconLit. Ceased with issues of 2004.

33 **Business dateline.** http://library.dialog .com/bluesheets/html/bl0635.html. ProQuest, ProQuest Information and Learning Company. [Ann Arbor, Mich.]: ProQuest. 1985–

HF54.7

Provides indexing and full text for 550 regional business publications from the U.S. and Canada. Especially useful for coverage of local firms, products and executives. Useful for economic conditions in specific cities, states, or regions; mergers and acquisitions; and company news. Available on multiple platforms including ProQuest, OCLC FirstSearch, and DIALOG.

34 **Business source elite.** http://www .ebscohost.com/academic/business-source -elite. EBSCO Publishing. Ipswich, Mass.: EBSCO. 1997– ISSN 1092-9754

338   HF5001

Comprehensive indexing of a wide range of business-related periodicals, reports and news sources. EBSCO publishes several versions of its business database product, with content that varies in extent and pricing. All include access to a *Regional business news* collection. All resources are delivered over the Web.

Business Source elite covers more than 1,100 business periodicals, including Harvard Business Review (47), and more than 10,000 Datamonitor company profiles. Over 1,000 journals are full text. Backfiles from 1985.

Business Source complete indexes some 2,000 peer-reviewed business journals and over 1,800 trade periodicals, many in full text, with some coverage from as early as 1886; over a million company profiles; market reports, industry reports and economic reports on individual countries; and 9,000 case studies.

Business Source premier covers some 2,200 periodicals, with some full text going back to 1965, and a smaller array of marketing, industry, company and country reports.

Business source corporate is a similar product marketed to companies, with full text from 2,700 periodicals, and numerous company, industry and country profiles and reports.

Successor to the print-format *Business periodicals index* (1959–) and online *Business abstracts* (1991–), published until 2011 by the H. W. Wilson Company. Incorporates older content formerly found in *Business periodicals index retrospective* (1913–1982).

A similar and competing product is ABI/Inform global (31).

35 **Econlit.** http://www.econlit.org/. American Economic Association. [Nashville, Tenn.]: American Economic Association. 1990–

Z7164.E2

Comprehensive index of and abstracts for economics literature from around the world, including journal articles, books, book reviews, collective volume articles, dissertations, and working papers. Some covered content is as early as 1886. Successor to coverage in the *Journal of economic literature* and *Index of economic articles in journals and collective volumes*. Most references are to English language publ. Available online on multiple platforms including EBSCO, Ovid/Silver Platter, and ProQuest.

36 **EconPapers.** http://econpapers.repec .org/. Sune Karlsson. Örebro, Sweden: Swedish Business School. Örebro University. 2004–

HB171

Search engine for RePEc: Research Papers in Economics (40), which contains over 500,000 working papers, 900,000 journal articles, 17,000 books, 18,000 chapters and 3,000 software items. More than 340,000 of the items are available online. Many of the working papers are available through EconLit (35) as well.

37 General businessfile ASAP. http://www
.gale.cengage.com/customer_service/
sample_searches/gbfasap.htm. Gale Group
(Firm). Farmington Hills, Mich.: Gale
Cengage. 1999–

016.07   HF5030

Includes a variety of business research sources in one
product: full text of selected newspaper and journal articles, indexing of other periodicals, directory
information for 200,000 companies, and Investext
investment reports. Some content extends back to
1980. Rolling coverage of one year of the *Wall Street
Journal*. Searchable by keywords in abstracts or full
text, author name, or subject term.

**38 International bibliography of
economics = bibliographie
internationale de sciences
économiques.** Fondation nationale
des sciences politiques, International
Economic Association., International
Committee for Social Sciences
Documentation., Unesco., International
Committee for Social Science Information
and Documentation. Paris: UNESCO,
1955– ISSN 0085-204X

016.33   Z7164.E2

An extensive and unique international list of books,
selected chapters from multi-authored books, pam-
phlets, 715 current journals, 200 defunct journals,
and official government publications that deal with
economic history, methodology and theory, international and domestic economic policy, the production of goods and services, prices and markets,
money and finance, social economics and public
economy. Best for its international coverage, as more
than half the journals covered are published outside
the U.S. or U.K. Some records date back to 1951.
Subject indexes in English and French. Part of the
larger IBSS (International bibliography of the social
sciences) series. Available in online form.

39 LexisNexis academic. http://www
.lexisnexis.com/en-us/products/lexisnexis
-academic.page. LexisNexis (Firm).
Bethesda, Md.: LexisNexis. 1984–

KF242.A1

Searchable full-text subscription database that
includes full text of articles from more than 2,500
newspapers, news from more than 300 local and
regional newspapers, blogs and other web sources
via WebNews, broadcast transcripts from the major
radio and TV networks; national and international
wire services; campus newspapers; polls and surveys; and over 600 newsletters. Non-English language news sources available in Spanish, French,
German, Italian, and Dutch. Dates of coverage vary
by individual source, with newspapers updated daily.
Legal content includes federal and U.S. state statutes
and cases, including Supreme Court decisions since
1790; some 800 law reviews; federal regulations;
Shepherd's citations; and selective international coverage. Business content includes company information for 80 million public, private and international
firms; profiles of 58 million executives; SEC filings;
and industry profiles. A comparable resource for
legal, news and business content is Westlaw (43).

40 RePEc: research papers in economics.
http://repec.org/. Kit Baum, Christian
Zimmermann. Helsinki, Finland:
University of Helsinki, Department of
Economics, Faculty of Social Sciences.
1994–

HB31

Maintained by volunteers, this website is "a decentralized bibliographic database of working papers,
journal articles, books, books' chapters and software components" based on "over 1,600 archives
from 81 countries" and "about 1.4 million research
pieces from 1,800 journals and 3,800 working paper
series."

41 The Wall Street Journal index. Dow
Jones (Firm). New York: Dow Jones,
1957– ISSN 1042-9840

332.05   HG1

Index coverage begins in 1955 and is based on the
final Eastern edition of the Wall Street journal (101)
newspaper. Each issue has two parts: (1) corporate
news indexed by company name; (2) general news
indexed by topic. Includes special sections for book
reviews, personalities, deaths, and theater reviews.
The last section of the index includes the daily Dow
Jones averages for each month of the year. Since
1981, v. 1 includes *Barron's index*, a subject and corporate index to *Barron's business and financial weekly*.
Since 1990, published monthly with quarterly and
annual cumulations. Former publication frequency
was monthly with annual cumulations. Annual

cumulations issued in 2 pts., 1980–2001. This is a traditional print format index to newspaper articles, and not to be confused with the "Wall Street Journal Dollar Index" of seven widely traded currencies.

Fully searchable page images of the complete *Wall Street Journal* 1889–1995 are available in ProQuest Historical Newspapers (an additional year is added each year). Searchable full text (although not original page images) is also available in a number of other commercial database services, including ProQuest Newspapers, Factiva (98), and ABI/Inform Global (31). Current daily news appears at WSJ.com (102).

42   Web of science. http://wokinfo.com/ products_tools/multidisciplinary/ webofscience/. Thomson Reuters. Philadelphia: Thomson Reuters. 2001–
                                                       Z7401

The Web of Science (WoS) database is the platform for Thomson Reuter's suite of databases. The *Web of Science Core Collection Citation Indexes* include the Science Citation Index, the Social Sciences Citation Index, the Arts and Humanities Citation Index and Book Citation Index, which are available separately. Other databases are available on the platform, such as chemical indexes, Journal Citation Reports, Essential Science Indicators, and nonproprietary databases such as Medline (1099) and CAB Abstracts. In addition to standard indexing, "Cited Reference Search" discovers all the articles in the database that have cited a particular article. "Related Records" retrieves records that have cited a source common to the chosen record. The "Author Search" function is a work in progress, attempting to cluster results to provide author name disambiguation. Offers strong analytical tools to assess a results set: "Analyze Results" to rank records by selected fields, and the "Create Citation Report" function includes a calculation of the h-index impact measurement of records in the set. Includes access to EndNote Basic bibliographic management software and to ResearcherID to manage author name disambiguation. Permits cross searching of all subscribed databases. One of the greatest strengths and weaknesses of the WoS is that coverage is largely restricted to core and high-impact journals. Coverage years vary by database. The Web of Science superceded the Web of Knowledge platform name in January 2014.

43   Westlaw. http://legalsolutions .thomsonreuters.com/law-products/.

West Publishing. Eagan, Minn.: West Publishing/Thomson Reuters. 1975–
One of the major online platforms for U.S. legal research, combined with full text searching of news, and business research content. Searchable full text of federal and state statutes, case law including Supreme Court opinions, administrative codes, and specialized legal content including some international coverage. Also includes periodical literature, from legal journals and law reviews to newspapers and magazines. This is the online equivalent of print format West legal volumes, and incorporates the West Key Number System which groups entries by topic. Available only to subscribers, including working professional attorneys, courts, and law schools with their libraries. News content benefits from the connection to Reuters. WestlawNext offers "Company Investigator" searching and report-making based on 30 million company profiles. A comparable resource is LexisNexis (39).

Book Reviews

44   Business information alert. Alert Publications. Chicago: Alert Publications, 1989–2011 ISSN 1042-0746
025   HF5001
From 1989–2011, provided reviews of print and electronic business resources, as well as news items, coverage of trends, and tips for business researchers. Ceased in 2011.

45   Economic history services. http://eh .net/. EH.Net. Oxford, Ohio: EH.Net. 1993–
330.9   HC21.E25
Owned by the Economic History Association and intended primarily for economic historians, historians of economics, economists, and historians. EH .net provides full text of book reviews and course syllabi, directory of economic historians, lists of conferences, an *Encyclopedia of economic and business history*, and access to historical economic data sets (such as Global Financial Data, 1880–1913 and historic labor statistics). Researchers may also register databases hosted on servers at other institutions.

The section "How Much Is That?" uses calculators and data sets to show the comparative value of money, including five ways to compare the worth of a U.S. dollar since 1790; the price of gold since

1257; estimated Consumer Price Index figures for the United States since 1774; the purchasing power of the British pound, since 1264; annual real and nominal GDP for the United States, since 1790; annual real and nominal GDP for the United Kingdom, since 1086; interest rate series for the United Kingdom and the United States, since 1790; and daily closing values of the Dow Jones Industrial Average (DJIA) since 1896.

46   The economist: world news, politics, economics, business and finance.
London: Economist Newspaper Ltd., 1843–. ill. ISSN 0013-0613
330.05   HG11
Coverage of political, economic and business events, world leaders, and science and technology. Economic and financial indicators (output, prices and jobs, *The Economist*commodity-price index, GDP growth forecasts, trade, exchange rates, budget balances and interest rates, markets, and stock markets), and emerging market indicators (overview, child mortality, economy, financial markets) are published regularly. Regular book reviews. Full online access available for a fee at http://www.economist.com/ and through various aggregator databases. *The economist* sponsors EIU.com (209).

47   Harvard business review. Graduate School of Business Administration. Boston: Graduate School of Business Administration, Harvard University, 1922–. ill. ISSN 0017-8012
330.904   HF5001
Articles, best practices, book reviews, and case studies on communication, finance and accounting, global business, innovation and entrepreneurship, leadership, management, organizational development, sales and marketing, strategy and execution, and technology and operations. Also available online, through Business Source Elite (34). In recent years, the publisher has imposed stricter controls over use of the content by library users at libraries with licensed access to the digital version through aggregators.

Encyclopedias

48   American economy: a historical encyclopedia. Rev. ed. Cynthia Northrup. Santa Barbara, Calif.: ABC-CLIO, 2011. 2 v.
ISBN 9781598844610
330.973003   HC102
This updated version of the 2003 edition includes more than 600 entries covering American economic history from colonial times to the present. Volume one provides biographical and topical entries including court cases, laws, events, and commodities. Volume two includes primary documents and in-depth essays covering larger concepts like advertising or education with lengthier lists of references. Selected bibliography. Index. Available as an e-book.

49   Bulls, bears, boom, and bust: a historical encyclopedia of American business concepts. John M. Dobson. Santa Barbara, Calif.: ABC-CLIO, 2007. 423 p., ill. ISBN 9781851095537
330.973003   HF3021
Contains 210 topical entries and 160 biographical sketches defining the most influential techniques, instruments, policies, and personalities in the American business system from colonial times to the present. Sections are divided into specific span of years and include a brief historical review to set the concepts and biographies in context. Concise entries include cross-references and further reading recommendations. In addition to a standard index, the book contains three appendixes—concepts and biographies by section; concepts by section and subject; and biographies by section and subject. Available as an e-book.

50   Class in America: an encyclopedia. Robert E. Weir. Westport, Conn.: Greenwood Press, 2007. 3 v., ill.
ISBN 9780313337192
305.50973   HN90.S6
Includes 525 signed entries on economic, sociological, historical, and policy aspects of class relations in the U.S., as well as biographies of key figures. Addresses topics such as consumption and consumerism, wages and income, wealth and poverty, and ethnic and racial issues. Bibliography. Index.

51   Coins and currency: An historical encyclopedia. Mary Ellen Snodgrass. Jefferson, N.C.: McFarland, 2003. xii, 562 p., ill. ISBN 9780786414505
737.403   CJ59

Contains 250 entries with historical commentary on coins and various other forms. Includes pictures of currency and biographical information about coin designers and creators of monetary systems. Entries are cross-referenced. Arranged alphabetically. Includes timeline, glossary, and bibliography. Also useful is *World monetary units: An historical dictionary, country by country* (198).

52   Economic history services. http://eh
.net/. EH.Net. Oxford, Ohio: EH.Net.
1993–
330.9   HC21.E25
Owned by the Economic History Association and intended primarily for economic historians, historians of economics, economists, and historians. EH .net provides full text of book reviews and course syllabi, directory of economic historians, lists of conferences, an *Encyclopedia of economic and business history*, and access to historical economic data sets (such as Global Financial Data, 1880–1913 and historic labor statistics). Researchers may also register databases hosted on servers at other institutions.

The section "How Much Is That?" uses calculators and data sets to show the comparative value of money, including five ways to compare the worth of a U.S. dollar since 1790; the price of gold since 1257; estimated Consumer Price Index figures for the United States since 1774; the purchasing power of the British pound, since 1264; annual real and nominal GDP for the United States, since 1790; annual real and nominal GDP for the United Kingdom, since 1086; interest rate series for the United Kingdom and the United States, since 1790; and daily closing values of the Dow Jones Industrial Average (DJIA) since 1896.

53   The economics book. Niall Kishtainy,
George Abbot. New York: DK Pub., 2012.
352 p. ISBN 9780756698270
330   HB 71
Explains the development and application of more than 100 commonly-encountered concepts and maxims in economics, for concepts such as private property, inflation, taxes, supply and demand, interest, and game theory. Explanations are lively, with illustrations, diagrams, and quotations. Glossary. Index.

**54   The economics of socialism:
principles governing the operation**

**of the centrally planned economies
under the new system. 4th enl. ed.**
Jozef Wilczynski. London; Boston: Allen
and Unwin, 1982. xvii, 238 p.
ISBN 9780043350447
330.947   HC244
Explanation of economic concepts under planned economies, including principles of planning, investment, distribution of profits, credit, economic incentives, consumption models, and pricing. Bibliographic references. Index.

**55   Encyclopedia of American business.
Rev. ed.** W. Davis Folsom, Stacia N.
VanDyne. New York: Facts On File, 2011.
2 v. (xvii, 844 p.) ISBN 9780816081127
338.097303   HF3021
Some 800 short articles in alphabetical order, covering topics in accounting, banking, finance, marketing and management that are most likely to be of interest to students. Identifies and discusses key principles, trade assocations and practices. Updates the 1st edition of 2004, with attention to topics of recent interest such as subprime mortgages and the 2008 recession. Bibliography. Index. Also available as an e-book.

**56   Encyclopedia of American business
history.** Charles R. Geisst. New York:
Facts On File, 2005
ISBN 9780816043507
338.097303   HF3021
Contains 400 entries on businesses and industries, business events, and leaders, as well as business and economic topics from 1776 to the present. Entries are cross-referenced and include recommended readings. Writing is accessible for students in high school, but coverage is complete enough to be useful to a much wider audience. Includes a chronology and 15 primary documents, including essays, legislative acts, and court judgments. Available as an e-book.

**57   Encyclopedia of business and finance.
2nd ed.** Burton S. Kaliski, Macmillan
Reference. Detroit, Mich.: Macmillan
Reference, 2007. 2 v.
0028660617   HF1001 650.03
Written for the novice but useful for anyone seeking background information on five key topics:

accounting, finance and banking, management, management of information systems, and marketing. The 310 essays include graphs, tables, photographs, and recommended readings. Alphabetically arranged entries range from the history of computing to green marketing and the Sarbanes-Oxley Act. The 3rd ed. is projected for publication in 2014. Available as an e-book.

58   Encyclopedia of business ethics and society. Robert W. Kolb. Thousand Oaks, Calif.: SAGE Publications, 2008. 5 v. (lxix, 2437 p.) ISBN 9781412916523
174/.403   HF5387
More than 800 signed articles in alphabetical order, each with suggestions for further reading. Addresses the application of ethics and accountability in accounting; corporate management; legislation and regulation; dealings with consumers and employees; and aspects of gender, race, and sexual orientation. Bibliography. Index. Available as an e-book.

59   Encyclopedia of consumption and waste: the social science of garbage. Carl A. Zimring, William L. Rathje. Thousand Oaks, Calif.: SAGE Reference, 2012. 2 v. (xxxiv, 1177 p.), ill. ISBN 9781412988193
363.72/803   HD4482
Includes some 390 signed articles in alphabetical order, with suggestions for further reading. Investigates the social, ecological and economic consequences of a consumer economy. Covers topics such as avoided costs, carbon accounting, marketing and consumption patterns, branding and packaging, the economics of waste disposal, landfills, industrial waste, biofuels, and recycling. Articles on conditions in each U.S. state, as well as international coverage. Interdisciplinary in concept, tapping sociology, anthropology, archaeology, environmental studies, and history. Chronology. Glossary. Index. Available as an e-book.

60   The encyclopedia of money. 2nd ed. Larry Allen. Santa Barbara, Calif.: ABC-CLIO, 2009. xvi, 520 p., ill. ISBN 9781598842517
332.403   HG216
Some 350 entries in alphabetical order cover aspects of currency, banking and monetary systems of all

kinds, including historical and international developments. Covers topics related to inflation and deflation, the gold standard, taxation, the money supply, currency speculation, interest rates, bonds, foreign exchange, government borrowing, paper money, monetary policy, the impact of wars on money, and key figures like John Maynard Keynes. Updated from the first edition of 1999, to include content related to the economic crisis of 2008–2009. Some content of interest has been removed, which is reason for keeping the earlier edition as well. Glossary. Bibliography. Index. Available as an e-book.

61   A financial history of the United States. 2nd ed. Jerry Markham. Armonk, N.Y.: M.E. Sharpe, 2011. 2 v., 912 p., ill. ISBN 9780765624314
332.0973   HB3722
Covers the period 2004–2009: the history, issues, regulations, and key financial developments. Volumes are divided by time period and cover Enron-era scandals, restructuring of the stock and derivative markets, rise of private equity and hedge funds, development of the mortgage market, and the residential housing boom and bust. Vol. 1: *From Enron-era scandals to the subprime crisis (2004–2006)*. Vol. 2: *From the subprime crisis to the Great Recession (2006–2009)*. Also includes notes, selective bibliography, cumulative name index, and cumulative subject index. Another 3-vol. work by the same author covers events from 1492–2001. Available as an e-book.

62   Gold: a cultural encyclopedia. Shannon L. Venable. Santa Barbara, Calif.: ABC-CLIO, 2011. xxii, 315 p., ill. ISBN 9780313384301
669   GT5170
Over 130 articles on the cultural, historical, and economic importance of gold in human societies, from antiquity to its present-day significance in technology and finance. Illustrations. Bibliography and suggestions for further reading. Index. Available as an e-book.

63   International encyclopedia of business and management. 2nd ed. Malcolm Warner, John P. Kotter. London: Thomson Learning, 2002. 8 v., xvii, 7160 p., ill. ISBN 9781861521613
650.03   HF101

Contains 750 entries, intended to clarify international management and management education topics for students and faculty in higher education. Interdisciplinary in scope, including concepts from psychology, sociology, mathematics, computer engineering, political science, and economics.

64   International encyclopedia of economic sociology. Jens Beckert, Milan Zafirovski. London; New York: Routledge, 2006. xxv, 773 p. ISBN 0415286735

306.3   HM548; HM35

Sociological analysis of the economy. 250 signed entries. Examines how economics and society are interrelated, including economic behavior and choice, ideas of key figures, consumption and markets, competition and cooperation, game theory, globalization, labor and management, money, non-market transfers, and issues of class, gender and race. Entries are cross-referenced and include succinct bibliographies. Index.

65   The new Palgrave dictionary of economics. 2nd ed. Steven N. Durlauf, Lawrence E. Blume. Basingstoke, Hampshire, U.K.; New York: Palgrave Macmillan, 2008. 8 v., 7344 p. ISBN 9780333786765

330.03   HB61

Successor to *Palgrave's dictionary of political economy*, first published 1894–96, and the 1987 4-vol. *New Palgrave: a dictionary of economics*. Heavily updated since the 1987 edition, and expanded to cover areas such as experimental and behavioral economics, game theory, international economics, and the impact of technology. Sophisticated encyclopedic coverage of modern economic thought, with signed entries written by 1,500 prominent economists, historians, philosophers, mathematicians, and statisticians. Articles present diverse philosophies, ideologies, and methodologies and discuss their origin, historical development, and philosophical foundation. Bibliographies accompany most entries. Index. Available as an e-book. Online version is continuously updated.

66   The Oxford encyclopedia of economic history. Joel Mokyr, Oxford University Press. New York: Oxford University Press, 2003. 5 v. ISBN 9780195105070

330.03   HC15

Authoritative five-volume set covering all aspects of economic history from ancient to modern times. Alphabetic arrangement of nearly 900 signed articles with bibliographies and cross-references. Major topics include geography, agriculture, production systems, business history, technology, demography, institutions, governments, markets, money, banking finance, labor, natural resources and the environment, and biographies. Separate listing of scholarly economic history internet sites. Index and topical outline of articles. Available as an e-book.

67   Problems of the planned economy: the New Palgrave. John Eatwell, Murray Milgate, Peter Newman. New York: Norton, 1990. xiii, 268 p. ISBN 9780393027365

330.124   HD82

Functions as an encyclopedia of socialist economics. Signed articles with suggestions for further reading are drawn from *The new Palgrave: A dictionary of economics* (1987). Covers concepts such as central planning, collective agriculture, command economies, planning, and prices and quantities under socialism. Biographical entries for important individuals.

68   Routledge encyclopedia of international political economy. R. J. Barry Jones. New York: Routledge, 2001. 3 v. ISBN 9780415145329

337.03   HF1359

Explanations for a wide range of issues, developments, people, terms, organizations, and concepts about the global political economy. Includes brief biographical sketches. Intended for students, scholars, and practitioners. Entries are signed and followed by suggested readings. Available as an e-book.

Dictionaries

69   The AMA dictionary of business and management. George Thomas Kurian. New York: Amacom, 2013. 292 [6] p. ISBN 9780814420287

650.03   HD30.15

A low-cost source for looking up some 6,000 business terms. Brief definitions for words and phrases, including acronyms and abbreviations, jargon and slang, legal terms, and a wide range of business and economic concepts in management, sales, marketing, finance and human resources. Includes profiles of historic figures. Cross-references. Index. Available as an e-book.

70   The American Heritage dictionary of business terms. David Logan Scott. Boston: Houghton Mifflin Harcourt, 2009. x, 594 p. ISBN 9780618755257

650.03   HF1001

Over 6,000 definitions. Covers the vocabulary of recent developments in Internet commerce, investment vehicles, globalization, retirement, insurance and benefits systems, as well as the basic vocabulary of finance, management, economics and accounting. One hundred case studies provide context for especially important concepts, such as "subprime loans." Practical advice from business professionals appears in some areas.

71   The anti-capitalist dictionary: movements, histories and motivations. David E. Lowes. Nova Scotia; Kuala Lumpur; London; New York: Fernwood; SIRD; Zed Books; Distributed in the USA exclusively by Palgrave Macmillan, 2006. x, 310 p. ISBN 9781842776827

330.03   HB61

About 150 articles in alphabetical order explaining the significance of terms found in criticisms of contemporary capitalism. Covers economic concepts, major global trade agreements, and historical references. Suggestions for further reading include Web resources. Timeline of relevant authors since the 1600s. Bibliography. Index. Available as an e-book.

72   Cambridge business English dictionary. Cambridge, U.K.; New York: Cambridge University Press, 2011. x, 947, 33 p., ill. (some col.) ISBN 9780521122504

650.03   HF1001

Unique dictionary of 35,000 business-related words, phrases and meanings designed specially for learners of English. Many terms include phonetics, use examples, and category labels. Select terms also include "Focus on Vocabulary" boxes identifying near-synonyms and theme related terms to assist users with word choice. Also includes help pages covering business communication and writing skills

such as interviewing and report writing, as well as general topics such as company structure and corporate social responsibility. Sections at the back cover symbols, countries/regions/ continents, world currencies, and major financial centers with their stock exchanges.

A free version is also available online at http://dictionary.cambridge.org/dictionary/business-english/ and includes audio pronunciations.

73   The Chartered Management Institute dictionary of business and management. Chartered Management Institute. London: Bloomsbury, 2003. ix, 660 p. ISBN 9780747562368

658.003   HF1001

Easy to read definitions for 6,000 international business terms, people, and phrases. Ranges from slang expressions like "herding cats" to management vocabulary such as "vertical linkage analysis." Multilingual glossary translates some terms into Chinese, French, German, Japanese and Spanish. Also published as *The ultimate business dictionary*.

74   A dictionary of business. 3rd ed., New ed. Oxford University Press. Oxford; New York: Oxford University Press, 2002. 545 p., ill. ISBN 9780198603979

650.03   HF1001

For business students and practitioners, with short definitions of terms and jargon in all fields of business, with more selective coverage of economics and law.

75   Dictionary of business and economics terms. 5th ed. Rev. ed. Jack P. Friedman. Hauppauge, N.Y.: Barron's Educational Series, 2012. 800 p. ISBN 9780764147579

330.03   HF1001

Aimed at students and laypeople, this revised and expanded edition provides concise definitions for over 8,000 terms related to numerous fields of business including taxation, computers and the Internet, finance, real estate, marketing, advertising, and international business. Also covers business research, key theories, statistical models, key legislation, and organizations and associations. Entries include brief definitions with examples and cross-references. Terms with field-dependent definitions are noted with the field and appropriate definition.

76   A dictionary of business and management. 5th ed. Jonathan Law. Oxford; New York: Oxford University Press, 2009. 598 p. ISBN 9780199234899

650.03   HD30.15

Contains 7,000 entries relating to business strategy, marketing, taxation, accounting, operations management, investment, banking and international finance. Non-American terms and phrases are defined, such as *zaibatsu* and "badges of trade." Readers should be aware that common phrases, such as balance sheet, may defined from a British or European perspective. Updates the 4th edition of 2006: additional entries reflect recent developments such as the financial crisis of 2008/2009. Available as an e-book, and through Oxford reference online.

77   Dictionary of business terms. Jae K. Shim. Mason, Ohio: Thomson, 2006. vi, 441 p. ISBN 9780324205459

650.03   HF1001

A good general dictionary, covering all areas of business and written in language accessible to the general public, as well as to the business student. Definitions often include charts, graphs, or formulas.

78   A dictionary of economics. 4th ed. John Black, Nigar. Hashimzade, Gareth D. Myles. Oxford; New York: Oxford University Press, 2012. 464 p., ill. ISBN 9780199696321

330.03   HB61

More than 3,400 definitions covering macroeconomics, microeconomics, finance, international trade and economic organizations. First published in 1997: now updated since the 3rd edition of 2009 to include more terms associated with the Great Recession. Appendices include lists of acronyms, Nobel Prize winners and relevant Web sites, and a guide to the Greek alphabet.

79   Dictionary of environmental economics. Anil Markandya, Renat Perlet, Pamela Mason, Tim Taylor. London; Sterling, Va.: Earthscan, 2001. ix, 196 p., ill. ISBN 1853835293

333.703   HC79.E5D53

Repr. 2002.

Defines more than 1,000 terms that address specific issues raised in environmental economics. Entries written to be understandable to students and lay persons, and include graphs, charts, equations, and tables when appropriate. Entries are one to two paragraphs long and include italicized cross-references, parenthetical citations, and *see also* references. General bibliography. Available electronically via NetLibrary.

80   Dictionary of international business terms. 3rd ed. John J. Capela, Stephen Hartman. Hauppauge, N.Y.: Barron's, 2004. ix, 626 p. ISBN 9780764124457

382.03   HD62.4

Nearly 5,000 terse definitions of business and economics terms. Appendixes with abbreviations, acronyms, contacts for major foreign markets, and U.S. Customs officers, regions, and districts. 2nd ed. (2000) available as an e-book.

81   Dictionary of international economics terms. John Owen Edward Clark. London: Les50ns Professional Pub, 2006. 300 p. ISBN 0852976852

330.03   HF1359

Defines concepts, jargon, and acronyms in economics, finance and business. Includes definitions such as accelerated depreciation, Andean Pact, coupon interest rate, marginal cost, shakeout, and X-inefficiency. Part of a series of dictionaries, which include: *Dictionary of international accounting terms, Dictionary of international banking and finance terms, Dictionary of international business terms, Dictionary of international insurance and finance terms,* and *Dictionary of international trade finance.* Some definitions are shared between the dictionaries in the series.

82   Elsevier's dictionary of financial and economic terms: Spanish-English and English-Spanish. Martha Uriona G. A., José Daniel Kwacz. Amsterdam, The Netherlands; New York: Elsevier, 1996. 311 p. ISBN 9780444822567

332.03   HG151

Explanations and definitions for terms in economics, finance and business, including jargon. Intended for practitioners.

83   An eponymous dictionary of economics: a guide to laws and theorems named after economists. Julio Segura, Carlos Rodríguez Braun.

Cheltenham, U.K.; Northampton, Mass.: Edward Elgar Publ., 2004. xxviii, 280 p., ill. ISBN 9781843760290

330.03   HB61

Over 300 thorough entries for well-known (Adam Smith's problem) and lesser known eponyms (Schmeidler's lemma), written by more than 200 authors. Suggestions for further reading. Alphabetical table of contents. Available as an e-book.

84   A Historical dictionary of American industrial language. William H. Mulligan. New York: Greenwood Press, 1988. xii, 332 p. ISBN 9780313241710

338.00321   TS9

Brief definitions drawn primarily from the period before World War I. An appendix lists terms by industry. Includes a list of contributors, bibliography, and index of institutions and people.

85   Understanding American business jargon: a dictionary. 2nd ed. W. Davis Folsom. Westport, Conn.: Greenwood Press, 2005. xviii, 364 p. ISBN 9780313334504

650.03   HF1001

Defines some 2,500 words, phrases, slang terms, acronyms and colloquial expressions used in the business world and places of work in the U.S., explained in context, and sometimes illustrated with quotations from sources like the *Wall Street Journal*. Bibliography.

Quotations

86   Book of business quotations. Bill Ridgers. Hoboken, N.J.: John Wiley & Sons, 2012. xvi, 240 p. ISBN 9781118185346

650   PN6084.B87

Business-related quotes from a wide range of persons, including Dickens, Lenin, Heidegger, P.T. Barnum, John Cleese, J.P. Morgan, and Warren Buffett. Detailed table of contents for topics, such as "competition," "marketing" and "office life." Also published as *Economist book of business quotations*. Index of speaker names. Available as an e-book.

87   A Dictionary of business quotations. Simon R. James, R. H. Parker. New York:

Simon and Schuster, 1990. x, 172 p. ISBN 9780132101547

082   PN6084.B87

Covers more than 215 topics. Setting this book of quotations apart from the rest are the quotes that business leaders have made about themselves. Author/source and keyword indexes.

88   The Elgar dictionary of economic quotations. Charles R. McCann. Cheltenham, U.K.: Edward Elgar Publishing, 2003. xi, 315 p. ISBN 9781840648201

330   PN6084.E36

Quotes from economists, as well as jurists, politicians, religious leaders, scientists, and others. Authoritative quotes intended for use in supporting economic arguments, but that also provide insight into how economists view diverse topics such as altruism, competition, corruption, equality, free trade, human nature, and taxes. Arranged alpabetically by author, making the index invaluable.

89   The Forbes book of business quotations: 10,000 thoughts on the business of life. 90th anniversary ed., completely rev. and updated ed. Ted Goodman. New York: Black Dog & Leventhal Publ., 2006. 704 p. ISBN 9781579127213

650   PN6084.B87

Quotes relevant to topics applicable in business situations, such as "hope" or "power" as well as "banking" or "capitalism." Cited persons, from Tacitus and Napoleon to Henry Ford and Malcolm Forbes, are drawn from a wide range of disciplines and careers, and from historical and modern eras. Detailed table of contents in alphabetical order by topic, from "ability" to "zeal." Index of speaker names.

90   The Wiley book of business quotations. Henry Ehrlich. New York: Wiley, 1998. xviii, 430 p. ISBN 9780471182078

650   PN6084.B87

Over 5,000 quotations from speeches and articles. Organized in 44 categories such as management, success, and geographical area. Brief context for each quote provided. Indexed by name and organization.

Periodicals

91   ABI/Inform global. http://www.il
.proquest.com/products_pq/descriptions/
abi_inform_global.shtml. ProQuest. Ann
Arbor, Mich.: ProQuest. 1971–

HF54.7.A25

ABI/Inform, an early and important entrant in the bibliographic database marketplace, has expanded coverage
and changed platforms over the years: access today of
course is via the Web. Indexing and abstracting of business periodicals, some economics periodicals, as well
as other periodicals related to business. Periodical coverage extends back as far as 1923 in some cases. Sold
in several versions: extent of content varies with price.

ABI/Inform global covers more than 3,700 publications, with more than 2,600 available in full text.
Includes 18,000 business-related dissertations,
some 5,000 business case studies, the *Wall Street
Journal* since 1984, and *EIU ViewsWire.*

ABI/Inform complete includes more than 6,000
periodicals, 30,000 business-related dissertations,
the *Economist* and *Wall Street Journal,* 100,000 working papers from sources like OECD, and analysis of
industries, markets and countries.

ABI/Inform research covers over 1,800 journals,
with more than 1,200 available in full text.

ABI/Inform dateline offers some 280 periodicals,
with more than 230 available in full text. These
include journals, newspapers, trade magazines and
regional sources.

A comparable and competing product is Business
source elite (34).

92   American economic review. American
Economic Association. Princeton, N.J.:
American Economic Association, 1911–.
ill. ISSN 0002-8282

HB1

Articles and shorter papers on a variety of economic
topics. Each May issue is devoted to the papers and
proceedings of the annual meeting of the American
Economic Association. Published also in online
form, and archived in JSTOR. Beginning in January
2014, *AER* will appear monthly.

**93   Business journals of the United
States.** William Harvey Fisher. New York:
Greenwood Press, 1991. ix, 318 p.

ISBN 9780313252921
016.33005   HF5001

Surveys over 100 business serials to create an overview of business publishing in the U.S. during the
19th and 20th cent. Serials are compared and important articles, special issues, and features are mentioned. Useful for historic research, especially for
information on where the journal is indexed, availability of microfilm copy or reprints, types of libraries
where located, and bibliographic notes. Some information, such as availability, may have changed since
publication, but this is a valuable starting point.

94   Business source elite. http://www
.ebscohost.com/academic/business-source
-elite. EBSCO Publishing. Ipswich, Mass.:
EBSCO. 1997– ISSN 1092-9754

338   HF5001

Comprehensive indexing of a wide range of business-
related periodicals, reports and news sources. EBSCO
publishes several versions of its business database
product, with content that varies in extent and pricing. All include access to a *Regional business news* collection. All resources are delivered over the Web.

Business Source elite covers more than 1,100 business periodicals, including Harvard Business Review
(47), and more than 10,000 Datamonitor company
profiles. Over 1,000 journals are full text. Backfiles
from 1985.

Business Source complete indexes some 2,000 peer-
reviewed business journals and over 1,800 trade periodicals, many in full text, with some coverage from as
early as 1886; over a million company profiles; market reports, industry reports and economic reports on
individual countries; and 9,000 case studies.

Business Source premier covers some 2,200 periodicals, with some full text going back to 1965, and
a smaller array of marketing, industry, company and
country reports.

Business source corporate is a similar product
marketed to companies, with full text from 2,700
periodicals, and numerous company, industry and
country profiles and reports.

Successor to the print-format *Business periodicals
index* (1959–) and online *Business abstracts* (1991–),
published until 2011 by the H. W. Wilson Company.
Incorporates older content formerly found in *Business
periodicals index retrospective* (1913–1982).

A similar and competing product is ABI/Inform
global (31).

95   **Business week.** New York: Bloomberg
L.P., 1929–. ill. ISSN 0007-7135
    650   HF5001
A good source for current news on companies and
industries, the impact of the economy on business,
investing, and markets. Various special issues cover
most innovative companies, investment outlook,
top global companies, best employers, and report
on philanthropy with top corporate givers. Much of
the print content is available for free at http://www
.businessweek.com/.

96   **Econometrica: Journal of the
Econometric Society.** Econometric
Society. Chicago: Econometric Society,
University of Chicago, 1933–. ports.,
diagrs. ISSN 0012-9682
    330.5   HB1
Includes articles on a wide range of economic topics, but *Econometrica* looks to publish articles that
unify the theoretical-quantitative and the empirical-
quantitative approaches to economics. At least one
co-author must be a member of the Econometric
Society. Published also in online form, and archived
in JSTOR.

97   **The economist: world news, politics,
economics, business and finance.**
London: Economist Newspaper Ltd.,
1843–. ill. ISSN 0013-0613
    330.05   HG11
Coverage of political, economic and business events,
world leaders, and science and technology. Economic and financial indicators (output, prices and jobs,
*The Economist*commodity-price index, GDP growth
forecasts, trade, exchange rates, budget balances
and interest rates, markets, and stock markets), and
emerging market indicators (overview, child mortality, economy, financial markets) are published
regularly. Regular book reviews. Full online access
available for a fee at http://www.economist.com/ and
through various aggregator databases. *The economist*
sponsors EIU.com (209).

98   **Factiva.** http://www.dowjones.com/
factiva/. Dow Jones & Co. New York: Dow
Jones and Reuters. [2001–]
    15.9   HG45
Full-text articles from wire services such as Dow
Jones and Reuters, major American and world

newspapers such as the *New York Times*, leading
business newspapers such as the *Wall Street Journal*,
and a wide range of periodicals including *Barron's*
and *Forbes*. Provides industry snapshots for more
than 100 categories such as insurance, steel production, or alternative fuels; current and recent stock
and currency price quotes (with graphing capability); and company snapshots for tens of thousands
of worldwide firms. Content is in 28 languages.

99   **Harvard business review.** Graduate
School of Business Administration.
Boston: Graduate School of Business
Administration, Harvard University, 1922–.
ill. ISSN 0017-8012
    330.904   HF5001
Articles, best practices, book reviews, and case studies on communication, finance and accounting,
global business, innovation and entrepreneurship,
leadership, management, organizational development, sales and marketing, strategy and execution, and technology and operations. Also available
online, through Business Source Elite (34). In recent
years, the publisher has imposed stricter controls
over use of the content by library users at libraries
with licensed access to the digital version through
aggregators.

100   **LexisNexis academic.** http://www
.lexisnexis.com/en-us/products/lexisnexis
-academic.page. LexisNexis (Firm).
Bethesda, Md.: LexisNexis. 1984–
                                                    KF242.A1
Searchable full-text subscription database that
includes full text of articles from more than 2,500
newspapers, news from more than 300 local and
regional newspapers, blogs and other web sources
via WebNews, broadcast transcripts from the major
radio and TV networks; national and international
wire services; campus newspapers; polls and surveys; and over 600 newsletters. Non-English language news sources available in Spanish, French,
German, Italian, and Dutch. Dates of coverage vary
by individual source, with newspapers updated daily.
Legal content includes federal and U.S. state statutes
and cases, including Supreme Court decisions since
1790; some 800 law reviews; federal regulations;
Shepherd's citations; and selective international coverage. Business content includes company information for 80 million public, private and international

firms; profiles of 58 million executives; SEC filings; and industry profiles. A comparable resource for legal, news and business content is Westlaw (43).

101   The Wall Street journal. Eastern ed.
Dow Jones. New York: Dow Jones, 1889–. ill. ISSN 0099-9660
332   HG1
The leading U.S. business newspaper, in print format. Articles on business, politics, the economy, technology, and industry, as well as editorials, regular columns, and book reviews. A great source of market data, such as stocks, stock indexes, commodities, international markets, exchange-traded funds, mutual funds, bonds, rates, and credit markets, commodities and futures, and currencies. Some content is freely available at WSJ.com (102), but full access requires a subscriptions. Content since 1955 is indexed in print volumes of the Wall Street journal index (41). Digital coverage since 1889 is offered in ProQuest historical newspapers.

102   The Wall Street journal: breaking news, business, financial and economic news, world news and video. http://online.wsj.com/. Dow Jones & Co. New York: Dow Jones & Co. 1996– ISSN 0099-9660
                                              HG1
WSJ.com is the website for the leading U.S. financial newspaper. Provides current news, market data, opinion, and related features. A mix of free and fee-based content: headlines are freely browsable, along with market highlights for stocks, currency, commodities, and interest rates. The Wall Street Journal index (41) provides controlled vocabulary searching for issues since 1955; digitized historical content since the founding of the print format Wall Street journal (101) in 1889 is available in ProQuest historical newspapers. A comparable source from the U.K. is the *Financial times* of London at http://www.ft.com/.

Directories

103   Academic business library directors. http://www.abld.org/. ABLD. Stanford, Calif.: ABLD. 1987–
Home page of ABLD, an organization made up of the directors of the fifty largest academic business libraries in the U.S. and Canada. Contact information for the major business libraries, bylaws, record of annual conference sites and dates. Links to an online guide to rankings of business schools, maintained by librarians at Wake Forest University.

104   The best . . . business schools.
Princeton Review (Firm). New York: Random House, 2004– ISSN 2168-9334
650/.071/173   HF1131
For each school, a two-page entry provides address, URL, telephone number, tuition figures, admissions criteria, and deadlines. Indicates areas of specialization, student body profile, and recent job placement information. Includes survey results from students. Essays on the application process and costs. Title varies slightly with number of recommended schools, for example, *The Best 295 Business Schools (2014 Edition)*. Indexes by name, location, cost, and MBA concentration.

105   Consultants and consulting organizations directory. Gale Research (Firm). Detroit: Gale Group, 1973–. 7 v. ISSN 0196-1292
658.4/6/025   HD69.C6
Organized into 14 general fields of consulting. Entries give contact information, brief description of activities, mergers and former names, geographic area served, and where possible, annual consulting revenue. Published annually since 1988, triennially since 1973. 2013 will see the 38th edition.

106   The directory of business information resources. Grey House Pub. Lakeville, Conn.: Grey House Pub., 1992– ISSN 1549-7224
016.65   HF54.52.U5
Identifies newsletters, trade magazines, trade shows, and organizations as information sources. Chapters cover nearly 100 areas of commerce, including prominent areas such as accounting and management, but also specialized sectors such as boating, glass & ceramics, and shoes. For publishers, associations and agencies, provides contact information including address, email address, telephone and URL, with descriptive blurb, and costs if relevant. Updated annually: the 21st ed. appeared in 2014. Entry index. Publisher index.

107 Directory of members. https://www
.aeaweb.org/ms2/dirSearch.php. American
Economic Association. Nashville, Tenn.:
American Economic Association. 1974–
ISSN 1066-3568
330.06073   HB119
Online successor to the *Telephone directory of members*. Search for individuals by name, field, institution, employer, alma mater, or geographic location.
Entries show members' contact information, fields
of specialization, current research interests, employment and degrees earned. The AEA home page at
http://www.aeaweb.org/ provides information about
the association, upcoming conferences, annotated
list of online "Resources for Economists" such
as data sources and links to other organizations,
and career advice. Access to some services limited
to members.

**108 The Directory of trade and
professional associations in the
European Union: = Répertoire
de . . . associations professionnelles
et commerciales dans l'Union
européenne.** Euroconfidential. London;
New York: Europa/European Union,
1994– ISSN 1742-4011
                                             HD2429.E88
Biennial. Gives contact information and publications
for 750 associations in the European Union. Also
gives contact information for 11,700 national member organizations and the Chambers of Commerce
in Europe. Indexes for: acronyms and abbreviations,
full names, keywords, and Standard Industrial Classification (SIC) codes.

109 Directory of U.S. labor organizations.
Courtney D. Gifford. Washington:
Bureau of National Affairs, 1983–
ISSN 0734-6786
331.8802573   HD6504
Annual. Lists some 30,000 unions affiliated with
AFL-CIO and other national, regional, state, and
local affiliates. Gives the structure, leadership, and
contact information for the unions. Index of unions
by common name and by abbreviations; index
of officers. Contact information includes names,
addresses, telephone and fax numbers, and URLs.
Provides updated information on union membership
nationally and by state, recent major work stoppages,

and results of union elections. Membership figures
use U.S. Bureau of Labor Statistics figures for a
breakdown by industry, occupation, race, age, and
gender.

**110 Economics departments, institutes
and research centers in the world.**
http://edirc.repec.org/. Christian
Zimmermann. St. Louis: Research Division
of the Federal Reserve Bank of St. Louis.
[1995–] 330
"EDIRC is a service hosted by the Research Division
of the Federal Reserve Bank of St. Louis." Free online
index to Web sites of 12,000 economics-related
institutions in more than 200 countries. Part of the
wider IDEAS site (http://ideas.repec.org/) which also
lists over 1,900 journals by title and publishers; and
39,000 authors by name, parent institution, and
field of interest.

**111 National trade and professional
associations of the United States.**
Craig Colgate, John J. Russell, Kathleen
Anders, Duncan Bell, David Epstein.
Washington: Columbia Books, 1966–
ISSN 0734-354X
061.3   HD2425
Entries for more than 7,500 national trade and
professional associations and labor unions, with
contact information including the primary executive, figures for staffing and annual budget, a summary of the group's history and purpose, and
statements of membership fees and upcoming
conferences. Separate directory lists 400 association management companies with the names of the
organizations they manage. Indexes by subject,
geographic location, budget size, name of executive officer, and acronym. Companion publication: *State and regional associations of the United
States* (113).

**112 Peterson's graduate programs
in business, education, health,
information studies, law and social
work.** Peterson's (Firm). Princeton, N.J.:
Peterson's, 1997–2012. ill.
ISSN 1088-9442
378.15530257   L901
The standard guide to graduate schools, with information on programs offered; degree requirements;

number and gender of faculty; number, gender, and ethnicity of students; average student age; percentage of students accepted; entrance requirements; application deadlines; application fee; costs; and financial aid. Ceased in print format with 2012, but similar content is available online at http://www.petersons.com/graduate-schools.aspx.

113   State and regional associations of the United States. Washington, D.C.: Columbia Books, 1989–
ISSN 1044-324X
380.102573   HD2425

Lists 8,000 major trade associations, professional societies, and labor organizations that have state or regional memberships. Fraternal, patriotic, charitable, hobby, and small organizations are excluded, making SRA significantly smaller than the Encyclopedia of associations which includes all types of nonprofit groups. Entries include address, telephone, fax, president, number of members and of staff, and when available annual budget, historical note, publ., and annual meetings. Arranged geographically with the following indexes: subject, budget, executive, acronym, and management firm.

For associations with national memberships, consult the companion directory: *National trade and professional associations of the United States* (111). Both titles are available online at http://www.associationexecs.com/.

114   The Wall Street Journal guide to the top business schools. Wall Street Journal, Harris Interactive (Firm). New York: Simon and Schuster, 2003–
ISSN 1544-2977
650   HF1101

Annual. Ranks business schools using recruiter surveys. Lists include top-ranked national, regional, and international programs, top schools for major industries, by academic discipline, for recruiting women, for recruiting minorities, and for recruiting MBAs with high ethical standards. Detailed profiles of full-time programs are included, with the school's ranking, admissions process, test scores, the industries and companies most likely to hire graduates, and expected first-year salaries.

115   World directory of trade and business journals. Euromonitor PLC. London:

Euromonitor PLC, 1996–1998
ISBN 9780863386299
016.338   Z7164.C81

Lists some 2,000 magazines, newsletters, and journals. Gives language, frequency, content, country coverage, format, publisher and contact information. Arranged into 80 industry categories, beginning with advertising and ending with wholesaling. Two indexes: A-Z index by country and publisher with publications, and A-Z index of journals by country. Especially useful for finding a source for news, organizational information, trends or statistics on a company or industry that is not gathered in a reference resource. Published as recently as 1998 (3rd edition).

116   Yearbook of international organizations online. http://www.uia.be/node/52. Union of International Associations. Brussels, Belgium: Union of International Associations. 2000–
314.2   JX1904

Available in print form annually as Yearbook of international organizations in 6 vols., and as a subscription database made up of four components:

At its core is International Organizations Online, a guide to more than 65,000 international nongovernmental organizations (INGOs) and intergovernmental organizations (IGOs) and selected subsidiary bodies. Covers all known IGOs, but the inclusion of NGOs is dependent on numerous criteria. Entries range from a few words in length to more than 10,000.

Biography Profiles Online consists of biographical entries on more than 24,000 individuals holding or having held significant positions in organizations profiled in International Organizations Online.

Statistics Online contains graphs and detailed tables on various aspects of IGOs and INGOs, such as their geographic distribution, fields of activity, dates founded, structure, language use, publishing output, and interrelationships. Periods covered vary; one time series begins in 312 CE.

Bibliography Online consists of bibliographic references to titles mentioned in International Organizations Online and to studies on IGOs and INGOs by scholars throughout the social sciences. Its value to users having access to such databases as WorldCat and Worldwide Political Science Abstracts is questionable.

Biographies

117 African-American business leaders: A biographical dictionary. John N. Ingham, Lynne B. Feldman. Westport, Conn.: Greenwood Press, 1994. xiv, 806 p. ISBN 9780313272530
338.64208996073   HC102.5.A2
Lengthy biographies for 123 African-American business leaders, with information on many individuals who do not appear in standard biographical sources. Each essay concludes with references list, some with primary sources. Includes bibliographic references and indexes. Available as an e-book.

118 American business leaders: From colonial times to the present. Neil A. Hamilton. Santa Barbara, Calif.: ABC-CLIO, 1999. 2 v., 791 p., ports. ISBN 9781576070024
338.092272   HC102.5.A2
Some 400 short entries with information on significant dates, family, education, discussion of entrepreneurial efforts, and brief bibliography. Arranged alphabetically, but with an index by industry. Available as an e-book.

119 American inventors, entrepreneurs, and business visionaries. Rev. ed. Charles W. Carey, Ian C. Friedman. New York: Facts On File, 2010. xxi, 455 p., ill. ISBN 9780816081462
609.2/273   CT214
Updated since the first edition of 2002, with more figures from the early 21st century. Profiles more than 300 Americans since the seventeenth century. Not all individuals are well known or achieved business success, making this a richer resource than the typical biographical source. Entries of 1–2 pages cover birth and death dates, life and innovations, with brief bibliographies. Indexes for invention, industry, and birth year. Available as an e-book.

120 A to Z of American women business leaders and entrepreneurs. Victoria Sherrow. New York: Facts on File, 2002. xx, 252 p., ill. ISBN 9780816045563
338.0082092273   HD6054.4.U6
Contains 135 profiles of well-known women throughout U.S. history. Entries of 1–2 pages cover

accomplishments, with a bit on each woman's life, and suggested further reading. A more complete source is *Encyclopedia of American women in business: from colonial times to the present* (132).

121 Biographical dictionary of American business leaders. John N. Ingham. Westport, Conn.: Greenwood Press, 1983. 4 v., xvi, 2026 p. ISBN 9780313213625
338.0922   HC102.5.A2
835 entries, with information on 1,159 leaders from colonial times to the early 1980s. Appendices by industry, company, birthplace and date, ethnic background and religion, place of business activity, and sex. Partially updated by Contemporary American business leaders: a biographical dictionary (126).

122 The biographical dictionary of British economists. Donald Rutherford. Bristol, U.K.: Thoemmes, 2004. 2 v., xxv, 1330 p. ISBN 9781843710301
330.092241   HB76
Covers 600 economists who lived before the 21st century, with a focus on those in the 20th century. Entries include well-known economists such as Friedrich Engels, but many are for less prominent figures.

123 A biographical dictionary of dissenting economists. 2nd ed. Philip Arestis, Malcolm C. Sawyer. Cheltenham, U.K.; Northampton, Mass.: E. Elgar, 2000. xiv, 722 p.
1858985609   HB76 330.0922
A mix of biographical and autobiographical entries on nearly 100 international economists. Autobiographical entries include economists' statements about their principal contributions to the discipline. Contains biographical information, information on economic philosophies, and compact bibliographic information. Available as an e-book.

124 A biographical dictionary of women economists. Robert W. Dimand, Mary Ann Dimand, Evelyn L. Forget. Cheltenham, U.K.; Northampton, Mass.: Edward Elgar, 2000. xxviii, 491 p. ISBN 9781852789640
330.0820922   HB76
More than 120 profiles of deceased or retired female economists from around the world. Entries include

biographical information, as well as information about the contributions made and the significance of those contributions. No index.

125   Business leader profiles for students.
Gale Research Inc. Farmington Hills, Mich.: Gale Research, 1999–2002. ill.
ISSN 1520-9296
650   HC102.5.A2
Vol. 1, issued in 1999, covers more than 200 individuals; updated by vol. 2 in 2002, with some 100 new profiles and updated information for 25 others. Entries range from 1,250 to 2,500 words in length. Summary biographies include an overview, personal life, career, details, a chronology, social and economic impact, and a bibliography. Photographs are often included. Also available as an e-book.

126   Contemporary American business leaders: a biographical dictionary.
John N. Ingham, Lynne B. Feldman. New York: Greenwood Press, 1990. xxxv, 788 p. ISBN 9780313257438
338.0922   HC102.5.A2
Contains 116 biographies of the major U.S. leaders from 1945–1989. Emphasizes business decisions made rather than personal lives. Entries are several pages long, with bibliographies. Appendixes include industry, company, place of business, place of birth, and black and women leaders. Indexed. Considered a companion to the *Biographical dictionary of American business leaders* (121).

127   Dictionary of labour biography. Joyce M. Bellamy, John Saville. London; [Clifton] N.J.: Macmillan; A. M. Kelley, 1972–2007. v. 1–13 ISBN 0678070083
331.0922   HD8393.A1
Ambitious biographical dictionary that intends to include "not only the national personalities of the British labour movement but also the activists at regional and local level."—*Introd.* Indeed, "everyone who made a contribution, however modest, to any organisation or movement, provided that certain basic details of their career can be established," is to be included. The period of coverage is from 1790 to the present, excluding living persons. Each volume is alphabetically arranged and includes biographies without regard to date of the biographee's activity. A consolidated index appears in each successive volume; a system of cross-references is also provided, referring to both earlier and later volumes. Vol. 6 includes a list of additions and corrections for v. 1–5.

128   Directory of members. https://www.aeaweb.org/ms2/dirSearch.php. American Economic Association. Nashville, Tenn.: American Economic Association. 1974–
ISSN 1066-3568
330.06073   HB119
Online successor to the *Telephone directory of members*. Search for individuals by name, field, institution, employer, alma mater, or geographic location. Entries show members' contact information, fields of specialization, current research interests, employment and degrees earned. The AEA home page at http://www.aeaweb.org/ provides information about the association, upcoming conferences, annotated list of online "Resources for Economists" such as data sources and links to other organizations, and career advice. Access to some services limited to members.

129   Distinguished Asian American business leaders. Naomi Hirahara. Westport, Conn.: Greenwood Press, 2003. viii, 242 p., ports. ISBN 9781573563444
338.0973092395   HC102.5.A2
Contains 96 profiles with education and career highlights, and the story of how they succeeded. Entries include further reading. Appendix for distinguished Asian American business leaders by field.

130   Distinguished women economists.
James Cicarelli, Julianne Cicarelli. Westport, Conn.: Greenwood Press, 2003. xxvi, 244 p. ISBN 9780313303319
330.0922   HB76
Contains 51 profiles of women selected from the 19th century to the present. Entries include an introduction, short biography, section on contributions to economics, and further reading. Most entries can be found in *A Biographical Dictionary of Women Economists* (124) or *Who's Who in Economics* by Blaug. Available as an e-book.

131   Economic thinkers: a biographical encyclopedia. David A. Dieterle. Santa Barbara, Calif.: Greenwood, 2013. xxxviii, 552 p., illustrations ISBN 9780313397462
330.092/2   HB76

Entries in alphabetical order cover more than 200 important economists from antiquity to the 21st century. Americans make up about half of the total. Introductory essay on the evolution of economic thought. Each entry summarizes the life and significance of one figure, with suggested readings by and about the person and their work. Lists of individuals by eras, countries, and economic concepts and philosophies. Appendix of Nobel prize winners. Glossary. Bibliography. Index. Available as an e-book.

132 Encyclopedia of American women in business: from colonial times to the present. Carol Krismann. Westport, Conn.: Greenwood Press, 2005. 2 v., 692 p. ISBN 9780313327575
338.0922   HD6054.4.U6
Contains 327 brief entries on American businesswomen and nearly 100 entries on topics related to their lives, such as affirmative action, child care, and civil rights. Coverage begins in the 18th century. Appendixes for *Fortune* 50 most powerful women in American business, 1998–2003; *Working Woman* top thirty woman-owned businesses, 1997–2001; businesswomen by ethnic group; businesswomen by historical periods; businesswomen by profession; and women in Junior Achievement's national business hall of fame. Good cross-references, bibliography, and index.

133 Fifty major economists. 3rd ed. Steven Pressman. London; New York: Routledge, 2014. 320 p. ISBN 9780415645096
330.092/2   HB76
Profiles with biographical sketches of seminal economists. Entries are in chronological order: the earliest figure included is Thomas Mun (1571–1641), and the most recent is Paul Krugman. Also included are Karl Marx, John Maynard Keynes, Friedrich Hayek, and John Kenneth Galbraith. Introductory essay places all figures in context of the development of economic thought. Each entry summarizes the life and ideas of the economist, with references to publications by and about them. Glossary of economic terms. Available as an e-book.

134 Great economists since Keynes: an introduction to the lives and works of one hundred modern economists. 2nd ed. Mark Blaug. Cheltenham, U.K.;

Northampton, Mass.: Edward Elgar, 1998. xiii, 312 p., ill. ISBN 9781858986920
330.0922   HB76
Blaug, a well known economic historian, describes the careers and contributions of key economists, with biographical and academic information, list of major works, photographs, and illustrations. Indexed by name and subject.

135 Historical encyclopedia of American women entrepreneurs: 1776 to the present. Jeannette M. Oppedisano. Westport, Conn.: Greenwood Press, 2000. xii, 283 p., ports. ISBN 9780313306471
338.04082092273   HF3023.A2
Eminently readable narratives that bring 100 women to life. Entries are short (2–3 pages) and include references. Index includes personal names, company names, and industries.

136 International directory of business biographies. Neil Schlager, Schlager Group. Detroit: St. James Press, 2005. 4 v., ill. ISBN 9781558625549
338.0922   HC29
Profiles over 600 business leaders. International in scope, with almost half the profiles on non-U.S. figures. Includes information on education, awards, family, career path, leadership style, impact, and business strategies. Four indexes (nationality, geographic, company and industry, and name) assist in locating information. Available as an e-book.

137 Leadership library on the internet. http://www.leadershipdirectories.com/. Leadership Directories, Inc. New York: Leadership Directories, Inc. 2002–
                            CT210
Profiles 400,000 individuals in the United States, including in government, business, professional, and nonprofit organizations. Includes contact information, education, religion, political affiliations, date and place of birth, and professional highlights. Includes contents of Federal yellow book, Congressional yellow book, State yellow book, Judicial yellow book, *Corporate yellow book*, and *Financial yellow book*; and Congressional staff directory, Federal staff directory, Judicial staff directory, and Federal-state court directory formerly published by CQ Press/SAGE.

138   Standard and Poor's register of corporations, directors, and executives. Standard and Poor's. New York: Standard and Poor's. ill. ISSN 0361-3623

332.67   HG4057

Annual. Information on public and private corporations, with current address, financial and marketing information, and biographies for corporate executives and directors. Useful for identifying corporate relationships and executive's business connections. Vol. 1 lists firms, v. 2 lists executives, v. 3 provides indexes including Standard Industrial Classification (SIC) codes and geography. Available online as part of *NetAdvantage*.

139   Who's who in economics. 4th ed. Mark Blaug, Howard R. Vane. Cheltenham, U.K.; Northampton, Mass.: Edward Elgar Publ., 2003. xxiv, 971 p. ISBN 9781840649925

330/.092/2   HB76

Profiles over 1,100 major economists, with detailed entries for more than 700 living persons who responded to requests for information. Entries include date of birth, credentials, current and past employment, fields of interest, and key publications. Updates the third edition of 1999. Available as an e-book.

140   Who's who in finance and business. Marquis Who's Who. New Providence, N.J.: Marquis Who's Who, 2005– ISSN 1930-3262

338   HF3023.A2W5; HC29.W46

Over 24,000 entries on executives in the U.S. and in 100 other countries and territories. Also has entries for administrators and professors in the top business schools in the U.S., Canada, and Mexico. Continues: 1936–59, *Who's who in commerce and industry*; 1961–1968/69, *World who's who in commerce and industry*; 1970/71, *World's who's who in commerce and industry*; and 1972/73–2003, *Who's who in finance and industry*. Included in Marquis who's who on the web.

Statistics

141   Business statistics of the United States: patterns of economic change. Cornelia J. Strawser. Lanham, Md.: Bernan Press, 1996–. ill. ISSN 1086-8488

338   HC101

Annual. Compiles data from other sources. Part A contains economic data such as GDP, income, government spending, energy figures, and stock prices. Pt. B offers industry profiles with numbers grouped by NAICS code, and for key sectors such as housing or retail sales. Pt. C has regional and state data. Highlights are more than 150 tables, 30 yr. of annual data and four yr. of monthly data, and information by city, state, region, and country. Index. A good general source to start with, if the Statistical Abstract of the United States (288) does not have what is needed. Available as an e-book.

142   Currency converter foreign exchange rates: OANDA. http://www.oanda.com/currency/converter/. OANDA. New York: OANDA Corp. 1996–

332.45   HG3851

One of several websites offering Forex information: a similar site is *XE currency converter* at http://www.xe.com/currencyconverter/. Provides current exchange rates for some 200 world currencies, including gold and Bitcoin; graphs and tables for recent figures; and resources supporting foreign exchange trading.

143   Data.gov: business. http://www.data.gov/business/. United States. General Services Administration. Washington: General Services Administration. 2009–

Online access to freely available data sets from the U.S government, in this case on topics in business. Part of the larger Data.gov website: other parts of that site cover finance (http://www.data.gov/finance) and manufacturing (http://www.data.gov/manufacturing). Information may appear in a variety of formats including XML, CSV, XLS or TXT. Includes an annual survey of manufactures, monthly house price indexes, interest rate statistics, U.S. natural gas prices, construction spending, and e-stats (reporting figures for online purchases).

144   Data-planet. http://homepage.data-planet.com/. Conquest Systems. Beltsville, Md.: Conquest Systems. 2010–

202   HA

Formerly marketed as *ProQuest Statistical Datasets*. Subscription-only. Presents data in chart, graph, map and/or table formats, for some two billion time series drawn from publications of 70 source organizations. Data has been standardized and restructured to allow comparisons: users can create comparative displays or time series, and export data. Content can be found by expanding a hierarchical display of categories such as Banking, Finance & Insurance, Criminal Justice & Law, Education, Energy Resources & Demand, Food & Agriculture, Government & Politics, Health & Vital Statistics, Housing & Construction, Industry & Commerce, International, Labor & Employment, Natural Resources & Environment, Population & Income, Prices & Cost of Living, Stocks & Commodities, and Transportation & Travel. Key economic indicators are available, as well as statistics related to current news events, and a list of sources. Controlled vocabulary.

145   Data: The World Bank. http://data .worldbank.org/. World Bank. Washington: World Bank. 2010–

HC21

Freely available source for global data. Searchable by keywords, or browsable by individual countries or groupings such as OECD members, topics such as aid effectiveness or financial sector, and specific indicators such as "investment in energy with private participation" or "share of women employed in the nonagricultural sector." Interface in English, French, Spanish, Arabic, or Chinese. Data can be downloaded, and displayed in map or graph formats.

146   Economic census. https://www.census .gov/econ/census/. U.S. Census Bureau. Washington: U.S. Dept. of Commerce. 1954–

317.3   HA181

Publishes extensive official statistics on business and the economy in the U.S. and overseas possessions, gathered every five years. As of 2014, statistics for 2007 are the latest available: figures for 2012 will be the next release. Covers wholesale and retail trade, construction, manufacturing, and service industries, but not agriculture (for which see the Census of agriculture). Originated with a variety of publications and assumed its current scope in 1992. PDF versions are available online at http://www.census.gov/ prod/www/economic_census.html for editions since 1977. Data is accessible through the American fact-finder (263) interface, from the U.S. Census Bureau. Industry research using the economic census (924) is a guide to use of these resources.

147   EIU CountryData. http://www.eiu.com/ site_info.asp?info_name=ps_countryData. Bureau van Dijk Electronic Publishing, Economist Intelligence Unit (Great Britain). [Bruxelles]: Bureau van Dijk. 1980–

HB3730

The emphasis here is on economic indicators—both historical time series and forecast figures—in categories such as demographics and income, GDP, fiscal and monetary, foreign payments, external debts, and external trade. Annual, quarterly, and monthly figures for 201 countries, with as many as 320 indicators for some countries, and figures from as early as 1980. Forecasts to the year 2030 are published on a monthly basis for 179 countries, and quarterly for 79 emerging market regions. Core reports cover demographics and income, gross domestic product (GDP), fiscal and monetary indicators, foreign payments, external debt stock, external debt service, and external trade. Also covers commodity prices and forecasts, and aggregated figures for 45 regions. Available via EIU Data Tool, Bureau van Dijk, and Alacra. Sometimes called *EIU country data*. This is a subscription database. For brief country summaries from EIU, consult EIU.com (209).

148   FRED. http://research.stlouisfed.org/ fred2/. Federal Reserve Bank of St. Louis. St. Louis: Federal Reserve Bank of St. Louis. 1997–

330.973   HC106

Currently offers data from more than 200,000 U.S. and international economic time series, drawn from over 60 sources. Organized into categories such as academic data; money, banking & finance; national accounts; population, employment & labor markets; production & business activity; and prices. The largest categories cover international data and U.S. regional data, and these two are broken down geographically by countries, states or regions. A source leading to figures such as consumer price indexes (CPIs), employment and population numbers, exchange rates, GDP, interest rates, PPIs, U.S. financial data, and more. Data varies in frequency (daily, weekly, biweekly, monthly, quarterly, annual) and may be seasonally adjusted. Time depth of the series varies. For older data files, see also ALFRED®: ArchivaL Federal Reserve Economic Data (http:// alfred.stlouisfed.org/).

149 ICPSR. http://www.icpsr.umich.edu/. Inter-University Consortium for Political and Social Research, Inter-university Consortium for Political and Social Research. Ann Arbor, Mich.: Institute for Social Research, University of Michigan. [1997–]
300.0285   H61.3
Archive of international social science data, including a large collection of economic data. In thematic collections grouped by topic are surveys of Census Enumerations; Community and Urban Studies; Conflict, Aggression, Violence, Wars; Economic Behavior and Attitudes; Education; Elites and Leadership; Geography and Environment; Government Structures, Policies, and Capabilities; Health Care and Facilities; Instructional Packages; International Systems; Legal Systems; Legislative and Deliberative Bodies; Mass Political Behavior and Attitudes; Organizational Behavior; Social Indicators; Social Institutions and Behavior; Publication-Related Archive; and External Data Resources. Data can be downloaded for SAS, SPSS and Stata. Full access is available to students, staff and faculty at 700 ICPSR member institutions; some content is freely available to the public, but may not emphasize economics.

150 ProQuest statistical abstract of the United States. ProQuest. Lanham, Md.: Bernan Press, 2013. 1025 p.
ISBN 9781598885910
317.3   HA 202
Successor to the important federal publication. When the U.S. government cut funding for the Statistical Abstract of the United States (288) published by the Census Bureau, over the objections of librarians and researchers, ProQuest launched this replacement edition as an annual publication beginning with 2013. Intentionally mimics the format, scope and organization of the original resource. Remains an excellent source for the most current possible data on population, government finance, the economy, and even for some international statistics. Original source publications for figures in tables are indicated. Appendixes include a guide to sources of statistics, state statistical abstracts, and foreign statistical abstracts; discussion of metropolitan and micropolitan statistical areas; and a table of weights and measures. Index. Also available in an online edition, from which the data tables can be retrieved in PDF. http://proquest.libguides.com/statisticalabstract

151 Statista. http://www.statista.com/.
Statista, Inc. New York: Statista, Inc. 2008–
                                        HF5415.2
Searchable subscription data resource. Covers demographics such as employment or the CPI; topical data on trends such as wind power or app stores; and downloadable industry reports for areas such as banking or retail (as defined by NAICS codes). Offers a glossary of statistical terms. Publishes a "chart of the day" which is freely available under a Creative Commons License.

152 Statistical yearbook: annuaire statistique. United Nations. New York: United Nations. 37 v. ISSN 0082-8459
310.5   HA12.5.U63
A summary of international statistics for the countries of the world, and continuing the *Statistical yearbook of the League of Nations*. Covers agriculture, forestry and fishing; communication; development assistance; education; energy; environment; finance; gender; international merchandise trade; international tourism; labour force; manufacturing; national accounts; population; prices; and science and technology. Tables may show figures for up to ten years. References are given to sources. A world summary was introduced beginning with v. 15 (1963), summarizing tables appearing in various chapters. Can be downloaded as a large PDF from http://unstats.un.org/unsd/syb/. The *Monthly bulletin of statistics online* complements this resource by providing current information.

153 UNdata. http://data.un.org. United Nations Statistics Division. New York: United Nations. 2008–
                                         HA155
Provides simultaneous access to datasets derived from 14 statistical databases produced within the U.N. System. Subject matter includes population, labor, education, energy, agriculture, industry, tourism, trade, and national accounts. Its content may be accessed in four ways. Both the keyword and advanced searches identify and retrieve data by source (e.g., Unesco statistics), year, country, region, and miscellaneous keyword, but the advanced search does so more precisely. The Explorer offers hierarchical navigation within each database. Finally, the user may browse profiles created for each country. UNdata also contains a statistical profile of each country. The UN Statistics Division (UNSD) will ultimately include the statistical resources of national

governments. UNdata usually hosts only part of a database's content, so it does not replace UN Comtrade (228), the National Accounts Main Aggregates Database, and other statistical systems created by the U.N. and related intergovernmental organizations. The lone exception is the UN Common Database (229), which has been rendered obsolete.

154   United States business history, 1602–1988: a chronology. Richard Robinson. New York: Greenwood Press, 1990. xii, 643 p. ISBN 9780313260957

338.0973   HC103

"Designed to provide a basic calendar of representative events . . . in the evolution of U.S. business."—*Pref.* Contains descriptive historical data, arranged by year, then under categories of general news and business news. Significant individuals, specific companies, inventions, trade unions, and key business, economic, and social developments are included. Brief bibliography; detailed index. Complemented by *Robinson's business history of the world: a chronology.*

155   U.S. Bureau of Labor Statistics. http://www.bls.gov/. Bureau of Labor Statistics. Washington: U.S. Department of Labor. 1995–

331.10212   HD8051

Home page of the official data-collecting agency in the field of labor statistics and economics: this includes tracking market activity, working conditions, and price changes. BLS produces the Consumer Price Index (CPI), Producer Price Index (PPI), Import and Export Price Indices, and the Consumer Expenditure Survey. Online reports cover inflation and prices, spending and time use, employment and unemployment, pay and benefits, productivity, workplace injuries, and comparisons with international figures. Offers "at a glance" snapshots covering the whole U.S. economy; regions, states and areas; and 100 specific industries.

156   The value of a dollar: colonial era to the Civil War, 1600–1865. Scott Derks, Tony Smith. Millerton, N.Y.: Grey House, 2005. 436 p., ill. ISBN 1592370942

338.520973   HB235.U6

Similar to *Value of a dollar, 1860–2014* (157): each chapter covers a different period of time. Each chapter includes background, historical snapshots, currency, selected incomes, services and fees, financial rates

and exchanges, commodities, selected prices, and miscellany. Slave trades are included through chapter four, 1800–1824. Useful for historical research, as well as an interesting glimpse into history.

157   The value of a dollar: prices and incomes in the United States, 1860–2014. 5th ed. Scott Derks. Amenia, N.Y.: Grey House Pub., 2014. 600 p. ISBN 9781619252547

338.5/20973   HB235.U6

Illustrates trends in prices. Each chapter covers a different period of time (every five years, since 1900) and includes historical chronology, consumer prices, typical investment returns, income for selected jobs, national average wages, and pricing for food and other items. Data is by city, county, or state. For information from earlier years, see The value of a dollar: colonial era to the Civil War, 1600–1865 (156). Content has been extended to add five more years since the 2009 edition, with new chapters covering wages, prices and investment yields in the U.S. through 2014. Bibliography. Index. Also available as an e-book.

Consumer Protection Information

158   Better business bureau. http://www.bbb.org/. Council of Better Business Bureaus. Arlington, Va.: Council of Better Business Bureaus. 1996–

TX335

Portal to home pages of the 112 independent BBB offices in cities of the U.S. and Canada. These groups provide directories and ratings of businesses and charities, register complaints, and attempt to mediate conflicts between businesses and consumers. BBB is not a government agency. Accreditation for businesses is voluntary. In some ways a precursor to social media-based rating and review sites like *Yelp* for local businesses, or *TripAdvisor* for hotels.

159   Consumer information | Federal Trade Commission. https://www.consumer.ftc.gov/. Federal Trade Commission. Washington: U.S. Federal Trade Commission. 2012–

HV6695

Home page for "the nation's consumer protection agency. The FTC works to prevent fraudulent, deceptive and unfair business practices in the marketplace." Information relating to money and credit, homes and mortgages, health and fitness, jobs and making money, and privacy and identity. Register of scam alerts. On the website, consumers can file complaints, sign up for the do-not-call registry, report identity theft, or obtain free credit reports.

160   Consumer protection — USA.gov.
http://www.usa.gov/topics/consumer
.shtml. General Services Administration.
Washington: U.S. General Services
Administration. 2011–

HC110

Includes an online Consumer Action Handbook with advice on topics such as ATM fraud, leasing a car, lemon laws, free credit reports, debt collectors, the do-not-call registry, student loans, health care, mortgages and refinancing, insurance, identity theft, travel tips, service contracts, and funerals. Sample letter of complaint. Directory of state and local consumer agencies. Lists of federal and tribal agencies. Part of the larger USA.gov site.

161   Consumer reports online. http://www
.consumerreports.org/cro/index.htm.
Consumers Union of United States.
[Yonkers, N.Y.]: Consumers Union of U.S.
1998–
640.73/0973   TX335.A1

Product ratings and reviews for products such as cars, appliances, electronic devices, home and garden tools, products for children, health care devices, and services ranging from insurance to airline travel. Online counterpart to the well-known *Consumer reports* magazine, founded in 1942. Access to ratings and recommendations is limited to subscribers, but buying tips and price comparisons are freely available.

162   FDA for consumers. http://www
.fda.gov/ForConsumers/default.htm.
FDA Consumer Health Information.
Silver Spring, Md.: U.S. Food and Drug
Administration. 2010–
640.73   HD9000.9.U5

Consumer information about products in these categories: animal and veterinary; cosmetics; drugs; food; medical devices; radiation-emitting products; tobacco; and vaccines, blood, and biologics. Tracks product recalls in these areas. Posts consumer updates. Part of the larger FDA site.

**163   Recalls.gov: your online resource for
recalls.** http://www.recalls.gov/. U.S.
Consumer Product Safety Commission.
Washington: U.S. Consumer Product
Safety Commission. 2003–
363.19   HF5415.9

Tracks official government recalls of unsafe, hazardous or defective consumer products including motor vehicles, boats, food, medicine, cosmetics, and environmental products. A joint effort of the U.S. Department of Agriculture, the Food and Drug Administration, the Coast Guard, the Environmental Protection Agency, the National Highway Traffic Safety Administration, and the Consumer Product Safety Commission (164). In English and Spanish.

**164   U.S. consumer product safety
commission.** http://www.cpsc.gov/. U.S.
Consumer Product Safety Commission.
Washington: U.S. Consumer Product
Safety Commission. 1996–
HC110

Home page for the U.S. agency "charged with protecting the public from unreasonable risks of injury or death associated with the use of the thousands of types of consumer products . . ." Searchable list of recalls (163). Guidelines for safety education. Full text of relevant laws, regulations, and standards. Statistics on injuries and deaths. Information for businesses, manufacturers, and importers.

Economic Conditions and World Trade

Guides and Handbooks

165 Exporters' encyclopaedia. Dun's
Marketing Services. New York: Dun and
Bradstreet International, 1982–2009.
maps ISSN 8755-013X
382.602573   HF3011
Ceased in 2009. Comprehensive world marketing
guide for 220 world markets. Designed as a guide to
possible markets and also as an instructional manual
for some practicalities (e.g. shipping and insurance).
Country profiles include communications, key contracts, trade regulations, documentation, marketing data, transportation, and business travel. Other
sections cover U.S. ports, U.S. foreign trade zones,
World Trade Center Association members, U.S. government agencies providing assistance to exporters,
foreign trade organizations, foreign communications,
and general export and shipping information.

166 Guide to foreign trade statistics.
http://www.census.gov/foreign-trade/
guide/. Bureau of the Census. Washington:
U.S. Dept. of Commerce. 1967–
ISSN 0565-0933
382.0973   HF105.B73a
Guide to various sources of foreign trade statistics
from the U.S. government. Most useful for definitions and links to relevant sources. Earlier editions
available in print.

**167 Handbook of United States economic
and financial indicators. Rev. ed.**
Frederick M. O'Hara, F. M. O'Hara.
Westport, Conn.: Greenwood Press, 2000.
x, 395 p. ISBN 9780313274503
330.973   HC106.8
Definitions for 284 economic and financial indicators, with calculations, derivations, use, and publishers. Appendixes for nonquantitative indicators, key
to printed sources, compilers of indicators, key to
electronic sources, and general reading. Available as
an e-book.

168 The index of economic freedom.
Heritage Foundation, Wall Street Journal
(Firm). Washington: The Heritage
Foundation, 1995–. maps
ISSN 1095-7308
338.9005   HB95
Ranks 185 countries, including Hong Kong, by the
extent of government involvement in the economy.
The more that a government is involved in constraint
in the production, distribution, or consumption
of goods and services, the less freedom the editors
believe is present. In addition to the score, 2-p. long
country profiles discuss trade policy, fiscal burden,
government intervention, monetary policy, foreign
investment, banking and finance, wages and prices,
property rights, regulation, and informal market. The
2007 ed. adds a chapter on regions. A Web version
is available at http://www.heritage.org/index/, with

interactive features tracking 10 benchmarks related to the rule of law, limited government, regulatory efficiency, and open markets: property rights, freedom from corruption, fiscal freedom, government spending, business freedom, labor freedom, monetary freedom, trade freedom, investment freedom, and financial freedom.

169   The secrets of economic indicators: hidden clues to future economic trends and investment opportunities. 3rd ed. Bernard Baumohl. Upper Saddle River, N.J.: FT Press, 2013. xxv, 468 p., ill. ISBN 9780132932073
330.01/12   HB3730

Information on the indicators with the greatest influence on markets, indicators that are best for forecasting the economy, major data sources, and information on interpreting economic indicators. Includes frequency of publication, release times, and revisions. Focus is primarily on U.S. indicators for employment, consumer spending, GDP, housing starts, the Federal Reserve, and prices; also includes descriptions of key international economic indicators, and a guide to important sources on the Web. Available as an e-book.

Reviews of Research and Trends

170   World development report. World Bank. [New York]: Oxford University Press, 1978–. ill., maps ISSN 0163-5085
330.9/172/4   HC59.7

Each annual report presents an overview and analysis of a currently relevant international economic development issue such as youth, jobs, or gender equity, or investment climate. The statistical "data annex" presents selected social, economic, and demographic data for more than 130 countries and multiple other regions. Also available online as PDFs through the World Bank at http://econ.worldbank.org/wdrs/.

171   World economic and social survey. United Nations, United Nations. New York: United Nations, 1994–
ISSN 1605-7910
330.9005   HC59

Analysis and economic data for long-term social and economic development issues. Chapters on the global outlook, international trade, financial flows to developing countries, regional developments and outlooks, and statistical tables. Includes a lengthy bibliography. Available online from the UN's Web site (http://www.un.org/esa/policy/publications/papers.htm). Also known as *WESS*. Formerly *World economic survey*, to 1993, and successor to an earlier League of Nations publication of that name.

Encyclopedias

172   Booms and busts: an encyclopedia of economic history from Tulipmania of the 1630s to the global financial crisis of the 21st century. James Ciment. Armonk, N.Y.: Sharpe, 2010. 3 v. ISBN 9780765682246
330.03   HB3722

Three-hundred-and-sixty signed articles in alphabetical order on concepts, theories, key personalities, government agencies, and national economies. Historical and global in scope, but emphasizes events in the U.S. and since the 20th century, such as the Great Depression and the financial crisis of 2008. Charts and tables. Chronology. Glossary. Bibliography. Index.

173   Business cycles and depressions: an encyclopedia. David Glasner, Thomas F. Cooley. New York: Garland, 1997. xv, 779 p., ill. ISBN 0824009444
338.54203   HB3711.B936

Contains 327 essays about economists, theories, and historic events, with selective bibliographies. Biographies focus on an individual economist's contributions to understanding business cycles. Well written, with good international coverage.

174   Crises and cycles in economic dictionaries and encyclopaedias. Daniele Besomi. London; New York: Routledge, 2012. xxiv, 676 p., ill. ISBN 9780415499033
338.5/42   HB3722

Summarizes coverage of crises and business cycles in major reference works of the last two centuries. Serves also as an essay on the history and development of dictionaries and encyclopedias as scholary tools. Surveys major economic and social science dictionaries and encyclopedias from France, Germany, Italy, Russia, the Netherlands and Great Britain, and their authors. Bibliography. Index. Available as an e-book.

175 Encyclopedia of business in today's world. Charles Wankel. Thousand Oaks, Calif.: SAGE Publications, 2009. 4 v. (lxiv, 2010 p.), ill. ISBN 9781412964272
650.03   HF1001
Almost 1,000 signed entries in alphabetical order, with suggestions for further reading. Covers key companies; major commercial countries; aspects of globalization and international agreements; practices in finance, marketing, accounting and management; legislation and legal factors; issues of ethics and social responsibility; and the impact of technology, all from a global perspective. Chronology. Extensive glossary. Appendix of WTO world trade statistics. Bibliography. Index. Also available as an e-book.

176 Encyclopedia of globalization. Roland Robertson, Jan Aart Scholte. New York: Routledge, 2007. 4 v.; xvii, 1559, I-37 p., ill., maps ISBN 0415973147
303.48203   JZ1318.E63
Contains nearly 400 entries, from acid rain to youth culture, to cover the multiple aspects of globalization affecting sectors of society around the world. Each volume includes a list of entries, reader's guide, and cumulative index. All entries contain a bibliography and recommend related entries or documents. Vol. 4 also includes primary source documents related to the entries; the CSGR Globalisation Index, which measures dimensions of globalization per country; and an additional selected bibliography arranged by subject areas. Also available as an e-book.

177 Encyclopedia of international development. Tim Forsyth. Abingdon, U.K.;New York: Routledge, 2005. xix, 826 p. ISBN 9780415253420
338.9003   HD82
Contains 600 entries on concepts, organizations, summits, policies, and leaders involved in international development. The authors take a wide view of the topic, including entries on religion, education, war, and reproductive rights. Entries are signed and include further reading. Index; cross-references.

178 Encyclopedia of sustainability. Robin Morris Collin, Robert W. Collin. Santa Barbara, Calif.: Greenwood Press, 2010. 3 v., ill. ISBN 9780313352638
333.7203   GE10.E528
Presents a balanced look at the "3-legged stool" of sustainability: Environment and Ecology, Business and Economics, and Equity and Fairness. The authors are law professors with extensive experience in the field and have produced a clear and comprehensive summary of the issues. Each volume includes five main chapters: Overview, Definitions and Contexts, Government and United Nations Involvement, Controversies, and Future Directions and Emerging Trends, along with a useful initial Guide to Related Topics and a complete index to the set.

Illustrations are appropriate. Has occasional sidebar biographies of people not often covered in standard environmental works. Can be used for quick reference, but most valuable for more in-depth coverage, especially of controversies and trends. Vol. 1 of *The Berkshire encyclopedia of sustainability*, which began publication in 2010, deals with some of the same fairness issues. Available online.

179 Encyclopedia of the developing world. Thomas M. Leonard. New York: Routledge, 2006. 3 v. ISBN 9781579583880
909.0972403   HC59.7
Contains 800 entries by 251 authors, which include country descriptions, biographies, and topical definitions, such as "capitalist economic model." Entries are signed and include references and further readings. Country entries discuss location, temperature, history, and the economy. Biographical entries include educational background, professional accomplishments, and impact on the economy. Entries are 1–3 p. long.

180 Encyclopedia of the global economy: a guide for students and researchers. David E. O'Connor. Westport, Conn.: Greenwood Press, 2006. 2 v., ill. ISBN 9780313335846
330.03   HF1359
Over 150 entries briefly cover issues and key individuals related to the global economy. Especially useful for the inclusion of tables, graphs, 59 key primary documents, and statistical data located in v. 2. For

historical perspective, see the *Timeline of key events in the global economy, 1776–2009*. Also has a glossary of selected terms, a list of global economy web sites, and a selected bibliography. Available as an e-book.

181   Encyclopedia of world poverty.
Mehmet Odekon. Thousand Oaks, Calif.:
SAGE Publications, 2006. 3 v., ill., maps
ISBN 9781412918077
362.503   HV12

Over 750 signed articles on the political, social, geographic, and economic characteristics of poverty in 191 countries. Definition and measurement of poverty in various contexts, as well as effects on special groups including women, children, and the elderly. Includes historical context, along with political and economic factors in specific countries and settings. Covers aid organizations. Biographies of individuals who have made significant contributions to the study or alleviation of poverty. Where available, country rankings on the Human Development Index and the Human Poverty Index are given. Chronology from antiquity to the present. Three appendixes: United Nations statistics on national poverty, World Trade organization statistics on national economics, and directory of poverty-relief organizations. Cross-references. Bibliographies. Index. Available as an e-book.

182   Encyclopedia of world trade: from ancient times to the present. Cynthia
Clark Northrup. Armonk, N.Y.: Sharpe
Reference, 2005. 4 v., ill., maps
ISBN 9780765680587
382.03   HF1373

With 450 entries, provides background to the development of world trade. Signed entries vary in coverage and scope, but include the highlights. Some entries are for an event, others for individuals, places, and even religions. Also includes primary documents.

183   Europa world plus. http://www
.europaworld.com/pub/about/. Europa
Publications Limited, Routledge, Taylor
& Francis Group. New York: Routledge;
Taylor and Francis Group. 2003–
                                           D443

Economic and political information for more than 250 countries and territories. Links to recent news are featured on the Web site home page. Includes

Europa world year book (184) and the *Europa regional surveys of the world* series:
   Africa south of the Sahara (337)
   Central and south-eastern Europe
   Eastern Europe, Russia and Central Asia (322)
   The Far East and Australasia
   The Middle East and North Africa (340)
   South America, Central America and the Caribbean (320)
   South Asia
   The USA and Canada (292)
   Western Europe

Country entries include country profile, geography, chronology, history, economy, country statistics, government and politics directory, society and media directory, business and commerce directory, and bibliography.

Unique to the online version is the comparative statistics section, which generates five years of multinational statistics on area and population, agriculture, industry, finance, external trade, and education in tables and charts downloaded as an HTML table, comma-separated values and in tab-separated values. The comparative statistics section uses different sources than the country statistics section, making data comparisons possible.

Print versions of some *Europa* content have appeared since 1926 and may be useful for historical and comparative purposes.

184   The Europa world year book. Europa
Publications Limited. London: Europa
Publications Limited, 1989–
ISSN 0956-2273
391.184   JN1

Despite the title, covers all countries of the world. Issued annually in two volumes, with v. 1 covering international organizations and the first group of alphabetically arranged country entries and v. 2 the remainder of the country entries. Information on the United Nations, its agencies, and other international organizations followed by detailed information about each country, arranged alphabetically in each volume, giving an introductory survey, a statistical survey, the government, political parties, the constitution, judicial system, diplomatic representation, religion, press, publishers, radio and television, finance, trade and industry, transport, and tourism. Vol. 1 ends with an index to international organizations; v. 2 includes a country index.

Published as *Europa year book* prior to 1989. Similar Europa publications with a regional focus are the *Regional surveys of the world*, including *Africa south of the Sahara* (337), *Central and south-eastern Europe*, *Eastern Europe, Russia, and Central Asia* (322), *The Far East and Australasia, The Middle East and North Africa* (340), *South America, Central America, and the Caribbean* (320), *South Asia, The USA and Canada* (292), and *Western Europe*. The electronic version of this resource, Europa World Plus (183), includes both the year book and the regional surveys as well as continual updates on recent elections, recent events, and a featured country. It also provides the capability to search and create tables of comparative statistics for the countries in the database.

185   The Federal Reserve System: an encyclopedia. R. W. Hafer. Westport, Conn.: Greenwood Press, 2005. xxxii, 451 p., ill. ISBN 0313328390
332.11097303   HG2563
Contains 250 well-written articles explaining the somewhat mysterious Federal Reserve System, its structure, process, and policies. Entries also cover people and key events related to the Federal Reserve. Appendixes provide the text of The Federal Reserve Act, Federal Reserve Regulations, and a list of the Membership of the Board of Governors: 1913–2004. Available as an e-book.

186   Globalization: encyclopedia of trade, labor, and politics. Ashish K. Vaidya. Santa Barbara, Calif.: ABC-CLIO, 2006. 2 v., ill. ISBN 9781576078266
337.03   JZ1318
Contains 94 entries about international trade since World War II, concentrating on the economic, business, legal, political and environmental aspects of international economic integration. Organized in four sections: basic trade and investment issues, impact of globalization in various economic sectors, roles of international blocs and agencies in furthering globalization, and social and political issues. Available as an e-book.

187   History of world trade since 1450. John J. MacCusker. Farmington Hills, Mich.: Macmillan Reference USA, 2006. 2 v. ISBN 9780028658407
382/.09   HF1379
Similar to *Encyclopedia of world trade: from ancient times to the present* (182), but more accessible for younger readers and with enough unique content to justify owning both sources. Over 400 signed entries, with cross-references and annotations for additional reading. Also available as an e-book.

188   The Oxford encyclopedia of economic history. Joel Mokyr, Oxford University Press. New York: Oxford University Press, 2003. 5 v. ISBN 9780195105070
330.03   HC15
Authoritative five-volume set covering all aspects of economic history from ancient to modern times. Alphabetic arrangement of nearly 900 signed articles with bibliographies and cross-references. Major topics include geography, agriculture, production systems, business history, technology, demography, institutions, governments, markets, money, banking finance, labor, natural resources and the environment, and biographies. Separate listing of scholarly economic history internet sites. Index and topical outline of articles. Available as an e-book.

189   St. James encyclopedia of labor history worldwide: major events in labor history and their impact. Neil Schlager. Detroit: St. James Press/Gale Group/Thomson Learning, 2004. 2 v., 1200 p., ill. ISBN 9781558625426
331.8   HD4839
More than 300 articles on topics such as significant strikes and laws dealing with labor and unions, with an emphasis on events in the United States and on the period from 1800 to the present. Some additional short biographical entries. Bibliography. Available as an e-book.

190   Trade unions of the world. 6th ed. John Harper Publishing. London: John Harper Publishing, 2005 ISBN 9780955114427
331.88025   HD6483
Political and economic background sketches for 186 countries, with an overview and history of trade union activities. Individual union entries including contact information, URLs, history, and international affiliations. Available as an e-book.

Dictionaries

191 **The concise encyclopedia of the
great recession 2007–2012. Rev. and
expanded ed., 2nd ed.** Jerry Martin
Rosenberg. Lanham, Md.: Scarecrow
Press, 2012 ISBN 9780810883406
330.9/051103   HB3743

Defines relevant terms, identifies major companies,
and discusses key sectors of the American economy,
fiscal policies and government responses to the crisis.
Presents numerous statistics. In alphabetical order,
with numerous cross-references: most entries are brief.
Updated since the 1st edition of 2010 to track events
into 2012. Bibliography. Index. Available as an e-book.

192 **Dictionary of international economics
terms.** John Owen Edward Clark.
London: Les50ns Professional Pub, 2006.
300 p. ISBN 0852976852
330.03   HF1359

Defines concepts, jargon, and acronyms in economics, finance and business. Includes definitions
such as accelerated depreciation, Andean Pact,
coupon interest rate, marginal cost, shakeout, and
X-inefficiency. Part of a series of dictionaries, which
include: *Dictionary of international accounting terms,
Dictionary of international banking and finance terms,
Dictionary of international business terms, Dictionary of
international insurance and finance terms,* and *Dictionary of international trade finance.* Some definitions are
shared between the dictionaries in the series.

193 **Dictionary of international trade.** Jerry
Martin Rosenberg. New York: Wiley, 1994.
xii, 314 p. ISBN 9780471597322
382.03   HF1373

More than 4,000 entries define terms, simple to
complex, sometimes offering more than one definition for an entry: "relatively simple for the layperson,
more developed and technical for the specialist."
Introd. contains cross-references. Includes an appendix of currency codes. Reissued with some changes
in 2004 as *Essential dictionary of international trade.*

194 **Dictionary of international trade:
handbook of the global trade
community, includes 34 key
appendices. 10th ed.** Edward G.

Hinkelman, Paul Denegri. Petaluma, Calif.:
World Trade Press, 2013. 792 p.
ISBN 9781618408754
382.03   HF1373

An A-Z guide to formal and informal vocabulary on
exporting, importing, banking, shipping, and other
matters relating to international trade. Definitions
make up half the book, with the other half devoted
to appendixes. Topics of appendixes include acronyms
and abbreviations, country codes, international dialing
guide, currencies of the world, business entities worldwide, weights and measures, ship illustrations, airplane
illustrations, truck and trailer illustrations, railcar illustrations, guide to air freight containers, guide to ocean
freight containers, world airports by IATA code, seaports of the world, guide to Incoterms 2000, guide to
letters of credit, resources for international trade, guide
to trade documentation, guide to international sourcing, key words in eight languages, global supply chain
security, and maps of the world in color.

195 **Dictionary of trade policy terms.
5th ed.** Walter Goode, World Trade
Organization, University of Adelaide.
Cambridge, U.K.: Cambridge University
Press, 2007. xi, 528 p.
ISBN 9780521885065
382.03   HF1373

Contains roughly 2,500 entries on terms, principles,
policies and practices, agreements, events, issues,
and theories related to international trade regulation
and negotiation. Covers the trade-related activities
of intergovernmental organizations and, to a lesser
degree, national governments. Includes in-text references and a bibliography. Though intended for the
generalist, specialists will also find it useful.

196 **Historical dictionary of organized
labor. 3rd ed.** J. C. Docherty, Jacobus
Hermanus Antonius van der Velden.
Lanham, Md.: Scarecrow Press, 2012.
xlvii, 448 p. ISBN 9780810861961
331.8803   HD4839

Contains 400 entries on countries, national and
international organizations, unions, and labor leaders. Revised and expanded since the edition of 2004,
with new entries covering trends globally and in the
United States. The introduction serves as a history
of organized labor. Extensive list of acronyms and
abbreviations. Chronology notes major events by

year, beginning in 1152 B.C. and ending with 2011. Bibliography includes URLs for relevant organizations. Complemented by the 2006 *Historical dictionary of socialism* by Docherty and Peter Lamb, which covers political theories and parties. Available as an e-book.

197 The new Palgrave dictionary of economics and the law. Peter Newman. London; New York: Macmillan Reference; Stockton Press, 2004. 3 v., ill. ISBN 9781561592159

330.03   K487.E3

Contains 399 signed articles with international coverage on the legal aspects of economics, such as airline deregulation and property rights. Includes statutes, treaties, directives, and cases. Written by 340 contributors from eight countries.

198 World monetary units: an historical dictionary, country by country. Howard M. Berlin. Jefferson, N.C.: McFarland, 2006. vii, 229 p. ISBN 9780786420803

332.403   HG216

Chronologies, etymologies, and orthographic information for 203 countries and four confederations. Arranged by country. Appendixes for Foreign language number systems, Families of monetary units, Monetary abbreviations and symbols, ISO–4217 currency codes, and Central banks. References and index. Also useful is *Coins and currency: an historical encyclopedia* (51).

Periodicals

199 The economist: world news, politics, economics, business and finance. London: Economist Newspaper Ltd., 1843–. ill. ISSN 0013-0613

330.05   HG11

Coverage of political, economic and business events, world leaders, and science and technology. Economic and financial indicators (output, prices and jobs, *The Economist* commodity-price index, GDP growth forecasts, trade, exchange rates, budget balances and interest rates, markets, and stock markets), and emerging market indicators (overview, child mortality, economy, financial markets) are published regularly. Regular book reviews. Full online access

available for a fee at http://www.economist.com/ and through various aggregator databases. *The economist* sponsors EIU.com (209).

200 International trade statistics yearbook. United Nations Statistical Office. New York: United Nations, 1985– ISSN 0498-0204

382.021   HF91

Four to five years of external trade data for select commodities and nearly 200 countries. Vol. 1 contains detailed data by country, with summary tables on trade relations of each with its region and of the world. Vol. 2 shows the economic world trade of certain commodities analyzed by region and country. Some editions available as e-books, including some links at the UN website at http://comtrade.un.org/pb/ (see "List of Yearbooks").

201 World economic outlook: a survey by the staff of the International Monetary Fund. International Monetary Fund. Washington: The International Monetary Fund, 1980–. ill. ISSN 0256-6877

338.5/443/09048   HC10

Reviews world economic conditions with short- to mid-term economic projections. Over half the publication consists of expository chapters, supplemented by tables and charts, that discuss industrial countries, developing countries, and economies in transition. The statistical appendix has 43 tables, giving output, inflation, financial policies, foreign trade, current account transactions and financing, external debt and debt service, and flow of funds summary. All reports since 1998 available online on the IMF website (http://www.imf.org/external/ns/cs.aspx?id=29/).

Atlases

202 Atlas of the world economy. Michael J. Freeman, Derek Howard Aldcroft. New York: Simon and Schuster, 1991. xv, 167 p., ill. ISBN 9780130507419

330.904   HC59

While dated, still interesting for visuals of world economy. Broken into eight broad categories (population, agriculture, energy, industry, national income, transport and trade, labor, and multinationals), with introductory comments and some 250 maps, charts, tables, and graphs.

203   The state of the world atlas. 8th ed.

Dan Smith. London: Earthscan, 2008. 144 p., col. ill., col. maps
ISBN 9781844075737
300.223   G1021

Visual display of the geographic distribution of measures such as life expectancy, education, urbanization, national income, foreign investment, energy trade, communications, tourism, debt and aid, military spending, political systems, malnutrition, smoking, water resources, waste, and energy use.

Statistics

204   Balance of payments statistics.

International Monetary Fund. Washington: International Monetary Fund, 1981–
ISSN 0252-3035
382.170212   HG3882

Continues, in part, *Balance of payments yearbook* (1947–80), which has data back to 1938. Includes information on 56 countries, organized into three parts: country tables; world and regional tables; and methodologies, compilation practices, and data sources. Contains detailed balance of payments and international investment position data, i.e., information about transactions in goods, services, and income between an economy and the rest of the world; changes in ownership in that country's monetary gold; special drawing rights (SDRs); and claims and liabilities to the rest of the world. Often used to help determine a country's short-term market potential. Also published online through the IMF eLibrary.

205   Bulletin of labour statistics.

International Labour Office. Geneva, Switzerland: The Office, 1965–2009. ill.
ISSN 0007-4950
331.0212   HD4826

Monthly and quarterly international labor data, including level of employment, numbers and percentages unemployed, average number of hours worked, average earnings or wage rates, and consumer prices. Covers 190 countries. Supplements the *Yearbook of labour statistics* (236) also from ILO. Ceased with issues of 2009.

206   The complete economic and demographic data source: CEDDS.

Woods and Poole Economics. Washington: Woods and Poole Economics, 1984–
ISSN 1044-2545
330.9730021   HC101

Based on results of the Woods and Poole regional forecasting model of every county and metropolitan area in the United States. Vol. 1 (1992) summarizes the results of the 1992 forecast, points out trends in regional economies, describes the database and methodology, and presents statistical tables that rank states, statistical areas, and counties in terms of population, employment, and income historically and over the forecast period, now extending to 2040. The remainder of v. 1 and the whole of v. 2 and 3 present detailed statistical tables for counties in each state, in alphabetical order by state. Also marketed in CD-ROM format.

207   Datastream advance. Datastream

International. New York: Thomson Reuters, 1995–
332.642   HG4551

Also known as Thomson Datastream or TDS. A wide array of current and historic global market and economic data. Covers 700 topics, with data going back 20 years. Includes: global and sector indexes, exchange-traded derivatives, investment research, fixed income and equity securities, current and historical fundamental data, foreign exchange and money markets data, real-time financial news from Dow Jones, closing prices for OTC bond instruments, forecast and historical economics data, and interest and exchange rates. Data can easily be compared and downloaded to Excel, Word, or PowerPoint.

208   Direction of trade statistics quarterly.

International Monetary Fund. Washington: International Monetary Fund, 1994–
1017–2734   HF1016 382

Presents current values for import and export of merchandise among member states of the IMF, disaggregated to show important trading partners. About 160 countries are covered. Figures are also combined to show trade flow between world regions. Figures are combined annually in the *Direction of trade statistics year book*. Successor to the quarterly *Direction of trade statistics* (1981–1994).

209 EIU.com. http://www.eiu.com/. Economist Intelligence Unit (Great Britain). London: Economist Intelligence Unit. 1996–

Recent news and trends for nearly 200 countries. Tabs lead to "country analysis" with summaries of recent political developments, economic trends, and the business environment in each nation; "risk analysis" with a credit risk assessment for each country; and "industry analysis" with sections for automotive, energy, healthcare, consumer goods, financial services, and telecommunications. Includes reports of the *Global forecasting service* organized by regions (North America, Japan, Western Europe, Transition Economies, Asia & Australasia, Latin America, and the Middle East & Africa); archived back issues of the *Country reports*; and older archived issues of *Country profiles* although new editions of this content ceased in 2008. Recent information is presented under the headings of Country analysis, Risk analysis and Industry Analysis. Similar to Political Risk Yearbook (226), but with more frequent updates. Key data include GDP, forecast GDP, exports, imports, inflation, exchange rates, interest rates, consumer and producer prices, deposit rate, lending rate, money market rate, select commodity prices, and select industry data. Many numbers can be downloaded into Excel. Archives available from 1996. For a larger array of indicators, consult EIU CountryData (147).

210 FAO statistical yearbook = Annuaire statistique de la FAO = Anuario estadístico de la FAO = Liang nong zu zhi tong ji nian jian. Food and Agriculture Organization of the United Nations. Rome, Italy: Food and Agriculture Organization of the United Nations, 2004– ISSN 1812-0571

338.1   HD1421

Profiles food and agriculture in 155 countries. Data is by topic or by country. Country tables begin with a socio-economic overview, then an overview of agricultural sectors, followed by details of agricultural resources, production, trade, prices, food consumption, and nutritional status. Combines *FAO bulletin of statistics*, *FAO yearbook: Production*, *FAO yearbook: Trade*, and *FAO yearbook: Fertilizer*.

Also available online at http://www.fao.org/docrep/009/a0490m/a0490m00.htm with related data in FAOSTAT.

211 FRED. http://research.stlouisfed.org/fred2/. Federal Reserve Bank of St. Louis. St. Louis: Federal Reserve Bank of St. Louis. 1997–

330.973   HC106

Currently offers data from more than 200,000 U.S. and international economic time series, drawn from over 60 sources. Organized into categories such as academic data; money, banking & finance; national accounts; population, employment & labor markets; production & business activity; and prices. The largest categories cover international data and U.S. regional data, and these two are broken down geographically by countries, states or regions. A source leading to figures such as consumer price indexes (CPIs), employment and population numbers, exchange rates, GDP, interest rates, PPIs, U.S. financial data, and more. Data varies in frequency (daily, weekly, biweekly, monthly, quarterly, annual) and may be seasonally adjusted. Time depth of the series varies. For older data files, see also ALFRED®: ArchivaL Federal Reserve Economic Data (http://alfred.stlouisfed.org/).

212 Government finance statistics yearbook. International Monetary Fund. Washington: International Monetary Fund, 1977– ISSN 0250-7374

336.0212   HJ101

Provides detailed tables for each country on revenue, grants, expenditure, lending minus repayments, financing, and debt of central governments. Also includes data on state and local governments. Annual time series beginning in 1972. Documentation can be found in supplements and *Government finance statistics manual* also from IMF.

213 Global development finance. World Bank. Washington: World Bank, 1997–. 2 v. ISSN 1020-5454

336.3/435/091724   HJ8899

External debt and financial flow data for the economies of 203 countries. Vol. 1 is *Analysis and outlook*, with financial flows to developing countries. Vol. 2 is *Summary and country tables* and includes summary data for regions and income groups. Indicators include external debt stocks and flows, major economic aggregates, key debt ratios, average terms of new commitments, and currency composition of long-term debt. Many tables of data and indicators are also available online via the "Data" tab on the World Bank's Web site.

214   Global financial data. https://www
.globalfinancialdata.com/. Global Financial
Data. San Juan Capistrano, Calif.: Global
Financial Data. 2003–
332.1   HG4501
Historical financial data, from as early as the 1200s,
based on original source publications, newspapers, and
archival materials. Provides 20,000 financial and economic data series for some 200 countries. Categories
include daily stock market data from 1962 (open, high,
low, close, volume, available in split adjusted or unadjusted format); state, national and international real
estate market data from 1830 (includes Median New
Home Prices—United States, Winans International
U.S. Real Estate Index—Price Only, Austria ATX Real
Estate Index, Shanghai SE Real Estate Index); international bond indices from 1862; central bank interest
yields; commercial paper yields; commodity indices;
commodity prices; consumer price indices; U.S and
European corporate bond yields, some from 1857;
international deposit rates; international exchange
rates, some from 1660; futures contracts; government
bond yields; gross domestic product; international
interbank interest rates from the 1980s; interest rate
swaps from 1988 (United States, Europe, Japan); U.S.
intraday data, daily from January 1933 to present; international lending rates, some from 1934; overnight and
call money rates, some from 1857 (monthly, weekly,
daily); international population; sector indices (consumer discretionary, consumer staples, energy, finance,
health care, industrials, information technology, materials, telecommunications, transports, utilities), stock
indices—preferred stocks; stock indices—composites;
stock indices—size and style; stock market—AMEX;
stock market—NASDAQ; stock market—NYSE; stock
market—OTC; stocks (capitalization, volume, dividend yields and P/E ratios, technical indicators); total
return indices—bills; total return indices—bonds;
total return indices—stocks; international treasury bill
yields; international unemployment rates, some from
1890; and international wholesale price indices.

**215   Household Spending: Who Spends
How Much on What. 18th. ed.** New
Strategist Publ. Ithaca, N.Y.: New Strategist
Publ., 2013 ISBN 9781940308074
ISSN 1097-962X
658   HC110.C6
Provides household and detailed spending statistics
organized by major product and service category

from unpublished data collected by the Bureau of
Labor Statistics' 2009 and 2010 Consumer Expenditure Survey. Chapters are arranged alphabetically by
spending category and cover hundreds of products
and services ranging from food and drink to utilities
and transportation. Each section includes a general
overview with statistics by age, income, household
type, region of residence, race and Hispanic origin,
and educational attainment. Appendixes include an
explanation of the Consumer Expenditure Survey;
percent reporting expenditure and amount spent;
spending by product and service ranked by amount
spent; and average amount spent for mortgage principal reduction and capital improvements. The index
is fairly comprehensive and a good entry point for
researchers looking for specific data.

216   ICPSR. http://www.icpsr.umich.edu/. Inter-
University Consortium for Political and
Social Research, Inter-university Consortium
for Political and Social Research. Ann
Arbor, Mich.: Institute for Social Research,
University of Michigan. [1997–]
300.0285   H61.3
Archive of international social science data, includ-
ing a large collection of economic data. In thematic
collections grouped by topic are surveys of Census
Enumerations; Community and Urban Studies;
Conflict, Aggression, Violence, Wars; Economic
Behavior and Attitudes; Education; Elites and Leadership; Geography and Environment; Government
Structures, Policies, and Capabilities; Health Care
and Facilities; Instructional Packages; International
Systems; Legal Systems; Legislative and Deliberative
Bodies; Mass Political Behavior and Attitudes; Organizational Behavior; Social Indicators; Social Institutions and Behavior; Publication-Related Archive; and
External Data Resources. Data can be downloaded
for SAS, SPSS and Stata. Full access is available to
students, staff and faculty at 700 ICPSR member
institutions; some content is freely available to the
public, but may not emphasize economics.

217   IMD world competitiveness yearbook.
IMD International. Lausanne, Switzerland:
International Institute for Management
Development, 2002–. ill. ISSN 1026-2628
337.05   HF1414
Ranks and analyzes how a nation's business and eco-
nomic environment effects the competitiveness of

enterprises. Provides data for 60 national and regional economies within 333 criteria, grouped into four categories: economic performance, government efficiency, business efficiency, and infrastructure. Country profiles include current challenges, competitiveness landscape, peer rankings, improvements, declines, strengths, weaknesses, government efficiency, business efficiency, and infrastructure. Data is gathered from international, regional, and national organizations, private institutes, and a survey conducted by the publisher. Also available in online form.

218 International financial statistics yearbook. English ed. International Monetary Fund. Washington: International Monetary Fund, 1979– ISSN 0250-7463
332/.02/12   HG61

Unified source for overview of financial statistics for nations of the world. Contains summary tables by subject (exchange rate agreements, interest rates, international trade, national accounts, commodity prices), followed by detailed tables for each country, describing its financial and monetary conditions. Updated by the monthly *International financial statistics* (1948–). Much of the data is available online from IMF at http://www.imf.org/external/data.htm.

219 International marketing data and statistics. Euromonitor International. London: Euromonitor, 1975/76–
ISSN 0308-2938
382.09   HA42

Demographic trends and forecasts and economic statistics for 161 non-European countries. Includes up to 30 years of data on cultural indicators, consumer market sizes and expenditures, labor force, foreign trade, health, energy, environment, IT and telecommunications, literacy and education, crime, retailing, travel and tourism, and consumer prices. Sources include the International Monetary Fund, United Nations, national statistical offices and national trade associations. Companion volume to *European marketing data and statistics* (323).

220 International trade statistics yearbook. United Nations Statistical Office. New York: United Nations, 1985–
ISSN 0498-0204
382.021   HF91

Four to five years of external trade data for select commodities and nearly 200 countries. Vol. 1 contains detailed data by country, with summary tables on trade relations of each with its region and of the world. Vol. 2 shows the economic world trade of certain commodities analyzed by region and country. Some editions available as e-books, including some links at the UN website at http://comtrade.un.org/pb/ (see "List of Yearbooks").

221 International yearbook of industrial statistics. United Nations Industrial Development Organization. Vienna, Austria; Aldershot, U.K.; Brookfield, Vt.: Edward Elgar, 1995–
ISSN 1025-8493
338.0021   HC10

Statistics on current performance and trends in the manufacturing sector worldwide, including employment patterns, wages, consumption, and gross output. Includes sections on summary tables, manufacturing sector, manufacturing divisions/branches, and country tables.

222 MarketLine business information centre. http://www.marketline.com/. MarketLine. London; New York: MarketLine. 1994–2010
                              HD2709

Merged with Business insights (793) in 2010 to form Marketline advantage (799).

Provided profiles of about large companies, industry segments, and countries, with an international scope. Company profile information included business descriptions and histories, major products and services, revenue analysis, key employees and biographies, locations and subsidiaries, company view (often taken from an annual report), SWOT analysis, and list of top competitors. Industry profiles were Datamonitor reports, with an executive summary, market overview, market value, market segmentation, competitve landscape, leading companies, and market forecast. Country profiles offered information on the economy, politics and government. Valued for international coverage of industry segments, with reports like "Beer in China." Shares of company profiles were 45 percent United States, 35 percent European, 15 percent Asian, and 5 percent from the rest of world.

223 National accounts statistics. United
Nations. New York: United Nations,
1985–
339.3   HC79.15

Detailed national accounts estimates from 200 countries and areas. Sections include *Main aggregates and
detailed tables*, *Analysis of main aggregates*, and *Government accounts and tables*. Data gathered from national
statistical services, and national and international
source publications. This source is invaluable for
providing data since 1950. Prepared by The Statistical Offices of the United Nations Secretariat. Continues *Yearbook of national accounts statistics (1957–81)*,
which superseded *Statistics of national income and
expenditure (1952–57)*. Also available through the
National Accounts Main Aggregates Database
(http://unstats.un.org/unsd/snaama/Introduction
.asp), with data from 1970 to the present.

224 OECD iLibrary. http://www.oecd-ilibrary
.org/. Organisation for Economic Cooperation and Development. Paris: OECD.
2000–
337   HC59.15

SourceOECD became *OECD iLibrary* in 2010. A subscription database featuring OECD books, reports,
working papers, serials, and statistical databases
on economic and social topics, as well as the environment, energy, and technological development.
Focuses mainly on the 30 OECD member states
and major nonmember developing countries, but
includes information for all nations of the world.
Content is in English and French.

Serials include journals; the OECD Factbook and
other statistical works; and titles that forecast and
analyze trends, such as the OECD Economic Outlook, *African economic outlook*, International Migration Outlook, and OECD-FAO Agricultural Outlook.

Current, themed databases include the OECD
Economic Outlook Database, SourceOECD Main
Economic Indicators, Banking Statistics, Education
Statistics, Globalisation, Indicators of Industry and
Services, Insurance, International Development, Inter-
national Direct Investment Statistics, International
Migration Statistics, the ITCS International Trade by
Commodity Database, Monthly Statistics of Interna-
tional Trade, the National Accounts Database, OECD
Health Data, OECD Statistics on International Trade
in Services, the Revenue Statistics of OECD Member
Countries Database, the Science and Technology

Database, the Social Expenditure Database, Structural
and Demographic Business Statistics, Taxing Wages
Statistics, and the Telecommunications Database. Statistical databases of the International Energy Agency
are also available via this source. OECD.Stat enables
users to query multiple databases simultaneously and
to export search results in several formats.

Also incorporates Future Trends, an index of
published and unpublished sources in more than a
dozen languages covering issues affecting the public
and private sectors. OECD also publishes glossaries.

225 Penn world table. https://pwt.sas.upenn
.edu/php_site/pwt_index.php. Alan W.
Heston, Robert Summers, Bettina Aten,
University of Pennsylvania. Philadelphia:
Center for International Comparisons of
Production, Income and Prices, University
of Pennsylvania. 2002–

International data on "purchasing power parity and
national income accounts converted to international
prices for 188 countries for some or all of the years
1950–2004." —*About PWT*. Variables are Population,
Exchange Rate, Purchasing Power, Parity over GDP,
Real Gross Domestic Product per Capita, Consumption
Share of CGPD, Government Share of CGDP, Invest-
ment Share of CGDP, Price Level of Gross Domestic
Product, Price Level of Consumption, Price Level of
Government, Price Level of Investment, Openness in
Current Prices, Ratio of GNP to GDP, CGDP Relative
to the United States, Real GDP per Capita (Constant
Prices: Laspeyres), Real GDP per capita (Constant
Prices: Chain Series), Real GDP Chain per Equiva-
lent Adult, Real GDP Chain per Worker, Real Gross
Domestic Income (RGDPL Adjusted for Terms of Trade
Changes), Openness in Constant Prices, Consumption
Share of RGDPL, Government Share of RGDPL, Invest-
ment Share of RGDPL, Growth Rate of Real GDP per
Capita (Constant Prices: Chain Series). Data is based on
World Development Indicators and National Accounts
of OECD countries. Data can be downloaded as SAS
and comma separated values (.csv).

226 Political risk yearbook online. http://
www.prsgroup.com/. PRS Group. East
Syracuse, N.Y.: PRS Group. 1999–
                                                    HG3879

Political and economic risk analysis for 106 countries. Reports are PDF files with a country forecast
(highlights, current data, comments and analysis,

forecast scenarios, political players), and country conditions (investment climate, climate for trade including political violence and legal framework, background on geography, history, social conditions, government, political conditions, and environmental trends). Includes forecasts for GDP growth, current account, inflation, political turmoil, investment and trade restrictions, and domesic and international economic problems. Also has statistics for foreign direct investment flows by source country and sector. In print, this resource consists of eight volumes, for North & Central America, the Middle East & North Africa, South America, Sub-Saharan Africa, Asia & the Pacific, West Europe, East Europe, and Central & South Asia.

227 Statistical yearbook: annuaire statistique. United Nations. New York: United Nations. 37 v. ISSN 0082-8459
310.5   HA12.5.U63

A summary of international statistics for the countries of the world, and continuing the *Statistical yearbook of the League of Nations*. Covers agriculture, forestry and fishing; communication; development assistance; education; energy; environment; finance; gender; international merchandise trade; international tourism; labour force; manufacturing; national accounts; population; prices; and science and technology. Tables may show figures for up to ten years. References are given to sources. A world summary was introduced beginning with v. 15 (1963), summarizing tables appearing in various chapters. Can be downloaded as a large PDF from http://unstats.un.org/unsd/syb/. The *Monthly bulletin of statistics online* complements this resource by providing current information.

228 UN comtrade. http://comtrade.un.org/. United Nations Statistical Division. New York: United Nations. 2003–
                                          HF1016

The largest repository of international trade data. Contains more than 1.5 billion records on imports and exports involving some 200 countries and other entities since 1962. A typical record identifies the type of transaction and the year it took place, the reporting country and partner (e.g., the importer and exporter), the commodity name and code, and the type of unit (e.g., volume in liters) and quantity reported. The Comtrade Knowledge Base contains manuals and other materials that facilitate the use

of this source. Updated continuously. Some search options are available only to subscribers, and nonsubscribers cannot download search results. The Comtrade portal also directs users to the UN Comtrade Yearbook, which provides trade statistics by country, region, and commodity in PDF format. Some Comtrade records may also be found in UNdata (153).

229 United Nations common database (UNCDB). http://unstats.un.org/. United Nations Statistics Division. New York: United Nations Statistics Division. 2003–2008

In 2008, UNCDB was replaced by UNdata (153), also from the United Nations Statistics Division. Formerly provided socioeconomic data from 55 sources on 274 countries and areas, with coverage since 1948.

230 World development indicators. World Bank. Washington: World Bank, 1978–. ill.
330.9/005   HC59.15

Compiled annually for 209 economies. Organized in six sections: world view, people, environment, economy, states and markets, and global links. Data back to 1960, from national statistical organizations, the World Bank, and other authoritative sources. Especially useful since data can be scaled, ranged against a particular year, viewed by percentage change, charted, and exported. Much data is also available online at http://data.worldbank.org/indicator/ broken out into agriculture & rural development, aid effectiveness, climate change, economic policy & external debt, education, energy & mining, environment, financial sector, gender, health, infrastructure, labor & social protection, poverty, private sector, public sector, science & technology, social development, and urban development.

231 World development report. World Bank. [New York]: Oxford University Press, 1978–. ill., maps ISSN 0163-5085
330.9/172/4   HC59.7

Each annual report presents an overview and analysis of a currently relevant international economic development issue such as youth, jobs, or gender equity, or investment climate. The statistical "data annex" presents selected social, economic, and demographic data for more than 130 countries and multiple other regions. Also available online as PDFs through the World Bank at http://econ.worldbank.org/wdrs/.

232 World economic and social survey.
United Nations, United Nations. New
York: United Nations, 1994–
ISSN 1605-7910
330.9005   HC59
Analysis and economic data for long-term social
and economic development issues. Chapters on the
global outlook, international trade, financial flows
to developing countries, regional developments and
outlooks, and statistical tables. Includes a lengthy
bibliography. Available online from the UN's
Web site (http://www.un.org/esa/policy/publications/
papers.htm). Also known as *WESS*. Formerly *World
economic survey*, to 1993, and successor to an earlier
League of Nations publication of that name.

**233 World economic outlook: a survey
by the staff of the International
Monetary Fund.** International Monetary
Fund. Washington: The International
Monetary Fund, 1980–. ill.
ISSN 0256-6877
338.5/443/09048   HC10
Reviews world economic conditions with short- to
mid-term economic projections. Over half the publication consists of expository chapters, supplemented
by tables and charts, that discuss industrial countries,
developing countries, and economies in transition.
The statistical appendix has 43 tables, giving output,
inflation, financial policies, foreign trade, current
account transactions and financing, external debt and
debt service, and flow of funds summary. All reports
since 1998 available online on the IMF website
(http://www.imf.org/external/ns/cs.aspx?id=29/).

234 World industry and market outlook.
Barnes Reports Division. Bath, Maine: C.
Barnes & Co., 2006–
338.0021   HC10
Published annually, this report provides worldwide
data on major and minor manufacturing, retail,
wholesale and services industries. Arranged by industry with tables covering current and forecasted estimates for establishments, employment and sales by
country. Beginning in 2014, reports will also include a
worldwide economic forecast with establishment and
sales changes plus projected changes in gross domestic product (GDP), population, inflation, unemployment, poverty, country debt and deficits, and imports
and exports. Available as PDF, spreadsheet (Excel), or

print format edition. Also available in EBSCO Business Source (34) from 2011 to present.

235 WRDS. https://wrds-web.wharton.upenn
.edu/wrds/. Wharton School. Philadelphia:
The Wharton School, University of
Pennsylvania. 1993–
                                  HG4026
Wharton research data services supports quantitative data
research through web access to a hosting service, for
a number of financial databases, including Compustat
(now *Research insight*) (573), CRSP (Center for Research
in Securities Prices), Dow Jones Averages, FDIC, Philadelphia Stock Exchange, Institutional Brokers Estimate
System (IBES), BankScope (888) from Bureau van Dijk,
CSMAR China Stock Market databases, Eventus, Global Insight, NYSE-TAQ, and OptionMetrics.

236 Yearbook of labour statistics.
International Labour Office. Geneva,
Switzerland: International Labour Office,
1936– ISSN 0084-3857
331.29   HD4826
Summarizes labor statistics on the economically active
population of 184 countries and territories. Covers
consumer price indexes, employment, wages and
hours of work, occupational injuries, strikes and lockouts, and household income and expenditures. In
English, French, and Spanish. Updated by *Bulletin of
labor statistics* (Geneva, 1965–, quarterly) (205). The
Retrospective edition on population census, 1945–89,
combines and adjusts data from previous ILO yearbooks with some new data derived from recent or
previously unpublished censuses. Beginning in 2007,
published in two parts: *Country profiles*, and *Time series*.

Internet Resources

237 Bureau of economic analysis. http://
www.bea.gov/. United States Bureau of
Economic Analysis. Washington: Bureau of
Economic Analysis. 1996–
330.09   HC103
Official U.S. government source for extensive economic data in downloadable Excel format. For U.S.
national accounts, includes tables for gross domestic
product (GDP), personal income and outlays, consumer spending, corporate profits, and fixed assets
value. For U.S. international trade, includes tables

for balance of payments, trade in goods and services, international services, international investment position, and direct investment and multinational companies. For regions of the U.S., tables include GDP by state and metropolitan area, state and local area personal income, RIMS II Regional Input-Output Multipliers, and economic information for coastal areas. For U.S. industries, tables include annual industry accounts (GDP by industry & input-output cccounts), benchmark input-output accounts, research and development satellite accounts, and travel and tourism satellite accounts. "U.S. Economy at a Glance" is a useful snapshot. Online source for *Survey of current business* (no longer published in print after 2013).

238 Country briefings. http://www
.economist.com/countries/. Economist
Intelligence Unit (EIU), Economist
Intelligence Unit (New York). New York:
Economist. 1995–2010
909.83   HC59.15
Ceased circa 2010: replaced by EIU's *Country forecast* service with coverage of individual countries, which can be found at EIU.com (209). Provided news from the *Economist* (46) print edition, country profiles, forecasts, statistics, political outlook, economic policy outlook, economic forecast, and economic structure for 60 countries.

**239 Doing business: measuring business
regulations.** http://www.doingbusiness
.org/. World Bank Group, International
Finance Corporation, Oxford University
Press. Washington; Oxford: World Bank;
International Finance Corp.; Oxford
University Press. 2003– ISSN 1729-2638
                                          K563.B87
Measures the impact and effectiveness of regulations, laws, and regulatory institutions around the world. Covers 11 indicator sets such as starting a business, getting credit, and enforcing contracts. Ranks the regulatory situation for the economies of 185 countries. Within some countries, analysis also is available for specific cities. Links to data, rankings and reports. Available in multiple languages.

240 Economic history services. http://eh
.net/. EH.Net. Oxford, Ohio: EH.Net.
1993–
330.9   HC21.E25

Owned by the Economic History Association and intended primarily for economic historians, historians of economics, economists, and historians. EH.net provides full text of book reviews and course syllabi, directory of economic historians, lists of conferences, an *Encyclopedia of economic and business history*, and access to historical economic data sets (such as Global Financial Data, 1880–1913 and historic labor statistics). Researchers may also register databases hosted on servers at other institutions.

The section "How Much Is That?" uses calculators and data sets to show the comparative value of money, including five ways to compare the worth of a U.S. dollar since 1790; the price of gold since 1257; estimated Consumer Price Index figures for the United States since 1774; the purchasing power of the British pound, since 1264; annual real and nominal GDP for the United States, since 1790; annual real and nominal GDP for the United Kingdom, since 1086; interest rate series for the United Kingdom and the United States, since 1790; and daily closing values of the Dow Jones Industrial Average (DJIA) since 1896.

**241 Export.gov: helping U.S. companies
export.** http://export.gov/. United States.
International Trade Administration.
Washington: International Trade
Administration, Dept. of Commerce.
2000–
                                          HF1416.5
U.S. government source for information and assistance on exporting into global markets. Incorporates input from the U.S. Commercial Service, the Export-Import Bank, and the Small Business Administration. Sections address industries, countries, market research, trade events, free trade agreements, international sales and marketing, international financing, international logistics, overseas licenses & regulations, trade data and analysis, and trade problems. Lists U.S. Export Assistance Centers in the U.S. and U.S. Commercial Service offices abroad. Publishes guides to specific countries, such as Doing business in China (358).

**242 GlobalEDGE: your source for global
business knowledge.** http://globaledge
.msu.edu/. Center for International
Business Education and Research
(CIBER). East Lansing, Mich.: Center
for International Business Education and

Research, Eli Broad Graduate School of Management, Michigan State University. 2001–

382   HF1379

Provides news, statistics and summary information about economic activity for trading blocs (such as NAFTA or the European Union), countries, U.S. states, and industries (such as energy or retail). The Reference Desk links to information sources from across the Web. Knowledge Tools allow interactive manipulation of data.

243   Manufacturing.net. http://www .manufacturing.net/. Advantage Business Media (Firm). Rockaway, N.J.: Advantage Business Media. 2000s–

Provides news, reports, links to resources, and networking related to manufacturing for a wide range of sectors, including aerospace, automotive, chemicals and petroleum, energy, food and beverage, materials handling, medical pharmaceuticals and biotechnology, software, and utilities. Includes aspects such as design and development needs, sustainability and environmental issues, facilities operations, labor relations, manufacturing technology, quality control, safety, and supply chain management. Has international focus.

244   Penn world table. https://pwt.sas.upenn .edu/php_site/pwt_index.php. Alan W. Heston, Robert Summers, Bettina Aten, University of Pennsylvania. Philadelphia: Center for International Comparisons of Production, Income and Prices, University of Pennsylvania. 2002–

International data on "purchasing power parity and national income accounts converted to international prices for 188 countries for some or all of the years 1950–2004." —*About PWT*. Variables are Population, Exchange Rate, Purchasing Power, Parity over GDP, Real Gross Domestic Product per Capita, Consumption Share of CGPD, Government Share of CGDP, Investment Share of CGDP, Price Level of Gross Domestic Product, Price Level of Consumption, Price Level of Government, Price Level of Investment, Openness in Current Prices, Ratio of GNP to GDP, CGDP Relative to the United States, Real GDP per Capita (Constant Prices: Laspeyres), Real GDP per capita (Constant Prices: Chain Series), Real GDP Chain per Equivalent Adult, Real GDP Chain

per Worker, Real Gross Domestic Income (RGDPL Adjusted for Terms of Trade Changes), Openness in Constant Prices, Consumption Share of RGDPL, Government Share of RGDPL, Investment Share of RGDPL, Growth Rate of Real GDP per Capita (Constant Prices: Chain Series). Data is based on World Development Indicators and National Accounts of OECD countries. Data can be downloaded as SAS and comma separated values (.csv).

245   Statistical sites on the World Wide Web. http://www.bls.gov/bls/other .htm. U.S. Bureau of Labor Statistics. Washington: U.S. Bureau of Labor Statistics. 1998–

Links to official government statistical offices all over the world, including Web sites from more than 140 countries and from international agencies such as Afristat, East African Community (EAC), European Union Eurostat, Food and Agriculture Organization (FAO), International Energy Agency (IEA), International Labour Organization (ILO), Organization for Economic Cooperation and Development (OECD iLibrary (224)), United Nations International Computing Centre, United Nations Statistical Division, UN Economic Commission for Europe (UN/ECE) Statistical Division, UN Industrial Development Organization Statistics, and World Health Organization Statistical Information System (WHOSIS (1072)). Also links to sites of major U.S. federal statistical agencies, including Bureau of Economic Analysis, Bureau of Justice Statistics, Bureau of Labor Statistics, Bureau of Transportation Statistics, Census Bureau, Economic Research Service, Energy Information Administration, National Agricultural Statistics Service, National Center for Education Statistics, National Center for Health Statistics, Statistics of Income from the IRS, and FedStats. Excellent starting point for researchers.

246   United Nations common database (UNCDB). http://unstats.un.org/. United Nations Statistics Division. New York: United Nations Statistics Division. 2003–2008

In 2008, UNCDB was replaced by UNdata (153), also from the United Nations Statistics Division. Formerly provided socioeconomic data from 55 sources on 274 countries and areas, with coverage since 1948.

3 *International Information*

Global Resources

247   Data: The World Bank. http://data
.worldbank.org/. World Bank. Washington:
World Bank. 2010–

HC21

Freely available source for global data. Searchable
by keywords, or browsable by individual countries
or groupings such as OECD members, topics such
as aid effectiveness or financial sector, and specific
indicators such as "investment in energy with private
participation" or "share of women employed in the
nonagricultural sector." Interface in English, French,
Spanish, Arabic, or Chinese. Data can be downloaded, and displayed in map or graph formats.

248   EIU.com. http://www.eiu.com/.
Economist Intelligence Unit (Great
Britain). London: Economist Intelligence
Unit. 1996–

Recent news and trends for nearly 200 countries. Tabs
lead to "country analysis" with summaries of recent
political developments, economic trends, and the
business environment in each nation; "risk analysis"
with a credit risk assessment for each country; and
"industry analysis" with sections for automotive, energy, healthcare, consumer goods, financial services, and
telecommunications. Includes reports of the *Global
forecasting service* organized by regions (North America,
Japan, Western Europe, Transition Economies, Asia
& Australasia, Latin America, and the Middle East &

Africa); archived back issues of the *Country reports*; and
older archived issues of *Country profiles* although new
editions of this content ceased in 2008. Recent information is presented under the headings of Country
analysis, Risk analysis and Industry Analysis. Similar to
Political Risk Yearbook (226), but with more frequent
updates. Key data include GDP, forecast GDP, exports,
imports, inflation, exchange rates, interest rates, consumer and producer prices, deposit rate, lending rate,
money market rate, select commodity prices, and select
industry data. Many numbers can be downloaded into
Excel. Archives available from 1996. For a larger array
of indicators, consult EIU CountryData (147).

249   EIU CountryData. http://www.eiu.com/
site_info.asp?info_name=ps_countryData.
Bureau van Dijk Electronic Publishing,
Economist Intelligence Unit (Great
Britain). [Bruxelles]: Bureau van Dijk.
1980–

HB3730

The emphasis here is on economic indicators—both
historical time series and forecast figures—in categories such as demographics and income, GDP, fiscal
and monetary, foreign payments, external debts, and
external trade. Annual, quarterly, and monthly figures
for 201 countries, with as many as 320 indicators for
some countries, and figures from as early as 1980.
Forecasts to the year 2030 are published on a monthly
basis for 179 countries, and quarterly for 79 emerging market regions. Core reports cover demographics

and income, gross domestic product (GDP), fiscal and monetary indicators, foreign payments, external debt stock, external debt service, and external trade. Also covers commodity prices and forecasts, and aggregated figures for 45 regions. Available via EIU Data Tool, Bureau van Dijk, and Alacra. Sometimes called *EIU country data*. This is a subscription database. For brief country summaries from EIU, consult EIU.com (209).

250 Europa world plus. http://www .europaworld.com/pub/about/. Europa Publications Limited, Routledge, Taylor & Francis Group. New York: Routledge; Taylor and Francis Group. 2003–
D443

Economic and political information for more than 250 countries and territories. Links to recent news are featured on the Web site home page. Includes *Europa world year book* (184) and the *Europa regional surveys of the world* series:

Africa south of the Sahara (337)
Central and south-eastern Europe
Eastern Europe, Russia and Central Asia (322)
The Far East and Australasia
The Middle East and North Africa (340)
South America, Central America and the Caribbean (320)
South Asia
The USA and Canada (292)
Western Europe

Country entries include country profile, geography, chronology, history, economy, country statistics, government and politics directory, society and media directory, business and commerce directory, and bibliography.

Unique to the online version is the comparative statistics section, which generates five years of multinational statistics on area and population, agriculture, industry, finance, external trade, and education in tables and charts downloaded as an HTML table, comma-separated values and in tab-separated values. The comparative statistics section uses different sources than the country statistics section, making data comparisons possible.

Print versions of some *Europa* content have appeared since 1926 and may be useful for historical and comparative purposes.

251 The Europa world year book. Europa Publications Limited. London: Europa

Publications Limited, 1989–
ISSN 0956-2273
391.184   JN1

Despite the title, covers all countries of the world. Issued annually in two volumes, with v. 1 covering international organizations and the first group of alphabetically arranged country entries and v. 2 the remainder of the country entries. Information on the United Nations, its agencies, and other international organizations followed by detailed information about each country, arranged alphabetically in each volume, giving an introductory survey, a statistical survey, the government, political parties, the constitution, judicial system, diplomatic representation, religion, press, publishers, radio and television, finance, trade and industry, transport, and tourism. Vol. 1 ends with an index to international organizations; v. 2 includes a country index.

Published as *Europa year book* prior to 1989. Similar Europa publications with a regional focus are the *Regional surveys of the world*, including *Africa south of the Sahara* (337), *Central and south-eastern Europe*, *Eastern Europe, Russia, and Central Asia* (322), *The Far East and Australasia*, *The Middle East and North Africa* (340), *South America, Central America, and the Caribbean* (320), *South Asia*, *The USA and Canada* (292), and *Western Europe*. The electronic version of this resource, Europa World Plus (183), includes both the year book and the regional surveys as well as continual updates on recent elections, recent events, and a featured country. It also provides the capability to search and create tables of comparative statistics for the countries in the database.

252 Global development finance. World Bank. Washington: World Bank, 1997–. 2 v. ISSN 1020-5454
336.3/435/091724   HJ8899

External debt and financial flow data for the economies of 203 countries. Vol. 1 is *Analysis and outlook*, with financial flows to developing countries. Vol. 2 is *Summary and country tables* and includes summary data for regions and income groups. Indicators include external debt stocks and flows, major economic aggregates, key debt ratios, average terms of new commitments, and currency composition of long-term debt. Many tables of data and indicators are also available online via the "Data" tab on the World Bank's Web site.

253 ICPSR. http://www.icpsr.umich.edu/.
Inter-University Consortium for Political
and Social Research, Inter-university
Consortium for Political and Social
Research. Ann Arbor, Mich.: Institute for
Social Research, University of Michigan.
[1997–]
300.0285   H61.3

Archive of international social science data, includ-
ing a large collection of economic data. In thematic
collections grouped by topic are surveys of Census
Enumerations; Community and Urban Studies;
Conflict, Aggression, Violence, Wars; Economic
Behavior and Attitudes; Education; Elites and Leadership; Geography and Environment; Government
Structures, Policies, and Capabilities; Health Care
and Facilities; Instructional Packages; International
Systems; Legal Systems; Legislative and Deliberative
Bodies; Mass Political Behavior and Attitudes; Organizational Behavior; Social Indicators; Social Institutions and Behavior; Publication-Related Archive; and
External Data Resources. Data can be downloaded
for SAS, SPSS and Stata. Full access is available to
students, staff and faculty at 700 ICPSR member
institutions; some content is freely available to the
public, but may not emphasize economics.

254 The index of economic freedom.
Heritage Foundation, Wall Street Journal
(Firm). Washington: The Heritage
Foundation, 1995–. maps
ISSN 1095-7308
338.9005   HB95

Ranks 185 countries, including Hong Kong, by the
extent of government involvement in the economy.
The more that a government is involved in constraint
in the production, distribution, or consumption
of goods and services, the less freedom the editors
believe is present. In addition to the score, 2-p. long
country profiles discuss trade policy, fiscal burden,
government intervention, monetary policy, foreign
investment, banking and finance, wages and prices,
property rights, regulation, and informal market.
The 2007 ed. adds a chapter on regions. A Web version is available at http://www.heritage.org/index/,
with interactive features tracking 10 benchmarks
related to the rule of law, limited government, regulatory efficiency, and open markets: property rights,
freedom from corruption, fiscal freedom, government spending, business freedom, labor freedom,
monetary freedom, trade freedom, investment freedom, and financial freedom.

**255 International financial statistics
yearbook. English ed.** International
Monetary Fund. Washington: International
Monetary Fund, 1979– ISSN 0250-7463
332/.02/12   HG61

Unified source for overview of financial statistics for
nations of the world. Contains summary tables by
subject (exchange rate agreements, interest rates,
international trade, national accounts, commodity
prices), followed by detailed tables for each country, describing its financial and monetary conditions. Updated by the monthly *International financial
statistics* (1948–). Much of the data is available
online from IMF at http://www.imf.org/external/
data.htm.

256 NationMaster.com. http://www
.nationmaster.com/index.php.
NationMaster.com. Woolwich, NSW,
Australia: Rapid Intelligence. 2003–
310.1   HA154

Gathers data in the public domain to prepare statistical comparisons between countries. The Web site
includes tabs for information about "Countries A-Z"
and for "Statistics." Statistical categories include
economy, education, health issues, immigration,
industry, labor, taxation, and transportation. Data is
displayed in easy-to-read bar graphs and color-coded
world maps. Sources of data are noted: typical sources range from official publications like the CIA's
World Factbook to entries from Wikipedia. This is a
companion to StateMaster.com.

257 OECD iLibrary. http://www.oecd-ilibrary
.org/. Organisation for Economic Cooperation and Development. Paris: OECD.
2000–
337   HC59.15

SourceOECD became *OECD iLibrary* in 2010. A subscription database featuring OECD books, reports,
working papers, serials, and statistical databases
on economic and social topics, as well as the environment, energy, and technological development.
Focuses mainly on the 30 OECD member states
and major nonmember developing countries, but
includes information for all nations of the world.
Content is in English and French.

Serials include journals; the OECD Factbook and other statistical works; and titles that forecast and analyze trends, such as the OECD Economic Outlook, *African economic outlook*, International Migration Outlook, and OECD-FAO Agricultural Outlook.

Current, themed databases include the OECD Economic Outlook Database, SourceOECD Main Economic Indicators, Banking Statistics, Education Statistics, Globalisation, Indicators of Industry and Services, Insurance, International Development, International Direct Investment Statistics, International Migration Statistics, the ITCS International Trade by Commodity Database, Monthly Statistics of International Trade, the National Accounts Database, OECD Health Data, OECD Statistics on International Trade in Services, the Revenue Statistics of OECD Member Countries Database, the Science and Technology Database, the Social Expenditure Database, Structural and Demographic Business Statistics, Taxing Wages Statistics, and the Telecommunications Database. Statistical databases of the International Energy Agency are also available via this source. OECD.Stat enables users to query multiple databases simultaneously and to export search results in several formats.

Also incorporates Future Trends, an index of published and unpublished sources in more than a dozen languages covering issues affecting the public and private sectors. OECD also publishes glossaries.

258 Political risk yearbook online. http://www.prsgroup.com/. PRS Group. East Syracuse, N.Y.: PRS Group. 1999–

HG3879

Political and economic risk analysis for 106 countries. Reports are PDF files with a country forecast (highlights, current data, comments and analysis, forecast scenarios, political players), and country conditions (investment climate, climate for trade including political violence and legal framework, background on geography, history, social conditions, government, political conditions, and environmental trends). Includes forecasts for GDP growth, current account, inflation, political turmoil, investment and trade restrictions, and domesic and international economic problems. Also has statistics for foreign direct investment flows by source country and sector. In print, this resource consists of eight volumes, for North & Central America, the Middle East & North Africa, South America, Sub-Saharan Africa, Asia & the Pacific, West Europe, East Europe, and Central & South Asia.

259 Statistical sites on the World Wide Web. http://www.bls.gov/bls/other.htm. U.S. Bureau of Labor Statistics. Washington: U.S. Bureau of Labor Statistics. 1998–

Links to official government statistical offices all over the world, including Web sites from more than 140 countries and from international agencies such as Afristat, East African Community (EAC), European Union Eurostat, Food and Agriculture Organization (FAO), International Energy Agency (IEA), International Labour Organization (ILO), Organization for Economic Cooperation and Development (OECD iLibrary (224)), United Nations International Computing Centre, United Nations Statistical Division, UN Economic Commission for Europe (UN/ECE) Statistical Division, UN Industrial Development Organization Statistics, and World Health Organization Statistical Information System (WHOSIS (1072)). Also links to sites of major U.S. federal statistical agencies, including Bureau of Economic Analysis, Bureau of Justice Statistics, Bureau of Labor Statistics, Bureau of Transportation Statistics, Census Bureau, Economic Research Service, Energy Information Administration, National Agricultural Statistics Service, National Center for Education Statistics, National Center for Health Statistics, Statistics of Income from the IRS, and FedStats. Excellent starting point for researchers.

260 Statistical yearbook: annuaire statistique. United Nations. New York: United Nations. 37 v. ISSN 0082-8459

310.5   HA12.5.U63

A summary of international statistics for the countries of the world, and continuing the *Statistical yearbook of the League of Nations*. Covers agriculture, forestry and fishing; communication; development assistance; education; energy; environment; finance; gender; international merchandise trade; international tourism; labour force; manufacturing; national accounts; population; prices; and science and technology. Tables may show figures for up to ten years. References are given to sources. A world summary was introduced beginning with v. 15 (1963), summarizing tables appearing in various chapters. Can be downloaded as a large PDF from http://unstats.un.org/unsd/syb/. The *Monthly bulletin of statistics online* complements this resource by providing current information.

261 UNdata. http://data.un.org. United Nations Statistics Division. New York: United Nations. 2008–

HA155

Provides simultaneous access to datasets derived from 14 statistical databases produced within the U.N. System. Subject matter includes population, labor, education, energy, agriculture, industry, tourism, trade, and national accounts. Its content may be accessed in four ways. Both the keyword and advanced searches identify and retrieve data by source (e.g., Unesco statistics), year, country, region, and miscellaneous keyword, but the advanced search does so more precisely. The Explorer offers hierarchical navigation within each database. Finally, the user may browse profiles created for each country. UNdata also contains a statistical profile of each country. The UN Statistics Division (UNSD) will ultimately include the statistical resources of national governments. UNdata usually hosts only part of a database's content, so it does not replace UN Comtrade (228), the National Accounts Main Aggregates Database, and other statistical systems created by the U.N. and related intergovernmental organizations. The lone exception is the UN Common Database (229), which has been rendered obsolete.

United States

262 Almanac of the 50 states. Information Publications. Burlington, Vt.: Information Publications, 1985– ISSN 0887-0519

317.3   HA203

Subtitle: *Basic data profiles with comparative tables.* Place of publication varies. In two parts: 1) statistical and demographic profiles of each of the 50 states, the District of Columbia, and the entire U.S., with tables of vital statistics, health, education, housing, government finance, etc.; 2) tables that rank the same areas according to 54 selected criteria such as population, households, doctors, hospitals, crime rate, etc. Sources of data are cited.

263 American factfinder. http://factfinder2 .census.gov/. U.S. Census Bureau. Washington: U.S. Census Bureau. [1999–]

317.3   HA181

American FactFinder (AFF) contains data on U.S. population and housing (from the decennial censuses from 2000 and 2010, as well as the American Community Survey) and economic data from the 2002 and 2007 Economic Censuses. In the new version of AFF the 1990 census has been removed. Social Explorer can be used to access the 1990 census and all other older census data. Users will find the current version significantly easier to user than the previous release. Before using FactFinder users should have a clear idea of the various Census programs and the data availability.

The Community Facts search reveals basic information for a state, county, city, or zip code. The simple Guided Search is a stepped approach to the complex available data. Experienced users will appreciate the Advanced Search functions, where users can start at any number of places including topics like Census program, Census dataset, population features (e.g. age, sex, education, employment, income), housing features (housing counts, financial characteristics), or if economic census data is desired, NAICS codes can be used. Durable URLs can be generated for most of the data tables, making it easy to refer to tables at a later time.

264 American incomes: demographics of who has money. 9th ed. New Strategist Publ. Ithaca, N.Y.: New Strategist Publ., 2014. 450 p, ill. ISBN 9781940308371

339.2   HC110.I5

Explores and explains the economic status of Americans by looking at household income trends by age, household type, race and ethnicity, education, region of residence, and work status. Arranged by chapters covering household income, men's income, women's income, discretionary income, wealth, and poverty. Ninth ed. of 2014 has data through 2012. The index is fairly comprehensive and a good entry point for researchers looking for specific data. Also available as PDF with spreadsheets or as e-book.

265 Bureau of economic analysis. http:// www.bea.gov/. United States Bureau of Economic Analysis. Washington: Bureau of Economic Analysis. 1996–

330.09   HC103

Official U.S. government source for extensive economic data in downloadable Excel format. For U.S. national accounts, includes tables for gross domestic product (GDP), personal income and outlays, consumer spending, corporate profits, and fixed assets value. For U.S. international trade, includes tables for balance of payments, trade in goods and services, international services, international investment position, and direct investment and multinational companies. For regions of the U.S., tables include GDP by state and metropolitan area, state and local area personal income, RIMS II Regional Input-Output Multipliers, and economic information for coastal areas. For U.S. industries, tables include annual industry accounts (GDP by industry & input-output cccounts), benchmark input-output accounts, research and development satellite accounts, and travel and tourism satellite accounts. "U.S. Economy at a Glance" is a useful snapshot. Online source for *Survey of current business* (no longer published in print after 2013).

266 Business statistics of the United States: patterns of economic change.
Cornelia J. Strawser. Lanham, Md.: Bernan Press, 1996–. ill. ISSN 1086-8488
338   HC101
Annual. Compiles data from other sources. Part A contains economic data such as GDP, income, government spending, energy figures, and stock prices. Pt. B offers industry profiles with numbers grouped by NAICS code, and for key sectors such as housing or retail sales. Pt. C has regional and state data. Highlights are more than 150 tables, 30 yr. of annual data and four yr. of monthly data, and information by city, state, region, and country. Index. A good general source to start with, if the Statistical Abstract of the United States (288) does not have what is needed. Available as an e-book.

267 BusinessUSA. http://business.usa.gov/.
U.S. Small Business Administration.
[Washington]: U.S. Small Business Administration. 2011–
338.7/406   HF3021
Official web portal for U.S. government information related to business matters. Organized around 12 topics: start a business, grow your business, access financing, begin exporting, expand exporting, help with hiring employees, find opportunities, browse resources for veterans, seek disaster assistance, learn about new health care changes, learn about taxes and credits, and invest in the USA. Browsable and searchable FAQs and a combined list of resources. Lists categorized by such topics as services, grants,

events, or rules. Replaces Business.gov. A subsection of the wider USA.gov portal which replaced *STAT-USA*, discontinued in 2010.

268 The complete economic and demographic data source: CEDDS.
Woods and Poole Economics. Washington: Woods and Poole Economics, 1984–
ISSN 1044-2545
330.9730021   HC101
Based on results of the Woods and Poole regional forecasting model of every county and metropolitan area in the United States. Vol. 1 (1992) summarizes the results of the 1992 forecast, points out trends in regional economies, describes the database and methodology, and presents statistical tables that rank states, statistical areas, and counties in terms of population, employment, and income historically and over the forecast period, now extending to 2040. The remainder of v. 1 and the whole of v. 2 and 3 present detailed statistical tables for counties in each state, in alphabetical order by state. Also marketed in CD-ROM format.

269 Consumer USA. Euromonitor Publications Limited. London: Euromonitor Publications Limited, 1988–2010 ISSN 0952-9543
339.47097305   HC101
Market-size time series for last five yr. and forecasted time series for upcoming five yr. for over 330 consumer markets, as well as economic, demographic, lifestyle, and purchasing data and analysis. Also lists manufacturer and brand shares for major consumer goods sectors. Print edition ceased with 2010, as Euromonitor moves to online products such as Passport GMID (804).

270 County and city data book. U.S. Bureau of the Census, U.S. Census Bureau. Washington: U.S. Dept. of Commerce, Bureau of the Census, 1949–. ill.
ISSN 0082-9455
317.3   HA202
A supplement to *Statistical abstract of the United States* (288); continues in part *Cities supplement* and also *County data book*. Presents the latest available census figures for each county, and for the larger cities in the United States. Also has summary figures for states, geographical regions, urbanized areas, standard metropolitan areas, and unincorporated places.

The 14th ed., dated 2007, is the latest as of early 2014. Also available online at http://www.census .gov/statab/www/ccdb.html.

271   County and city extra: annual metro, city, and county data book. Bernan Press. Lanham, Md.: Bernan Press, 1992–. maps ISSN 1059-9096
917.305   HA203
Covers states, counties, metropolitan areas and congressional districts as well as statistics for urban places with populations of 25,000 or more. Includes statistics on education, income, construction, labor, agriculture, crime, etc. Available as an e-book. Bernan is also publishing a successor to State and metropolitan area data book (286) as a complement to this series.

272   Economic census. https://www.census .gov/econ/census/. U.S. Census Bureau. Washington: U.S. Dept. of Commerce. 1954–
317.3   HA181
Publishes extensive official statistics on business and the economy in the U.S. and overseas possessions, gathered every five years. As of 2014, statistics for 2007 are the latest available: figures for 2012 will be the next release. Covers wholesale and retail trade, construction, manufacturing, and service industries, but not agriculture (for which see the Census of agriculture). Originated with a variety of publications and assumed its current scope in 1992. PDF versions are available online at http://www.census.gov/ prod/www/economic_census.html for editions since 1977. Data is accessible through the American factfinder (263) interface, from the U.S. Census Bureau. Industry research using the economic census (924) is a guide to use of these resources.

273   Economic indicators. United States Council of Economic Advisers. Washington: United States G.P.O., 1948–
ISSN 0013-0125
330.973005   HC101.A186
Basic statistical series on U.S. prices, wages, production, business activity, purchasing power, credit, money and Federal finance, as well as international statistics like industrial production and consumer prices for major industrial countries.
    Monthly data is online from 1995 to the present at http://www.gpo.gov/fdsys/browse/collection .action?collectionCode=ECONI.

274   Economic report of the President transmitted to the Congress. Council of Economic Advisers. Washington: G.P.O., 1947–. ill. ISSN 0193-1180
330.973   HC106.5
Review of the nation's economic condition, documented by statistics. Special attention is paid to economic trends, the state of employment and production, real income, and Federal budget outlays. Reports since 1995 are available online at http://www.gpo.gov/ fdsys/browse/collection.action?collectionCode=ERP and since 1947 from the non-official site at http:// fraser.stlouisfed.org/publications/ERP/.

275   Federal reserve bulletin. Board of Governors of the Federal Reserve System. Washington: G.P.O., 1915–
ISSN 0014-9209
332.110973   HG2401.A5
The most complete current information, including statistics, on financial conditions in the United States. Includes bank asset quality, bank assets and liabilities, bank structure data, business finance, exchange rates, flow of funds accounts, household finance, industrial activity, interest rates, and money stock and reserve balances. Also reports on financial developments in foreign countries. Since 2005, no longer published in print. Current *Bulletins* and an archive back to 1996 are available online at http:// www.federalreserve.gov/pubs/bulletin/default.htm.

276   The Federal Reserve System: an encyclopedia. R. W. Hafer. Westport, Conn.: Greenwood Press, 2005. xxxii, 451 p., ill. ISBN 0313328390
332.11097303   HG2563
Contains 250 well-written articles explaining the somewhat mysterious Federal Reserve System, its structure, process, and policies. Entries also cover people and key events related to the Federal Reserve. Appendixes provide the text of The Federal Reserve Act, Federal Reserve Regulations, and a list of the Membership of the Board of Governors: 1913–2004. Available as an e-book.

277   FedBizOpps.gov: federal business opportunities. https://www.fbo .gov/. United States. General Services Administration. Washington: United States. U.S. General Services

Administration. Office of Acquisition Systems. 2002–

JK1673

Searchable database of United States government business contract opportunities: "the single government point-of-entry (GPE) for Federal government procurement opportunities over $25,000." Replaced *Commerce business daily* in 2002. FBO can be searched by keyword, solicitation number, procurement type, date, response deadline, contract award date, place of performance (by state or ZIP code), NAICS code, or agency/office location.

278   Handbook of U.S. labor statistics: employment, earnings, prices, productivity, and other labor data.
Bernan Press. Lanham, Md.: Bernan Press, 1997– ISSN 1526-2553
331.0973021   HD8051.H36

While this data can be found in other Bureau of Labor Statistics sources such as http://www.bls.gov/, these print volumes conveniently place the most useful labor statistics in one source. Includes statistics on employment (status, earnings, characteristics, experience, contingent and alternative work arrangements), projections by industry and occupation, productivity and costs, compensation, prices and living conditions, consumer expenditures, safety and health, labor management relations, and foreign labor and prices. Available as an e-book.

279   Historical statistics of the United States. http://hsus.cambridge.org/.
Richard Sutch, Susan B. Carter. New York: Cambridge University Press

Standard source for American historical data. No uniform end date for tables, but many end in the late 1990s. Examples of tables include population, work, labor, education, health, and government finance. Tables are easily searched and can be downloaded into Excel or CSV formats. Also in print as a five-vol. set.

280   International historical statistics: the Americas, 1750–2005. 6th ed.
B. R. Mitchell. Houndmills, Basingstoke, Hampshire, U.K.: Palgrave Macmillan, 2007. xix, 875 p. ISBN 9780230005136
317   HA175

Updates the fifth edition of 2003. A companion to the author's International historical statistics: Europe

(325) and International historical statistics: Africa, Asia & Oceania (339). Presents comparative statistics for all countries of North, Central and South America. Tables are grouped in broad subject areas, and (when available) include figures for population, vital statistics, the labor force, agriculture, industry, external trade, transport and communication, prices, education, finances, and national accounts. Based on official publications. Introductory summary traces changes in borders. Table for conversion of weights and measures. A combined online version of the three works is available, with figures to 2010.

281   National compensation survey. http://www.bls.gov/ncs/home.htm. U.S. Dept. of Labor, Bureau of Labor Statistics. Washington: Bureau of Labor Statistics. 1998–

HD4976.A735N38

Summarizes wages, earnings, and hours for cities, regions, and the nation. "Wage data are shown by industry, occupational group, full-time and part-time status, union and nonunion status, establishment size, time and incentive status, and job level." —*Summary*. Also includes benefits and the Employment Cost Index, which is released quarterly.

282   ProQuest statistical abstract of the United States. ProQuest. Lanham, Md.: Bernan Press, 2013. 1025 p.
ISBN 9781598885910
317.3   HA202

Successor to the important federal publication. When the U.S. government cut funding for the Statistical Abstract of the United States (288) published by the Census Bureau, over the objections of librarians and researchers, ProQuest launched this replacement edition as an annual publication beginning with 2013. Intentionally mimics the format, scope and organization of the original resource. Remains an excellent source for the most current possible data on population, government finance, the economy, and even for some international statistics. Original source publications for figures in tables are indicated. Appendixes include a guide to sources of statistics, state statistical abstracts, and foreign statistical abstracts; discussion of metropolitan and micropolitan statistical areas; and a table of weights and measures. Index. Also available in an online edition, from which the data tables can be retrieved in PDF. http://proquest.libguides.com/statisticalabstract

283 Small business economic trends.
http://www.nfib.com/surveys/small
-business-economic-trends/. NFIB
Education Foundation. Washington:
National Federation of Independent
Business. 1993– ISSN 1080-0816
HD2346.U5
Monthly report of economic indicators such as optimism, earnings, sales, prices, employment, compensation, credit conditions, inventories, and capital
outlays. Information comes from a survey of members of the National Federation of Independent Business. The website also provides news and advocacy
materials.

284 The small business economy. http://
www.sba.gov/advocacy/849/6282. Small
Business Administration. Washington:
U.S. Government Printing Office. 1982–
ISSN 1932-3573
338.7 HD2346.U5
Annual review, including small business trends,
demographics, financing, federal procurement,
women in business, regulations, and data. Tables,
available online as PDFs. Data includes U.S. Business Counts and Turnover Measures, Macroeconomic Indicators for, Business Turnover by State,
Opening and Closing Establishments, and Characteristics of Self-Employed Individuals. Published as
The State of Small Business from 1982–2000.

285 State and local government finances.
http://www.census.gov/govs/local/. U.S.
Bureau of the Census. Washington: U.S.
Census Bureau. 1992–
HJ275
A census of U.S. state and local gov. finances is
taken every five years, with an annual survey for the
intervening years. Figures for 2011 are available as of
2014. The statistics in spreadsheet format cover gov.
financial activity in four broad categories of revenue,
expenditure, debt, and assets. A print version is also
available.

**286 State and metropolitan area data
book.** U.S. Census Bureau, U. Bureau of
the Census. Washington: U.S. Dept. of
Commerce, Bureau of the Census, 1979–
2010. ill. ISSN 0276-6566
317.3 HA202

A supplement to *Statistical abstract of the United
States* (288).
In three main parts. First part is data for individual states and for the United States as a whole. Statistical items include population and vital statistics,
health, education, employment, income, government, social welfare, crime, construction, housing,
banking, elections, energy, transportation, natural
resources, trade, and services. Second part is similar
data for metropolitan areas arranged alphabetically.
Third part is data for metropolitan areas ranked by
population-size categories. Five appendixes provide
information on standard metropolitan statistical
areas ranked by population size, effects of population change, estimates of states and congressional
districts population and voting age population, etc.
Ceased with edition of 2010, for which a PDF
version is available online at http://www.census.gov/
compendia/databooks/pdf_version.html. Beginning
with 2013, Bernan Press is issuing the same title as a
non-government publication.

287 The state of working America.
Economic Policy Institute. Washington:
Economic Policy Institute, 1988–. ill.
ISSN 1054-2159
330.973008623 HD8051
Biennial covering family incomes, wages, taxes,
unemployment, wealth, and poverty. Includes data
and commentary. Commentary places the numbers
in context, as well as explains how the data could be
interpreted and used. EPI is an advocacy organization
for low- to moderate-income families. The text of the
12th edition is online at http://stateofworkingamerica
.org/subjects/overview/?reader.

**288 Statistical abstract of the United
States.** U.S. Dept. of the Treasury, Bureau
of Statistics, U.S. Dept. of Commerce and
Labor, Bureau of Statistics, U.S. Bureau
of Foreign and Domestic Commerce,
U.S. Bureau of the Census, U.S. Census
Bureau. Washington: U.S. G.P.O., 1878–
2012. ill. ISSN 0081-4741
317.3 HA202
A single-volume work presenting quantitative summary statistics on the political, social, and economic
organization of the United States. Statistics given
in the tables cover a period of several years. Indispensable in any library: it serves not only as a first

source for statistics of national importance but also as a guide to further information, as references are given to the sources of all tables. Includes a table of contents arranged by broad subject areas and a detailed alphabetical index. Also available online from the Census Bureau at http://www.census.gov/compendia/statab/.

In 2011, the Census Bureau announced that publication of the Statistical Abstract would cease after the 2012 edition due to federal budget cuts. In 2012, ProQuest announced plans to publish equivalent print and online versions. Under the title ProQuest Statistical Abstract of the United States (150), this new work began to appear with 2013.

Supplement: *County and city data book* (270).

289 Survey of current business. http://www.bea.gov/scb/index.htm. Bureau of Economic Analysis. Washington: U.S. Dept. of Commerce. 2007– ISSN 0039-6222
330.5   HC101

Published in print from 1921–2014; beginning February 2014, only in online form. Includes articles on current trends, charts and tables for national, international, industry and regional data; and link to *BEA current and historical data* in PDF. Descriptive and statistical material on basic income and trade developments in the United States. Covers prices, foreign trade, commodities, industries, etc.

290 United States business history, 1602–1988: a chronology. Richard Robinson. New York: Greenwood Press, 1990. xii, 643 p. ISBN 9780313260957
338.0973   HC103

"Designed to provide a basic calendar of representative events . . . in the evolution of U.S. business." —*Pref.* Contains descriptive historical data, arranged by year, then under categories of general news and business news. Significant individuals, specific companies, inventions, trade unions, and key business, economic, and social developments are included. Brief bibliography; detailed index. Complemented by *Robinson's business history of the world: a chronology.*

291 United States economy at a glance. http://www.bls.gov/eag/eag.us.htm. U.S. Bureau of Labor Statistics. Washington: U.S. Bureau of Labor Statistics. 1998–
HA155

Snapshots of key economic data related to jobs, including recent monthly employment, price and earnings figures, and quarterly productivity and employment costs. Browsable for the U.S. as a whole, by region, by state, and for many metropolitan areas. Provides graphs and tabular numbers for download. Useful tools such as maps of data and an inflation calculator.

292 The USA and Canada. Europa Publications, Routledge. London; New York: Routledge, 1989–. maps
ISSN 0956-0904
330.9730927   E838

Besides a brief historical overview, includes statistical information on geography, economy, population, vital statistics, labor, health, agriculture, trade and industry, transportation, and education for each nation in the region. One of nine regional surveys associated with Europa World Plus (183).

293 U.S. Bureau of Labor Statistics. http://www.bls.gov/. Bureau of Labor Statistics. Washington: U.S. Department of Labor. 1995–
331.10212   HD8051

Home page of the official data-collecting agency in the field of labor statistics and economics: this includes tracking market activity, working conditions, and price changes. BLS produces the Consumer Price Index (CPI), Producer Price Index (PPI), Import and Export Price Indices, and the Consumer Expenditure Survey. Online reports cover inflation and prices, spending and time use, employment and unemployment, pay and benefits, productivity, workplace injuries, and comparisons with international figures. Offers "at a glance" snapshots covering the whole U.S. economy; regions, states and areas; and 100 specific industries.

294 U.S. Chamber of Commerce. https://www.uschamber.com/. Washington: U.S. Chamber of Commerce. 1997–
HF295

Home page of the highest-spending lobbying organization in the U.S.: "We advocate for pro-business policies that create jobs and grow our economy." Presents programs, services, and legislative positions. Provides statements and issue briefs on relevant topics such as health care, taxes, or regulatory reform.

Includes a directory of local and state chambers of commerce.

295   The value of a dollar: colonial era to the Civil War, 1600–1865. Scott Derks, Tony Smith. Millerton, N.Y.: Grey House, 2005. 436 p., ill. ISBN 1592370942

338.520973   HB235.U6

Similar to *Value of a dollar*, 1860–2014 (157): each chapter covers a different period of time. Each chapter includes background, historical snapshots, currency, selected incomes, services and fees, financial rates and exchanges, commodities, selected prices, and miscellany. Slave trades are included through chapter four, 1800–1824. Useful for historical research, as well as an interesting glimpse into history.

296   The value of a dollar: prices and incomes in the United States, 1860–2014. 5th ed. Scott Derks. Amenia, N.Y.: Grey House Pub., 2014. 600 p. ISBN 9781619252547

338.5/20973   HB235.U6

Illustrates trends in prices. Each chapter covers a different period of time (every five years, since 1900) and includes historical chronology, consumer prices, typical investment returns, income for selected jobs, national average wages, and pricing for food and other items. Data is by city, county, or state. For information from earlier years, see The value of a dollar: colonial era to the Civil War, 1600–1865 (156). Content has been extended to add five more years since the 2009 edition, with new chapters covering wages, prices and investment yields in the U.S. through 2014. Bibliography. Index. Also available as an e-book.

Canada

297   The Canada year book. Census and Statistics Office (Canada). Ottawa, Canada: Census and Statistics Office, 1906–. ill. (some fold., some col.), maps (some fold., some col.) ISSN 0068-8142

317.1   HA744

Subtitle (varies): *Statistical annual of the resources, demography, institutions and social and economic conditions of Canada*. Some volumes cover two years. Volumes for 1905–71 issued by the agency under its earlier name,

Canada, Bureau of Statistics. Presents official data on history, constitution and government, institutions, population, production, industry, trade, transportation, finance, labor, administration, and general social and economic conditions. Current year books are available in print only. The first century of *Canada year books*, 1867–1967, are available free online at http://www65.statcan.gc.ca/acyb_r000-eng.htm.

298   Canadian almanac and directory. Toronto: Grey House Canada, 1848–. maps (part fold.) ISSN 0068-8193

971.0025   AY414

167th ed., 2014. Previous title: *Canadian almanac and legal and court directory*.

Contains reliable legal, commercial, governmental, statistical, astronomical, departmental, ecclesiastical, financial, educational, and general information with charts and color photographs plus election results. Available as an e-book.

299   Canadian economic observer. Historical statistical supplement: L'Observateur économique canadien. Supplément statistique historique. Statistics Canada. Ottawa, Canada: Statistics Canada, 1988–2012 ISSN 0838-0236

330.9710021   HC111

Annual data for all series reported monthly in the *Canadian Economic Observer*, including national accounts, prices, international and domestic trade, labor, and financial markets. Provincial detail given for employment earnings, retail trade, housing, and consumer price indexes. Ceased in print with edition of 2012. Available as an e-book.

300   Canada business network. http://www.canadabusiness.ca/eng/. Ottawa, Canada: Industry Canada. 2004–

Offers information for those planning, starting, financing, managing or growing a business in Canada, the largest international trade partner of the U.S. Links to online resources and texts. Sponsored by agencies of all Canadian provinces. Also called *Canada business: services for entrepreneurs*. Available in French or English.

301   CANSIM, Canadian socio-economic information management system.

http://www5.statcan.gc.ca/cansim/home
-accueil?lang=eng. Statistics Canada.
Ottawa, Canada: Statistics Canada
(Statistique Canada). 1979–
ISSN 0706-0858
016.3171   HA37
"Statistics Canada's key socioeconomic database."
Part of the larger Statistics Canada site. Over 35 million time series on Canadian economic, social,
financial, and monetary issues. Includes agriculture,
construction and housing, demography, domestic
trade, health and social conditions, energy, environment and natural resources, finance, household
expenditures, international trade, justice, labor,
manufacturing, prices and price indexes, service
industries, national accounts, transportation, travel
and tourism, education, and culture. Daily updates.

302 Doing business in Canada. http://
    www.bakermckenzie.com/Doing-Business
    -in-Canada-2011-11-01-2011/. Baker &
    McKenzie LLP (Firm). Toronto: Baker
    & McKenzie LLP. 2011
A 203-page PDF document available for free download. One of several online texts offered by international firms: for a similar work see PKF's Doing
business in Canada (303). Covers corporate law,
income tax and other taxes, joint ventures, customs
and trade for import and export, regulation of foreign
investment, advertising rules, intellectual property,
financing, labor law, pensions, immigration, real
property, environmental issues, and the court system in Canada, the largest international trade partner
of the U.S.

303 Doing business in Canada. http://www
    .pkf.com/publications/doing-business
    -in/pkf-doing-business-in-canada. PKF
    International Limited (Firm). London: PKF
    International Limited. [2008]
Forty-six-page PDF document available for free
download. One of several online texts offered by
international firms: for a similar work see Baker &
McKenzie's Doing business in Canada (302). Provides an overview of geography, the political and
legal system, the economy, controls on currency
and securities, and financial services, with additional
detail about the regulatory environment, consumer
protection, immigration, forms of business organizations, partnerships, taxation, and accounting

practices in Canada, the largest international trade
partner of the U.S.

**304 Doing business in Canada: 2013
    country commercial guide for U.S.
    companies.** http://www.buyusainfo.net/
    docs/x_87649.pdf. U.S. Commercial
    Service. Washington: U.S. Department of
    Commerce. 2013
Seventy-six-page PDF document available for free
download: http://www.buyusainfo.net/ is a service
of the U.S. government. Provides an overview of the
political and economic system, the investment and
financing climate, leading sectors for U.S. exports,
trade and customs regulations, and tips for business
travel, including contact information for associations
and official bodies in Canada, the largest international trade partner of the U.S.

**305 International historical statistics:
    the Americas, 1750–2005. 6th ed.**
    B. R. Mitchell. Houndmills, Basingstoke,
    Hampshire, U.K.: Palgrave Macmillan,
    2007. xix, 875 p. ISBN 9780230005136
    317   HA175
Updates the fifth edition of 2003. A companion
to the author's International historical statistics:
Europe (325) and International historical statistics:
Africa, Asia & Oceania (339). Presents comparative
statistics for all countries of North, Central and South
America. Tables are grouped in broad subject areas,
and (when available) include figures for population,
vital statistics, the labor force, agriculture, industry, external trade, transport and communication,
prices, education, finances, and national accounts.
Based on official publications. Introductory summary traces changes in borders. Table for conversion of weights and measures. A combined online
version of the three works is available, with figures
to 2010.

**306 Market research handbook: manuel
    statistique pour études de marché.**
    Canada Statistics Canada. Ottawa,
    Canada: Dominion Bureau of Statistics,
    Merchandising and Services Division =
    Bureau fédéral de la statistique, Division
    du commerce et des services, 1969–2008.
    ill. ISSN 0590-9325
    658.83971   HC111

Annual summary of Canadian national and international trade statistics. Includes data for national and 25 metropolitan markets, with demographic and economic projections. Organized into 11 sections: user's guide, population, labor market and income, consumer expenditures, housing and household characteristics, macroeconomic and financial statistics, international trade, business and industry statistics, census metropolitan areas and census agglomerations, glossary and alphabetic index. Ceased with the edition of 2008.

307 The USA and Canada. Europa Publications, Routledge. London; New York: Routledge, 1989–. maps
ISSN 0956-0904
330.9730927   E838

Besides a brief historical overview, includes statistical information on geography, economy, population, vital statistics, labor, health, agriculture, trade and industry, transportation, and education for each nation in the region. One of nine regional surveys associated with Europa World Plus (183).

Central and Latin America

308 Anuario estadístico de América Latina: statistical yearbook for Latin America. United Nations. Santiago, Chile: United Nations, Economic Commission for Latin America, 1973–1984. 8 v.
ISSN 0251-9445
300.8   JX1977

Socioeconomic statistics for Latin America, organized into four sections: 1. Social statistics, 2. Economic statistics, 3. Statistics on natural resources and the environment, 4. Technical notes. Statistics are generally for ten years, but also include forecasts. "The printed version of the *Yearbook* contains a selection of tables which seek to provide statistical information from the regional perspective, with emphasis on the international comparability of data such as national accounts statistics in dollars."—*Introd*. Succeeded by Anuario estadístico de América Latina y el Caribe (309).

309 Anuario estadístico de América Latina y el Caribe = Statistical yearbook for Latin America and the Caribbean.

http://www.eclac.cl/cgi-bin/getProd.asp?xml=/deype/agrupadores_xml/aes250.xml. United Nations, Economic Commission for Latin America and the Caribbean. [Santiago, Chile]: Economic Commission for Latin America and the Caribbean. 1986– ISSN 0251-9445
300.8   JX1977

More than 130 indicators summarize the past and present social and economic development of 33 Latin American and Caribbean countries. Some historical data series begin in 1950. Includes technical notes with definitions, methodology, information sources, and comments on each indicator. Great for relatively current Latin American data. Successor to Anuario estadístico de América Latina (308). Editions of 1998 to the present are online at the CEPAL site. Print version is available, including earlier years, but has fewer detailed indicators.

310 Consumer Latin America. Euromonitor Publications Limited. London: Euromonitor Publications Limited, 1993–2010. ill. ISSN 1359-0979
330.98   HC130.C6

Market-size time series for last five yr. and forecasted time series for upcoming five yr.for over 330 consumer markets in six Latin American countries (Argentina, Brazil, Chile, Colombia, Mexico, and Venezuela), as well as economic, demographic, lifestyle, and purchasing data and analysis. Also lists manufacturer and brand shares for major consumer goods sectors. Print edition ceased with 2010, as Euromonitor moves to online products such as Passport GMID (804).

311 Doing business in Mexico. http://www.bakermckenzie.com/BKMexicoDBI13/. Baker & McKenzie Abogados, S.C. (Firm). Monterrey, Nuevo Leon, Mexico: Baker & McKenzie Abogados, S.C. 2013

Eighty-eight-page PDF document available for free download. One of several online texts offered by international firms: for a similar work see PKF's Doing business in Mexico (312). Covers investment law, the IMMEX or Maquiladora Program, taxation, corporate law, labor law, environmental issues, and intellectual property law in Mexico, the third largest international trade partner of the U.S. Also available in Spanish.

312   Doing business in Mexico. http://www
.pkf.com/publications/doing-business
-in/pkf-doing-business-in-mexico. PKF
International Limited (Firm). London: PKF
International Limited. [2010]

Forty-three-page PDF document available for free
download. One of several online texts offered by
international firms: for a similar work see Baker &
McKenzie's Doing business in Mexico (311). Provides an overview of geography, the political system,
communications, the regulatory environment, laws
affecting companies, and import/export controls,
with additional detail about forms of corporations,
partnerships, accounting practices, and taxation in
Mexico, the third largest international trade partner
of the U.S.

**313   Doing business in Mexico: 2013
country commercial guide for U.S.
companies.** http://www.buyusainfo.net/
docs/x_5309176.pdf. U.S. Commercial
Service. Washington: U.S. Department of
Commerce. 2013

One-hundred-and-thirty-six-page PDF document
available for free download: http://www.buyusainfo
.net/ is a service of the U.S. government. Provides an
overview of politics and the economy, the climate for
investment and financing, trade and customs regulations, and leading sectors for U.S. exports to Mexico,
the third largest international trade partner of the
U.S. Tips for business travel deal with business etiquette, visas, health, telephone service, transportation, and holidays. Includes contact information for
U.S. consular officials, government ministries, and
local chambers of commerce.

**314   Economic and social progress in Latin
America.** Inter-American Development
Bank. Washington: Inter-American
Development Bank, 1972–2008. ill.
ISSN 0095-2850
330.98003   HC125

Reviews economic and political progress in Latin
America, with development, economics, and finance
data. Print edition ceased with 2008. The IDB
web site at http://www.iadb.org/en/inter-american
-development-bank,2837.html provides online
access to many current reports in English, Spanish,
or Portuguese on topics such as transportation and
agriculture.

**315   Economic survey of Latin America
and the Caribbean.** United Nations.
Economic Commission for Latin America
and the Caribbean. Santiago, Chile:
United Nations, 1984–. ill.
ISSN 0257-2184
330.980005   HC161

Presents a summary of the international economy,
details the regional economy, outlines economic policy,
domestic performance, and the economic conditions of
each country in the region. With a lengthy statistical
appendix, this is a rich source of data. Part one reports
on performance of regional economies; part two deals
with long-term aspects of economic development.
Includes "Country notes" and statistics. Recent editions in English or Spanish can be downloaded from
the CEPAL / ECLAC web site at http://www.eclac.org/
(search by title in the 'Publications' facet).

316   HAPI online. http://hapi.gseis.ucla
.edu. UCLA Latin American Center. Los
Angeles: UCLA Latin American Center.
1997–
973.046805   F1408

The online version of HAPI: Hispanic American periodicals index. As of 2013, HAPI covers more than 350
peer reviewed journals with content on Latin America, the Caribbean, Brazil, and U.S. Latinos. Historically, more than 600 periodicals have been indexed.
Includes citations to articles, book reviews (through
2001), documents, and original literary works. Languages covered are English, Spanish, Portuguese,
French, German, and Italian. Initially, indexing
began with 1975, but a retrospective project bridged
the gap with the cessation of Index to Latin American
periodical literature, 1929–1960. The database has a
thesaurus and provides links to some full text.

**317   International historical statistics:
the Americas, 1750–2005. 6th ed.**
B. R. Mitchell. Houndmills, Basingstoke,
Hampshire, U.K.: Palgrave Macmillan,
2007. xix, 875 p. ISBN 9780230005136
317   HA175

Updates the fifth edition of 2003. A companion to
the author's International historical statistics: Europe
(325) and International historical statistics: Africa,
Asia & Oceania (339). Presents comparative statistics for all countries of North, Central and South
America. Tables are grouped in broad subject areas,

and (when available) include figures for population, vital statistics, the labor force, agriculture, industry, external trade, transport and communication, prices, education, finances, and national accounts. Based on official publications. Introductory summary traces changes in borders. Table for conversion of weights and measures. A combined online version of the three works is available, with figures to 2010.

318   LANIC. http://lanic.utexas.edu/. Latin American Network Information Center, Lozano Long Institute of Latin American Studies. Austin, Tex.: Latin American Network Information Center. 1992–
980.7   AP63; F1408 025.04;
Excellent directory of online resources from and about Latin America. Arranged both by country and by topic: provides links to resources on the economy, education, society & culture, arts, libraries, social sciences, geography & environment, etc. The 'Media, News and Communications' subsection of the site includes listings of academic journals and magazines, many of them electronic. Hosts a variety of digital projects, such as the Government Documents Archive, the Open Archives Portal to Latin American gray literature in the social sciences, and LAPTOC (Latin American Periodicals Tables of Contents), which provides a searchable database to the tables of contents of more than 800 periodicals.

319   MOxLAD. http://moxlad.fcs.edu.uy/. Pablo Astorga, Ame Berges, E. V. K. Fitzgerald, Rosemary Thorp, Latin American Centre, Oxford University, Programa de Historia Económica y Social (PHES), Universidad de la Republica. Montevideo, Uruguay: Universidad de la República del Uruguay. 2002–
HC125
Funded by the Inter-American Development Bank, with statistical series for economic and social indicators for 20 countries from 1870–2010. Includes Population and Demographics; Labour Force; Industry; Transport and Communications Infrastructure; External Trade; Finance; National Accounts; Nominal Exchange Rate;

Consumer and Producer Price Indices; and Commodity Price Indices and Weighted Commodity Price Indices. Until 2012, known as *Oxford Latin American economic history database* and housed at Oxford.

320   South America, Central America and the Caribbean. Europa. London: Europa, 1985–. maps ISSN 0268-0661
980   F1401.S68
Covers 43 countries and territories in three parts: (1) "Background to the region," which includes essays by scholars on such topics as religion, indigenous peoples, debt and the IMF, El Niño, and the Andean Regional Initiative; (2) "Country surveys," providing an overview of history, the economy, politics, and demographics as well as statistical surveys, a directory, and a bibliography; (3) "The region," which lists regional organizations, major commodities, and research institutes and contains a bibliography of periodical titles. Index to regional organizations. One of nine regional surveys available online with a subscription to Europa World Plus (183).

Europe

321   Consumer Europe. 26th ed. Euromonitor PLC. London: Euromonitor International, 2011–
339.4/7   HD7022
Annual. Formed by the merger of *Consumer Western Europe* and *Consumer Eastern Europe*. Indicates relative size of market for hundreds of consumer products. The current 2014 volume has data covering 2007–2012 and forecasts to 2017. Value figures in both local currency and U.S. dollars. Includes the following categories: alcoholic drinks, apparel, consumer appliances and electronics, consumer health products, eyewear, fresh food, home and garden products, hot drinks, packaged food, pet care, retail paper goods, soft drinks, tobacco, and toys and games. Provides the following national socio-economic indicators for context: population, health, foreign trade, household characteristics, income, and consumer expenditure. Covers 27 countries: Austria, Belgium, Bulgaria, Croatia, the Czech Republic, Denmark, Finland, France, Germany, Greece, Hungary, Ireland, Italy, Lithuania, the Netherlands, Norway, Poland, Portugal, Romania, Russia, Slovakia, Spain, Sweden, Switzerland, Turkey, Ukraine and the United Kingdom. Available in online format.

322   Eastern Europe, Russia and Central Asia. Europa Publications Limited, Routledge. London: Routledge, 2000–. maps ISSN 1470-5702
947.086   HC244.A1

Brief historical overviews for each nation in the region, followed by statistical information on geography, economy, population, vital statistics, labor, health, agriculture, trade and industry, transportation, and education. Useful directory sections and valuable statistical surveys. Annual since 2000. Continues *Eastern Europe and the Commonwealth of Independent States* (1992–1999).

323 European marketing data and statistics. Euromonitor. London; Chicago: Euromonitor International, 1962– ISSN 0071-2930
338.094   HA1107

Demographic trends and forecasts, and economic statistics for 45 European countries, including Russia and Turkey. Includes time series data on advertising, agricultural resources and output, automotives and transport, banking and finance, consumer expenditure, consumer market sizes, consumer prices and costs, economic indicators, education, energy resources and output, environmental data, external trade, health, home ownership, household profiles, income and deductions, industry, IT and telecommunications, labor, media and leisure, population, retailing, and travel and tourism. Sources include the International Monetary Fund, United Nations, national statistical offices, and national trade associations. Companion volume to *International marketing data and statistics* (219). Current edition also available as a PDF download.

324 Eurostat yearbook. Statistical Office of the European Communities, Office for Official Publications of the European Communities. Luxembourg, Belgium: Office for Official Publications of the European Communities, 1995–. ill. ISSN 1681-4789
314.05   HA1107

Economic, social, business, and environmental data for the European Union and its Member States, as well as major trade partners. In seven chapters: Statisticians for Europe; People in Europe; The economy (national accounts, prices and wages, balance of payments, international trade in goods); The environment; Science and technology; Sectors and enterprises (business structures at a glance, industry and construction, distributive trade, financial markets, transport, tourism, energy); and Agriculture,

forestry, and fisheries. Appendixes include a glossary, geonomenclature, classification of economic activities, classification of commodities, and a list of abbreviations and acronyms. The most recent edition is available online under 'Publications' at http://epp.eurostat.ec.europa.eu/portal/page/portal/eurostat/home/ along with other statistics.

325 International historical statistics: Europe, 1750–2005. 6th ed. B. R. Mitchell. Houndmills, Basingstoke, Hampshire, U.K.; New York: Palgrave Macmillan, 2007. xvii, 960 p. ISBN 9780230005143
314   HA1107

Updates the 5th edition of 2003. A companion to the author's International historical statistics: Africa, Asia & Oceania (339) and International historical statistics: the Americas (288). Presents comparative statistics for all countries of Western, Central and Eastern Europe, including Russia. Tables are grouped in broad subject areas, and (when available) include figures for population, vital statistics, the labor force, agriculture, industry, external trade, transport and communication, prices, education, finances, and national accounts. Based on official publications. Introductory summaries trace changes in borders and currencies. Table for conversion of weights and measures. A combined online version of the three works is available, with figures to 2010.

326 Major companies of Europe. Graham & Whiteside. Farmington Hills, Mich.: Gale Cengage, 1982– ISSN 0266-934X
338.740254   HC241.2

Covers major companies and related service and professional organizations. Provides directory information, officers, products or services, parent company, number of employees, and summary financial information. Other similar titles from the same publisher: *Major companies of the Arab world, Major companies of central and eastern Europe and the commonwealth of independent states, Major companies of the Far East and Australasia, Major companies of Africa south of the Sahara, Major chemical and petrochemical companies of the world, Major energy companies of the world, Major financial institutions of the world, Major food and drink companies of the world, Major information technology companies of the world, Major pharmaceutical and biotechnology companies of the world*, and *Major telecommunications companies of the world*.

327 Nordic statistical yearbook = Nordisk statistisk årsbok. Nordic Council of Ministers. Copenhagen, Denmark: Nordic Council of Ministers, 1997–. ill.
ISSN 1398-0017

HA1461

Provides comprehensive statistics of various aspects of life in the five Nordic countries, i.e. Denmark, Finland, Iceland, Norway, and Sweden, as well as independent Greenland, Faroe Islands, and the Åland Islands. Chapters cover area, climate, population, labor, industry, trade, and finance. Published in English and Swedish. Available as an e-book.

328 Russia and Eurasia facts and figures annual. Gulf Breeze, Fla.: Academic International Press, 1993–2002
ISSN 1074-1658
314.7   DK266.A2

Covers individual countries from the former USSR with tables on key areas of public finances, trade, economy, health, energy, industry, etc. Major sections are preceded by overview of key personnel and events. Continues the series *USSR facts and figures*.

Great Britain

329 British historical statistics. B. R. Mitchell. Cambridge, U.K.; New York: Cambridge University Press, 1988. xi, 886 p. ISBN 9780521330084
314.1   HA1134

A cumulation and expansion of Mitchell's *Abstract of British historical statistics* and Mitchell and H. G. Jones's *Second abstract of British historical statistics*. Emphasizes social and economic history, including population and vital statistics, transportation and communications, public finance, and financial institutions. Each of the 16 chapters contains information on sources and coverage. Includes some of the earliest available data; most tables cover to about 1980.

330 Consumer Europe. 26th ed. Euromonitor PLC. London: Euromonitor International, 2011–
339.4/7   HD7022

Annual. Formed by the merger of *Consumer Western Europe* and *Consumer Eastern Europe*. Indicates relative size of market for hundreds of consumer

products. The current 2014 volume has data covering 2007–2012 and forecasts to 2017. Value figures in both local currency and U.S. dollars. Includes the following categories: alcoholic drinks, apparel, consumer appliances and electronics, consumer health products, eyewear, fresh food, home and garden products, hot drinks, packaged food, pet care, retail paper goods, soft drinks, tobacco, and toys and games. Provides the following national socioeconomic indicators for context: population, health, foreign trade, household characteristics, income, and consumer expenditure. Covers 27 countries: Austria, Belgium, Bulgaria, Croatia, the Czech Republic, Denmark, Finland, France, Germany, Greece, Hungary, Ireland, Italy, Lithuania, the Netherlands, Norway, Poland, Portugal, Romania, Russia, Slovakia, Spain, Sweden, Switzerland, Turkey, Ukraine and the United Kingdom. Available in online format.

331 International historical statistics: Europe, 1750–2005. 6th ed. B. R. Mitchell. Houndmills, Basingstoke, Hampshire, U.K.; New York: Palgrave Macmillan, 2007. xvii, 960 p.
ISBN 9780230005143
314   HA1107

Updates the 5th edition of 2003. A companion to the author's International historical statistics: Africa, Asia & Oceania (339) and International historical statistics: the Americas (288). Presents comparative statistics for all countries of Western, Central and Eastern Europe, including Russia. Tables are grouped in broad subject areas, and (when available) include figures for population, vital statistics, the labor force, agriculture, industry, external trade, transport and communication, prices, education, finances, and national accounts. Based on official publications. Introductory summaries trace changes in borders and currencies. Table for conversion of weights and measures. A combined online version of the three works is available, with figures to 2010.

332 The value of a pound: prices and incomes in Britain 1900–1993. Oksana Newman, Allan Foster. New York; London: Gale Research International, 1995. xiv, 306 p. ISBN 9781873477311
338.5280210941   HD7023.G7;

A similar format to The value of a dollar by Derks, with statistics on earnings and employment, consumer expenditures, finance and economics, a chronology of events, and historic introduction to provide context. Chapters are arranged by decade, beginning in 1900 and ending in 1993. For an interesting look at life and economic value in 19th-century England, see Daniel Pool's *What Jane Austen ate and Charles Dickens knew*.

Africa

333 Africa development indicators. http://data.worldbank.org/data-catalog/africa-development-indicators. World Bank Group. Washington: World Bank Group. 2007–

HC800.A1

The most extensive statistical database on the 53 countries of Africa, both North Africa and Sub-Saharan Africa. Indicators. Contains more than 940 time series on population, births, and deaths; migration and refugees; health; social topics, including education, literacy, health care, sanitation and access to potable water, contraception, crime and corruption, poverty and income, and gender equality; Internet access; ownership of computers, cell phones, and vehicles; prices and expenditures; the labor force and employment; the environment, natural resources, and energy and water use; agriculture, manufacturing, and the service sector; GDP; exports and imports; balance of payments; development assistance and external debt; government finance; investment; money and banking; transportation and communication infrastructure; political stability; and governance.

The longest time series begin in 1960; some cover only the last few years. Data availability varies from one country to another.

The search for statistical series seeks exact phrases and is sensitive to punctuation. Therefore, one cannot retrieve "population, total" by entering "population total". Search results may be charted and mapped. Continuously updated.

Now provided free onilne by World Bank. Also issued annually in print as *Africa development indicators* (334).

334 Africa development indicators. United Nations Development Programme, World Bank, International Bank for Reconstruction and Development. Washington: World Bank, 1992–. ill.
ISSN 1020-2927
330.960021   HC800.A1

Statistical data for the 53 countries of Africa, both North Africa and Sub-Saharan Africa. Indicators for national accounts (value added in agriculture, industry and services, total consumption, gross private and public investment, GDP, resource balance); prices and exchange rates (GDP deflator, consumer price index, official exchange rate, SDR exchange rate index, currency conversion factor, parallel market exchange rate, ratio of parallel markets to official exchange rates, real effective exchange rate index); money and banking (domestic credit, credit to the private sector and the government, net foreign assets, growth of money supply, discount rate and real discount rate, commercial bank lending rate and commercial bank deposit rate); external sector (balance of payments, prices, and commodity trade); external debt and related flows (amortization, interest payments, debt and debt payments, and debt and debt service ratios); government finance (debt and surplus, expenditure, revenue, grants, foreign financing, taxes, and revenue); Agriculture (nominal producer prices, food price index, food production index, nonfood production index, food production per capita index, volume of food output, by major food crop, value of agricultural exports, cereal production, crop production index, fertilizer use, fertilizer imports, area under permanent crops, agricultural yields, by major crop, and incidence of drought); power, communications, and transportation (electric power consumption per capita, energy production and use, telephone, radio, and television availability, personal computers and internet use, vehicle ownership, roads, railroads, airplanes); doing business (cost of starting and closing a business, registering property, contract enforcement, investor protection); labor force and employment (number and structure of the labor force); aid flows, social indicators (poverty, income distribution, literacy, survival, education, economic opportunities); environmental indicators; Heavily Indebted Poor Countries (HIPC) initiative; household welfare (by individual country); privatization of public enterprises.

Companion CD-ROM, World Bank Africa Database, has time series from 1970. Also available online (333).

335   African development report. African
Development Bank. Abidjan, Ivory Coast:
African Development Bank, 1989–
330.96005   HC800.A1
An annual thematic publication. Part I includes
general overview essays, financial statistics, regional
profiles, and outlooks. Part II provides interpreta-
tive essays and a bibliography. Part III presents economic and social statistics. The data represent all 53
countries that are members of the African Development Bank, covering both Sub-Saharan and North
Africa. Print version ceased with edition of 2010, but
reports since 1999 can be downloaded from http://
www.afdb.org/en/documents/publications/african
-development-report/.

336   African statistical yearbook: *Annuaire*
statistique pour l'Afrique. United Nations.
Addis Ababa, Ethiopia: Economic
Commission for Africa, United Nations,
1974– ISSN 0252-5488
330.9600212   HA1955
African nations are arranged in alphabetical order,
with tables grouped in nine chapters: population and
employment, national accounts, agriculture and fishing, industry, transport and communications, foreign
trade, prices, finance, and social statistics. Covers 54
nations of North and Sub-Saharan Africa, now including South Sudan. A cooperative project of the African
Development Bank, the African Union Commission,
and the United Nations Economic Commission
for Africa (UNECA). Recent reports can be downloaded from http://www.afdb.org/en/documents/
publications/african-statistical-yearbook/.

337   Africa south of the Sahara. Europa
Publications Ltd., Routledge. London;
New York: Routledge, 1971–. maps
ISSN 0065-3896
916.7   DT351.A37
Annual; published since 1971. An introductory
"General survey" consists of signed essays on history, economic trends, and sociopolitical reforms.
Fifty-two country surveys each include the following
sections: physical and social geography; recent history; economy; statistical survey; directory; and bibliography. Many statistics are reproduced from United
Nations, International Monetary Fund, and other
organizations. "Regional information" includes organizations and commodities. Bibliography and index.

Also available online at Europa World Plus (183) with
additional features and more current content.

338   Arab world competitiveness report.
World Economic Forum. Geneva,
Switzerland: World Economic Forum,
2007– 320.9174927 1403948011
Annual, published in cooperation with OECD. Issue
for 2011–2012 can be downloaded at http://www3
.weforum.org/docs/WEF_AWC_Report_2011-12
.pdf. Discusses issues of trade, investment and devel-
opment. Older volumes contain country profiles for
Algeria, Bahrain, Egypt, Jordan, Kuwait, Lebanon,
Libya, Libyan Arab Jamahiriya, Morocco, Oman,
Qatar, Saudi Arabia, Syria, Syrian Arab Republic,
Tunisia, United Arab Emirates, and Yemen.

339   International historical statistics:
Africa, Asia and Oceania, 1750–2005.
5th ed. B. R. Mitchell. Houndmills,
Basingstoke, Hampshire, U.K.: Palgrave
Macmillan, 2007. xxvii, 1175 p.
ISBN 9780230005150
310   HA4675
Updates the 4th edition of 2003. A companion to the
author's International historical statistics: Europe (325)
and International historical statistics: the Americas
(288). Presents comparative statistics for all countries
of the Pacific region, Africa and Asia, including West
Asian and Middle Eastern states such as Turkey and
Israel. Tables are grouped in broad subject areas, and
(when available) include figures for population, vital
statistics, the labor force, agriculture, industry, external
trade, transport and communication, prices, education, finances, and national accounts. Based on official
publications. Introductory summaries trace changes in
borders and currencies. Table for conversion of weights
and measures. A combined online version of the three
works is available, with figures to 2010.

340   The Middle East and North Africa.
Europa Publications Limited. London:
Europa Publications, 1964–. ill., maps
ISSN 0076-8502
961.048   DS49
Annual. Covers Algeria, Bahrain, Cyprus, Egypt, Iran,
Iraq, Israel, Jordan, Kuwait, Lebanon, Libya, Moroc-
co and Western Sahara, Oman, Qatar, Saudi Arabia,
Syria, Tunisia, Turkey, United Arab Emirates, and
Yemen. Each country includes sections on physical

and social geography, recent history, and economy, along with a statistical survey, directory, and bibliography. Many statistics are reproduced from the United Nations, International Monetary Fund, and other organizations. The introductory general survey consists of signed essays on regional history, economic trends, and social and political reforms. Includes organizations and commodities. Bibliography. Index. Also available online at Europa World Plus (183) with additional features and more current content.

Middle East

341   The ABA practical guide to drafting basic Islamic finance contracts. Dena H. Elkhatib. Chicago: American Bar Association, Section of International Law, 2012. xiii, 97 p., ill. ISBN 9781614386193
346.07   KBP940.2

Introduces financial concepts under *sharia* law. Defines the basic elements in Islamic contracts, and the types of Islamic finance structures. Appendix outlines structures in chart form.

342   Arab world competitiveness report. World Economic Forum. Geneva, Switzerland: World Economic Forum, 2007– ISBN 1403948011
320.9174927

Annual, published in cooperation with OECD. Issue for 2011–2012 can be downloaded at http://www3.weforum.org/docs/WEF_AWC_Report_2011-12.pdf. Discusses issues of trade, investment and development. Older volumes contain country profiles for Algeria, Bahrain, Egypt, Jordan, Kuwait, Lebanon, Libya, Libyan Arab Jamahiriya, Morocco, Oman, Qatar, Saudi Arabia, Syria, Syrian Arab Republic, Tunisia, United Arab Emirates, and Yemen.

343   Consumer Middle East. Euromonitor PLC. London: Euromonitor PLC, 1998–2007
658.834C7583   HC415.15.Z9

Market-size time series for last five yr. and forecasted time series for upcoming five yr. for over 330 consumer markets, as well as economic, demographic, lifestyle, and purchasing data and analysis. Also lists manufacturer and brand shares for major consumer goods sectors. Covers Algeria, Egypt, Israel, Jordan,

Kuwait, Morocco, Saudi Arabia, Tunisia, Turkey, United Arab Emirates, with information on political structure, main industries, and the economy. Tables rank per capita consumer market sizes by country. Print edition ceased with 2007, as Euromonitor moves to online products such as Passport GMID (804).

344   Frequently asked questions in Islamic finance. Brian Kettell. Hoboken, N.J.: Wiley, 2010. xxix, 304 p., ill.
ISBN 9780470748602
332.1091767   HG3368.A6

Defines and interprets concepts of *riba* (interest), *takaful* (insurance reimbursement), *sukuk* (financial certificates), profit-loss sharing, and other key terms. Procedures, practices, and guidelines for banking and financial transactions under *sharia* law and Quranic principles. Identifies key regional agencies and institutions. Index. Available as an e-book.

345   Handbook of Islamic banking. Kabir Hassan, Mervyn Lewis. Cheltenham, U.K.; Northampton, Mass.: Edward Elgar, 2007. xviii, 443 p., ill. ISBN 9781845420833
332.10917/67   HG3368.A6

Twenty-five chapters by experts summarizing current trends. Coverage extends beyond banks to include insurance, leasing, mutual funds, stocks speculation, and regulatory issues. Glossary of Arabic terms. Index.

346   Information sources on Islamic banking and economics, 1980–1990. Syed Nazim Ali, Naseem N. Ali. London: Kegan Paul International, 1994. x, 352 p., ill. ISBN 9780710304865
016.3321/0917/671   HG3368.A6

Opening chapters introduce the concept of Islamic banking, and relevant sources from theses to databases to journal articles. Lists more than 1,500 works published between 1980 and 1992. Covers publications in English, Arabic, French, German, Persian, and Turkish. Keyword index. Author index.

347   International historical statistics: Africa, Asia and Oceania, 1750–2005. 5th ed. B. R. Mitchell. Houndmills, Basingstoke, Hampshire, U.K.: Palgrave Macmillan, 2007. xxvii, 1175 p
ISBN 9780230005150
310   HA4675

Updates the 4th edition of 2003. A companion to the author's International historical statistics: Europe (325) and International historical statistics: the Americas (288). Presents comparative statistics for all countries of the Pacific region, Africa and Asia, including West Asian and Middle Eastern states such as Turkey and Israel. Tables are grouped in broad subject areas, and (when available) include figures for population, vital statistics, the labor force, agriculture, industry, external trade, transport and communication, prices, education, finances, and national accounts. Based on official publications. Introductory summaries trace changes in borders and currencies. Table for conversion of weights and measures. A combined online version of the three works is available, with figures to 2010.

348   Islamic economics and finance: a bibliography. Javed Ahmad Khan. London; New York: Mansell, 1995. xi, 157 p. ISBN 9780720122190
016.330917/671   HB126.4
Identifies some 1,600 books, articles, dissertations, theses, and conference papers published from the 1980s up to 1993. There are no annotations, but entries are grouped in topical chapters such as "Performance of Islamic Banks" or "Islamic Critique of Other Economic Systems." Appendix lists a dozen relevant serials. Subject index. Author index.

349   Islamic economics and finance: a glossary. 2nd ed. Muhammad Akram Khan. London; New York: Routledge, 2003. xi, 195 p. ISBN 9780415318884
330.03   HB61
Defines terms in areas such as banking, insurance, auditing, accounting, and taxation that are used in economic and financial transactions under *sharia* law. Short entries identify key institutions and organizations, as well as key words and phrases primarily drawn from English and Arabic, but also including Urdu, Turkish, and Malaysian. Key to transliteration of Arabic script. First edition published in 1990 as *Glossary of Islamic economics*.

350   Islamic finance in a nutshell: a guide for non-specialists. Brian Kettell. Hoboken, N.J.: Wiley, 2010. xvii, 341 p., ill. ISBN 9780470748619
332.1091767   HG187.4

Discusses banking practices under Quranic principles, *sharia* law, and the profit loss sharing concept. Analyzes methods applied to balance sheets, contracts, and alternatives to conventional interest. Appendix lists 500 leading Islamic financial institutions. Index. Available as an e-book.

351   The Middle East and North Africa. Europa Publications Limited. London: Europa Publications, 1964–. ill., maps
ISSN 0076-8502
961.048   DS49
Annual. Covers Algeria, Bahrain, Cyprus, Egypt, Iran, Iraq, Israel, Jordan, Kuwait, Lebanon, Libya, Morocco and Western Sahara, Oman, Qatar, Saudi Arabia, Syria, Tunisia, Turkey, United Arab Emirates, and Yemen. Each country includes sections on physical and social geography, recent history, and economy, along with a statistical survey, directory, and bibliography. Many statistics are reproduced from the United Nations, International Monetary Fund, and other organizations. The introductory general survey consists of signed essays on regional history, economic trends, and social and political reforms. Includes organizations and commodities. Bibliography. Index. Also available online at Europa World Plus (183) with additional features and more current content.

Asia

352   Asian Development Bank. http://www.adb.org/. [Asian Development Bank]. Mandaluyong City, Philippines: Asian Development Bank. 1998–
330.95/005   HC411
Home page for Asian Development Bank (ADB), a multilateral development institution owned by 67 members, 48 from the Asia-Pacific region and 19 from other areas. Its aim is to help its member countries improve the welfare of the region's people, especially the nearly two billion who live on less than two dollars U.S. each day. Asia-Pacific remains home to two-thirds of the poor in the world. Annually, ADB lends about $6 billion dollars U.S. and supports technical assistance of some $180 million U.S. With headquarters in Manila, it also has 26 other offices around the world.

Of special note are the open publications, many on this website, of applications and documentation for many ADB projects. Most international aid projects supported by other bodies are done largely or altogether out of view. It is extremely useful to be able to study such documentation when trying to understand work which may be undertaken to alleviate poverty, especially within an international perspective. Also publishes *Asian development outlook: ADO*, an annual economic report on ADB member countries.

353 Asia's 10,000 largest companies: marketing and financial information on Asia's top companies. Oxford, U.K.: ELC International, 2006–
ISBN 9781907128127
338.74095   HG4234.85

Lists leading companies in banking, agriculture, mining, construction, business and personal services, electronics manufacturing, industrial manufacturing, food, beverage, tobacco, chemicals, petroleum, pharmaceuticals, wholesale, retail, transportation and oil, publishing, communications, hotels and restaurants, insurance, investment, real estate, and utilities. Entries give SIC code, sales, profit, employees, sales per employee, assets, equity, equity as a percentage of assets, and year established. Ranks Asia's 500 most profitable companies, 500 biggest money losers, and 100 largest companies by industry sector.

354 China securities market investment yearbook. GTA Securities Research Institute. Hong Kong, China: GTA Securities Research Institute, 2005–. ill.
HG5781

Provides a review of China's securities market from 1990–2004, and gives data from 2004. Chapters include: China securities market overview, 1990–2004; statistics for SSE and SZSE index; stock market monthly statistics, 2004; rankings for 2004; transition statistics, 2004; China fund market 1998–2004; statistics of delisted securities, 1990–2004; securities law; company law; historical exchange rate, 1990–2004; and major securities agencies in China.

355 China's provincial statistics, 1949–1989. T`ien-tung Hsüeh, Qiang Li, Shucheng Liu. Boulder, Colo.: Westview Press, 1993. xxiii, 595 p.
ISBN 9780813387321
330.95105021   HC427.92

Divided into two parts. In pt. 1, statistics are under individual provinces. Pt. 2 covers autonomous regions and municipalities. Over 15 key components are covered, such as national income, investment, consumption, public finance, trade, labor, education, and population. Appendixes provide explanatory notes on key variables with separate English alphabetical and Chinese phonetical indexes.

356 China statistical yearbook. English ed. China Statistical Information & Consultancy Service Centre, International Centre for the Advancement of Science & Technology, University of Illinois at Chicago. Hong Kong, China; Beijing, China: International Centre for the Advancement of Science & Technology; China Statistical Information & Consultancy Service Centre, 1988–1994
ISSN 1052-9225
315.105   HA4631

Arranged in 25 sections covering demographics, finance and economics, industry and commerce, trade and tourism, education, and culture and health. Ceased in print format with edition of 1994, but continues online as China statistical database (366).

357 Directory for doing business in Japan. http://www.jetro.go.jp/en/invest/directory/. Nihon Bo eki Shinko kai. Tokyo: Japan External Trade Organization (JETRO). 1998–
382.029452   HF3823

Lists Japanese companies and associations involved in international trade, as well as products. Gives contact information, representative, type of business, year established, capital, annual sales, number of employees, bank reference, product/service imported or exported. Searchable by business type and geograhic location. JETRO publishes in print *Japan trade directory (Nihon Bo eki Shinko kai)*.

358 Doing business in China. http://export.gov/china/build/groups/public/@eg_cn/documents/webcontent/eg_cn_025684.pdf. U.S. Commercial Service. Washington: U.S. Department of Commerce. 2012
HF3120

PDF document available for free download. Covers export practices, investments, market research, business travel, and the general environment for business in the People's Republic of China: political, economic and cultural. Includes current statistics, and contact information and URLs for local ministries, trade fairs, and U.S. government offices operating in China.

359   Doing business in China. http://www
.pkf.com/publications/doing-business
-in/pkf-doing-business-in-china. PKF
International Limited (Firm). London: PKF
International Limited. [2010]

HF3120

Forty-one-page PDF document available for free download. Provides an overview of geography, language, communications, the constitution and legal system, major exports and imports, and sources of finance, with additional detail about types of business structures, joint ventures and partnerships, foreign owned enterprises, official policies on foreign investment, control of foreign exchange and imports, grants and incentives, taxation, customs duties, and necessary permits for residency and work by international personnel in China, the second largest international trade partner of the U.S.

**360   Eastern Europe, Russia and Central
Asia.** Europa Publications Limited,
Routledge. London: Routledge, 2000–.
maps ISSN 1470-5702

947.086   HC244.A1

Brief historical overviews for each nation in the region, followed by statistical information on geography, economy, population, vital statistics, labor, health, agriculture, trade and industry, transportation, and education. Useful directory sections and valuable statistical surveys. Annual since 2000. Continues *Eastern Europe and the Commonwealth of Independent States* (1992–1999).

**361   Economic and social survey of Asia
and the Pacific.** United Nations;
Economic and Social Commission for Asia
and the Pacific. Bangkok, Thailand: United
Nations, 1974– ISSN 0252-5704

330.95042   HC411

Examines policy issues impacting the region, global and regional economic developments, macroeconomic performance, and poverty reduction

strategies. Full of tables with economic data. Annual reports since 1999 available online at http://www
.unescap.org/pdd/publications/index_survey.asp.

**362   Encyclopedia of Japanese business
and management.** Allan Bird. London;
New York: Routledge, 2002. xix, 500 p.
ISBN 9780415189453

650.0952   HF1001

Written for the specialist and student alike, with articles on economics, finance, management, government institutions, history, human resource management, industries, companies, social entities, business personalities, industrial relations, Japanese business overseas, manufacturing, marketing, and research and development. The encyclopedia is a good mix of expected information (history of the labor movement) and the unexpected (such as the article on office ladies, young, single women in clerical jobs). Entries range between 150 and 2,000 words in length. Entries are signed and some have recommended further reading. Available as an e-book.

**363   International historical statistics:
Africa, Asia and Oceania, 1750–2005.
5th ed.** B. R. Mitchell. Houndmills,
Basingstoke, Hampshire, U.K.: Palgrave
Macmillan, 2007. xxvii, 1175 p.
ISBN 9780230005150

310   HA4675

Updates the 4th edition of 2003. A companion to the author's *International historical statistics: Europe* (325) and *International historical statistics: the Americas* (288). Presents comparative statistics for all countries of the Pacific region, Africa and Asia, including West Asian and Middle Eastern states such as Turkey and Israel. Tables are grouped in broad subject areas, and (when available) include figures for population, vital statistics, the labor force, agriculture, industry, external trade, transport and communication, prices, education, finances, and national accounts. Based on official publications. Introductory summaries trace changes in borders and currencies. Table for conversion of weights and measures. A combined online version of the three works is available, with figures to 2010.

364   Japan statistical yearbook. http://
www.stat.go.jp/english/data/nenkan/
index.htm. Ministry of Internal Affairs

and Communication, Statistics Bureau, Director-General for Policy Planning (Statistical Standards), Statistical Research and Training Institute. Tokyo: Statistics Bureau; Statistical Research and Training Institutes. 2010– ISSN 0389-9004

315.2   HA4621

Online resource has 27 areas of information with data on climate, land, and population topics, including marital status, age, and education levels. Other statistics include housing, agriculture, natural resources, industry and trade, labor, health education, and energy. Tables on culture include libraries, museums, media, sports, religion, and crime. Tables in PDF or Microsoft Excel format. Statistics presented in both English and Japanese. Published in print format since 1949.

365   **Key indicators of developing Asian and Pacific countries.** Economics and Development Resource Center, Asian Development Bank. Manila, Philippines; Hong Kong, China: ADB; Oxford University Press, 1970–2002 ISSN 0116-3000

HC411

Presents economic and financial statistics for Asian and Pacific countries. Each year's publication also has a specific focus (*Measuring policy effectiveness in health and education*, *Labor markets in Asia: promoting full, productive, and decent employment*, *Poverty in Asia: measurement, estimates, and prospects*, etc.). Categories for data include: poverty, inequality, and human development; education indicators; environment indicators; health and nutrition indicators; mortality and reproductive health; population; population by age group; labor and employment by gender and economic activity; land use; agriculture production; total and per capita GNI; shares of major sectors in GDP; expenditure shares in GDP; domestic saving, capital formation, and resource gap; growth rates of GDP and major sectors; inflation rates; growth rates of merchandise exports and imports; foreign trade indicators; direction of trade: merchandise exports and imports; government finance indicators; money supply indicators; foreign direct investment, net inflows; international reserves indicators; external debt and debt service payments; debt indicators; official flows from all sources to DMCs; net private flows from all sources to DMC's; and aggregate net resource flows

from all sources to DMC's. Ceased in print with edition of 2002, but continues online at http://www.adb .org/publications/series/key-indicators-for-asia-and -the-pacific as *Key indicators for Asia and the Pacific.*

366   **National Bureau of Statistics of China.** http://www.stats.gov.cn/english/. National Bureau of Statistics of China. Beijing, China: National Bureau of Statistics of China. 2006–

Publishes *China statistical database*, including links to 2010 census of population. English website of federal statistical agency for the People's Republic of China. Main access point to statistics is by frequency published (monthly, quarterly, yearly), with a separate access point for census data.

367   **The national economic atlas of China.** Chung-kuo k o hsüeh yüan. Hong Kong; New York: Oxford University Press, 1994. 1 atlas (xvi, 314 p.), color maps ISBN 0195857364

912.43   G2306.G1

A separate volume of the National Atlas Series, which will consist of additional volumes focused on agriculture, the physical environment, history, and a general atlas. This work contains 265 high-quality color maps arranged within the following categories: (1) resources; (2) population; (3) general economy; (4) agriculture; (5) industry; (6) transportation, post, and telecommunications; (7) building, urban construction, and environmental protection; (8) commerce, foreign trade, tourism, and finance; (9) education, science, sports, culture, and public health; and (10) regional comprehensive economy. Translated work includes four handbooks of descriptive notes to maps bound separately in pockets. Comprehensive in nature and provides an excellent overview for anyone interested in studying the Chinese economy.

Pacific Area

368   **Economic and social survey of Asia and the Pacific.** United Nations; Economic and Social Commission for Asia and the Pacific. Bangkok, Thailand: United Nations, 1974– ISSN 0252-5704

330.95042   HC411

Examines policy issues impacting the region, global and regional economic developments, macroeconomic performance, and poverty reduction strategies. Full of tables with economic data. Annual reports since 1999 available online at http://www.unescap.org/pdd/publications/index_survey.asp.

369 International historical statistics: Africa, Asia and Oceania, 1750–2005. 5th ed. B. R. Mitchell. Houndmills, Basingstoke, Hampshire, U.K.: Palgrave Macmillan, 2007. xxvii, 1175 p.
ISBN 9780230005150
310   HA4675

Updates the 4th edition of 2003. A companion to the author's International historical statistics: Europe (325) and International historical statistics: the Americas (288). Presents comparative statistics for all countries of the Pacific region, Africa and Asia, including West Asian and Middle Eastern states such as Turkey and Israel. Tables are grouped in broad subject areas, and (when available) include figures for population, vital statistics, the labor force, agriculture, industry, external trade, transport and communication, prices, education, finances, and national accounts. Based on official publications. Introductory summaries trace changes in borders and currencies. Table for conversion of weights and measures. A combined online version of the three works is available, with figures to 2010.

370 Key indicators of developing Asian and Pacific countries. Economics and Development Resource Center, Asian Development Bank. Manila, Philippines; Hong Kong, China: ADB; Oxford University Press, 1970–2002
ISSN 0116-3000
                              HC411

Presents economic and financial statistics for Asian and Pacific countries. Each year's publication also has a specific focus (*Measuring policy effectiveness in health and education*, *Labor markets in Asia: promoting full, productive, and decent employment*, *Poverty in Asia: measurement, estimates, and prospects*, etc.). Categories for data include: poverty, inequality, and human development; education indicators; environment indicators; health and nutrition indicators; mortality and reproductive health; population; population by age group; labor and employment by gender and economic activity; land use; agriculture production; total and per capita GNI; shares of major sectors in GDP; expenditure shares in GDP; domestic saving, capital formation, and resource gap; growth rates of GDP and major sectors; inflation rates; growth rates of merchandise exports and imports; foreign trade indicators; direction of trade: merchandise exports and imports; government finance indicators; money supply indicators; foreign direct investment, net inflows; international reserves indicators; external debt and debt service payments; debt indicators; official flows from all sources to DMCs; net private flows from all sources to DMC's; and aggregate net resource flows from all sources to DMC's. Ceased in print with edition of 2002, but continues online at http://www.adb.org/publications/series/key-indicators-for-asia-and-the-pacific as *Key indicators for Asia and the Pacific*.

4 *Functional Areas of Business*

Accounting and Taxation

Guides and Handbooks

371 Accountants' handbook. 12th ed.
Lynford Graham, D. R. Carmichael.
Hoboken, N.J.: Wiley, 2012. 2 v., ill.
ISBN 9780471790419
657   HF5621
Latest edition of an authoritative handbook. Covers accounting standards and organizations, financial statements (presentation, analysis, areas), specialized industries, compensation and benefits, special areas of accounting, and topics in auditing and management information systems. Kept up-to-date with annual supplements. Updated coverage in this edition includes changes in FASB Codification and the International Financial Reporting Standards, and developments in fair value, fraud risk, and health care. Available as an e-book.

372 Accounting desk book. 22nd ed.
Lois R. Plank, Donald Morris, William H. Behrenfeld, Tom M. Plank, Douglas L. Blensly, Lois R Plank. Chicago: CCH, 2012. ill. ISBN 9780808031659
657/.05   HF5601
Organized by topical area (information systems, standards, statement of cash flows, cost accounting, etc.). Useful for practitioners or advanced accounting students who are looking for guidance on the

application of accounting standards, rules, and guidelines. Includes information on international accounting standards.

373 Accounting handbook. 5th ed. J. G. Siegel, J. K. Shim. Hauppauge, N.Y.: Barron's Educational Series, 2010.
1046 p., ill. ISBN 9780764162701
657   HF5635
This updated edition provides a practical overview of accounting principles and practices with illustrations and examples and a dictionary of related terms. An overview of financial accounting includes financial statements, reporting requirements, and accounting principles and standards. Additional chapters cover individual income tax preparation and planning, auditing, personal financial planning, accounting for governments and nonprofits, information technology, quantitative methods, international accounting and standards, and forensic accounting. Also includes appendices covering the Sarbanes-Oxley Act.

374 AICPA audit and accounting manual: Nonauthoritative technical practice aids. American Institute of Certified Public Accountants. Chicago: Commerce Clearing House, 1979– ISSN 1535-6264
657   HF5667
Intended for the practitioner, but useful for students. Explains practices, techniques, and procedures.

Includes practice aids, sample letters, and internal control checklists.

375 The Economist numbers guide: the essentials of business numeracy.
6th ed. Richard Stutely. London: Profile Books Ltd., 2013. vii, 256 p., ill.
ISBN 9781846689031
650/.01/513   HF5691

Introduction to numerical methods and quantitative techniques used in mathematics, statistics, business, accounting, and economics. Explains methods of analyzing and solving problems in finance, and the use of numbers in business forecasting and decision-making. Uses charts, graphs, tables, figures and examples to explain in layman's terms. Appendix is a dictionary of relevant terms, with cross-references to the main section. Index.

376 Federal accounting handbook: policies, standards, procedures, practices. 2nd ed. Cornelius E. Tierney. Hoboken, N.J.: Wiley, 2007
ISBN 9780471739289
657.83500973   HJ9801

Written in accessible language for anyone interested in federal accounting. Pt. 1 focuses on financial management in the federal government, with chapters on legislation and policy, the Chief Financial Officers Act of 1990, the federal budget, accounting events, budgetary and proprietary accounting practices, the Department of the Treasury, federal financial and information systems, and federal financial statements. Pt. 2 focuses on accounting practices for federal activities and transactions, with chapters on pay, leave and allowances, contracts, expenditures, receipts, reimbursements and refunds, assets, liabilities, net entity position, nonappropriated fund activities, and grants. The appendix concentrates on federal government and the Sarbanes-Oxley Act of 2002.

377 Handbook of accounting and auditing. Frank C. Minter, Barry Jay Epstein, Michael P. Krzus. Boston: Warren, Gorham, and Lamont, 1982–. various pagings, ill.
657.02   HF5635

Covers the many changes that continue to deluge the profession, with specific attention to Generally Accepted Accounting Principles (GAAP) and Generally Accepted Auditing Standards (GAAS). Organized in six sections: (1) overview of financial accounting, (2) audit function, (3) major areas of financial accounting and auditing, (4) accounting for specialized industries, (5) comprehensive coverage of the financial services industry, and (6) major accounting institutions. Index. Kept up-to-date by cumulative supplements, each containing a cumulative index. Also available online through Checkpoint (415).

378 International handbook of financial reporting. 3rd ed. Nexia International. London: Tolley, 2002. 422 p.
ISBN 9780754511502
657.3   HF5681.B2

Written by accountants and intended for practitioners, with general information on accounting reporting standards and practices in 33 European countries. Organized alphabetically.

379 Mathematical formulas for economists. 4th ed. Bernd Luderer, Volker Nollau, Klaus Vetters. Heidelberg, [Germany]; New York: Springer, 2010. x, 198 p., ill. ISBN 9783642040788
330.0151   HB135

Defines formulas and differential equations used in economics, finance, and accounting, including definitions for the notations used in formulas. Gives basic formulas, as well as alternate formulas. Assumes some prior knowledge. Enlarged from the 3rd edition of 2007 "to include methods of rank statistics and the analysis of variance (ANOVA) and covariance." Bibliography. Index. Available as an e-book.

380 TRANSACC: transnational accounting. 2nd ed. Dieter Ordelheide, KPMG International. Basingstoke, U.K.: Palgrave, 2001. 4 v. ISBN 9781561592463
657   HF5626

An invaluable source for accounting practices for individual and group accounts in 21 countries, for rules from the European Union, and for International Accounting Standards. Most covered countries are European, but includes the United States, Argentina, Australia, Canada, and Japan. The 2nd ed. added Argentina, Finland, Italy, Norway and Portugal. In addition to lengthy entries on individual countries, two reference matrices provide a comparative glance across countries: one for recognition and valuation rules, the other for principles of consolidation. Each matrix provides International Accounting Standards, and refers to the relevant section in the set. Glossary defines 500 terms in English with translations into 11 other languages.

381   The ultimate accountants' reference: including GAAP, IRS and SEC regulations, leases, and more.
3rd ed. Steven M. Bragg. Hoboken, N.J.: Wiley, 2010. xxviii, 783 p., ill.
ISBN 9780470572542
657.0973   HF5616.U5

Intended for the practicing accountant, but also useful for students. Provides good background information for accounting topics. Organized into chapters on the role and structure of accounting, accounting rules and regulations, accounting reports, balance sheets and income statements, accounting management, financial management, and related topics such as mergers, IPOs, taxation, and bankruptcy. Appendixes with a sample chart of accounts, interest tables, formulas and explanations for ratios, dictionary of terms, and due diligence checklist. Index. Available as an e-book.

382   Wiley CPA exam review. O. Ray Whittington. Hoboken, N.J.: Wiley, 2005–. 4 v., ill.
657   KF889.5

Study material, primarily in the form of practice questions based on past tests, for those preparing for certified public accountant examinations. Separate volumes cover current AICPA requirements in auditing and attestation (AUD); business environment and concepts (BEC); financial accounting and reporting (FAR); and regulation (REG). Updated annually.

Reviews of Research and Trends

383   Accounting trends and techniques. American Institute of Certified Public Accountants. New York: American Institute of Certified Public Accountants, 1945/47–2011 ISSN 1531-4340
657   HF5681.B2

Annual survey of accounting practices. Used to analyze accounting information disclosed in stockholders' reports. Organized around the financial statement (balance sheet, income statement, statement of cash flows), including information from the independent auditors' report. Includes appendix for the 600 companies surveyed, plus index for companies, pronouncements, and subjects. Ceased with 2011.

384   More than a numbers game: A brief history of accounting. Thomas A. King. Hoboken, N.J.: John Wiley & Sons, 2006
ISBN 9780470008737
657.0973   HF5616.U5

With chapters on double entry, railroads, taxes, costs, disclosure, standards, science, inflation, volatility, intangibles, debt, options, earnings, and SOX (Sarbanes-Oxley), this is an engaging glimpse at the events that have shaped modern U.S. accounting. Especially useful for the context it provides. Available as an e-book.

Indexes; Abstract Journals

385   Accounting and tax. http://www.proquest.com/products-services/pq_accounting.html. ProQuest. Ann Arbor, Mich.: Proquest. 2006–
                                            HF5635

Comprehensive coverage of accounting and tax, with nearly 500 sources, including top accounting journals like the *Accounting review* (398) and the *Journal of accounting research* (401). Has accounting standards from FASB, GASB, and IASB, with International Financial Reporting Standards, SIC Interpretations, IFRC Interpretations, pronouncements, statements, technical bulletins, interpretations, board opinions, American Institute of Certified Public Accountants (AICPA) Interpretations, and Emerging Issues Task Force (EITF) abstracts. A handy glossary of terms appears within the text of the FASB, GASB, and IASB documents. Other features include links to related standards and SmartView, a split screen displaying the table of contents and the text of the standards. Another Web-based tax resource is *BNA tax and accounting center*.

386   Accounting articles. Commerce Clearing House. Chicago: Commerce Clearing House, 1965–
016.657   HF563

Unique coverage of major accounting and taxation articles and books, as well as some coverage of finance and financial services. Organized by subject. Author index.

387 Bibliography of works on accounting by American authors. Harry C. Bentley, Ruth S. Leonard. Mansfield Centre, Conn.: Martino, 2005 ISBN 1578985439
016.657   Z7164.C81B5;HF5635
Reprint of a 1934 bibliography of 1,500 books on accounting and bookkeeping published from 1796 to 1934. Vol. 1 covers 1796 to 1900, Vol. 2 covers 1901–1934. Some citations include an annotation, but most only provide bibliographic information. Author index. Subject index.

388 ProQuest accounting and tax. http://www.proquest.com/products-services/pq_accounting.html. ProQuest. Ann Arbor, Mich.: ProQuest. 2006–
HF5636
Successor to the print format *Accounting and tax index*. Analyzes content (often with full text) from trade periodicals and scholarly journals, including all the journals published by the American Accounting Association; relevant publications from major sources such as CCH and AICPA; works on tax law; more than 1,500 dissertations on accounting topics; selected conference proceedings; and over 7,000 working papers from the Social Science Research Network.

389 Rutgers accounting web. http://raw.rutgers.edu/. Rutgers Accounting Research Center, Rutgers Business School. Newark, N.J.: Rutgers Accounting Research Center. 1994–
HF5625.7
Online resources for accounting and finance, including an "Accounting Digital Library" with links to streaming lectures for accounting courses, and an "Accounting Research Directory" that indexes publications since 1963.

Encyclopedias

390 Encyclopedia of business and finance. 2nd ed. Burton S. Kaliski, Macmillan Reference. Detroit, Mich.: Macmillan Reference, 2007. 2 v. ISBN 0028660617
650.03   HF1001

Written for the novice but useful for anyone seeking background information on five key topics: accounting, finance and banking, management, management of information systems, and marketing. The 310 essays include graphs, tables, photographs, and recommended readings. Alphabetically arranged entries range from the history of computing to green marketing and the Sarbanes-Oxley Act. The 3rd ed. is projected for publication in 2014. Available as an e-book.

391 Encyclopedia of management. 7th ed. Sonya D. Hill. Detroit: Gale, Cengage Learning, 2012. xxx, 1133 p. ISBN 9781414459042
658.003   HD30.15
Covers functional areas such as corporate planning and strategic management, emerging topics in management, entrepreneurship, financial management and accounting, general management, human resources management, innovation and technology, international management, leadership, legal issues, management science and operations, management information systems, performance measures and assessment, personal growth and development for managers, production and operations management, quality management and total quality management, supply chain management, and training and development. More than 300 essays in alphabetical order, written by academics and business professionals, with cross-references and recommended reading lists. New content reflects trends such as the use of handheld devices for Internet-based tools, social networking, network security, venture capital and entrepreneurship, and business in China. Includes a glossary of terms. Index. Available as an e-book.

392 The encyclopedia of taxation and tax policy. 2nd ed. Joseph J. Cordes, Robert D. Ebel, Jane Gravelle, Urban Institute. Washington: Urban Institute Press, 2005. xvii, 499 p., ill ISBN 9780877667520
336.2/003   HJ2305
Alphabetically arranged, with over 200 essays on tax policy, tax structure, tax compliance, and tax administration, with some coverage of public finance. Written by tax professionals, academicians, and administrators, almost all of whom are members of the National Tax Association. Entries are brief, but cover definitions, background, and relevance. Most entries include

recommended readings. The 2nd ed. adds 45 new entries and updates entries with legislative changes.

Dictionaries

393   The complete dictionary of accounting and bookkeeping terms explained simply. Cindy Ferraino. Ocala, Fla.: Atlantic Publ. Group, 2011. 288 p., ill. ISBN 9781601383259
657.03   HF5636

Over 2,000 terms plus a glossary of acronyms. Intended for small business owners, beginning bookkeepers, students and general readers. Bibligraphy. Index.

394   A dictionary of accounting. 4th ed. Jonathan Law. New York: Oxford University Press, 2010. 439 p. ISBN 9780199563050
657.03   HF5621

3,600 definitions for terms, concepts and jargon used in all aspects of accounting, including management accounting, financial accounting, direct and indirect taxation, auditing, corporate finance, and accounting organizations. Written from a British perspective. Some definitions include clarifying examples. Most entries are brief, but seven "features" provide more extended discussion of bankruptcy law; assessment of damages; the UK Data Protection Act of 1998; European Economic and Monetary Union; the London-based FTSE Indexes; international standard setters; and mortgage law. Written for accounting students and professionals. No index, but good cross-references. Updates the 3rd edition of 2005, with new content reflecting recent legislation and corporate scandals, the financial crisis of 2008, and expanded international coverage. URLs for major web resources. Available as an e-book.

395   Dictionary of accounting terms. 5th ed. Jae K. Shim, Joel G. Siegel. Hauppauge, N.Y.: Barron's, 2010. v, 523 p, ill. ISBN 9780764143106
657.03   HF5621

Over 2,500 accounting terms in alphabetical order related to financial statements, taxes, and related IT technology.

Updates the 4th edition of 2005. Available as an e-book.

396   The international dictionary of accounting acronyms. Library ed. Thomas W. Morris. Chicago: Glenlake Pub. Co.; Fitzroy Dearborn Publishers, 1998. viii, 155 p. ISBN 9781884964565
657.03   HF5621

Contains 2,000 currently used acronyms from accounting and related disciplines, with brief explanation of the acronym's meaning. Appendix for monetary units, with country, currency, and symbols. Alphabetically arranged with no index. Available as an e-book.

397   Kohler's dictionary for accountants. 6th ed. Eric Louis Kohler, William W. Cooper, Yuji Ijiri. Englewood Cliffs, N.J.: Prentice-Hall, 1983. xi, 574 p. ISBN 9780135166581
657.0321   HF5621

A classic dictionary for accounting and still a relevant resource. Contains explanations and definitions for 2,600 terms. Kohler was chair of the American Institute of Accountants' Committee on Terminology, which may explain why his definitions are so meaningful. Accounting has changed since publication in 1983, so no collection should rely solely upon this source, but many will find entries here easier to understand than those in other newer dictionaries.

Periodicals

398   The accounting review. American Accounting Association, American Association of University Instructors in Accounting. Sarasota, Fla.: American Accounting Association, 1926–
ISSN 0001-4826
381.805   HF5601

Published by the American Accounting Association (403), with research articles in all areas of accounting for a primary audience of academicians and graduate students. A typical issue has articles on reporting incentives in European firms, the value of cash flow news on SEC filings, the evolution of stock option accounting, the influence of venture capitalists on IPO earnings, the existence and extent of abnormal accrual anomaly, and the effects of regulations on auditor-provided tax services. Most articles have a U.S. bent, but some occasionally venture into international topics.

399   Cabell's directory of publishing opportunities in accounting. David W. E. Cabell, Deborah L. English. Beaumont, Tex.: Cabell Pub. Co., 2000–
ISSN 2157-0795
657   HF5601

Alphabetical list of periodicals in accounting, with information for authors about circulation data, publication guidelines, where to submit, journal acceptance rate, manuscript topics and guidelines for format, length, and style. The same firm publishes similar directories covering management, economics and finance, and marketing. Available as an e-book.

400   Journal of accounting and economics. William E. Simon Graduate School of Business Administration, University of Rochester. Amsterdam, The Netherlands: Elsevier, 1979–. ill.
ISSN 0165-4101
                                       HF5601

Articles that apply economic theory to accounting, including discussions of the role of accounting within the firm, in capital markets, and in financial contracts. Intended audience is academicians and accounting practicners. Available in online form.

401   Journal of accounting research. London School of Economics and Political Science, University of London, Accounting Research Center, Booth School of Business, University of Chicago. Hoboken, N.J.: Wiley, 1963–. ill.
ISSN 0021-8456
657.05   HF5601

Publishes theoretical, empirical, and clinical research in all areas of accounting. Four regular issues plus one conference issue (published in May) covering the previous year's annual accounting research conference from the Institute of Professional Accounting at the University of Chicago's Graduate School of Business. Typical articles cover international accounting standards, insider trading and voluntary disclosure, stock returns, ownership concentration in privatized firms, the press as a watchdog for accounting fraud, and auditors' responses to political connections in Malaysia.

Organizations and Associations

402   AICPA online. http://www.aicpa.org/. American Institute of Certified Public Accountants. New York: American Institute of Certified Public Accountants. 1998–
                                       HF5601

"The American Institute of Certified Public Accountants is the national, professional organization for all Certified Public Accountants." —*AICPA Mission.* Includes professional resources; conferences, publications, CPE, and the AICPA library; magazines and newsletters; information on becoming a CPA; career development and workplace issues; consumer information; AICPA Media Center; current news; and information on legislative activities and state licensing issues impacting CPAs. The professional resources area has the AICPA Code of Professional Conduct and Ethics Code, AICPA standards (Statements on Auditing Standards SAS 1–114, Statements on Standards for Attestation Engagements SSARS 1–14, Statements on Quality Control Standards 2, 3, and 5), and links to FASB, IASB, IFAC, GASB, SEC, the GAO, FASAB, and PCAOB websites.

403   American Accounting Association. http://aaahq.org/. American Accounting Association. Sarasota, Fla.: American Accounting Association. 1998–
657.025759   HF5601.A7

Founded in 1916, the assoc.'s purpose is to "influence ways of thinking about professional practice, education, business issues and standard setting." —*Mission and Shared Values.* AAA has been present on the Web since 1998.

Includes information on assoc. journals (*The Accounting Review* (398)*, Issues in Accounting Education, Accounting Horizons*), faculty development resources, awards, a placement service, links to other accounting sites and assoc., and a discussion forum.

Accounting Standards

404   Accounting and tax. http://www.proquest.com/products-services/pq_accounting.html. ProQuest. Ann Arbor, Mich.: Proquest. 2006–
                                       HF5635

Comprehensive coverage of accounting and tax, with nearly 500 sources, including top accounting journals like the *Accounting review* (398) and the *Journal of accounting research* (401). Has accounting standards from FASB, GASB, and IASB, with International Financial Reporting Standards, SIC Interpretations, IFRC Interpretations, pronouncements, statements, technical bulletins, interpretations, board opinions, American Institute of Certified Public Accountants (AICPA) Interpretations, and Emerging Issues Task Force (EITF) abstracts. A handy glossary of terms appears within the text of the FASB, GASB, and IASB documents. Other features include links to related standards and SmartView, a split screen displaying the table of contents and the text of the standards. Another Web-based tax resource is *BNA tax and accounting center*.

405 Accounting standards. Financial Accounting Standards Board, American Institute of Certified Public Accountants. Stamford, Conn.: Financial Accounting Standards Board, 1982–2009
ISSN 0888-7896
657.0218   HF5616.U5
The Financial Accounting Standards Board is recognized by the Securities and Exchange Commission (SEC) and the American Institute of Certified Public Accountants (AICPA) as the designated authority for U.S. private sector accounting standards. Major publications such as *Accounting standards: original pronouncements*, *Accounting standards: Current text . . .* , *Accounting standards: statement of financial accounting standards*, *FASB interpretation* and *FASB report* ceased in print format with issues of 2009: instead full text is available through the FASB website at http://www.fasb.org/home. Advanced versions of the online service are also marketed. FASB standards are also available in online services including Accounting research manager (411) and Comperio (408).

406 AICPA online. http://www.aicpa.org/. American Institute of Certified Public Accountants. New York: American Institute of Certified Public Accountants. 1998–
                                HF5601
"The American Institute of Certified Public Accountants is the national, professional organization for all Certified Public Accountants." —*AICPA Mission.*

Includes professional resources; conferences, publications, CPE, and the AICPA library; magazines and newsletters; information on becoming a CPA; career development and workplace issues; consumer information; AICPA Media Center; current news; and information on legislative activities and state licensing issues impacting CPAs. The professional resources area has the AICPA Code of Professional Conduct and Ethics Code, AICPA standards (Statements on Auditing Standards SAS 1–114, Statements on Standards for Attestation Engagements SSARS 1–14, Statements on Quality Control Standards 2, 3, and 5), and links to FASB, IASB, IFAC, GASB, SEC, the GAO, FASAB, and PCAOB websites.

407 Codification of auditing standards. American Institute of Certified Public Accountants, Public Company Accounting Oversight Board. New York: American Institute of Certified Public Accountants, 2004–
                                HF5667
Annual. Presents American Institute of Certified Public Accountants (AICPA) auditing and attestation standards (*Statements on Auditing Standards*), as well as interpretations and amendments, which are applicable to nonissuers. Arranged by subject. The AICPA web site at http://www.aicpa.org/ also has full text of major documents.

408 Comperio. http://www.pwc.com/Extweb/aboutus.nsf/docid/58B 3A4A2F1C2053680256E2800357A82. PricewaterhouseCoopers (Firm). Tampa, Fla.: PricewaterhouseCoopers. 2004–
Full text of global financial reporting and accounting literature for Australia, Canada, Finland, the Netherlands, South Africa, Switzerland, the United Kingdom and the United States. Also has international documents, with International Financial Reporting Standards, International Accounting Standards, IFRS Exposure Drafts, Checklists, Practice Aids, and Interpretations, SIC Interpretations, International Standards on Auditing, IFAC Code of Ethics, International Public Sector Accounting Standards, and even the occasional text of a speech.

For the United States, it includes American Institute of Certified Public Accountants (AICPA) Professional Standards, Statements of Position Practice Bulletins, Issues Papers, Audit and Accounting Guides, Audit

Risk Alerts, COSO Report, and Exposure Drafts and Response Letters; Financial Accounting Standards Board (FASB) Statements and Interpretations, Technical Bulletins, Accounting Research Bulletins, APB Opinions and Statements, Implementations Guides, Special Reports, Exposure Drafts; GASB documents; Securities and Exchange Commission (SEC) Securities Act of 1933, Securities Exchange Act of 1934, Investment Advisor's Act of 1940, Investment Company Act of 1940; PricewaterhouseCoopers SEC Volume; Emerging Issues Task Force (EITF) Abstracts, Minutes, and Issues Summaries; Independence Standards Board (ISB) Standards and Interpretations; Derivatives Implementation Group (DIG) Issues and discussion; PricewaterhouseCoopers Guidance and Interpretations, Accounting and Reporting Manual, Montgomery's Auditing, Twelfth Edition, Accounting and Auditing DataLines, and Implementation Guides.

Search by organization (like Australian Accounting Standards Board), territory, topic (ranges from assurance to strategic monitoring risk), document type (ranges from best practice to news and views), and publication.

409   IAS plus. http://www.iasplus.com/. Deloitte Touche Tohmatsu Limited (Firm). New York: Deloitte Touche Tohmatsu Limited. 2007–

It's all about the international accounting standards at IAS Plus. Organized into IFRS News, Standards (summaries of IFRS 1–8, IAS 1–41), Interpretations (summaries of documents issued by the International Financial Reporting Interpretations Committee), IASB Agenda, IASB Structure, Newsletter, Financials (IFRS Financial Statements, Disclosure Checklist, Compliance Questionnaire), links to 200 websites about International Financial Reporting Standards (including governmental and regulatory organizations, international organizations, securities exchanges, professional accountancy organizations, standard-setting bodies), Countries-Regions (table showing the country requirements for use of International Financial Reporting Standards as the primary GAAP, as used by domestic listed and unlisted companies), and Resources (odds and ends such as information on the International Valuation Standards Committee, IFAD Activities, IFAC Public Sector Committee, IFRS Reference Materials, Comment Letters to IASB, and tools like a 14-year calendar), and a currency converter.

410   International accounting/financial reporting standards guide. New York: Aspen, 2004– ISSN 1550-7181
657   HF5626
Information and commentary on IFRS (422) reporting standards issued by the International Accounting Standards Board (IASB). Organized into three parts: pt.1 is an overview of the IASB, pt. 2 provides commentary on general standards, pt. 3 gives industry standards (agriculture, banks and other financial institutions, and insurance contracts). Each year's edition covers new International Financials Reporting Standards (IFRS's) and amendments to standards. Practice pointers are weaved into the text and explain how to apply the standards. Formerly *Miller international accounting/financial reporting standards guide*. Also available through CCH's Tax Research NetWork and Accounting Research Manager (411).

Accounting Practices

411   Accounting research manager. http://www.accountingresearchmanager.com/. CCH Incorporated. Riverwoods, Ill.: Wolters Kluwer. 2004–
                                                        HF5626
Includes a dizzying array of authoritative and interpretive financial reporting literature. Divided into accounting, SEC, auditing, and government sections, each with standards, interpretations, and examples. The acccounting section has documents from the Financial Accounting Standards Board (FASB), Emerging Issues Task Force (EITF), and International Accounting Standards Board (IASB). The SEC section includes Regulations S-X and S-K, Forms 10-K and 10-Q, SABs, Sarbanes-Oxley, Public Company Accounting Oversight Board (PCAOB), and Regulation S-B. The audit section includes AICPA, Public Company Accounting Oversight Board (PCAOB), U.S. Department of Housing and Urban Development, Office of Management and Budgets (OMB), and American Institute of Certified Public Accountants (AICPA). The government section includes GASB, GAO, and OMB.

Documents are color coded: white for authoritative, beige for interpretation, blue for proposed, and green for SEC. They also show amendments, deletions, or suspensions. SEC filings since 1994, available in Word, Adobe Acrobat, and Excel. Highlights current developments and events on the home page.

An online tutorial and regularly scheduled live tutorials are available and recommended to master the database. Updated five times a day.

412   CCH Internet tax research network.
http://www.cchgroup.com/. CCH (Firm).
Chicago: CCH. 1999–

Organized into fully searchable libraries: accounting/auditing, federal, state, financial and estate, special entities, pension and payroll international, and perform plus II. Each library is organized into subsections that include current features and journals; CCH explanations and analysis; Treatises; Primary Sources; Practice aids; Archives; and Topical indexes. Perhaps most used for federal tax materials, but also addresses state taxes (has all State Tax Reporters), sales tax, financial and estate planning, business entities, international (treaties), tax forms, practice aids, and calculators for accountants.

The Federal library includes legislative materials, Federal Tax Code, Federal Tax Regulations, Cases, Tax Court and other trial court cases, U.S. Circuit Courts of Appeal, U.S. Supreme Court, IRS Publications (Revenue rulings, Revenue procedures, IRS notices, IRS announcements, Letter rulings, IRS positions, and Internal revenue manual), Standard Federal Tax Reporter, Federal Estate/Gift Tax Reporter, and Federal Excise Tax Reporter.

Search includes citation, check citator, news, and a thesaurus.

413   Comperio. http://www.pwc.com/Extweb/
aboutus.nsf/docid/58B3A4A2F1C2
053680256E2800357A82.
PricewaterhouseCoopers (Firm). Tampa,
Fla.: PricewaterhouseCoopers. 2004–

Full text of global financial reporting and accounting literature for Australia, Canada, Finland, the Netherlands, South Africa, Switzerland, the United Kingdom and the United States. Also has international documents, with International Financial Reporting Standards, International Accounting Standards, IFRS Exposure Drafts, Checklists, Practice Aids, and Interpretations, SIC Interpretations, International Standards on Auditing, IFAC Code of Ethics, International Public Sector Accounting Standards, and even the occasional text of a speech.

For the United States, it includes American Institute of Certified Public Accountants (AICPA) Professional Standards, Statements of Position Practice Bulletins,

Issues Papers, Audit and Accounting Guides, Audit Risk Alerts, COSO Report, and Exposure Drafts and Response Letters; Financial Accounting Standards Board (FASB) Statements and Interpretations, Technical Bulletins, Accounting Research Bulletins, APB Opinions and Statements, Implementations Guides, Special Reports, Exposure Drafts; GASB documents; Securities and Exchange Commission (SEC) Securities Act of 1933, Securities Exchange Act of 1934, Investment Advisor's Act of 1940, Investment Company Act of 1940; PricewaterhouseCoopers SEC Volume; Emerging Issues Task Force (EITF) Abstracts, Minutes, and Issues Summaries; Independence Standards Board (ISB) Standards and Interpretations; Derivatives Implementation Group (DIG) Issues and discussion; PricewaterhouseCoopers Guidance and Interpretations, Accounting and Reporting Manual, Montgomery's Auditing, Twelfth Edition, Accounting and Auditing DataLines, and Implementation Guides.

Search by organization (like Australian Accounting Standards Board), territory, topic (ranges from assurance to strategic monitoring risk), document type (ranges from best practice to news and views), and publication.

**414   Handbook of accounting and
auditing.** Frank C. Minter, Barry Jay
Epstein, Michael P. Krzus. Boston: Warren,
Gorham, and Lamont, 1982–. various
pagings, ill.
657.02   HF5635

Covers the many changes that continue to deluge the profession, with specific attention to Generally Accepted Accounting Principles (GAAP) and Generally Accepted Auditing Standards (GAAS). Organized in six sections: (1) overview of financial accounting, (2) audit function, (3) major areas of financial accounting and auditing, (4) accounting for specialized industries, (5) comprehensive coverage of the financial services industry, and (6) major accounting institutions. Index. Kept up-to-date by cumulative supplements, each containing a cumulative index. Also available online through Checkpoint (415).

415   Thomson Reuters checkpoint. http://
ria.thomsonreuters.com/. RIA Group.
Fort Worth, Tex.: Thomson Reuters Tax &
Accounting. [1998–]

Formerly *RIA checkpoint*. Accessible by subscription. Integrates RIA tax and accounting publications that provide primary tax documents and secondary analysis into one online resource with the federal tax code (from 1990), regulations, committee reports, rulings (1954 to present), Internal Revenue Bulletins (1996 to present), WG&L tax treatises and journals, IBFD Materials, state tax guides and laws, and federal tax case histories (1860 to present).

Sections of Checkpoint are Tax News, Federal Tax Library, State and Local Tax Library, International Tax Library, Pensions and Benefits Library, Estate Planning Library, Payroll Library, WG&L Financial Reporting and Management (FRM) Library, Accounting and Auditing Library, Checkpoint Archives, and Continuing Professional Education (CPE). Major publications and primary documents are *RIA daily updates, the BNA daily tax report, Federal tax coordinator* (416), *United States tax reporter, Federal tax handbook, Tax planning and practice guides, Federal income taxation of corporations and shareholders, WG&L tax dictionary, RIA worldwide tax law, Comtax news* (2001–5), *International taxes weekly newsletter* (1999–2006), *WG&L international transfer pricing treatises, RIA's executive compensation analysis, ERISA, DOL and PBGC regulations and committee reports,* SEC compliance documents, GAAP compliance documents, AICPA documents (Professional Standards, Technical Practice Aids, Audit and Accounting Guides), FASB documents (Original Pronouncements, Original Pronouncements as amended including Implementation Guides and FASB Staff Positions, Current Text, Emerging Issues Task Force, Derivative Instruments and Hedging Activities, Exposure Drafts, Business Reporting Research Project, FASB Reports, Action Alerts, Proposed Documents, Topical Index), GASB documents (Original Pronouncements, Implementation Guides, Exposure Drafts, Topical Index), IASB (IASC Foundation Constitution, Standards, Interpretations, Implementation Guidance for IFRS and IAS, Proposal Stage Documents, News, Glossary), PCAOB documents (Advance PCAOB, Final Releases, Proposals, Final and Proposed Rules, Auditing Standards, Interim Auditing Standards, Interim Attestation Standards, Interim Quality Control Standards, Interim Ethics Standards, Interim Independence Standards, Registration System, Ethics Code), *Advance Sarbanes-Oxley cases* (2003 to present), and the *Handbook of accounting and auditing* (377).

Many of these resources are also available through Westlaw, CCH's Accounting Research Manager (411) or Tax Research Network.

Tax Services

416   Federal tax coordinator 2d. Research Institute of America. New York: Research Institute of America, 1977–
10603343   KF6285

Easy to understand analysis of tax laws (income, gift, estate, and excise), regulations, IRS rulings, and releases, as well as text of the Internal Revenue Code and Treasury Regulations; issued as a multi-volume loose-leaf service, with annotations and analysis. Arranged by subject, with a good index. Updated weekly. Similar to *CCH Standard Federal Tax Reporter* (417). Available through RIA Checkpoint (415) and Westlaw. Preceded by *Federal tax coordinator* which began in 1941.

417   Standard federal tax reporter. Commerce Clearing House, United States., United States., CCH Incorporated. Chicago: Commerce Clearing House, 1945– ISSN 0162-3494
343.7304   KF6285

The best known tax service, with analysis and primary documents for federal tax law (such as personal income, corporate income, business expenses and deductions, mergers and acquisitions, employee benefit plans, tax accounting, exempt organizations, capital gains and losses). Primary documents include: Internal Revenue code sections, regulations and proposed regulations, and excerpts of committee reports. Most used for CCH explanations of federal tax law and the annotations of cases and rulings that go back to 1913. Arranged by code section, with four topical indexes, each in a separate volume: in the *Index* volume; in *Internal Revenue Code*, v. 1; and the cumulative index in the *New Matters* volume. Updated weekly. Available through CCH Tax Research NetWork and LexisNexis. Similar to RIA's *Federal Tax Coordinator 2d* (416).

International Accounting Resources

418   Comperio. http://www.pwc.com/Extweb/aboutus.nsf/docid/58B3A4A2F1C20536 80256E2800357A82. PricewaterhouseCoopers (Firm). Tampa, Fla.: PricewaterhouseCoopers. 2004–

Full text of global financial reporting and accounting literature for Australia, Canada, Finland, the

Netherlands, South Africa, Switzerland, the United Kingdom and the United States. Also has international documents, with · International Financial Reporting Standards, International Accounting Standards, IFRS Exposure Drafts, Checklists, Practice Aids, and Interpretations, SIC Interpretations, International Standards on Auditing, IFAC Code of Ethics, International Public Sector Accounting Standards, and even the occassional text of a speech.

For the United States, it includes American Institute of Certified Public Accountants (AICPA) Professional Standards, Statements of Position Practice Bulletins, Issues Papers, Audit and Accounting Guides, Audit Risk Alerts, COSO Report, and Exposure Drafts and Response Letters; Financial Accounting Standards Board (FASB) Statements and Interpretations, Technical Bulletins, Accounting Research Bulletins, APB Opinions and Statements, Implementations Guides, Special Reports, Exposure Drafts; GASB documents; Securities and Exchange Commission (SEC) Securities Act of 1933, Securities Exchange Act of 1934, Investment Advisor's Act of 1940, Investment Company Act of 1940; PricewaterhouseCoopers SEC Volume; Emerging Issues Task Force (EITF) Abstracts, Minutes, and Issues Summaries; Independence Standards Board (ISB) Standards and Interpretations; Derivatives Implementation Group (DIG) Issues and discussion; PricewaterhouseCoopers Guidance and Interpretations, Accounting and Reporting Manual, Montgomery's Auditing, Twelfth Edition, Accounting and Auditing DataLines, and Implementation Guides.

Search by organization (like Australian Accounting Standards Board), territory, topic (ranges from assurance to strategic monitoring risk), document type (ranges from best practice to news and views), and publication.

419   Deloitte international tax and business guides. http://www.deloitte.com/taxguides. Deloitte (Firm). New York: Deloitte Touche Tohmatsu Limited. 2007–

Information on laws and regulations for doing business in 50 countries, with coverage of investment climate (economic structure, banking and financing, foreign trade), business and regulatory environment (registration and licensing, price controls, monopolies and restraint of trade, intellectual property, mergers and acquisitions, accounting standards), foreign investment (foreign investment incentives and restrictions, exchange controls), choice of business entity (principal forms of doing business, establishing a branch, setting up a company), corporate and individual taxation (taxable income and rates, capital gains, foreign income and tax treaties, transfer pricing, turnover and other indirect taxes and duties, tax compliance and administration), employment law (employees' rights and remuneration, wages and benefits, termination of employment), and entry requirements. Snapshots are available for 100 countries, giving country profiles, with economic indicators, tax rates, business forms, and labor environment.

420   IAS plus. http://www.iasplus.com/. Deloitte Touche Tohmatsu Limited (Firm). New York: Deloitte Touche Tohmatsu Limited. 2007–

It's all about the international accounting standards at IAS Plus. Organized into IFRS News, Standards (summaries of IFRS 1–8, IAS 1–41), Interpretations (summaries of documents issued by the International Financial Reporting Interpretations Committee), IASB Agenda, IASB Structure, Newsletter, Financials (IFRS Financial Statements, Disclosure Checklist, Compliance Questionnaire), links to 200 websites about International Financial Reporting Standards (including governmental and regulatory organizations, international organizations, securities exchanges, professional accountancy organizations, standard-setting bodies), Countries-Regions (table showing the country requirements for use of International Financial Reporting Standards as the primary GAAP, as used by domestic listed and unlisted companies), and Resources (odds and ends such as information on the International Valuation Standards Committee, IFAD Activities, IFAC Public Sector Committee, IFRS Reference Materials, Comment Letters to IASB, and tools like a 14-year calendar), and a currency converter.

421   International accounting/financial reporting standards guide. New York: Aspen, 2004– ISSN 1550-7181
657   HF5626

Information and commentary on IFRS (422) reporting standards issued by the International Accounting Standards Board (IASB). Organized into three parts: pt.1 is an overview of the IASB, pt. 2 provides commentary on general standards, pt. 3 gives industry standards (agriculture, banks and other financial institutions, and insurance contracts). Each year's edition covers new International Financials Reporting Standards (IFRS's) and amendments to standards. Practice pointers are weaved into the text and explain how to apply the standards. Formerly *Miller international accounting/financial reporting standards guide*. Also available through CCH's Tax Research NetWork and Accounting Research Manager (411).

422   International financial reporting standards. International Accounting Standards Board. London: International Accounting Standards Board, 2003–. ill.
657.0218   HF5626

International Financial Reporting Standards (IFRS) currently are issued by the International Accounting Standards Board (IASB). The print editions contain the complete consolidated text of the latest version of Standards, including International Accounting Standards (IAS's), IFRIC and Standard Industrial Classification (SIC) Interpretations, and IASB issued supporting documents. Also includes a glossary and an index. Summaries and other information are available online at http://www.ifrs.org/Pages/default .aspx. Also available online through services such as Comperio (408) and Accounting Research Manager (411). International accounting/financial reporting standards guide (410) and similar guides are in print.

Internet Resources

423   Rutgers accounting web. http://raw .rutgers.edu/. Rutgers Accounting Research Center, Rutgers Business School. Newark, N.J.: Rutgers Accounting Research Center. 1994–
                                 HF5625.7

Online resources for accounting and finance, including an "Accounting Digital Library" with links to streaming lectures for accounting courses, and an "Accounting Research Directory" that indexes publications since 1963.

Business Law

Guides and Handbooks

424   The business guide to legal literacy: What every manager should know

about the law. Hanna Hasl-Kelchner. San Francisco: Jossey-Bass, 2006. xii, 372 p., ill. ISBN 9780787982553
346.7307   KF390.B84

Uses real-life stories to increase understanding about how the law impacts business. Written by a corporate lawyer who taught business law to MBA students at Duke University. Pt. 1 addresses legal risk; pt. 2, actions that employees should take; and pt. 3, actions that organizations should take. Appendixes include a legal primer. Written for managers, but useful for anyone trying to grasp legal risks. Available as an e-book.

425   The employer's legal handbook. Fred Steingold. Berkeley, Calif.: Nolo Press, 1994–. ill. ISSN 2163–033X
344   KF3455

Updated every two years: the 11th edition appeared in 2013. Practical coverage of topics in hiring, personnel practices, wages and hours, employee benefits, taxes, family and medical leave, health and safety, illegal discrimination, workers with disabilities, termination, employee privacy, independent contractors, unions, lawyers and legal research. Appendixes for labor departments and agencies, state drug and alcohol testing laws, state laws on employee arrest and conviction records, state laws on access to personnel records, state minimum wage laws for tipped and regular employees, state meal and rest breaks, state health insurance continuation laws, state family and medical leave laws, right-to-know laws (hazardous chemicals), state laws prohibiting discrimination in employment, agencies that enforce laws prohibiting discrimination in employment, and state laws that control final paychecks. Available as an e-book.

426   The law of securities regulation. 6th ed. Thomas Lee Hazen. St. Paul, Minn.: Thomson/West, 2009. xxxiii, 862 p. ISBN 9780314187970
                                 KF1439

Introduces and summarizes U.S. securities laws: regularly updated to reflect evolution of the law. Covers laws based on the Securities Act of 1933, with other chapters on related topics such as IPOs, tender offers, market regulation, broker-dealer disputes, fraud and civil liability, insider trading, and protection of bondholders. Bibliographic references. Index. One volume abridgment of the seven volume *Treatise on securities regulation* by the same author.

427 The legal environment of business and online commerce: business ethics, e-commerce, regulatory, and international issues. 7th ed. Henry R. Cheeseman. Upper Saddle River, N.J.: Pearson/Prentice Hall, 2013. xx, 628 p., col. ill., maps ISBN 9780132870887
346.7307   KF889
Relies on study of cases to consider the impact of the legal environment and government regulation on e-commerce. Covers the general legal and ethical environment, traditional contracts and electronic commerce, agency and business organizations, employment and equal opportunity law, the regulatory environment, and property and bankruptcy issues, as well as specifics such as cyber crime, intellectual property and cyber piracy, e-contracts, and e-securities.

428 The portable bankruptcy code and rules. Sally M. Henry, ABA Section of Business Law. Chicago: American Bar Association, 1996–
ISSN 1527-4144
346.7307/8   KF1510.99
Annual publication of the American Bar Association, with complete text of the U.S. federal bankruptcy code and the bankruptcy rules with forms. Includes updates to relevant sections of Titles 18 and 28. Comprehensive indexing.

429 Understanding international business and financial transactions. 3rd ed. Jerold A. Friedland. New Providence, N.J.: LexisNexis, 2010. xvi, 367, [7] p., ill. ISBN 9781422478417
346.7307   KF390.B8
Includes chapters on money, currency and finance, rules of international trade, United States trade law, international sales, operating in foreign markets, and taxation of international transactions. Updated to reflect the impact of the financial crisis of 2008. Friedland, a law professor at DePaul University, presents an overview of international business law. Index. Available as an e-book.

Encyclopedias

430 Affirmative action: An encyclopedia. James A. Beckman. Westport, Conn.: Greenwood Press, 2004. 2 v., 1074 p., ill. ISBN 9781573565196
331.133097303   HF5549.5.A34
Entries on affirmative action from legal, political science, historical, and sociological perspectives. Contributors are both academics and practitioners, providing a balanced perspective. Appendixes include full text of the 2003 *Gratz v. Bollinger* and *Grutter v. Bollinger* decisions. Selective bibliography and index. Available as an e-book.

431 Encyclopedia of law and economics. 2nd ed. Gerrit de Geest. Cheltenham, U.K.; Northampton, Mass.: Edward Elgar, 2009–
346.03   K487.E3
Replaces the five-volume first edition of 2000. Individual volumes are the work of separate editors, and at this time include v. 1, Tort law and economics; v. 2, Labor and employment law and economics; v. 3, Criminal law and economics; v. 4, Antitrust law and economics; v. 5, Property law and economics; and v. 6, Contract law and economics. The revised edition is intended to reach twelve volumes. Each volume consists of signed chapters by experts, reviewing current legal literature. Bibliographies in each chapter. Index in each volume.

Many of the essays in the five volumes of the first edition are available online at http://encyclo.findlaw.com/: v. 1, The history and methodology of law and economics; v. 2, Civil law and economics; v. 3, The regulation of contracts; v. 4, The economics of public and tax law; and v. 5, The economics of crime and litigation.

432 Encyclopedia of management. 7th ed. Sonya D. Hill. Detroit: Gale, Cengage Learning, 2012. xxx, 1133 p. ISBN 9781414459042
658.003   HD30.15
Covers functional areas such as corporate planning and strategic management, emerging topics in management, entrepreneurship, financial management and accounting, general management, human resources management, innovation and technology, international management, leadership, legal issues, management

science and operations, management information systems, performance measures and assessment, personal growth and development for managers, production and operations management, quality management and total quality management, supply chain management, and training and development. More than 300 essays in alphabetical order, written by academics and business professionals, with cross-references and recommended reading lists. New content reflects trends such as the use of handheld devices for Internet-based tools, social networking, network security, venture capital and entrepreneurship, and business in China. Includes a glossary of terms. Index. Available as an e-book.

433 The encyclopedia of taxation and tax policy. 2nd ed. Joseph J. Cordes, Robert D. Ebel, Jane Gravelle, Urban Institute. Washington: Urban Institute Press, 2005. xvii, 499 p., ill ISBN 9780877667520
336.2/003   HJ2305
Alphabetically arranged, with over 200 essays on tax policy, tax structure, tax compliance, and tax administration, with some coverage of public finance. Written by tax professionals, academicians, and administrators, almost all of whom are members of the National Tax Association. Entries are brief, but cover definitions, background, and relevance. Most entries include recommended readings. The 2nd ed. adds 45 new entries and updates entries with legislative changes.

434 Encyclopedia of white-collar crime. Jurg Gerber, Eric L. Jensen. Westport, Conn.: Greenwood Press, 2006
ISBN 9780313335242
364.168097303   HV6768
More than 500 entries giving history, definitions, law, investigations, prosecutions, biographical sketches, and events. Arranged in 17 topics: business fraud and crimes, companies, consumers, countries and regions, criminology and justice, financial and securities fraud, government, laws, medical and healthcare fraud, people, political scandals, pollution, products, regulation, scams and swindles, war profiteering, and work-related crimes. Includes cross-references, further readings, and a chronology of events. Available as an e-book.

435 McCarthy's desk encyclopedia of intellectual property. 3rd ed. J. Thomas McCarthy, Roger E. Schechter, David J. Franklyn. Washington: Bureau of National Affairs, 2004. xxi, 736 p.
ISBN 9781570184017
346.7304/8   KF2976.4
Definitions for 800 words, phrases, conventions and statutes in the areas of patents, trademarks, copyright, trade secrets, entertainment, and computer law. McCarthy is a professor at the University of San Francisco School of Law. Arranged alphabetically, with references to relevant cases and statutes. Appendixes list the superintendents and commissioners of patents and trademarks from 1802 to the present, the assistant commissioners of trademarks from 1953 to the present, annual patent applications filed and issued between 1790 and 1994, annual trademark registrations and renewals between 1870 and 1994, and the registers of copyrights from 1897 to the present.

Dictionaries

436 A dictionary of human resource management. 2nd ed. Edmund Heery, Mike Noon. Oxford; New York: Oxford University Press, 2008. xxvi, 552 p.
ISBN 9780199298761
658.3003   HF5549.A23
Provides definitions for 1,400 words and phrases, including 300 new entries since the edition of 2001. Covers legal, technical, and theoretical terms, including catch phrases and jargon. Includes vocabulary from psychology, sociology, and economics. Major themes include employee resourcing, work organization, employee development, discrimination, health, collective bargaining, and laws and regulations. Written from a British perspective. Cross-references. Bibliography. Available as an e-book.

437 A handbook of business law terms. Bryan A. Garner, David W. Schultz. St. Paul, Minn.: West Group, 1999. iii, 637 p.
ISBN 9780314239358
346.730703   KF390.B84
Clear definitions for more than 3,000 words and phrases in business law. Useful for both students and business practitioners.

438 The new Palgrave dictionary of economics and the law. Peter Newman. London; New York: Macmillan Reference; Stockton Press, 2004. 3 v., ill. ISBN 9781561592159

330.03   K487.E3

Contains 399 signed articles with international coverage on the legal aspects of economics, such as airline deregulation and property rights. Includes statutes, treaties, directives, and cases. Written by 340 contributors from eight countries.

Periodicals

439 American business law journal. Academy of Legal Studies in Business. Hoboken, N.J.: Wiley-Blackwell, 1963– ISSN 0002-7766

347.306705   KF872 346.730705;

Covers the full range of business law topics. Published by the Academy of Legal Studies in Business, an association of business and corporate law educators who teach outside of law schools. Intended for students and professors. Available online.

440 Federal register. http://www.gpo.gov/fdsys/browse/collection.action?collection Code=FR. U.S. National Archives and Records Administration, Office of the Federal Register. Washington: National Archives and Records Administration, Office of the Federal Register ISSN 0097-6326

353.005   KF70

Official repository for the daily publication of all newly adopted rules and regulations, proposed rules, and notices of federal agencies and organizations, executive orders, and other presidential documents. When a regulation is codified, it is part of the *Code of federal regulations* (454). As many federal rules, codes, and regulations affect business establishments, this is a necessary resource. For example, information on business rates and terms, trademarks, or even the *Federal register* notice describing changes adopted for NAICS 2007.

Online access to issues 1994 (v. 59) through the most current. Issues prior to 1994 available at Federal depository libraries.

Subscriber access to the complete digitized *Federal register*, from its earliest date of publication, is available from HeinOnline.

441 Review of banking and financial law. Morin Center for Banking and Financial Law. Boston: Boston University School of Law, 2008– 1544–4627   KF967.R48

Annual. Edited by law students at Boston University's Morin Center for Banking and Financial Law, with articles written by professors and practitioners. Covers banking, securities, financial services, and administrative and general corporate law. Available online. Successor to *Annual review of banking and financial law* (2004–2007).

Organizations and Associations

442 American Bar Association. http://www.americanbar.org/groups/business_law.html. American Bar Association Section of Business Law. Chicago: American Bar Association. 1996–

K1000

Home page includes news, program materials, publications (*Business Law Today, The Business Lawyer*, and various monographs), event calendar, and committee links.

443 Association of Corporate Counsel (ACC). http://www.acc.com/. Association of Corporate Counsel. Washington: Association of Corporate Counsel. 1997–

Intended for in-house counsel, the site offers research (virtual library with legal forms, statistics and surveys, compliance and ethics), education, member directory, ACC publications (*ACC Docket, European and Canadian Briefings*), public policy, and career resources.

Topical Law Services

444 BNA's bankruptcy law reporter. Bureau of National Affairs. Washington: Bureau of National Affairs, 1989–. loose-leaf ISSN 1044-7474

347.3067805   KF1507 346.7307805;

Covers state and federal bankruptcy law, with filings, forms, motions, decisions, and legislation. Also available online through Bloomberg BNA's *Bankruptcy law resource center*.

445   CCH Internet tax research network.
http://www.cchgroup.com/. CCH (Firm).
Chicago: CCH. 1999–
Organized into fully searchable libraries: accounting/
auditing, federal, state, financial and estate, special entities, pension and payroll international, and
perform plus II. Each library is organized into subsections that include current features and journals;
CCH explanations and analysis; Treatises; Primary
Sources; Practice aids; Archives; and Topical indexes.
Perhaps most used for federal tax materials, but also
addresses state taxes (has all State Tax Reporters),
sales tax, financial and estate planning, business
entities, international (treaties), tax forms, practice
aids, and calculators for accountants.

The Federal library includes legislative materials,
Federal Tax Code, Federal Tax Regulations, Cases,
Tax Court and other trial court cases, U.S. Circuit
Courts of Appeal, U.S. Supreme Court, IRS Publications (Revenue rulings, Revenue procedures, IRS
notices, IRS announcements, Letter rulings, IRS positions, and Internal revenue manual), Standard Federal Tax Reporter, Federal Estate/Gift Tax Reporter,
and Federal Excise Tax Reporter.

Search includes citation, check citator, news, and
a thesaurus.

**446   Contemporary corporation forms. 2nd
ed.** Aspen Law and Business. New York:
Aspen Law and Business, 1998–. 5 v.
(loose-leaf), ill., forms ISBN 1567066623
346.730660269   KF1411
Compiles 500 actual documents from law firms,
intended to serve as templates. Targets all types of corporations and even those interested in forming a corporation. Forms cover shareholder agreements, warrants,
options, dividends, spin-offs, mergers and acquisitions,
initial public offerings, bylaws, and more. Forms are
cross-referenced with relevant state corporation law.

447   Federal tax coordinator 2d. Research
Institute of America. New York: Research
Institute of America, 1977–
10603343   KF6285
Easy to understand analysis of tax laws (income,
gift, estate, and excise), regulations, IRS rulings, and
releases, as well as text of the Internal Revenue Code
and Treasury Regulations; issued as a multi-volume
loose-leaf service, with annotations and analysis.
Arranged by subject, with a good index. Updated

weekly. Similar to *CCH Standard Federal Tax Reporter*
(417). Available through RIA Checkpoint (415) and
Westlaw. Preceded by *Federal tax coordinator* which
began in 1941.

**448   Labor and Employment Law Resource
Center.** http://laborandemploymentlaw
.bna.com/. Bureau of National Affairs.
Arlington, Va.: Bureau of National Affairs.
[1999–] ISSN 2156-2849
331   KF3319
Cases, summaries of developments, manuals, and
explanations of U.S. federal and state laws in areas like
arbitration, collective bargaining, wages and hours, fair
employment, disability and employee rights. Includes
Daily labor report, comparative *State law chart builder*,
information on labor-management relations with decisions from 1984,and fair employment practices from
1965, BNA's *Labor Relations Reporter*, *HR Policy Handbook*, and *Client Letters, Checklists, and Forms*. Formerly
BNA's labor & employment law library. BNA also publishes an online *Human resources library* addressing
practical management of topics such as benefits, training and labor relations; and the *LaborPlus* database
with sections for NLRB Elections, Work Stoppages,
Unfair Labor Practices, Contract Settlement Summaries, and private sector Contract Listings.

449   Policies and practice: HR series.
Thomson West (Firm). Eagan, Minn.:
Thomson West, 2004–. 3 v.
                HF5549
Covers HR management, with sections on recordkeeping, hiring, termination, fair employment practices,
productivity, performance appraisal, training, communication, work rules and discipline, grievances,
labor relations, compensation, benefits, work/life
integration strategies, leaves of absence, safety and
occupational health, substance abuse, and security.
Includes forms and sample policies.

450   Standard federal tax reporter.
Commerce Clearing House, United
States., United States., CCH Incorporated.
Chicago: Commerce Clearing House,
1945– ISSN 0162-3494
343.7304   KF6285
The best known tax service, with analysis and primary documents for federal tax law (such as personal
income, corporate income, business expenses and

deductions, mergers and acquisitions, employee benefit plans, tax accounting, exempt organizations, capital gains and losses). Primary documents include: Internal Revenue code sections, regulations and proposed regulations, and excerpts of committee reports. Most used for CCH explanations of federal tax law and the annotations of cases and rulings that go back to 1913. Arranged by code section, with four topical indexes, each in a separate volume: in the *Index* volume; in *Internal Revenue Code*, v. 1; and the cumulative index in the *New Matters* volume. Updated weekly. Available through CCH Tax Research NetWork and LexisNexis. Similar to RIA's *Federal Tax Coordinator 2d* (416).

451   Thomson Reuters checkpoint. http:// ria.thomsonreuters.com/. RIA Group. Fort Worth, Tex.: Thomson Reuters Tax & Accounting. [1998–]

Formerly *RIA checkpoint*. Accessible by subscription. Integrates RIA tax and accounting publications that provide primary tax documents and secondary analysis into one online resource with the federal tax code (from 1990), regulations, committee reports, rulings (1954 to present), Internal Revenue Bulletins (1996 to present), WG&L tax treatises and journals, IBFD Materials, state tax guides and laws, and federal tax case histories (1860 to present).

Sections of Checkpoint are Tax News, Federal Tax Library, State and Local Tax Library, International Tax Library, Pensions and Benefits Library, Estate Planning Library, Payroll Library, WG&L Financial Reporting and Management (FRM) Library, Accounting and Auditing Library, Checkpoint Archives, and Continuing Professional Education (CPE). Major publications and primary documents are *RIA daily updates, the BNA daily tax report, Federal tax coordinator* (416), *United States tax reporter, Federal tax handbook, Tax planning and practice guides, Federal income taxation of corporations and shareholders, WG&L tax dictionary, RIA worldwide tax law, Comtax news* (2001–5), *International taxes weekly newsletter* (1999–2006), *WG&L international transfer pricing treatises, RIA's executive compensation analysis, ERISA, DOL and PBGC regulations and committee reports,* SEC compliance documents, GAAP compliance documents, AICPA documents (Professional Standards, Technical Practice Aids, Audit and Accounting Guides), FASB documents (Original Pronouncements, Original Pronouncements as amended including Implementation Guides and FASB Staff Positions, Current Text, Emerging Issues Task Force, Derivative Instruments and Hedging Activities, Exposure Drafts, Business Reporting Research Project, FASB Reports, Action Alerts, Proposed Documents, Topical Index), GASB documents (Original Pronouncements, Implementation Guides, Exposure Drafts, Topical Index), IASB (IASC Foundation Constitution, Standards, Interpretations, Implementation Guidance for IFRS and IAS, Proposal Stage Documents, News, Glossary), PCAOB documents (Advance PCAOB, Final Releases, Proposals, Final and Proposed Rules, Auditing Standards, Interim Auditing Standards, Interim Attestation Standards, Interim Quality Control Standards, Interim Ethics Standards, Interim Independence Standards, Registration System, Ethics Code), *Advance Sarbanes-Oxley cases* (2003 to present), and the *Handbook of accounting and auditing* (377).

Many of these resources are also available through Westlaw, CCH's Accounting Research Manager (411) or Tax Research Network.

452   Trade regulation reporter. 13th ed. Commerce Clearing House. Chicago: Commerce Clearing House, 1988–. 7 v., loose-leaf, ill.
347.3038   KF1606.5 343.7308;

Coverage of news and texts involving U.S. antitrust cases and pending consent decrees. Includes the text of court decisions for government and private antitrust litigation, and relevant antitrust legislation and regulations, with summaries of federal and state statutes, the Supreme Court docket, advisory material, policy pronouncements, case settlements, government antitrust decrees, and analysis of enforcement and procedures used by the Justice Department, the FTC, the states and corporations. Available in online form.

453   West's bankruptcy reporter. West Publishing Company. Eagan, Minn.: West, 1980– ISSN 0199-5782
346.7307802642   KF1515.A2

Text of reported decisions of the U.S. Bankruptcy Courts and the U.S. District Courts, with coverage of U.S. Supreme Court and U.S. Courts of Appeals opinions and decisions on bankruptcy cases. Cases are augmented with headnotes, describing each holding of a judicial opinion. Available online via Westlaw (43).

Internet Resources

454 **Code of federal regulations.** http://
www.gpo.gov/fdsys/browse/collectionCfr
.action?collectionCode=CFR. U.S.
National Archives and Records
Administration Office of the Federal
Register. Washington: National Archives
and Records Administration Office of the
Federal Register ISSN 1946-4975

342   KF70

Cited as *CFR*. Supersedes *Code of federal regulations of
the United States of America . . .* (1st ed., 1938).

A subject arrangement of administrative agency
rules and regulations, in paper format consisting
of more than 200 paperback volumes revised and
reissued each year on a staggered, quarterly basis.
Arranged in a subject scheme of 50 titles divided
into chapters, each of which contains the regulations of a specific agency. A list in the back of each
volume lists the title and chapter of each agency's
regulations. Title 3 contains presidential documents,
including proclamations and executive orders. An
"Index and finding aids" volume provides access by
agency name and subject.

New rules as they are promulgated appear in the
daily *Federal register* (440). Each issue has a cumulative table for the month, noting which parts of the
CFR are affected by new regulations. An index by
agency is published monthly and cumulates references since the beginning of the year.

Free electronic access to the *CFR* and the *Federal
register* is available from the website of the Government Printing Office (GPO). The *CFR* is available at
permanent URL http://purl.access.gpo.gov/GPO/
LPS494 both in HTML and PDF formats. The *Federal
register* is available at http://purl.access.gpo.gov/GPO/
LPS1756. The GPO also makes available the *e-CFR,*
which keeps the text of the *CFR* fully updated with
the new rules published in the *Federal register*. The
e-CFR is usually only 2–3 days behind; the currency is
indicated in bold red type at the top of the home page.

An electronic version of the *CFR* in PDF format,
complete back to its earliest publication in 1938, is
available on HeinOnline, as is the *Federal register*.

455 **Deloitte international tax and
business guides.** http://www.deloitte
.com/taxguides. Deloitte (Firm). New

York: Deloitte Touche Tohmatsu Limited.
2007–

Information on laws and regulations for doing business in 50 countries, with coverage of investment
climate (economic structure, banking and financing,
foreign trade), business and regulatory environment
(registration and licensing, price controls, monopolies and restraint of trade, intellectual property,
mergers and acquisitions, accounting standards),
foreign investment (foreign investment incentives
and restrictions, exchange controls), choice of business entity (principal forms of doing business, establishing a branch, setting up a company), corporate
and individual taxation (taxable income and rates,
capital gains, foreign income and tax treaties, transfer
pricing, turnover and other indirect taxes and duties,
tax compliance and administration), employment
law (employees' rights and remuneration, wages
and benefits, termination of employment), and
entry requirements. Snapshots are available for 100
countries, giving country profiles, with economic
indicators, tax rates, business forms, and labor
environment.

456 **Harmonized tariff schedule of
the United States.** http://www.usitc
.gov/tata/hts/bychapter/index.htm.
U.S. International Trade Commission.
Washington: International Trade
Commission. [1987–] ISSN 1066-0925

343.73056   KF6654.599

Approximately 5,000 six- to ten-digit product-based
numbers arranged into 99 chapters, plus appendixes.
The HTS classifies imported merchandise for rate of
duty and for statistical purposes and is used by most
countries. Three additional statistical annexes are
Schedule C, Classification of Country and Territory
Designations for U.S. Import Statistics; International
Standard Country Codes; and Schedule D, Customs
District and Port Codes.

457 **LLRX.com.** http://www.llrx.com/. Sabrina I.
Pacifici. Silver Spring, Md.: Law Library
Resource XChange. 1996–

KF272

An online guide to legal resources, especially court
rules, forms, and dockets, this site also has path-
finders, presentations, and articles with tips on legal
research, information management, government
resources, and competitive intelligence.

Electronic Commerce

Guides and Handbooks

**458   Gale e-commerce sourcebook. 2nd
ed.** Virgil L. Burton III. Farmington Hills,
Mich.: Gale Cengage Learning, 2012. x,
580 p. ISBN 9780787674212

381   HF5548.32

Updates the 1st edition of 2003. Intended for students, researchers or entrepreneurs. Organized into three sections: advice on "How To" topics such as accounting, B2B, incubators, and payment systems; a directory of relevant associations, consultants, publications and organizations; and a directory of 250 major e-commerce companies indicating revenue, number of employees, a basic description, and contact information including URLs. Index includes organization and personal names, industry terms and subject terms. Available as an e-book.

**459   Handbook of quantitative supply
chain analysis: modeling in the
e-business era.** David Simchi-Levi, S.
David Wu, Zuo-Jun Shen. Boston: Kluwer,
2004. xiii, 817 p., ill.
ISBN 9781402079528

658.70151   HD38.5

Includes trends, theory, and practice. Organized into five parts: emerging paradigms for supply chain analysis; auctions and bidding; supply chain coordinations in e-business; multi-channel coordination; and network design, IT, and financial services. Strong coverage of game theory as it applies to supply chains.

**460   The legal environment of business
and online commerce: business
ethics, e-commerce, regulatory, and
international issues. 7th ed.** Henry R.
Cheeseman. Upper Saddle River, N.J.:
Pearson/Prentice Hall, 2013. xx, 628 p.,
col. ill., maps ISBN 9780132870887

346.7307   KF889

Relies on study of cases to consider the impact of the legal environment and government regulation on e-commerce. Covers the general legal and ethical environment, traditional contracts and electronic commerce, agency and business organizations, employment and equal opportunity law, the regulatory environment, and property and bankruptcy issues, as well as specifics such as cyber crime, intellectual property and cyber piracy, e-contracts, and e-securities.

**461   Plunkett's e-commerce and internet
business almanac.** Jack W. Plunkett.
Houston, Tex.: Plunkett Research, 2001–.
ill. ISSN 1548-5447

338.7   HF5548.32

Annual. Like all the Plunkett almanacs, contains data on 300 major companies. Company profiles include types of business, brands and affiliates, contacts, employee benefits and top salaries, sales and profit numbers, growth plans, and competitive advantage. Especially useful for the industry statistics and rankings at the front of the volume. Also contains a glossary of key words and phrases. Available as an e-book.

Encyclopedias

**462   Dictionary of e-business: a definitive
guide to technology and business
terms. 2nd ed.** Francis Botto. Chichester,
U.K.; Hoboken, N.J.: Wiley, 2003. ix,
368 p., ill. ISBN 9780470844700

658.84   HF5548.32

Definitions and some short articles explain terms and concepts related to electronic commerce and the Internet. Available as an e-book.

**463   Encyclopedia of e-commerce,
e-government, and mobile commerce.**
Mehdi Khosrowpour. Hershey, Pa.: Idea
Group Reference, 2006
ISBN 9781591407997

381.14203   HF5548.32

Nearly 200 contributions from over 300 authors from around the world. Alphabetically arranged by topic, with good cross references. Topics include e-collaboration technologies and applications, e-commerce technologies and applications, e-commerce management and social issues, e-government technologies and applications, e-government management and social issues, e-healthcare technologies and applications, e-learning technologies and applications, e-technologies security and privacy, mobile commerce technologies and applications, mobile commerce management and social issues, virtual communities and enterprises, and web portals and services. Available as an e-book.

464 **Gale encyclopedia of e-commerce. 2nd ed.** Laurie J. Fundukian. Farmington Hills, Mich.: Gale Cengage Learning, 2012. 2 v. (xxi, 882 p.) ISBN 9780787690984
381/.17203   HF5548.32

Updates the first edition of 2002, with coverage of innovations such as e-books, Facebook, and YouTube. Some 480 entries on e-commerce include profiles of individuals, organizations and companies, coverage of significant events, a timeline of the development of e-commerce through 2011, and entries related to Cyber Monday, PayPal, encryption, Internet metrics, scalability, privacy, and security. Bibliography. Index. Available as an e-book.

Internet Resources

465 **ClickZ.** http://www.clickz.com/. Incisive Interactive Marketing LLC (Firm). New York: Incisive Interactive Marketing LLC. [2006–]
                                 HF5548.32

A treasure trove of statistics and trends about internet marketing, including advertising, business to business, broadband, demographics, education, e-mail and spam, entertainment, finance, geographics, government/politics, hardware, health care, professional, retailing, search tools, security, small/medium enterprises, software and IT, traffic patterns, and wireless. Some data back to 1999. Because ClickZ links to outside sources, some URLs can lead to broken links. Formerly called *CyberAtlas*, and *ClickZ Stats*.

466 **Emarketer.** http://www.emarketer.com/. eMarketer (Organization). New York: eMarketer. 1996–
658.84   HF5548.32

Reports marketing information with an emphasis on online media, internet commerce and digital marketing. Reports are grouped by topic (such as advertising, B2B contacts, or mobile devices), by industry (such as consumer products, travel, or retail), and by geography (such as North America, Asia-Pacific, or Western Europe). Aggregates data from 2,800 sources, with summaries in reports and articles. Sources

include Accenture, ACNielsen, *Advertising age* (731), Harris Poll, Juniper Research, Jupitermedia, Mediamark Research Inc. (MRI), Rand Corporation, Pew Internet & American Life Project, Red Hat, Red Herring, as well as various advertising and marketing associations. The data is searchable, making this a good source for online marketing and e-commerce statistics.

467 **E-stats.** http://www.census.gov/econ/estats/. U.S. Bureau of the Census. [Suitland, Md.]: U.S. Dept. of Commerce. 2001– ISSN 1943-0434
381   HF5548.32

Invaluable free Census Bureau resource presenting e-commerce data on shipments, sales, and revenue from multiple Census Bureau surveys of NAICS industries accounting for 70 percent of U.S. economic activity (not included are "agriculture, mining, utilities, construction, agents, brokers, electronic markets in wholesale trade, and approximately one-third of service-related industries"). Some tables are available in Excel. Also provides research papers and reports.

468 **Web marketing today.** http://www .wilsonweb.com/wmt/. Wilson Internet Services. Rocklin, Calif.: Wilson Internet Services. 1995– 384 1094-8112

Links to articles and other resources for web marketing and e-commerce. Categories for Industry Case Studies, Business to Business (B2B), Online Transactions, E-Commerce Environmental Design, Store-Building "Cart" Software, Website Promotion, Business Site Environmental Design, Paid Advertising, E-Mail Marketing, Miscellaneous Web Marketing, and Local Web Marketing. Access is a mix of fee and free.

Entrepreneurship/ Small Business

Guides and Handbooks

469 **Accounting and finance for your small business. 2nd ed.** Steven M. Bragg, E. James Burton. Hoboken, N.J.: Wiley, 2006. xv, 296 p., ill. ISBN 9780471771562
658   HD31

Contains information on tasks that should be accomplished before starting a business, and tasks and tips for operating an existing small business. Techniques and strategies for accounting, taxes, finance, and reporting. Also available as an e-book.

470 Anatomy of a business plan: the step-by-step guide to building your business and securing your company's future. 8th ed. Linda Pinson. Tustin, Calif.: Out of Your Mind . . . and into the Marketplace, 2013. xii, 372 p., ill. ISBN 9780944205556
658.4012   HD30.28

Updated to reflect current practices and the impact of online activity. Walks through the components of a business plan, explaining the purpose of all sections and the ways to write them. Advice about organization, marketing, financing and taxes; includes a section for nonprofits. Appendixes with blank forms and five complete sample business plans. Index. Available as an e-book.

471 The Blackwell handbook of entrepreneurship. Donald L. Sexton, Hans Landström, Blackwell Publishers, Nova Southeastern University. Oxford, U.K.; Malden, Mass.: Blackwell Business; Nova Southeastern University, 2000. xxiv, 468 p., ill. ISBN 9780631215738
658.421   HB615

Summarizes the scholarly literature on entrepreneurship and identifies gaps in entrepreneurship research. International in scope, comparing and contrasting American and European models of entrepreneurship. Typical chapters cover administrative climate as a factor, venture capital, networking, and growth. Of use to graduate students and researchers in the growing subfield of entrepreneurship scholarship. Available as an e-book.

472 Business plans handbook: A compilation of actual business plans developed by small businesses throughout North America. Gale Research Inc. Detroit: Gale Research, 1995– ISSN 1084-4473
658.401205   HD62.7

Annual. Real examples of company business plans across industries. Useful for entrepreneurs looking for

capital and for students writing mock business plans. Lists of small business organizations, agencies, and consultants, glossary of small business terms, and a bibliography. Available as an e-book in Gale Virtual Reference Library and in Small business resource center (486).

473 The Entrepreneur's reference guide to small business information. http://www.loc.gov/rr/business/guide/guide2/guide2_main.html. Aileen M. J. Marshall, Ellen Terrell, Business Reference Services Division, Library of Congress. Washington: Library of Congress. 2010
016.65802/2   HD62.7

Free online bibliography of major reference sources with full bibliographic citations, call numbers, and some annotations. Organized into chapters about getting started, raising capital, managing your business, human resources, marketing, doing business with government, international opportunities, sources of statistics, company and industry research, dictionaries, directories, and databases. Guide to business-related Library of Congress subject headings.

474 The guru guide to entrepreneurship: a concise guide to the best ideas from the world's top entrepreneurs. Joseph H. Boyett, Jimmie T. Boyett. New York: Wiley, 2001. xvi, 370 p. ISBN 9780471390848
658.421   HB615

Compiles the views of 70 entrepreneurs on basic questions relating to establishing and running your own business. The authors have synthesized ideas from more than 250 books and over 2,500 articles. These expert opinions are organized around six themes that cover the following issues: traits essential for entrepreneurial success, finding ideas for businesses, raising money, attracting customers, keeping customers, and managing people. An appendix includes biographical sketches of each of the 70 entrepreneurs profiled. Available as an e-book.

475 Harvard business review on entrepreneurship. Harvard Business Review. Boston: Harvard Business School Press, 1999. v, 217 p. ISBN 9780875849102
658.421   HD62.5

This volume, part of "The Harvard Business Review Paperback Series", is a collection of reprinted articles from The *Harvard Business Review* relating to entrepreneurship. All have been written by prominent faculty specializing in entrepreneurship or by business practitioners with extensive experience in this area. Contains a good collection of interesting articles that cover basic (e.g., writing a business plan) to advanced (e.g., marketing technological innovations) topics. Additionally, multiple viewpoints are represented. Available as an e-book.

476 The Oxford handbook of entrepreneurship. Mark Casson. Oxford; New York: Oxford University Press, 2006. xviii, 790 p., ill.

658.4   HB615

Reviews the state of research about entrepreneurs, startups, innovation, decision-making, financing, growth, global markets, and opportunities for women and minorities. Signed articles cite, summarize and discuss publications. Also available as an e-book.

477 The Oxford handbook of venture capital. Douglas Cumming. New York: Oxford University Press, 2012. xix, 1031 p., ill. ISBN 9780195391596

22   HG4751 332/.04154

Thirty-two signed chapters by experts review current academic writing about the financing of innovative start-up companies. Five sections deal with structures that support fundraising success, screening and the due diligence that precedes investment, the financial contracts that implement investment decisions, the impact of venture capital on the performance of new firms, and regional differences in financing for innovative start-up companies. Bibliography. Index.

478 Vault Reports guide to starting your own business. Jonathan Reed Aspatore, H. S. Hamadeh, Samer Hamadeh, Mark Oldman, Vault Reports. Boston: Houghton Mifflin, 1998. 296 p., ill. ISBN 9780395861707

658.041   HD62.5

Provides sound advice on all stages of establishing your own business, from developing a plan to filing tax forms. Aspatore has written several books on entrepreneurship including a handbook for students who want to start businesses while in college. Vault Reports, a company specializing in career advice, always offers an insider's perspective on the issue at hand. Aspatore achieves this through the inclusion of interviews with entrepreneurs from a wide range of industries. Readers will also find the sample business plan useful.

479 Venture capital: the definitive guide for entrepreneurs, investors, and practitioners. Joel Cardis. New York: Wiley, 2001. xv, 320 p., ill. ISBN 9780471398134

658.15224   HG4751

Detailed guide to venture capital clearly explains what venture capitalists look for and includes an insider's perspective on this type of start-up funding for entrepreneurs. The content is useful to small business owners in need of seed money in the range of $500,000 to growing companies hoping to secure funding in the $20 million range. Pt. 1 outlines the homework that entrepreneurs need to do before they seek funding. Pt. 2 focuses on getting funded. Multiple appendixes are included: checklists, sample agreements, a listing of online entrepreneurial resources, and a directory of venture capital resources for women and minorities.

Reviews of Research and Trends

480 Advances in entrepreneurship, firm emergence, and growth. Jerome A. Katz, Andrew C. Corbett. Bingley, U.K.: Emerald Group Publishing Limited, 1993–. ill. ISSN 1074-7540

658.42105   HB615

Annual. Brings together studies relating to the impact of entrepreneurial activities on U.S. economic development. These research findings are relevant to the academic and business communities; especially pertinent to practicing entrepreneurs. Volumes cover all aspects of entrepreneurship, from entrepreneurial education to the impact of government regulation. Available in online form.

481 Advances in the study of entrepreneurship, innovation, and economic growth. Greenwich, Conn.: JAI Press, 1986–. ill. ISSN 1048-4736

338.0405   HB615

Annual monographic seriesL each volume addresses a topic such as technology or intellectual property. Edited papers from top researchers, useful as summaries. Papers were presented at the Colloquium on Entrepreneurship Education and Technology Transfer, organized by the McGuire Center for Entrepreneurship at the University of Arizona. Available in online form.

Encyclopedias

482   Encyclopedia of emerging industries. 6th ed. Gale Research, Inc. Detroit: Gale, 2011. x, 1219 p., ill. ISBN 9781414486871
338/.003   HD2324

Discusses business ideas in sectors with recent or potential growth such as health care or education, and new opportunities in existing industries related to trends such as "green" practices, the use of mobile devices, and developments in e-commerce. Provides an industry overview including organizational structure and work force needs, discussion of historical trends, sketches of pioneer figures and industry leaders, and comments about global marketplace issues and research and development, followed by suggestions for further reading. General index and industry index. Also available as an e-book.

483   Encyclopedia of management. 7th ed. Sonya D. Hill. Detroit: Gale, Cengage Learning, 2012. xxx, 1133 p. ISBN 9781414459042
658.003   HD30.15

Covers functional areas such as corporate planning and strategic management, emerging topics in management, entrepreneurship, financial management and accounting, general management, human resources management, innovation and technology, international management, leadership, legal issues, management science and operations, management information systems, performance measures and assessment, personal growth and development for managers, production and operations management, quality management and total quality management, supply chain management, and training and development. More than 300 essays in alphabetical order, written by academics and business professionals, with cross-references and recommended reading lists. New content reflects trends such as the use

of handheld devices for Internet-based tools, social networking, network security, venture capital and entrepreneurship, and business in China. Includes a glossary of terms. Index. Available as an e-book.

484   Encyclopedia of new venture management. Matthew R. Marvel. Thousand Oaks, Calif.: SAGE, 2012. xxviii, 512 p., ill. ISBN 9781412990813
658.1/103   HD62.5

Over 190 signed entries in alphabetical order, with suggestions for further reading. Addresses the contributions of entrepreneurs and small business to innovation. Includes topics such as personal characteristics of entrepreneurs, decision-making, marketing, management, human resources, financing, franchising, incubators and technology transfer, and minority participation. Chronology. Glossary. Bibliography. Appendix lists think tanks that support the study of entrepreneurship. Index. Also available as an e-book.

485   Encyclopedia of small business. 4th ed. Virgil L. Burton III, Gale/Cengage Learning (Firm). Farmington Hills, Mich.: Gale/Cengage Learning, 2011. 2 v. (xiv, xi, 1414 p.) ISBN 9781414420288
658.02/2   HD62.7

Some 600 articles on topics related to planning, financing, hiring and human resources, marketing, legal matters, taxes, and sales and retail, each with suggestions for further reading. Identifies major government and trade association entities. Index. Updates the 3rd edition of 2007. Also available as an e-book, and as part of *Small business resource center*.

486   Small business resource center. http://www.galegroup.com/SmallBusiness/about.htm. Gale Group. Farmington Hills, Mich.: Gale Group. 2007–
                                      HD62.5

Combines reference sources, journals, trade magazines, and books relevant to students or individuals interested in small businesses or entrepreneurship. Includes books like *Franchising for dummies* (2006) and *Entrepreneur and small business problem solver* (2005), as well as reference books like the *Business plans handbook* (472) series, the *Encyclopedia of business information sources* (2006) (8), *Encyclopedia of business and finance* (2007) (57), and the *Encyclopedia of small business* (2002). Trade magazines and journals include *Black enterprise, Direct marketing, Entrepreneur, Financial management, Journal of small business management, Kiplinger business forecasts, Quarterly journal of business and economics, Small business economics,* and *The tax adviser.*

Directories

487   Bond's franchise guide. Source Book Publications. Oakland, Calif.: Source Book Publications, 1995–. ill. ISSN 1089-8794
381.1302573   HF5429.235.U5
Annual. Profiles for close to 900 franchisors, grouped in 29 franchise industry categories. Includes background, capital requirements, initial training and other start-up assistance provided, franchisee evaluation criteria, and specific areas of geographic criteria. Additional content about service providers, consultants and attorneys. Index.

488   The Corporate finance sourcebook. National Register Publishing (Firm). Berkeley Heights, N.J.: National Register Publishing, 1979– ISSN 0163-3031
332.02573   HG4057
Annual directory of firms involved in capital investments and financial services (e.g., venture capital, private lenders, commercial and financial factors, business intermediaries, leasing companies and corporate real estate, commercial, U.S.-based foreign, and investments banks and trusts, securities analysts and CPA/auditing firms). Entries include personnel, financial information, type of investor or service, minimum investment, funds available, average number of deals completed annually, industry preferences, and exit criteria. Indexed by name of company, personnel, and geography.

489   The directory of venture capital and private equity firms, domestic and international. Millerton, N.Y.: Grey House, 2003– ISSN 1549-702X
332   HG4751
Annual. With over 3,000 entries, this surpasses *Galante's venture capital and private equity directory* for coverage of venture capital firms. Includes contact information, mission statement, industry group and geographic preferences, average and minimum

investments and investment criteria. Particularly useful for finding portfolio companies, and educational and professional history of key executives. Formerly *Fitzroy Dearborn international directory of venture capital funds.* Available as an online database.

490   National minority and women-owned business directory. Diversity Information Resources, Inc. Minneapolis, Minn.: Diversity Information Resources, 2004–. ill. ISSN 1553-6025
338   HD2358.5.U6
Annual. Contains 9,000 entries in 84 industries with contact information, URL, products/services, year established, minority type, number of employees, annual sales, and certification. Indexed by company.

491   Small business sourcebook. Gale Research Company. Detroit: Gale Research, 1983– ISSN 0883-3397
658.02207073   HD2346.U5
Annual since 1991. Vol. 1 is organized by state and gives small business profiles that include sources of information for about 350 different types of businesses, e.g., start-up information, primary associations, statistical sources, trade periodicals, trade shows, and conventions. Vol. 2 contains sources for general topics common to the operation of any small business (funding, consultants, sources of supply, etc.). It also contains directories and descriptions of sources of assistance offered by state organizations and federal government agencies, a glossary, and master index.

492   World chamber of commerce directory. Johnson Publishing Co. Loveland, Colo.: World Chamber of Commerce Directory, 1958– ISSN 1048-2849
380.106   HF294
Lists U.S. chambers of commerce by state and city, giving mailing address, telephone and fax numbers, name of president, number of members, and local population. Similar information is provided for state boards of tourism, convention and visitors bureaus, economic development organizations, Canadian chambers of commerce, American chambers of commerce abroad, foreign tourist information bureaus, and foreign chambers of commerce in the U.S. and abroad. Also lists key diplomats, U.S. and foreign embassy addresses.

Organizations and Associations

493   International franchise association.
http://www.franchise.org/. International
Franchise Association. Washington:
International Franchise Association.
[1998–]

Home page for advocacy group for franchising.
Includes lists for over 1,000 franchise opportunities, searchable by category, level of desired investment, and type of franchise. Provides text for issues
of *Franchising world*, and a directory of suppliers and
services. Also offers advice for getting started and
current news.

494   U.S. small business administration.
http://www.sbaonline.sba.gov/. U.S. Small
Business Administration. Washington: U.S.
Small Business Administration. [1997?–]
658.02   HD2346.U5

This well-known agency offers information about starting, financing and managing a new business. Intended
for entrepreneurs. Sections address business planning,
management, loans and other financing sources, and
contracting opportunities. Includes forms, access to
online training tools, and pointers to regulations, loan
information, and SBA resources by region and state.

Biographies

**495   American inventors, entrepreneurs,
and business visionaries. Rev. ed.**
Charles W. Carey, Ian C. Friedman. New
York: Facts On File, 2010. xxi, 455 p., ill.
ISBN 9780816081462
609.2/273   CT214

Updated since the first edition of 2002, with more
figures from the early 21st century. Profiles more
than 300 Americans since the seventeenth century.
Not all individuals are well known or achieved business success, making this a richer resource than the
typical biographical source. Entries of 1–2 pages
cover birth and death dates, life and innovations,
with brief bibliographies. Indexes for invention,
industry, and birth year. Available as an e-book.

496   So who the heck was Oscar Mayer?.
Doug Gelbert. New York: Barricade

Books, 1996. 400 p., ill.
ISBN 9781569800829
338.0092273B   HC102.5.A2

Gelbert reveals the person and story behind 200 well-
known brand names such as Armour, Bacardi, Marshall
Field and Harley-Davidson. Brief biographical sketches
(averaging one to two pages in length) are cleverly categorized under themes such as "In the Kitchen," "From
the Bottle," "In the Closet," and "At the Game." Not
only fun to read but thoroughly researched.

**497   United States entrepreneurs and the
companies they built: an index to
biographies in collected works.** Wahib
Nasrallah. Westport, Conn.: Praeger, 2003.
366 p. ISBN 9780313323324
016.338092273   HC102.5.A2

Citations for biographies of 1,700 people, analyzing
120 sources. Organized by name of entrepreneur.
No annotations are provided. Indexed by corporation. Available as an e-book.

Internet Resources

498   Entrepreneur.com. http://www
.entrepreneur.com/. Entrepreneur.com
(Firm). Irvine, Calif.: Entrepreneur Media,
Inc. 2000–
338   HB615

Gives clear how-to advice in all the areas of concern
to a small business owner. Sections include: Starting a Business for startup basics and business plans;
Run and Grow your Business for human resources,
growth strategies and leadership; Money for financing, accounting and taxes; Sales & Marketing for
branding, networking and social media; Technology for software and security; Franchises for opportunities; The 'Treps for news about innovators and
entrepreneurs; and Ask Entrepreneur for an FAQ
database.

499   Entrepreneurial studies source.
http://www.ebscohost.com/academic/
entrepreneurial-studies-source. EBSCO
Publishing (Firm). Ipswich, Mass.: EBSCO
Publishing. 2010–
                                HD2346.U5

Full text from more than 100 periodicals and published conference proceedings, and more than 100

reference books. Includes case studies and company profiles. Provides streaming access to more than 600 presentations in video format, with transcripts. Covers business planning, innovation, management, marketing, product development, and fundraising.

500 Proquest entrepreneurship. http://www .proquest.com/en-US/catalogs/databases/ detail/pq_entrep.shtml. ProQuest (Firm). Ann Arbor, Mich.: ProQuest. 2008–

HD62.5

Draws on full text from journals, books, dissertations, working papers and conference proceedings. Also provides a "toolkit" of forms and templates, sample business plans, and tips from experienced entrepreneurs. Updated weekly. Users can create customized reports using company and market information. Over 650 source publications are listed. Sources of content include BizMiner, *Hoover's company records*, SEC reports, *Advertising age*, *Black enterprise*, *Fortune*, and a variety of international publications.

501 Small business economic trends. http://www.nfib.com/surveys/small -business-economic-trends/. NFIB Education Foundation. Washington: National Federation of Independent Business. 1993– ISSN 1080-0816

HD2346.U5

Monthly report of economic indicators such as optimism, earnings, sales, prices, employment, compensation, credit conditions, inventories, and capital outlays. Information comes from a survey of members of the National Federation of Independent Business. The website also provides news and advocacy materials.

502 The small business economy. http:// www.sba.gov/advocacy/849/6282. Small Business Administration. Washington: U.S. Government Printing Office. 1982– ISSN 1932-3573

338.7   HD2346.U5

Annual review, including small business trends, demographics, financing, federal procurement, women in business, regulations, and data. Tables, available online as PDFs. Data includes U.S. Business Counts and Turnover Measures, Macroeconomic Indicators for, Business Turnover by State, Opening and Closing Establishments, and Characteristics of

Self-Employed Individuals. Published as *The State of Small Business* from 1982–2000.

Finance and Investments

503 The value line investment survey. U.S. ed. Value Line. New York: Value Line, 1936–. diagrs. ISSN 0042-2401

332.6305   HG4501.V26

In three parts: ratings and reports, selection and opinion, and summary and index. Ratings and reports provides stock analysis for some 1,700 stocks and is a good source for betas, quarterly dividends, earnings per share, and other ratios. Also includes 90 short industry reviews. Selection and opinion analyzes the economy and stock markets, providing stock picks. Summary and index provides screening data on stocks and industries. Available also in online format.

Guides and Handbooks

504 Barron's finance and investment handbook. 8th ed. John Downes, Jordan Elliot Goodman. Hauppauge, N.Y.: Barron's Educational Series, 2010. xii, 1152 p., ill. ISBN 9780764162695

332.67/8   HG173

Presents a wide array of background information on financial institutions, finance, and investing. Arranged in five parts. Pt. I: 30 investment opportunities (from annuities to zero coupon bonds); pt. II: how to read an annual report; pt. III: how to read the financial news; pt. IV: dictionary of finance and investment (about 800 pages); and pt. V: finance and investing ready reference (sources of information and assistance in the U.S. and Canada, lists of major financial institutions and mutual funds, historical data on various stock exchanges and other financial data, and lists for publicly traded companies on the NYSE and NASDAQ 100). Appendixes for currencies of the world, abbreviations and acronyms, and selected further readings. Index. Available as an e-book.

505 Commodities price locator. Karen J. Chapman. Phoenix: Oryx Press, 1989. xxx, 135 p. ISBN 9780897743662

016.332644   HF1040.7

More than 150 government, trade, financial, and other serials that publish commodities price information are listed alphabetically by commodity and briefly annotated. An appendix lists databases (none of which appear in the main list) that contain commodities prices. The emphasis is on cash ("spot") prices paid for commodities received rather than on commodities futures prices, which are not covered. While dated, much of the information is still of use.

506   Commodity futures trading: bibliography. Chicago Board of Trade. Chicago: Chicago Board of Trade, 1967–1995
016.3326328   Z7164.C83C64; HG6046
In three sections: (1) books, monographs, and material provided by commodity exchanges; (2) resource material, i.e., scholarly journal articles and government publications; (3) trade, or popular press articles. Each section is subdivided by specific topics or commodity. No index. Ceased with 1995.

507   The Economist numbers guide: the essentials of business numeracy. 6th ed. Richard Stutely. London: Profile Books Ltd., 2013. vii, 256 p., ill. ISBN 9781846689031
650/.01/513   HF5691
Introduction to numerical methods and quantitative techniques used in mathematics, statistics, business, accounting, and economics. Explains methods of analyzing and solving problems in finance, and the use of numbers in business forecasting and decision-making. Uses charts, graphs, tables, figures and examples to explain in layman's terms. Appendix is a dictionary of relevant terms, with cross-references to the main section. Index.

508   The handbook of European fixed income securities. Frank J. Fabozzi, Moorad Choudhry. Hoboken, N.J.: J. Wiley, 2004. xiv, 1010 p., ill. ISBN 9780471430391
332.632044   HG4650
A well written guide to European financial markets, including government and corporate bond market instruments and institutions. In five sections. Section 1: background to fixed income securities, bondholder and shareholder value, bond pricing and yield measures, measuring interest rate risk. Section 2: Euro government bond market, Eurobond market, German Pfandbrief and European covered bonds market,

inflation linked bonds, United Kingdom gilts market, European repo market, mortgage backed securities, credit card and auto consumer loan ABS, and structured credit. Section 3: interest rate futures and options, pricing options on interest rate instruments, interest rate swaps, credit derivatives, and credit default swaps. Section 4: portfolio management for fixed incomes, portfolio strategies, and analysis and evaluation of corporate bonds. Section 5 covers legal considerations. Available as an e-book.

509   Handbook of Islamic banking. Kabir Hassan, Mervyn Lewis. Cheltenham, U.K.; Northampton, Mass.: Edward Elgar, 2007. xviii, 443 p., ill. ISBN 9781845420833
332.10917/67   HG3368.A6
Twenty-five chapters by experts summarizing current trends. Coverage extends beyond banks to include insurance, leasing, mutual funds, stocks speculation, and regulatory issues. Glossary of Arabic terms. Index.

510   Handbooks in economics. North-Holland Pub. Co. Amsterdam, The Netherlands; New York: Elsevier, 1981–. ill. ISSN 0169-7218
030   HC21
Surveys of recent literature in economics, written by scholars in the field. Each handbook focuses on a different topic. Titles in this growing series to date include: *Handbook of agricultural economics, Handbook of computational economics, Handbook of defense economics, Handbook of development economics, Handbook of econometrics, Handbook of the economics of finance, Handbook of environmental economics, Handbook of game theory with economic applications, Handbook of health economics, Handbook of income distribution, Handbook of industrial organization, Handbook of international economics, Handbook of labor economics, Handbook of macroeconomics, Handbook of mathematical economics, Handbook of monetary economics, Handbook of natural resource and energy economics, Handbook of population and family economics, Handbook of public economics, Handbook of regional and urban economics*, and *Handbook of social choice and welfare*. Available as e-books.

511   The law of securities regulation. 6th ed. Thomas Lee Hazen. St. Paul, Minn.: Thomson/West, 2009. xxxiii, 862 p. ISBN 9780314187970
KF1439

Introduces and summarizes U.S. securities laws: regularly updated to reflect evolution of the law. Covers laws based on the Securities Act of 1933, with other chapters on related topics such as IPOs, tender offers, market regulation, broker-dealer disputes, fraud and civil liability, insider trading, and protection of bondholders. Bibliographic references. Index. One volume abridgment of the seven volume *Treatise on securities regulation* by the same author.

512 Mathematical formulas for economists. 4th ed. Bernd Luderer, Volker Nollau, Klaus Vetters. Heidelberg, [Germany]; New York: Springer, 2010. x, 198 p., ill. ISBN 9783642040788
330.0151   HB135

Defines formulas and differential equations used in economics, finance, and accounting, including definitions for the notations used in formulas. Gives basic formulas, as well as alternate formulas. Assumes some prior knowledge. Enlarged from the 3rd edition of 2007 "to include methods of rank statistics and the analysis of variance (ANOVA) and covariance." Bibliography. Index. Available as an e-book.

513 Money and exchange in Europe and America, 1600–1775: a handbook. John J. McCusker, Institute of Early American History and Culture. Chapel Hill, N.C.: University of North Carolina Press, 1978. xi, 367 p., ill. ISBN 9780807812846
332.450212   HG219

Explains the economic role of money in colonial America. "Aims to provide sufficient information of a technical and statistical nature to allow the reader to convert a sum stated in one money into its equivalent in another." p. 3. Conversion tables.

514 Morningstar investment research center. http://www.morningstar.com/. Morningstar (Firm). Chicago: Morningstar. 1999–

Morningstar.com provides reports and screening for more than 15,000 mutual funds and for stocks traded on the New York Stock Exchange, NASDAQ®, and the American Stock Exchange. Mutual fund reports give a snapshot; data interpreter; analyst report to make sense of the data; stewardship grade (rates corporate culture, board quality, manager incentives, fees, and regulatory issues); three-, five-,

and ten- year Morningstar rating; ten years of performance returns; seven years of quarterly returns; seven years of investor returns; tax analysis; risk measures; portfolio; management; fees and expenses; and purchase information, including minimum investments and brokerage availability. Stock reports give a snapshot, quote, analyst report, Morningstar rating, data interpreter, valuation ratios (price/earnings, price/book, price/sales, price/cash flows, and dividend yield perectage calculated for the stock, industry, S&P 500, and stock's five-year average), ten years of basic financial statements and two years of quarterly sales and income, key ratios, charts, five years of dividends, splits, and returns, owners and estimates, and links to the SEC filings. Analyst reports are available for only 1,000 stocks and 2,000 mutual funds, and are archived from 2001 for stocks and from 1993 for mutual funds. Includes an investment glossary and training courses.

515 MRI bankers' guide to foreign currency. Monetary Research International. Houston, Tex.: Monetary Research International, 1991–. ill. ISSN 1055-3851
769.55024332   HG353

Describes the currency of more than 220 countries. Includes exchange restrictions, current exchange rates, and information on where the currency is used. Used most for the color images of paper notes and traveler's checks.

516 Stock trader's almanac. Yale Hirsch, Jeffrey Hirsch. Hoboken, N.J.: Wiley, 1967– ISSN 1553-4812
332.63   HG4637

Most used for the annotated calendar noting daily historical trading tendencies. A bull or bear appears on days with significant historical directional tendencies. Unusual in that it covers the best performing months or days.

Encyclopedias

517 Encyclopedia of business and finance. 2nd ed. Burton S. Kaliski, Macmillan Reference. Detroit, Mich.: Macmillan Reference, 2007. 2 v. ISBN 0028660617
650.03   HF1001

Written for the novice but useful for anyone seeking background information on five key topics: accounting, finance and banking, management, management of information systems, and marketing. The 310 essays include graphs, tables, photographs, and recommended readings. Alphabetically arranged entries range from the history of computing to green marketing and the Sarbanes-Oxley Act. The 3rd ed. is projected for publication in 2014. Available as an e-book.

518 Encyclopedia of municipal bonds: a reference guide to market events, structures, dynamics, and investment knowledge. Joe Mysak. Hoboken, N.J.: Bloomberg Press/Wiley, 2012. xx, 215 p. ISBN 9781118006757
332.63/23303   HG4726

Identifies and defines over 200 terms drawn from technical, economic, political and historical perspectives, in alphabetical order. Includes capsule histories of significant events and key legislation. Some entries are brief, others run to multiple pages with bibliographies. Available as an e-book.

519 The encyclopedia of technical market indicators. 2nd ed. Robert W. Colby. New York: McGraw-Hill, 2003. xii, 820 p., ill. ISBN 9780070120570
332.632220973   HG4915

Detailed information on over 100 indicators for sophisticated investors or advanced finance students. Essays focus on methods of evaluating technical market indicators, and there are descriptions of stock market performance (e.g., advance/decline divergence oscillator, confidence index, presidential election cycle), arranged alphabetically. Entries vary in length: most occupy at least half a page. Charts, graphs, and other ill. are frequent. Appendix of indicator interpretation definitions, index.

520 The Federal Reserve System: an encyclopedia. R. W. Hafer. Westport, Conn.: Greenwood Press, 2005. xxxii, 451 p., ill. ISBN 0313328390
332.11097303   HG2563

Contains 250 well-written articles explaining the somewhat mysterious Federal Reserve System, its structure, process, and policies. Entries also cover people and key events related to the Federal Reserve.

Appendixes provide the text of The Federal Reserve Act, Federal Reserve Regulations, and a list of the Membership of the Board of Governors: 1913–2004. Available as an e-book.

521 The international encyclopedia of mutual funds, closed-end funds, and real estate investment trusts. Peter Madlem, Thomas K. Sykes. Chicago: Glenlake; Fitzroy Dearborn, 2000. 367 p. ISBN 9780814404720
332.6327   HG4530

Over 5,000 entries in two section: mutual funds (how they operate, how to invest, categories) and closed-end funds (what they are, regulations, discounts, rights offerings, and categories). Good background information for investors. Available as an e-book.

522 Swaps/financial derivatives: products, pricing, applications, and risk management. 3rd ed. Satyajit Das. Singapore: Wiley, 2004. 4 v., ill., charts ISBN 9780470821091
332.6457   HG6024.A3

Explains the role and function of swaps and derivatives, as well as the derivatives themselves, in a way useful to an advanced student or to practitioner. Includes description of interest rates, yield curve modeling, options pricing, volatility, determination and behavior of swap spreads, risk management principles, market risk, credit risk, derivative trading, exotic options, new derivative markets, and the structure and evolution of derivative markets.

523 The world financial system. 2nd ed. Robert D. Fraser, Christopher Long. Harlow, Essex, U.K.; Detroit: Longman Current Affairs, 1992. xii, 508 p. ISBN 9780582096523
332.042   HG3881

Pt. 1 discusses the evolution of the world financial system, developments such as the Marshall Plan, the formation of the International Monetary Fund (IMF), and currency movements, with statistical tables and texts of significant agreements excerpted or printed in their entirety. Pt. 2, International economic organizations, lists over 50 organizations grouped geographically under four headings (general, monetary, developmental, and trade), with extensive discussion of the organization's background, objectives, membership, and structure in addition to standard directory information. Index.

Dictionaries

524 Barron's finance and investment handbook. 8th ed. John Downes, Jordan Elliot Goodman. Hauppauge, N.Y.: Barron's Educational Series, 2010. xii, 1152 p., ill. ISBN 9780764162695
332.67/8   HG173

Presents a wide array of background information on financial institutions, finance, and investing. Arranged in five parts. Pt. I: 30 investment opportunities (from annuities to zero coupon bonds); pt. II: how to read an annual report; pt. III: how to read the financial news; pt. IV: dictionary of finance and investment (about 800 pages); and pt. V: finance and investing ready reference (sources of information and assistance in the U.S. and Canada, lists of major financial institutions and mutual funds, historical data on various stock exchanges and other financial data, and lists for publicly traded companies on the NYSE and NASDAQ 100). Appendixes for currencies of the world, abbreviations and acronyms, and selected further readings. Index. Available as an e-book.

525 Common stock newspaper abbreviations and trading symbols. Howard R. Jarrell. Metuchen, N.J.: Scarecrow Press, 1989. x, 413 p., [1] leaf of plates, ill. ISBN 9780810822559
332.63220973   HG4636

Lists Associated Press abbreviations, primary stock exchange / market on which traded, and ticker symbols for more than 6,300 companies selling common stock on the New York or American Stock Exchanges, or traded in the 6,300 companies selling common stock on the New York or American Stock Exchanges, or traded in the over-the-counter National Association of Securities Dealers Automated Quotations (NASDAQ) market. Separate sections provide access by company name, AP newspaper abbreviation, and ticker symbol. A 1991 supplement covers some 2,400 changes and new listings that occurred after the original volume was compiled. For current symbols, several online sources exist, for example *Company directory: globally traded assets* at http://www.macroaxis.com/invest/companyDirectory/.

526 Dictionary of finance and investment terms. 8th ed. John Downes, Jordan Elliot Goodman. Hauppauge, N.Y.: Barrons's Educational Series, 2010. ix, 865 p, ill ISBN 9780764143045
332.03   HG151

Remains a useful financial dictionary, with 5,000 definitions and a list of key abbreviations and acronyms. Updated since the 7th edition of 2006 to include terms that have come into use since the Great Recession began in 2008, as well as recent financial regulations. Intended for students and members of the general public. Includes a list of financial abbreviations and acronyms. Available as an e-book.

527 Dictionary of financial abbreviations. John Paxton. New York: Fitzroy Dearborn, 2002 ISBN 9781579583972
332.03   HG151.3

Every discipline has a unique set of abbreviations. This dictionary defines over 4,000 abbreviations and acronyms for finance, including international institutions, regulatory bodies, trade unions and associations, and currencies. Most entries are about a paragraph long, but where needed, there are lengthier explanations.

528 Elsevier's banking dictionary in seven languages: English, American, French, Italian, Spanish, Portuguese, Dutch, and German. 3rd rev. and enl. ed. Julio Ricci. Amsterdam, The Netherlands; New York: Elsevier, 1990. 359 p. ISBN 9780444880673
332.1/03   HG151

A polyglot dictionary for banking and finance arranged on an English-language base with equivalent terms in the other languages. The third revision of Elsevier's banking dictionary in seven languages, adding Portuguese to the list of languages. More than 2,400 terms; indexed by terms in the other languages.

529 The futures markets dictionary. George Steinbeck, Rosemary Erickson. New York: New York Institute of Finance, 1988. xv, 191 p., ill. ISBN 9780133458770
332.644   HG6024.A3

Describes key words and phrases used in the commodities, options, forwards, and actuals markets. Explains how to read futures quotations. Many definitions contain examples, illustrations, and cross-references.

530 The handbook of international financial terms. http://www.oxfordreference.com/. Peter Moles, Nicholas Terry. [New York]: Oxford University Press. 2005
ISBN 9780198294818
332.04203 HG3881

8,500 brief definitions on finance and accounting, including international stock exchanges, option strategies, and laws. Some definitions include examples. Extensive list of acronyms and abbreviations. List of international currency codes. Also available in print.

531 International dictionary of finance. 4th ed. Graham Bannock, W. A. P. Manser. London: Profile Books, 2003. vi, 287 p. ISBN 9781861974785
332.03 HG151

Covers international finance, as well as domestic finance in various countries. Concentrates on the U.S. and the United Kingdom. Includes foreign language terms. Definitions range from one word to one-half page in length, depending on the complexity of the concept.

532 The new Palgrave dictionary of money and finance. Peter Newman, Murray Milgate, John Eatwell. London; New York: Macmillan Press; Stockton Press, 1992. 3 v., ill. ISBN 9780333527221
332.03 HG151

With 1,008 well-written articles on banking, monetary theory, finance, and financial economics, this serves as an indispensable reference source. Includes abbreviations and acronyms. Articles are signed and most include a bibliography.

533 Online trader's dictionary: the most up-to-date and authoritative compendium of financial terms. R. J. Shook. Franklin Lakes, N.J.: Career Press, 2002. 508 p. ISBN 9781564145673
332.63203 HG4515.95

Nearly 7,000 terms on investing and the Internet. Includes lesser known phrases such as *casino society*, as well as better known phrases like *best-of-breed*. All

definitions are short, but are written for the novice and expert alike. Available as an e-book.

534 The Palgrave Macmillan dictionary of finance, investment, and banking. Erik Banks. Basingstoke [England]; New York: Palgrave Macmillan, 2010. xxxi, 565 p., ill. ISBN 9780230238299
332.03 HG151

Defines over 5,000 terms associated with banking, finance, investments, insurance, and accounting. Current coverage reflects the Great Recession and global issues such as finance in the Islamic world and carbon/emissions trading. A separate list points to acronyms, colloquialisms and non-English language terms. Appendix lists financial accounting and reporting standards. Additional features on a companion web site.

535 Wall Street words: An A to Z guide to investment terms for today's investor. 3rd ed. David Logan Scott. Boston: Houghton Mifflin, 2003
ISBN 9780618176519
332.603 HG4513

Contains definitions of 4,500 terms, 100 of which are supplemented by case studies. Also features 50 investment tips from experts, typical examples of technical analysis chart patterns, and a brief bibliography. Available as an e-book.

536 Webster's new world finance and investment dictionary. Barbara Etzel. Indianapolis, Ind.: Wiley, 2003. viii, 369 p., ill. ISBN 9780764526350
332.03 HG151

Contains 3,500 international financial terms from accounting, finance, banking, economics, investing, financial markets, real estate, and securities, briefly described. Available as an e-book.

Periodicals

537 Banking information source. http://www.proquest.com/en-US/catalogs/databases/detail/pq_banking_info.shtml. ProQuest Information and Learning Company. Ann Arbor, Mich.: ProQuest Information and Learning
HG181

Indexes some 690 periodicals, including scholarly journals and trade publications, with full text of recent years for more than 500 titles. Information about automation, marketing, credit unions, international banking, investment banking, pension funds, private banking, savings and loan institutions, and women and minorities in banking. Also available through Dialog.

538   Barron's. Chicopee, Mass.: Dow Jones & Co., 1994–. ill. ISSN 1077-8039
332   HG1
Weekly trade periodical with reports on stocks, bonds, mutual fund and hedge fund performance; also reviews and ranks brokers and fund managers. Some free information available at the magazine's website at http://online.barrons.com/home-page. Also available in online format, and through aggregators such as Factiva (98).

539   Hulbert financial digest. Mark Hulbert. Washington: Hulbert Financial Digest, Inc., 1980– ISSN 1042-4261
332   HG4515.9
A unique guide to 180 financial newsletters, tracking their performance and risk level. Reports on the performance of recommended portfolios during 5, 10, 15, and 20 year periods. Available as a for-fee online service.

540   The review of financial studies.
http://rfs.oxfordjournals.org/. Society for Financial Studies, Society for Financial Studies. New York: Oxford University Press. 1988– ISSN 0893-9454
                                              HG1.R45
One of the top journals in financial economics, it publishes theoretical and empirical research in financial economics. Sponsored by the Society for Financial Studies, with irregular, but lengthy book reviews. E-mail alerts can be set up for table of contents or to track topics and authors. Also available in print format.

Directories

541   America's corporate finance directory.
LexisNexis Group (Firm). Atlanta, Ga.: LexisNexis Group, 1994–
ISSN 1080-1227
338.7402573   HG4057

Annual. Covers major publicly and privately owned companies, with contact information, financial data, and lists of key company officers. Indexes of individuals by financial responsibility and all personnel, and of companies by SIC code and geographical location, and as parent companies and subsidiaries.

542   Annual guide to stocks. Financial Information, Inc. Jersey City, N.J.: Financial Information, 1997–
                                              HG4512
International coverage of listed and unlisted stocks, with place of incorporation, par value, CUSIP number, transfer agent, transfer charge, dividend disbursing agent, capital structure, and dividends. Companion to the Directory of obsolete securities: annual guide to stocks (547), which annually compiles information on defunct corporations.

543   The bank directory. Accuity (Firm). Skokie, Ill.: Accuity, 2005–. 5 v.
ISSN 1941-6369
332.1/025/73   HG2441
Annual. Successor to *Thomson bank directory*. Provides information for U.S. and international banks, including national routing codes, personnel, basic financials, credit ratings, standard settlement instructions, and industry statistics and rankings. Also available through various aggregator databases.

544   The Bond Buyer's municipal marketplace: directory. National ed.
Thomson Financial Publishing. Skokie, Ill.: Thomson Financial, 1993–. ill.
ISSN 1079-2260
332.6323302573   HG4907
Lists municipal bond firms and professionals (dealers, underwriters, financial advisers, public fund managers, municipal derivatives specialists, bond attorneys, tax controversy representation, credit enhancers, corporate trust departments, arbitrage rebate, rating agencies, and municipal issuers). Ranks underwriters, financial advisers, bond counsels, leading credit enhancers and credit issuers, and corporate trust departments. Published twice a year. Also available online.

545   The Corporate finance sourcebook.
National Register Publishing (Firm).

Berkeley Heights, N.J.: National Register Publishing, 1979– ISSN 0163-3031
332.02573   HG4057

Annual directory of firms involved in capital investments and financial services (e.g., venture capital, private lenders, commercial and financial factors, business intermediaries, leasing companies and corporate real estate, commercial, U.S.-based foreign, and investments banks and trusts, securities analysts and CPA/auditing firms). Entries include personnel, financial information, type of investor or service, minimum investment, funds available, average number of deals completed annually, industry preferences, and exit criteria. Indexed by name of company, personnel, and geography.

546   Credit union directory. http://purl
.access.gpo.gov/GPO/LPS208. National Credit Union Administration. Alexandria, Va.: National Credit Union Administration. 1996– ISSN 0196-3678
334/.22/02573   HG2037

Information from NCUA on U.S. credit unions, except "state-chartered natural person credit unions that are either uninsured or covered by private insurance corporations." —*Pref.* Gives charter number, address, name of CEO/manager, telephone number, assets, loans, net worth ratio, percent share growth, percent loan growth, loans/assets ratio, investments/assets ratio, number of members, and number of full-time employees. Also includes national statistics.

547   Directory of obsolete securities. Jersey City, N.J.: Financial Information, 1970– ISSN 0085-0551
332.67   HG4961

Used to identify old stock certificates. Records are chronological, with details of the final action rendering the security obsolete. Companion to the *Annual guide to stocks* (542).

548   Directory of world futures and options: a guide to international futures and options exchanges and products. M. J. M. Robertson. New York: Prentice Hall, 1990. 1 v. (various pagings) ISBN 9780132178785
332.645   HG6024.A3

Arranged by regions of the world. Each entry contains stock exchange directory information, a brief history of the exchange, a description of what futures and options contracts are available, and details of how each commodity is traded. Includes where trades are quoted, if available. Indexed by exchange name, category, and product type. Glossary.

549   North American financial institutions directory. North American ed ed. Thomson Financial Publishing, Accuity (Firm). Skokie, Ill.: Thomson Financial, 2000–. maps ISSN 1529-1367
332.10257   HG1536

Covers Canada, the U.S., Central America, the Caribbean, and Mexico. Entries vary in length from very brief to extensive, the latter providing information about branches and corporate and financial structure. A separate section lists banks by name and gives ranked lists of banks, commercial banks, savings and loan banks, and credit unions. Includes directories of associations, the Federal Reserve System, pertinent government organizations (e.g., the Secret Service), and a limited directory of the largest international banks.

550   Registered investment advisors edirectory. http://www.mmdwebaccess
.com/RIA.htm. Money Market Directories, Inc. Charlottesville, Va.: Standard & Poor's. 2006–
332.6/2   HG4907

Lists 17,000 firms and their investment and mutual fund advisors, with information on type of accounts handled, investment style, and strategy. Also ranks advisors by assets managed. Formerly available in print as the *Directory of registered investment advisors*.

551   Standard and Poor's security dealers of North America. Standard and Poor's Corporation. New York: Standard and Poor's, 1923– ISSN 1087-3325
332.620257   HG4907

Aims to provide an up-to-date directory of all stock and bond dealers in the United States and Canada. Indexed by location, new address, and discontinued listing. Previously issued under variant titles.

Organizations and Associations

552   American association of individual investors. http://www.aaii.com/.

American Association of Individual Investors. Chicago: American Association of Individual Investors. 2002–

HG4930.I49

Home page for assoc. founded in 1978 to support individual investors. Sections of the web site include the *AAII journal* and resources dealing with getting started, financial planning, investing, model portfolios, stock screens, asset allocation and surveys. Some resources are available only to members.

553 American finance association. http:// www.afajof.org/. American Finance Association. Berkeley, Calif.: American Finance Association. 1998–

Home page for assoc. founded in 1939 to serve the interests of those interested in finance and financial economics. The website has a history of finance, Worldwide Directory of Finance Faculty, news, job and career advice, and a link to *The Journal of Finance*, one of the top journals in the field. Membership required for some content.

554 Bank for international settlements. http://www.bis.org/. Bank for International Settlements. [Basel, Switzerland]: Bank for International Settlements

332.11   HG1811

"The mission of the Bank for International Settlements (BIS) is to serve central banks in their pursuit of monetary and financial stability, to foster international cooperation in those areas and to act as a bank for central banks." —*About BIS*. Website includes a directory of central bank websites; speeches by central bankers; working papers; banking statistics from central banks in 40 countries; securities statistics; derivatives statistics, including Herfindahl indices; effective exchange rates for 61 economies, with data since 1964; foreign exchange statistics; external debt statistics; and payment statistics from 1993 to the present. The latest *Annual report* can be downloaded from the website, as well as *Working papers* and other publications.

555 Better investing. http://www.better -investing.org/. National Association of Investors Corp. Madison Heights, Mich.: National Association of Investors Corp. 2007– 332.607

Founded in 1951 to "empower our members to make better investment decisions by providing unbiased,

objective education, tools and support, and a proven investment methodology." —*About*. The site supports this mission with tools and resources (publications, courses, online tools, data services, research, events), personal finance (budget, banking, credit, financial planning, fun money, frugal marketplace, insurance), and investment clubs.

556 FDIC. http://www.fdic.gov/. Federal Deposit Insurance Corporation. Washington: Federal Deposit Insurance Corporation. [1996–]

HG1662.U5

Home page for the Federal Deposit Insurance Corporation, which insures deposits, examines financial institutions for soundness and consumer protection, and manages receiverships. Website is organized into: Deposit Insurance, Consumer Protection, Industry Analysis, Regulation & Examinations, Asset Sales, and News & Events. Includes Call Reports and Thrift Financial Reports from 1998 to the present; an institution directory for federally insured institutions; Summary of Deposits; Quarterly Banking Profile with figures since December 31, 1994; statistics on banking and depository institutions; and laws and regulations.

Statistics

557 BigCharts. http://bigcharts.marketwatch .com/. MarketWatch, Inc. San Francisco: MarketWatch, Inc. 1998–

HG4638

Best known for historic stock quotes, BigCharts has information on over 50,000 symbols, including current information on all NYSE, Nasdaq, AMEX, and OTC stocks, all NASDAQ quoted mutual funds, as well as leading financial indexes and international exchanges. The current information includes company profiles, company financials, news, charts, analyst estimates, analysis, and intraday stock screeners. Historic quotes include open, closing, high and low prices, volume traded, split adjusted price, and adjustment factor since 1970.

558 China securities market investment yearbook. GTA Securities Research Institute. Hong Kong, China: GTA Securities Research Institute, 2005–. ill.

HG5781

Provides a review of China's securities market from 1990–2004, and gives data from 2004. Chapters include: China securities market overview, 1990–2004; statistics for SSE and SZSE index; stock market monthly statistics, 2004; rankings for 2004; transition statistics, 2004; China fund market 1998–2004; statistics of delisted securities, 1990–2004; securities law; company law; historical exchange rate, 1990–2004; and major securities agencies in China.

559 The CRB commodity yearbook.
Commodity Research Bureau (U.S.),
Bridge/Commodity Research Bureau. New
York: Wiley, 1994–. ill. ISSN 1076-2906
332.6328   HF1041
Provides background information and statistical data on 100 domestic and international agricultural and industrial commodities, and on financial and stock index futures. Includes seasonal patterns and historical data from the prior ten yr., with some tables going back 100 yr. Organized alphabetically by commodity, with articles on each commodity that describe the commodity and give pricing trends and factors affecting price. Data sources are primarily U.S. official publications, with some from U.N., trade association, and international organization publications. Includes feature articles discussing current issues. Also available on CD-Rom.

560 CRSP databases. http://www.crsp.com/.
Center for Research in Security Prices.
Chicago: University of Chicago. Center for
Research in Security Prices. 1964–
                            HG4636
One of the best sources for current and historical security data for the NYSE (daily from July 1962; monthly from Dec. 1925), AMEX (daily from July 1962; monthly from July 1962), and NASDAQ (daily from July 1972; monthly from Dec. 1972) stock markets. Data subsets include: CRSP U.S. stock database (NYSE, AMEX, NASD, S&P, annual/quarterly/monthly/daily); CRSP U.S. Government Bond Fixed Term Index Series: monthly and daily; CRSP U.S. Treasury Risk-Free Rates File; and CRSP Fama-Bliss Discount Bond Files for prices and yields. Also available through Wharton Research Data Services (WRDS).

561 Datastream advance. Datastream
International. New York: Thomson
Reuters, 1995–
332.642   HG4551

Also known as Thomson Datastream or TDS. A wide array of current and historic global market and economic data. Covers 700 topics, with data going back 20 years. Includes: global and sector indexes, exchange-traded derivatives, investment research, fixed income and equity securities, current and historical fundamental data, foreign exchange and money markets data, real-time financial news from Dow Jones, closing prices for OTC bond instruments, forecast and historical economics data, and interest and exchange rates. Data can easily be compared and downloaded to Excel, Word, or PowerPoint.

562 The Dow Jones averages, 1885–
1995. Phyllis S. Pierce. Chicago: Irwin
Professional, 1996. 1 v. (unpaged), ill.
ISBN 9780786309740
332.632220973   HG4915
Chronology of the development of the Dow Jones Averages. Presents daily figures, beginning with the 14-stock average (combining railroads and industrials) in 1885 and ending with 1995 daily averages for industrials, transportation, utilities, and bonds. Supersedes earlier volumes.

563 Estimates. http://thomsonreuters.com/
estimates/. Thomson Reuters. New York:
Thomson Reuters. 2008–
332.6   HG4501
Provides historical broker analyst information for more than 20,000 companies, as far back as 1976 for U.S. firms, since 1985 for Canada; since 1987 for Europe, the Middle East, Africa and the Asia/Pacific region; and since 1992 for Latin America. Forecasts include sales, revenue, net income, earnings, and dividends. Includes content from the Institutional Brokers Estimate System or I/B/E/S.

564 Fact book. Securities Industry and
Financial Markets Association. New
York: Securities Industry and Financial
Markets Association, 2007–
ISSN 1945-4449
332.6   HG4910
Annual. Provides information on capital markets, the securities industry, market activity, investor participation, global markets, savings, and investment. Good for finding statistics on corporate underwriting and private placements, capital raised for U.S. business, initial public offerings by state, total

U.S. mergers and acquisitions, securities industry employment by firm category, securities industry profitability, pre-tax profit margins and return on equity, stock market capitalization, stock exchange activity, compound annual rates of return by decade for stocks, bonds and treasuries, and value of international securities offerings. Some data goes back to 1965. Successor to *Securities industry fact book*.

565 Federal reserve bulletin. Board of
Governors of the Federal Reserve System.
Washington: G.P.O., 1915–
ISSN 0014-9209
332.110973   HG2401.A5

The most complete current information, including statistics, on financial conditions in the United States. Includes bank asset quality, bank assets and liabilities, bank structure data, business finance, exchange rates, flow of funds accounts, household finance, industrial activity, interest rates, and money stock and reserve balances. Also reports on financial developments in foreign countries. Since 2005, no longer published in print. Current *Bulletins* and an archive back to 1996 are available online at http://www.federalreserve.gov/pubs/bulletin/default.htm.

566 The financial services fact book.
Insurance Information Institute, Financial Services Roundtable. New York: Insurance Information Institute [and] Financial Services Roundtable, 2002–. ill.
ISSN 1537-6257
658   HG181

Current information on insurance, banking, securities, and the financial services industry as a whole. Includes statistics on U.S. savings, investment and debt ownership, consumer fraud and identity theft, convergence of financial services companies, IT spending, and the growth of online commerce. The most current Fact book is available at http://www2.iii.org/financial/.

567 Global financial data. https://www.globalfinancialdata.com/. Global Financial Data. San Juan Capistrano, Calif.: Global Financial Data. 2003–
332.1   HG4501

Historical financial data, from as early as the 1200s, based on original source publications, newspapers, and archival materials. Provides 20,000 financial and economic data series for some 200 countries. Categories include daily stock market data from 1962 (open, high, low, close, volume, available in split adjusted or unadjusted format); state, national and international real estate market data from 1830 (includes Median New Home Prices—United States, Winans International U.S. Real Estate Index—Price Only, Austria ATX Real Estate Index, Shanghai SE Real Estate Index); international bond indices from 1862; central bank interest yields; commercial paper yields; commodity indices; commodity prices; consumer price indices; U.S and European corporate bond yields, some from 1857; international deposit rates; international exchange rates, some from 1660; futures contracts; government bond yields; gross domestic product; international interbank interest rates from the 1980s; interest rate swaps from 1988 (United States, Europe, Japan); U.S. intraday data, daily from January 1933 to present; international lending rates, some from 1934; overnight and call money rates, some from 1857 (monthly, weekly, daily); international population; sector indices (consumer discretionary, consumer staples, energy, finance, health care, industrials, information technology, materials, telecommunications, transports, utilities), stock indices—preferred stocks; stock indices—composites; stock indices—size and style; stock market—AMEX; stock market—NASDAQ; stock market—NYSE; stock market—OTC; stocks (capitalization, volume, dividend yields and P/E ratios, technical indicators); total return indices—bills; total return indices—bonds; total return indices—stocks; international treasury bill yields; international unemployment rates, some from 1890; and international wholesale price indices.

568 Global stock markets factbook.
Standard and Poor's Corporation. New York: Standard and Poor's, 2003–. ill.
ISSN 1530-678X
332   HG5993

Data on stock markets in developing and underdeveloped countries. Includes an overview with summary tables and charts, data on S&P emerging market indexes, market profiles for some 50 emerging markets, a global directory of emerging stock markets, and investor information on taxation and regulation. Most often used for the stock market index data.

569 Mergerstat review. Merrill Lynch
Business Brokerage and Valuation, W.T.
Grimm and Co., Houlihan, Lokey,

Howard, and Zukin. Chicago: The Company, 1982–. ill. ISSN 1071-4065
338.830973   HD2746.5

Annual review of mergers and acquisitions. Pt. 1 is statistical analysis with aggregate announcements, composition of aggregate net merger and acquisition announcements, method of payment, P/E offered, divestitures, publicly traded sellers, privately owned sellers, foreign sellers, aggressive buyers, financial advisor ranking, legal advisor ranking, top managers, and termination fees. Pt. 2 is industry analysis with highlights, industry groups, spotlights giving industry activity for the two most active industries by Standard Industrial Classification (SIC) code, multiples (TIC/EBITDA, P/E), premiums, composition, and cross-border activity. Pt. 3 is a geographical analysis with U.S. buyers and sellers by state, and foreign buyers and sellers. Pt. 4 is current year rosters with completed and pending transactions with pricing disclosed, canceled transactions with pricing disclosed, transactions with termination fees disclosed, and the composition of the Mergerstat $1 billion club. Pt. 5 is a historical review with a 25-year statistical review, record holders, 100 largest announcements in history, and largest announcements by industry. Pt. 6 lists transactions by seller SIC code. There is also a glossary of terms. Available as an e-book, as *Mergerstat M&A Database*.

570   Morningstar investment research center.
http://www.morningstar.com/. Morningstar (Firm). Chicago: Morningstar. 1999–

Morningstar.com provides reports and screening for more than 15,000 mutual funds and for stocks traded on the New York Stock Exchange, NASDAQ®, and the American Stock Exchange. Mutual fund reports give a snapshot; data interpreter; analyst report to make sense of the data; stewardship grade (rates corporate culture, board quality, manager incentives, fees, and regulatory issues); three-, five-, and ten- year Morningstar rating; ten years of performance returns; seven years of quarterly returns; seven years of investor returns; tax analysis; risk measures; portfolio; management; fees and expenses; and purchase information, including minimum investments and brokerage availability. Stock reports give a snapshot, quote, analyst report, Morningstar rating, data interpreter, valuation ratios (price/earnings, price/book, price/sales, price/cash flows, and dividend yield perectage calculated for the stock, industry, S&P 500, and stock's five-year average), ten years of basic financial statements and

two years of quarterly sales and income, key ratios, charts, five years of dividends, splits, and returns, owners and estimates, and links to the SEC filings. Analyst reports are available for only 1,000 stocks and 2,000 mutual funds, and are archived from 2001 for stocks and from 1993 for mutual funds. Includes an investment glossary and training courses.

571   National accounts statistics. United Nations. New York: United Nations, 1985–
339.3   HC79.I5

Detailed national accounts estimates from 200 countries and areas. Sections include *Main aggregates and detailed tables*, *Analysis of main aggregates*, and *Government accounts and tables*. Data gathered from national statistical services, and national and international source publications. This source is invaluable for providing data since 1950. Prepared by The Statistical Offices of the United Nations Secretariat. Continues *Yearbook of national accounts statistics (1957–81)*, which superseded *Statistics of national income and expenditure (1952–57)*. Also available through the National Accounts Main Aggregates Database (http://unstats.un.org/unsd/snaama/Introduction .asp), with data from 1970 to the present.

572   Natural resource commodities: a century of statistics, prices, output, consumption, foreign trade, and employment in the United States, 1870–1973. Robert S. Manthy, Joan R. Tron, Resources for the Future. Baltimore: Johns Hopkins University Press, 1978. xiii, 240 p., graphs ISBN 9780801821424
333   HF1052

An update of Resources for the Future's *Trends in natural resource commodities* by Neal Potter and Francis Christy, Jr. (1962). In five sections: (1) methodology; (2) highlights; (3) detailed agricultural, mineral, and forest commodity summaries, emphasizing the post-1950 period; (4) individual data series for 200 natural resources commodities, from 1870 to 1973; (5) documented sources and explanatory notes for the data tables.

573   Research insight. https://www.capitaliq .com/home.aspx. Capital IQ (Firm). New York: Standard and Poor's. 1998–
657.3   HG4001

Research Insight is the new interface to Compustat. An essential resource with the most recent 20 years of U.S. and Canadian financial statement data and monthly closing stock price data, six months of daily stock prices, and GlobalVantage, the most recent 10 years of financial data for companies in 80 countries. Not an easy database to use; complex screening is possible, which becomes easier from within Excel. Screening can be done for data items in financial reports. Choose from quarterly or annual financials, and from nearly every data item within a financial report. Over 100 preformatted reports are available (EVAntage, company highlights, cash flow statements, combined reports, common size statements, institutional holdings). Data is also available for geographic areas, industry composites, aggregates, and stock indexes, and about 7,000 inactive companies.

574 S&P index directory. Standard & Poor's Corporation. New York: Standard & Poor's, 2008– ISSN 1949–291X
338.7/4/0973   HG4057
Annual. Summary information for companies in the S&P 500, S&P MidCap 400, and S&P SmallCap 600 lists. Successor to *Stock market encyclopedia* and separate directories for companies on those Standard and Poor's lists.

575 Standard & Poor's 500 guide. Standard and Poor's Corporation. New York: McGraw-Hill, 1994–. ill.
338.7/4/097305   HG4057
Annual. Presents summary information for stocks in the 500 "blue chip" companies that make up the S&P 500 list. Companies are assigned to sectors, industry groups, industries and sub-industries. Charts and tables show recent stock performance, revenue, earnings per share, dividend history, and financial data.

576 Stock trader's almanac. Yale Hirsch, Jeffrey Hirsch. Hoboken, N.J.: Wiley, 1967– ISSN 1553-4812
332.63   HG4637
Most used for the annotated calendar noting daily historical trading tendencies. A bull or bear appears on days with significant historical directional tendencies. Unusual in that it covers the best performing months or days.

577 Survey of current business. http:// www.bea.gov/scb/index.htm. Bureau of Economic Analysis. Washington: U.S. Dept. of Commerce. 2007–
ISSN 0039-6222
330.5   HC101
Published in print from 1921–2014; beginning February 2014, only in online form. Includes articles on current trends, charts and tables for national, international, industry and regional data; and link to *BEA current and historical data* in PDF. Descriptive and statistical material on basic income and trade developments in the United States. Covers prices, foreign trade, commodities, industries, etc.

578 The value line investment survey: small and mid-cap. Expanded ed.
Value Line. New York: Value Line, 1995–
ISSN 1080-7705
332.605   HG4501.V262
Reports on 1,800 small and mid-cap stocks, with consensus earning estimates and basic financials. Each issue profiles 130–140 companies, with business descriptions, corporate developments, betas, total shareholder return, four years of quarterly sales, quarterly dividends, and quarterly earnings per share data, as well as other ratio and financial data. In two parts: ratings and reports, and summary and index. Used primarily for investing, as well as by researchers for gathering financial data. The expanded edition is now called *Small/mid-cap edition*. Available in an online version.

579 WONDA: William O'Neil direct access. http://wondacharts.williamoneil .com/vantage/. William O'Neil + Company, Inc. Los Angeles: William O'Neil + Company, Inc. 1999–
                                HG4636
Fee-based resource typically available in professional settings or at graduate schools of business. Analyzes financial data for U.S. and international companies for investment purposes. Data is based on sources such as company financial statements, annual and quarterly cash flow reports, and industry financial figures. Supports analysis of individual companies, a comparative group of companies, or an investment portfolio. Downloadable using *WONDA vantage*. A similar high-end for-fee service is offered by Bloomberg Finance LP, as *Bloomberg professional*, often called the "Bloomberg Terminal."

580 WRDS. https://wrds-web.wharton.upenn
.edu/wrds/. Wharton School. Philadelphia:
The Wharton School, University of
Pennsylvania. 1993–

HG4026

Wharton research data services supports quantitative
data research through web access to a hosting service, for a number of financial databases, including Compustat (now *Research insight*) (573), CRSP
(Center for Research in Securities Prices), Dow Jones
Averages, FDIC, Philadelphia Stock Exchange, Institutional Brokers Estimate System (IBES), BankScope
(888) from Bureau van Dijk, CSMAR China Stock
Market databases, Eventus, Global Insight, NYSE-
TAQ, and OptionMetrics.

Internet Resources

581 Business insights. http://www
.cengagesites.com/literature/782/gale
-business-insights-global-essentials/. Gale
(Firm). [Farmington Hills, Mich.]: Gale
Cengage Learning. 2000–

HG4001

Until 2012, known as *Business and company resource
center*. Redesigned at that time to support better
searching across multiple kinds of content, manipulation of data to create custom charts, and advanced
user tools such as text-to-speech and translation
into more than 30 languages for the interface and
some content. Web interface highlights company
and industry information, comparison charts, and a
glossary. Provides information about market share,
market analysis and product trends, and allows comparison of companies. Content drawn from more
than 3,900 periodicals (journals, newspapers, and
trade publications); two million investment reports;
25,000 industry reports and 500 longer industry
profiles with more detail; 2,500 market research
reports; over 10,000 company histories from *International directory of company histories* (906) and more
than 2,000 company chronologies; 500,000 shorter
company profiles; 65,000 articles from *Business rankings annual* (909); and listings of 70,000 associations.

582 Yahoo finance. http://finance.yahoo
.com/. Yahoo! Inc. Sunnyvale, Calif.:
Yahoo! Inc. 1994–

HG4515.94

A rich source of financial information, with company
profiles, SEC filings, annual reports, stock quotes,
news, analysis, conference call calendar, industry
statistics and news, and information for the personal investor. The focus is on financial information
about U.S. and Canadian companies and industries,
but international information, such as indices and
currency information, is also available, especially
through the portals to Yahoo!Finance for other countries (linked from the bottom of the entry page). Historical quotes for stocks, bonds, and money markets
are since 1970 and give daily, weekly, and monthly
closing prices, and dividends. Most content is free:
occasionally links to fee-based information. Comparable websites are *MSN money* at http://money.msn
.com/ and *CNN money* at http://money.cnn.com/.

Human Resources, Labor and Unions

Guides and Handbooks

583 The employer's legal handbook. Fred
Steingold. Berkeley, Calif.: Nolo Press,
1994–. ill. ISSN 2163–033X
344   KF3455

Updated every two years: the 11th edition appeared
in 2013. Practical coverage of topics in hiring, personnel practices, wages and hours, employee benefits,
taxes, family and medical leave, health and safety,
illegal discrimination, workers with disabilities, termination, employee privacy, independent contractors, unions, lawyers and legal research. Appendixes
for labor departments and agencies, state drug and
alcohol testing laws, state laws on employee arrest
and conviction records, state laws on access to personnel records, state minimum wage laws for tipped
and regular employees, state meal and rest breaks,
state health insurance continuation laws, state family
and medical leave laws, right-to-know laws (hazardous chemicals), state laws prohibiting discrimination
in employment, agencies that enforce laws prohibiting discrimination in employment, and state laws
that control final paychecks. Available as an e-book.

**584 The essential HR handbook: a quick
and handy resource for any manager
or HR professional.** Sharon Armstrong,

Barbara Mitchell. Franklin Lakes, N.J.: Career Press, 2008. 255 p.
ISBN 9781564149909
658.3   HF5549

Covers strategic planning, mission statements, staffing decisions, orientation and training, performance evaluation, pay and benefits, employee relations, and legal topics such as FMLA and ADA. Appendix with sample job descriptions and forms. Glossary. Bibliography. Index. Available as an e-book.

585   Everyday HR: a human resources handbook for academic library staff. Gail Munde. Chicago: Neal-Schuman, 2013. xci, 183 p. ISBN 9781555707989
023   Z675.U5

Intended specifically for personnel managers in American academic libraries. Covers basic employment law, positions, supervising, conflict resolution, search committees, and tenure and continuous employment decisions. Bibliography. Index.

586   The handbook of human resource management education: Promoting an effective and efficient curriculum. Vida Gulbinas Scarpello. Thousand Oaks, Calif.: SAGE Publications, 2008. xv, 464 p.
ISBN 9781412954907
658.300711   HF5549.17

Twenty-three chapters in nine sections address the history of Human Resource Management (HRM) education, the context for educators working with students in a variety of subject disciplines (business, labor, psychology), and professional considerations. Sections include development of the HRM field and HRM education; HR master's programs in industrial relations and in organizational psychology; thoughts on HR education in psychology departments; HR education in business schools; new emphasis on international HRM education; neglected topics in HRM education; micro- and macro-organizational concepts relevant to HRM; stakeholder views of HRM education; HR success constraints; and HR professional success and parting thoughts. Relevant for education collections as well, due to the increasing number of human resource education programs in schools of education. Name and subject indexes. Available as an e-book.

**587   The job description handbook.
3rd ed.** Marjorie Mader-Clark. Berkeley,

Calif.: Nolo Press, 2013. 249 p., ill.
ISBN 9781413318555
658.3/06   HF5549.5.J613

Covers job analysis, legal issues, interviewing and hiring. Provides sample job descriptions for a range of positions. Index.

588   Labor law: a basic guide to the National Labor Relations Act. David E. Strecker. Boca Raton, Fla.: CRC Press, 2011. xvi, 181 p., port., forms
ISBN 9781439855942
344.7301   KF3369

Intended for supervisors, HR managers, and business owners. Discusses laws and regulations for interaction with labor unions, union employees, and collective bargaining situations in the U.S. History and development of labor law; union elections; role of the NLRB; contract negotiation; grievances and arbitration; unfair labor practices; and strikes.

589   Lawyers' medical cyclopedia of personal injuries and allied specialties. 5th ed. Richard M. Patterson. Newark, N.J.: LexisNexis, c2002–c2005. v., ill. ISBN 1558340378
                            RA1022.U6L38

First ed., 1958–62; 4th ed., 1977–99 (10 v.). Publication of the current (5th) ed. in progress.

"Authoritative reference for attorneys involved in personal injury, medical malpractice, workers' compensation, social security, disability income, and health insurance cases . . . Offers in-depth information and caselaw on hundreds of medical and surgical specialties . . . written by physicians skilled at translating complex anatomy, physiology, and medical treatment into clear language" (*Publ. notes*). Kept up to date by pocket parts and revised volumes. Includes bibliographical references and indexes.

590   Managing library employees: a how-to-do-it manual. Mary J. Stanley. New York: Neal-Schuman Publ., 2008. xi, 247 p. ISBN 9781555706289
023/.9   Z682.S76

Intended as "a basic orientation in human resources management for librarians"—*Pref.* Covers federal laws; recruitment and selection of staff; training, retention, and professional development; compensation and benefits; performance appraisal; problem employees; conflict resolution and discipline; communication; technology in human resources management; and change management. Includes sample forms, checklists, and bibliographic references. More specialized works on employee relations include *Managing student assistants: a how-to-do-it manual for librarians* by Sweetman and *Managing library volunteers*, Second edition by Driggers and Dumas.

591 The Oxford handbook of human resource management. Peter Boxall, John Purcell, Patrick Wright. Oxford; New York: Oxford University Press, 2007. xv, 658 p., ill. ISBN 9780199282517
658.3 HF5549.17

Twenty-nine signed essays addressing issues such as the social and organizational purposes behind HR work; practical aspects such as recruitment, training, pay and evaluation; the impact of contemporary developments such as information technology and globalization; and the connection of HR work to business performance. Essays discuss recent publications, with bibliographic citations. Supported by figures and tables. Index.

592 Policies and practice: HR series. Thomson West (Firm). Eagan, Minn.: Thomson West, 2004–. 3 v.
HF5549

Covers HR management, with sections on recordkeeping, hiring, termination, fair employment practices, productivity, performance appraisal, training, communication, work rules and discipline, grievances, labor relations, compensation, benefits, work/life integration strategies, leaves of absence, safety and occupational health, substance abuse, and security. Includes forms and sample policies.

593 The Praeger handbook of human resource management. Ann Maycunich Gilley. Westport, Conn.: Praeger, 2009. 2 v. (xix, 651 p.), ill. ISBN 9780313350153
658.3 HF5549

Volume 1 covers topics such as recruiting, training, evaluation, pay and benefits, and employment law. Volume 2 looks at the role of HR in leadership, organizational development, change management, collective bargaining, and policy-making. Bibliography. Index. Available as an e-book.

594 Psychological testing at work: How to use, interpret, and get the most out of the newest tests in personality, learning styles, aptitudes, interests, and more!. Edward Hoffman. New York: McGraw-Hill, 2002. xiii, 209 p. ISBN 9780071360791
658.31125 HF5549.5.E5

Explains the purpose, construction, validity, and usefulness of 42 of today's most popular assessment tools. Focus is on interpreting and getting the most out of tests of personality, learning style, aptitudes, and interests. Offers in-depth, practical coverage of numerous well-established means of personality assessment to identify successful workers, aid in management and leadership training, as well as team building, and determining an employee's level of job satisfaction and likelihood of burnout. Contains glossary, bibliography, index of psychological tests, and general index. Available as an e-book.

595 Reassignment under the ADA: must an employer hire a minimally qualified, disabled employee over a more qualified, non-disabled applicant?: a legal research guide. Amy R. Stein. Buffalo, N.Y.: William S. Hein & Co, 2009. xvii, 43 leaves ISBN 9780837717203
344.7301/59 KF3469

Legal factors in reassignment and reasonable accommodation for hiring under the Americans with Disabilities Act. Supports research into the state of the law and different judicial approaches to the issues. Includes citations and summaries pointing to relevant sources including statutes, court cases, law reviews and legal encyclopedias.

596 The SAGE handbook of human resource management. Adrian Wilkinson, Nick A. Bacon, Tom Redman, Scott Snell. Los Angeles: SAGE, 2009. xx, 592 p., ill. ISBN 9781412928298
658.3 HF5549.15

Thirty-three signed essays by experts, on aspects of HR practice. Includes historical and strategic concepts behind HR; specific task areas such as recruitment, training, compensation, discipline and collective bargaining; contemporary issues such as ethics and work/life balance; and the differences between large and small companies, or the public and private sectors.

Summarizes and cites the current literature, drawing on studies in business, economics, psychology, politics, and sociology. Index. Available as an e-book.

597 Smart policies for workplace technologies: email, blogs, cell phones and more. 3rd ed. Lisa Guerin, Richard Stim. Berkeley, Calif.: Nolo Press, 2013. 241 p., ill. ISBN 9781413318432
651.7   HF5549.5.P39
Addresses legal, security and management aspects of personnel policies for the use of technology at work. Covers remote access to computers, password security, email, web surfing on the job, working from home, instant messaging, blogs and other social media, cell phones, portable devices, and camera phones. Looks ahead to coming capabilities such as biometrics and expanded use of RFID. Index.

598 Your rights in the workplace. Barbara Kate Repa, Lisa Guerin. Berkeley, Calif.: Nolo Press, 1991–. ill. ISSN 2152-6508
344.01   KF3455.Z9
Updated regularly to reflect changes in the law: the 10th edition is announced for 2014. Covers the Fair Labor Standards Act, calculation of earnings due, health insurance, FMLA, privacy, OSHA, injuries and workers' compensation, the Equal Pay Act and other anti-discriminatory legislation, firing and dismissal, filing a complaint, suing, collective bargaining, and more. Index.

Statistical Sources

599 The almanac of American employers: market research, statistics and trends pertaining to the leading corporate employers in America. Jack W. Plunkett. Houston, Tex.: Plunkett Research, 1985–
ISSN 1088-3150
338.7/4/02573   HF5382.75.U6
A comprehensive guide to the labor market in the U.S., with profiles of more than 500 major companies, both private and public. Unique features include information on companies most likely to hire women and minorities, company hiring patterns (will hire MBA's, engineers, liberal arts majors, etc.), and company profiles that give textual information including corporate culture and plans for growth. Historical and projected

statistics are updated in each edition, and include a U.S. Employment Overview; Total Employees, All Nonfarm Payrolls, Private Industry & Government; U.S. Civilian Labor Force; Number of People Employed and Unemployed, U.S.; Unemployed Jobseekers by Sex, Reason for Unemployment & Active Job Search Methods Used; U.S. Labor Force Ages 16 to 24 Years Old by School Enrollment, Educational Attainment, Sex, Race & Ethnicity; Medical Care Benefits in the U.S.: Access, Participation and Take-Up Rates; Retirement Benefits in the U.S.: Access, Participation and Take-Up Rates; Top 30 U.S. Occupations by Numerical Change in Job Growth; Top 30 U.S. Occupations by Percent Change in Job Growth; Occupations with the Largest Expected Employment Increases, U.S.; and Occupations with the Fastest Expected Decline. For the top "American Employers 500" list of firms, shows lists by Number of Employees, By Revenues, and By Profits; and organized by Industry List With Codes, Index of Companies Within Industry Groups, Alphabetical Index, Index of U.S. Headquarters Location by State, Index by Regions of the U.S. Where the Firms Have Locations, Index of Firms with International Operations, and Index of Firms Noted as Hot Spots for Advancement for Women & Minorities. Suggests Seven Keys for Job Seekers (Financial Stability, Growth Plan, Research and Development Programs, Product Launch and Production, Marketing and Distribution Methods, Employee Benefits, Quality of Work Factors, Other Considerations).

600 Bulletin of labour statistics. International Labour Office. Geneva, Switzerland: The Office, 1965–2009. ill. ISSN 0007-4950
331.0212   HD4826
Monthly and quarterly international labor data, including level of employment, numbers and percentages unemployed, average number of hours worked, average earnings or wage rates, and consumer prices. Covers 190 countries. Supplements the *Yearbook of labour statistics* (236) also from ILO. Ceased with issues of 2009.

601 Handbook of U.S. labor statistics: employment, earnings, prices, productivity, and other labor data. Bernan Press. Lanham, Md.: Bernan Press, 1997– ISSN 1526-2553
331.0973021   HD8051.H36

While this data can be found in other Bureau of Labor Statistics sources such as http://www.bls.gov/, these print volumes conveniently place the most useful labor statistics in one source. Includes statistics on employment (status, earnings, characteristics, experience, contingent and alternative work arrangements), projections by industry and occupation, productivity and costs, compensation, prices and living conditions, consumer expenditures, safety and health, labor management relations, and foreign labor and prices. Available as an e-book.

602 ILOSTAT. http://www.ilo.org/ilostat/.
International Labour Organisation (ILO).
Geneva, Switzerland: International Labour
Organisation. 2010–
                                    HD4826
Global labor statistics with over 100 indicators, based on official data from 230 participating countries, areas, and territories. May include monthly, quarterly or semi-annual figures for population, labor force, employment and unemployment, persons outside the labor force, youth, working time, earnings and employment-related income, occupational injuries, trade unions and collective bargaining, strikes and lockouts, the working poor, and labor inspection. This database is gradually replacing LABORSTA (625).

**603 Union membership and coverage
       database.** http://www.unionstats.com/.
Barry T. Hirsch, David A. Macpherson. San
Antonio, Tex.: Trinity University. 2002–
331.88   HD6504
Statistics on private and public sector labor union membership in the U.S., compiled from the Current Population Survey (CPS). Data is presented at the national level since 1973, the state level since 1983, for metropolitan areas since 1986, and by industry or occupation since 1983. Links to related websites.

604 United States economy at a glance.
http://www.bls.gov/eag/eag.us.htm. U.S.
Bureau of Labor Statistics. Washington:
U.S. Bureau of Labor Statistics. 1998–
                                    HA155
Snapshots of key economic data related to jobs, including recent monthly employment, price and earnings figures, and quarterly productivity and employment costs. Browsable for the U.S. as a whole, by region, by state, and for many metropolitan areas.

Provides graphs and tabular numbers for download. Useful tools such as maps of data and an inflation calculator.

605 Yearbook of labour statistics.
International Labour Office. Geneva,
Switzerland: International Labour Office,
1936– ISSN 0084-3857
331.29   HD4826
Summarizes labor statistics on the economically active population of 184 countries and territories. Covers consumer price indexes, employment, wages and hours of work, occupational injuries, strikes and lockouts, and household income and expenditures. In English, French, and Spanish. Updated by *Bulletin of labor statistics* (Geneva, 1965–, quarterly) (205). The *Retrospective edition on population census*, 1945–89, combines and adjusts data from previous ILO yearbooks with some new data derived from recent or previously unpublished censuses. Beginning in 2007, published in two parts: *Country profiles*, and *Time series*.

Directories

606 Directory of U.S. labor organizations.
Courtney D. Gifford. Washington: Bureau
of National Affairs, 1983–
ISSN 0734-6786
331.8802573   HD6504
Annual. Lists some 30,000 unions affiliated with AFL-CIO and other national, regional, state, and local affiliates. Gives the structure, leadership, and contact information for the unions. Index of unions by common name and by abbreviations; index of officers. Contact information includes names, addresses, telephone and fax numbers, and URLs. Provides updated information on union membership nationally and by state, recent major work stoppages, and results of union elections. Membership figures use U.S. Bureau of Labor Statistics figures for a breakdown by industry, occupation, race, age, and gender.

**607 National trade and professional
       associations of the United States.**
Craig Colgate, John J. Russell, Kathleen
Anders, Duncan Bell, David Epstein.
Washington: Columbia Books, 1966–
ISSN 0734-354X
061.3   HD2425

Entries for more than 7,500 national trade and professional associations and labor unions, with contact information including the primary executive, figures for staffing and annual budget, a summary of the group's history and purpose, and statements of membership fees and upcoming conferences. Separate directory lists 400 association management companies with the names of the organizations they manage. Indexes by subject, geographic location, budget size, name of executive officer, and acronym. Companion publication: *State and regional associations of the United States* (113).

608   Washington representatives.
Washington: Columbia Books, 1979–
ISSN 0192-060X
328.73078025   JK1118

A compilation of Washington representatives of the major national associations, labor unions, and U.S. companies, as well as registered foreign agents, lobbyists, lawyers, law firms, and special interest groups together with their clients and areas of legislative and regulatory concern. Generally in three parts: alphabetically arranged entries with contact information for individuals; alphabetical list of companies and organizations with contact information; and list of federal government departments and agencies with names of personnel responsible for legislative affairs. Includes the text of the Federal Regulation of Lobbying Act. Subject and foreign interests indexes.

Dictionaries and Encyclopedias

609   Chronology of labor in the United States. Russell O. Wright. Jefferson, N.C.: McFarland & Co., 2003. ix, 136 p.
ISBN 9780786414444
331.088/0973/02   HD6508

Notable events in the joint growth of U.S. industries and labor unions from 1850 to 2000, including the occupational shift from farms to manufacturing to service occupations, children and women in the labor force, hours of work and wages, safety issues, and unemployment. Introductory historical essay. Appendices include statistics on percentage of union membership in the work force 1930–2000, the decline in U.S. farm workers 1820–1994, and the percentage of women in the U.S. work force 1870–2000; list of work stoppages involving 1,000 workers

or more 1960–2000; and short biographies of key labor leaders. Bibliography. Index.

610   A dictionary of human resource management. 2nd ed. Edmund Heery, Mike Noon. Oxford; New York: Oxford University Press, 2008. xxvi, 552 p.
ISBN 9780199298761
658.3003   HF5549.A23

Provides definitions for 1,400 words and phrases, including 300 new entries since the edition of 2001. Covers legal, technical, and theoretical terms, including catch phrases and jargon. Includes vocabulary from psychology, sociology, and economics. Major themes include employee resourcing, work organization, employee development, discrimination, health, collective bargaining, and laws and regulations. Written from a British perspective. Cross-references. Bibliography. Available as an e-book.

611   Encyclopaedia of occupational health and safety. 4th ed. Jeanne Mager Stellman, International Labour Organization. Geneva, Switzerland: International Labour Organization, 1998. v. 2–4, ill. ISBN 9221092038
616.980303   RC963.A3.E53

Prepared under the auspices of the International Labour Organization.

First ed., 1930, had title *Occupation and health*; 2nd ed., 1971; 3rd ed., 1983. Sometimes cited as *ILO encyclopedia of occupational health and safety*.

Contents: v. 1, *The body*; v. 2, *Hazards*; v. 3, *Chemicals, industries and occupations*; v. 4, *Guides, indexes* (index by subject, index to chemicals, and guide to units and abbreviations), directory of experts.

Consists of a collection of signed articles on the basic information available in the field by international specialists, with recent bibliographic references. In 105 chapters, entries cover various aspects of toxicology, occupational illnesses and injuries, diseases of migrant workers, and institutions active in the field of occupational health. Preventive safety measures are stressed, and technical and social solutions to problems are offered. Intends to provide "theoretical and ethical underpinnings to the ongoing work of achieving the goal of social justice in a global economy"—*Pref.*

Table of contents with search interface to access words and phrases in the text (http://www.ilocis .org/en/contilo.html).

612 The encyclopedia of human resource management. William J. Rothwell, Robert K. Prescott, Jed Lindholm, Karen K. Yarrish, Aileen G. Zaballero, George M. Benscoter. San Francisco: Pfeiffer, 2012. 3 v., ill. ISBN 9780470257739
658.3003   HF5549.A23

Volume 1 covers overarching issues such as affirmative action, pay gaps, merit pay, work/life balance, collective bargaining, and grievances. Volume 2 deals with recruitment, development of talent, and analysis of performance by individuals and organizations. Volume 3 consists of essays on themes of leadership and the role of HR in organizations. Index in each volume. Available as an e-book.

613 The encyclopedia of strikes in American history. Aaron Brenner, Benjamin Day, Immanuel Ness. Armonk, N.Y.: M.E. Sharpe, 2009. xxxix, 750 p., ill. ISBN 9780765613301
331.892/97303   HD5324

Some 65 articles covering significant strikes from the 1870s to the present, as well as thematic essays on the theory and practice of strikes, working-class culture, strike waves in U.S. history, and contrasting developments in the public and private economic sectors. Timeline of relevant events since 1636. Bibliography. Index. Available as an e-book.

614 Encyclopedia of U.S. labor and working-class history. Eric Arnesen. New York: Routledge, 2007. 3 v. (xxxvii, 1561 p.), ill. ISBN 9780415968263
331.0973/03   HD8066

Some 650 signed articles with suggestions for further readings, on topics from the colonial era to the present. Covers important unions and other organizations, key leaders, themes in various historical periods, working conditions, major strikes, anti-union activities, the role of the U.S. government in labor matters, the rise and decline of labor as a political force, and issues of race, religion, ethnicity and gender. Index.

615 Historical dictionary of organized labor. 3rd ed. J. C. Docherty, Jacobus Hermanus Antonius van der Velden. Lanham, Md.: Scarecrow Press, 2012. xlvii, 448 p. ISBN 9780810861961
331.8803   HD4839

Contains 400 entries on countries, national and international organizations, unions, and labor leaders. Revised and expanded since the edition of 2004, with new entries covering trends globally and in the United States. The introduction serves as a history of organized labor. Extensive list of acronyms and abbreviations. Chronology notes major events by year, beginning in 1152 B.C. and ending with 2011. Bibliography includes URLs for relevant organizations. Complemented by the 2006 *Historical dictionary of socialism* by Docherty and Peter Lamb, which covers political theories and parties. Available as an e-book.

616 International encyclopaedia for labour law and industrial relations. R. Blanpain. Deventer, The Netherlands: Kluwer, 1977–. 13 v.
344.01   K1705

A collection of nat. monographs surveying the laws governing individual workers and collective organizations in more than 55 countries, as well as chs. on internat. and European labor law. Also includes vols. providing the texts of internat. instruments, case law from internat. tribunals, and legislation from some 20 countries. Each section has a separate index. A section on the European Works Council is also separately available.

In recent years, the same publisher and editor-in-chief have launched several similar works in other subject areas, under the series title "International encyclopaedia of laws." These have the potential to become important transnational reference sources, though to date none has provided coverage of more than a handful of countries. When completed, this new set will include approx. 50 nat. monographs of about 200–250 p. each.

Titles include *Commercial and economic law*, Jules Stuyck, ed. (1993–); *Constitutional law*, Andre Alen, ed. (1992–); *Contracts*, Jacques Herbots, ed. (1993–); *Corporations and partnerships*, Koen Geeris, ed. (1991–); *Criminal law*, Lieven Dupont and Cyrille Fijnaut, eds. (1993–); *Environmental law*, Marc Boes, ed. (1991–); *Insurance law*, Simon Fredericq and Herman Cousy, eds. (1992–); and *Medical law*, Herman Nys, ed. (1993–).

A full listing of available vols. can be found online at http://www.ielaws.com/. Continuously updated.

617 **Roberts' dictionary of industrial relations. 4th ed.** Harold S. Roberts. Washington: Bureau of National Affairs, 1994. xix, 874 p. ISBN 9780871797773
331/.03   HD4839
Defines some 4,000 words and phrases related to labor, HR, and industrial relations. Numerous cross-references. Definitions are tied to source quotations. Bibliography.

618 **St. James encyclopedia of labor history worldwide: major events in labor history and their impact.** Neil Schlager. Detroit: St. James Press/Gale Group/Thomson Learning, 2004. 2 v., 1200 p., ill. ISBN 9781558625426
331.8   HD4839
More than 300 articles on topics such as significant strikes and laws dealing with labor and unions, with an emphasis on events in the United States and on the period from 1800 to the present. Some additional short biographical entries. Bibliography. Available as an e-book.

619 **Trade unions of the world. 6th ed.** John Harper Publishing. London: John Harper Publishing, 2005
ISBN 9780955114427
331.88025   HD6483
Political and economic background sketches for 186 countries, with an overview and history of trade union activities. Individual union entries including contact information, URLs, history, and international affiliations. Available as an e-book.

620 **United States business history, 1602–1988: a chronology.** Richard Robinson. New York: Greenwood Press, 1990. xii, 643 p. ISBN 9780313260957
338.0973   HC103
"Designed to provide a basic calendar of representative events . . . in the evolution of U.S. business." —*Pref.* Contains descriptive historical data, arranged by year, then under categories of general news and business news. Significant individuals, specific companies, inventions, trade unions, and key business, economic, and social developments are included. Brief bibliography; detailed index. Complemented by *Robinson's business history of the world: a chronology.*

621 **Workers in America: a historical encyclopedia.** Robert E. Weir. Santa Barbara, Calif.: ABC-CLIO, 2013. 2 v. (xxiii, 920 p.), ill. ISBN 9781598847185
331.0973   HD8066
Covers the history of American unions and the organized labor movement up to the present, including biographical entries for key figures, the history of major organizations, influential events such as strikes and court cases, the development of workers rights and employee benefits, and the role of government. Includes suggestions for further reading. Revised edition of *Historical encyclopedia of American labor.* Chronology. Index. Available as an e-book.

Internet Resources

622 **AFL-CIO: America's unions.** http://www.aflcio.org/. American Federation of Labor and Congress of Industrial Organizations. Washington: AFL-CIO. 1996–
331.8   HD8055.A5
Home page for the largest advocacy group for labor unions in the U.S.: "the AFL-CIO represents millions of working people who belong to unions and have the benefits of union membership." Provides position statements on issues such as collective bargaining, health care, workplace rights, retirement security, and job safety. Web site tracks the status of federal legislation and voting records of members of Congress.

623 **Cases and decisions: NLRB.** http://www.nlrb.gov/cases-decisions. National Labor Relations Board (NLRB). Washington: U.S. National Labor Relations Board. 1998–
331.154   KF3362.A2
From the home page of the NLRB: full text of board decisions; administrative law judge decisions; advice memos; appellate court briefs and motions; contempt, compliance, and special litigation branch briefs; invitations to file briefs; weekly summaries of decisions; and regional election decisions. Also links to a list of other reference sources, an FAQ, fact sheets, and an array of graphs and data related to union elections and prevention of unfair labor practices. Some of this content has been published in print since 1936.

624 Labor & Employment Law Resource Center. http://laborandemploymentlaw.bna.com/. Bureau of National Affairs. Arlington, Va.: Bureau of National Affairs. [1999–] ISSN 2156-2849

331   KF3319

Cases, summaries of developments, manuals, and explanations of U.S. federal and state laws in areas like arbitration, collective bargaining, wages and hours, fair employment, disability and employee rights. Includes *Daily labor report*, comparative *State law chart builder*, information on labor-management relations with decisions from 1984,and fair employment practices from 1965, BNA's *Labor Relations Reporter*, *HR Policy Handbook*, and *Client Letters, Checklists, and Forms.* Formerly *BNA's labor & employment law library*. BNA also publishes an online *Human resources library* addressing practical management of topics such as benefits, training and labor relations; and the *LaborPlus* database with sections for NLRB Elections, Work Stoppages, Unfair Labor Practices, Contract Settlement Summaries, and private sector Contract Listings.

625 LABORSTA Internet. http://laborsta.ilo.org/. International Labour Organization Bureau of Statistics. Geneva, Switzerland: International Labour Organization. [1998–]

HD4826

Offers country-level time-series data on employment and unemployment, the size and composition of the workforce, labor costs, wages, hours of work, strikes and lockouts, international labor migration, consumer prices, household income and expenditures, and occupational injuries. Most series consisting of annual data begin coverage in 1969. Monthly and quarterly time series, which exist for employment, unemployment, hours of work, wages, and prices, start in 1976. Data for developing countries and for the early years in most series are incomplete. Also includes links to online labor force surveys and the websites of IGO statistical offices and programs, national statistical offices, and labor ministries. Provides longer time series than the *Bulletin of labour statistics* (205) and *Yearbook of labour statistics* (236) but lacks the country profiles found in the latter. Some LABORSTA series are also available in UNdata (153). Content is being shifted to the new ILOSTAT (602) database.

626 National compensation survey. http://www.bls.gov/ncs/home.htm. U.S. Dept. of Labor, Bureau of Labor Statistics. Washington: Bureau of Labor Statistics. 1998–

HD4976.A735N38

Summarizes wages, earnings, and hours for cities, regions, and the nation. "Wage data are shown by industry, occupational group, full-time and part-time status, union and nonunion status, establishment size, time and incentive status, and job level." —*Summary*. Also includes benefits and the Employment Cost Index, which is released quarterly.

627 NATLEX. http://www.ilo.org/dyn/natlex/natlex_browse.home. International Labour Organization. [Geneva, Switzerland]: International Labour Organization (ILO). 1999–

K1705

Contains over 65,000 records for the legal and regulatory documents of more than 190 countries and over 160 territories and provinces on work, social security, and workers' rights related to these topics. More than 540 directives, decisions, regulations, and recommendations of the European Union and over 170 conventions and protocols are also covered. The record for each text is indexed by subject and keyword and includes the document's title, the date it was signed or adopted, a citation, and at least one descriptor. The date of its entry into force, a link to the text on the Internet, and a link to one or more records for amended documents may also be provided. Each record appears in only English, French, or Spanish. Records for most countries in which none of these languages is an official language are in English. Content is moving to NORMLEX (628).

628 NORMLEX. http://www.ilo.org/dyn/normlex/en/. International Labour Organization. [Geneva, Switzerland]: International Labour Organization. 2012–

K1704.2

Contains more than 380 ILO labor standards—conventions and recommendations (nonbinding guidelines) regarding work, employment, and social security—and thousands of documents about the application and violation of these standards from

1919 to date. Displays names of conventions and recommendations chronologically and by subject, and provides ratification information for all conventions by country. The advanced search provides access to documents by type of text, associated convention, country, and date, as well as keyword in the title and full text. Many types of documents in this database are unique to the ILO, so the pages describing them should be consulted. Since 2012, includes the former NATLEX, APPLIS, ILOLEX and Libsynd databases.

629 Occupational outlook handbook.
http://www.bls.gov/ooh/. United States
Bureau of Labor Statistics. Washington:
U.S. Department of Labor. 1998–
331   HD8051

Biennial official government estimate of trends and potential employment in 800 occupations. Browsable by major Occupation Groups (such as Healthcare or Media & Communication), by rate of pay, by projected rate of job growth, by projected absolute number of new jobs, or alphabetically. Searchable by rate of pay, level of required education, and anticipated numbers of new openings. Entries for each occupation indicate median pay, required education or credentials, number of jobs nationally, and anticipated growth. Launched in print in 1949, and available on the Web since 1998. Reprints (932) are sold by private publishers as well.

**630 Occupational Safety and Health
Administration (OSHA).** http://www
.osha.gov/. Occupational Safety and
Health Administration. Washington: U.S.
Dept of Labor, Occupational Safety and
Health Administration. 199?–
344.73   KF3570.Z9

Access to OSHA programs and services. Includes information on OSHA standards on safety, preventing injuries, and protecting the health of American workers. Provides access to the OSHA occupational chemical database (http://www.osha .gov/chemicaldata/), originally developed by OSHA in cooperation with EPA. Safety and health topics include biological agents (avian flu, food-borne disease, ricin, etc.), OSHA standards for carcinogens, construction (key standards and compliance activities), emergency preparedness (e.g., national safety and health standards for emergency responders),

ergonomics (with focus on musculoskeletal disorders), hazard communication (e.g., workplace chemical safety programs), maritime industry, and many other subjects (see A-Z index http://www.osha.gov/ html/a-z-index.html).

631 U.S. Bureau of Labor Statistics. http://
www.bls.gov/. Bureau of Labor Statistics.
Washington: U.S. Department of Labor.
1995–
331.10212   HD8051

Home page of the official data-collecting agency in the field of labor statistics and economics: this includes tracking market activity, working conditions, and price changes. BLS produces the Consumer Price Index (CPI), Producer Price Index (PPI), Import and Export Price Indices, and the Consumer Expenditure Survey. Online reports cover inflation and prices, spending and time use, employment and unemployment, pay and benefits, productivity, workplace injuries, and comparisons with international figures. Offers "at a glance" snapshots covering the whole U.S. economy; regions, states and areas; and 100 specific industries.

International Business

Guides and Handbooks

**632 The Blackwell handbook of cross-
cultural management.** Martin J.
Gannon, Karen L. Newman. Oxford, U.K.;
Malden, Mass.: Blackwell Business, 2002.
xxiii, 509 p., ill. ISBN 9780631214304
658.049   HD62.4

Overview of theory and research findings. Organized into six sections: pt. 1: Frameworks for cross-cultural management; pt. 2: Strategy, structure, and interorganizational relationships; pt 3: Managing human resources across cultures; pt. 4: Motivation, rewards, and leadership behavior; pt. 5: Interpersonal processes; and pt. 6: Corporate culture and values.

**633 Craighead's international business,
travel, and relocation guide to . . .
countries.** Gale Research Inc. Detroit:
Gale Research, 1991–. maps
ISSN 1058-3904
910.202   HF5549.5.E45

Biennial guide to the political, economic and business environment, and everyday life in 84 countries. The most recent is the 12th edition of 2004/05. Entries are by country and include business customs and protocols, gift-giving, work ethic, employment conditions, power structure and hierarchy, attitude toward foreigners, tips for establishing a business presence, and even information on establishing a social life and finding a home. Similar to the *Price-WaterhouseCoopers guides*.

634   Exporters' encyclopaedia. Dun's
    Marketing Services. New York: Dun and
    Bradstreet International, 1982–2009.
    maps ISSN 8755-013X
    382.602573   HF3011

Ceased in 2009. Comprehensive world marketing guide for 220 world markets. Designed as a guide to possible markets and also as an instructional manual for some practicalities (e.g. shipping and insurance). Country profiles include communications, key contracts, trade regulations, documentation, marketing data, transportation, and business travel. Other sections cover U.S. ports, U.S. foreign trade zones, World Trade Center Association members, U.S. government agencies providing assistance to exporters, foreign trade organizations, foreign communications, and general export and shipping information.

**635   Global business etiquette: a guide
    to international communication and
    customs. 2nd ed.** Jeanette S. Martin,
    Lillian H. Chaney. Santa Barbara, Calif.:
    Praeger, 2012. xi, 229 p.
    ISBN 9780313397172
    395.5/2   HF5389

Designed to orient the business traveler to local customs. Includes chapters on the following: travel customs and tips; language, greetings, introductions, and business cards; socializing; gestures and other nonverbal communicators; dress and appearance; cultural attitudes and behaviors; dining and tipping customs; conversational customs and manners; and oral and written communication customs and etiquette. This new edition includes chapters on etiquette for international businesswomen and international negotiation etiquette, and added information about clothing norms, and the significance of objects and symbols. Concentrates on

the customs of the United States' top ten trading partners, now including Brazil. Index. Available as an e-book.

**636   International business information:
    how to find it, how to use it.
    2nd ed.** Ruth A. Pagell, Michael Halperin.
    New York; Chicago: AMACOM;
    Glenlake, 1999. xvii, 445 p., ill.
    ISBN 9781573560504
    016.33   HF54.5

"Describes key international business publications and databases, and provides the subject background needed to understand them."— *Pref*. While dated, many of the resources are still applicable. Most sources are English-language directories, yearbooks, reports, and electronic files that describe companies, industries, markets, and international transactions. Extensively illustrated with examples and tables. Appendixes, title and subject index.

**637   Kiss, bow, or shake hands: sales
    and marketing—the essential
    cultural guide—from presentations
    and promotions to communicating
    and closing.** Terri Morrison, Wayne A.
    Conaway. New York: McGraw-Hill, 2012.
    xvii, 284 p. ISBN 9780071714044
    395.52   HF5389

Successor to related titles of 1995 and 2006. Serves as a guide to business etiquette for those engaged in international business. Entries cover Argentina, Australia, Brazil, Canada, China, France, Germany, India, Indonesia, Italy, Japan, Mexico, Russia, Saudi Arabia, South Africa, South Korea, Turkey, the United Arab Emirates, the United Kingdom, and the U.S. (the 2006 edition covered about 60 countries, and remains useful for those places not covered here). Includes chapters covering background information, tips on doing business in the culture of each country, political context, language, cultural orientation (negotiation style, cognitive styles, value system), and business practices (punctuality, appointments, local time, entertainment). Cultural norms addressed include advertising, arrival time for meetings, business cards, eye contact, greetings, handshakes, smoking, and social distance. Appendixes cover tips on dining, drinking, delicacies, and "dangerous diversions." Available as an e-book.

638 The Oxford handbook of international business. 2nd ed. Alan M. Rugman. Oxford; New York: Oxford University Press, 2009. xix, 857 p., ill., plans ISBN 9780199234257
658.8/4   HF1379

Updated since the edition of 2001. Twenty-eight signed chapters written by academics, summarizing current publishing about aspects of international business. Organized into six sections: history and theory of the multinational enterprise (MNE); the political and regulatory environment; strategy and international management; managing the MNE; area studies (emphasizing East Asia); and methodological issues. Indexes by author and subject. Available as an e-book.

Encyclopedias

639 Biographical dictionary of management. Morgen Witzel. Bristol, U.K.: Thoemmes, 2001. 2 v. ISBN 9781855068711
658.00922   HD30.15

Contains 600 entries on leaders and scholars from around the world, who have made major contributions to business from the beginning of civilization to modern times. Written by some 50 international scholars, who note the work, scholarship, and contributions each individual has produced.

640 Encyclopedia of Japanese business and management. Allan Bird. London; New York: Routledge, 2002. xix, 500 p. ISBN 9780415189453
650.0952   HF1001

Written for the specialist and student alike, with articles on economics, finance, management, government institutions, history, human resource management, industries, companies, social entities, business personalities, industrial relations, Japanese business overseas, manufacturing, marketing, and research and development. The encyclopedia is a good mix of expected information (history of the labor movement) and the unexpected (such as the article on office ladies, young, single women in clerical jobs). Entries range between 150 and 2,000 words in length. Entries are signed and some have recommended further reading. Available as an e-book.

641 Encyclopedia of management. 7th ed. Sonya D. Hill. Detroit: Gale, Cengage Learning, 2012. xxx, 1133 p. ISBN 9781414459042
658.003   HD30.15

Covers functional areas such as corporate planning and strategic management, emerging topics in management, entrepreneurship, financial management and accounting, general management, human resources management, innovation and technology, international management, leadership, legal issues, management science and operations, management information systems, performance measures and assessment, personal growth and development for managers, production and operations management, quality management and total quality management, supply chain management, and training and development. More than 300 essays in alphabetical order, written by academics and business professionals, with cross-references and recommended reading lists. New content reflects trends such as the use of handheld devices for Internet-based tools, social networking, network security, venture capital and entrepreneurship, and business in China. Includes a glossary of terms. Index. Available as an e-book.

642 Global companies in the twentieth century: selected archival histories. Malcolm McIntosh, Ruth Thomas. London; New York: Routledge, 2001. 9 v., ill., maps ISBN 0415181100
338.88   HD2755.5

While *Global Companies* examines a select set of companies (BBC, Levi Strauss and Co., Broken Hill Proprietary Company, Barclays, BP Amoco, Rio Tinto, Cable and Wireless, Marks and Spencer, and Royal Dutch/Shell), it does so thoroughly. Uses company archival documents to analyze how the companies have changed and adapted over time.

643 International encyclopedia of business and management. 2nd ed. Malcolm Warner, John P. Kotter. London: Thomson Learning, 2002. 8 v., xvii, 7160 p., ill. ISBN 9781861521613
650.03   HF101

Contains 750 entries, intended to clarify international management and management education topics for students and faculty in higher education. Interdisciplinary in scope, including concepts from psychology, sociology, mathematics, computer engineering, political science, and economics.

Dictionaries

644 Dictionary of international business terms. 3rd ed. John J. Capela, Stephen Hartman. Hauppauge, N.Y.: Barron's, 2004. ix, 626 p. ISBN 9780764124457
382.03   HD62.4
Nearly 5,000 terse definitions of business and economics terms. Appendixes with abbreviations, acronyms, contacts for major foreign markets, and U.S. Customs officers, regions, and districts. 2nd ed. (2000) available as an e-book.

645 Dictionary of international economics terms. John Owen Edward Clark. London: Les50ns Professional Pub, 2006. 300 p. ISBN 0852976852
330.03   HF1359
Defines concepts, jargon, and acronyms in economics, finance and business. Includes definitions such as accelerated depreciation, Andean Pact, coupon interest rate, marginal cost, shakeout, and X-inefficiency. Part of a series of dictionaries, which include: *Dictionary of international accounting terms*, *Dictionary of international banking and finance terms*, *Dictionary of international business terms*, *Dictionary of international insurance and finance terms*, and *Dictionary of international trade finance*. Some definitions are shared between the dictionaries in the series.

646 Dictionary of international trade: handbook of the global trade community, includes 34 key appendices. 10th ed. Edward G. Hinkelman, Paul Denegri. Petaluma, Calif.: World Trade Press, 2013. 792 p. ISBN 9781618408754
382.03   HF1373
An A-Z guide to formal and informal vocabulary on exporting, importing, banking, shipping, and other matters relating to international trade. Definitions make up half the book, with the other half devoted to appendixes. Topics of appendixes include acronyms and abbreviations, country codes, international dialing guide, currencies of the world, business entities worldwide, weights and measures, ship illustrations, airplane illustrations, truck and trailer illustrations, railcar

illustrations, guide to air freight containers, guide to ocean freight containers, world airports by IATA code, seaports of the world, guide to Incoterms 2000, guide to letters of credit, resources for international trade, guide to trade documentation, guide to international sourcing, key words in eight languages, global supply chain security, and maps of the world in color.

647 Elsevier's dictionary of financial and economic terms: Spanish-English and English-Spanish. Martha Uriona G. A., José Daniel Kwacz. Amsterdam, The Netherlands; New York: Elsevier, 1996. 311 p. ISBN 9780444822567
332.03   HG151
Explanations and definitions for terms in economics, finance and business, including jargon. Intended for practitioners.

648 The handbook of international financial terms. http://www.oxfordreference.com/. Peter Moles, Nicholas Terry. [New York]: Oxford University Press. 2005 ISBN 9780198294818
332.04203   HG3881
8,500 brief definitions on finance and accounting, including international stock exchanges, option strategies, and laws. Some definitions include examples. Extensive list of acronyms and abbreviations. List of international currency codes. Also available in print.

649 International dictionary of finance. 4th ed. Graham Bannock, W. A. P. Manser. London: Profile Books, 2003. vi, 287 p. ISBN 9781861974785
332.03   HG151
Covers international finance, as well as domestic finance in various countries. Concentrates on the U.S. and the United Kingdom. Includes foreign language terms. Definitions range from one word to one-half page in length, depending on the complexity of the concept.

650 Language of trade. http://usinfo.org/enus/economy/trade/langtrade.html. Merritt R. Blakeslee, Carlos A. Garcia, U.S. Dept. of State, Office of International Information Programs. Washington: U.S. Dept. of State, Office of International Information Programs. [2000]
382.03   HF1002.5

Contains a glossary of trade terminology, a list of acronyms used in international trade, and a chronology of major events in international trade since 1916. Most glossary entries are a short paragraph in length and include links to other entries. The glossary and acronyms are also cross-linked. Also available in print edition.

Directories

651 Asia's 10,000 largest companies: marketing and financial information on Asia's top companies. Oxford, U.K.: ELC International, 2006– ISBN 9781907128127
338.74095   HG4234.85

Lists leading companies in banking, agriculture, mining, construction, business and personal services, electronics manufacturing, industrial manufacturing, food, beverage, tobacco, chemicals, petroleum, pharmaceuticals, wholesale, retail, transportation and oil, publishing, communications, hotels and restaurants, insurance, investment, real estate, and utilities. Entries give SIC code, sales, profit, employees, sales per employee, assets, equity, equity as a percentage of assets, and year established. Ranks Asia's 500 most profitable companies, 500 biggest money losers, and 100 largest companies by industry sector.

652 D and B principal international businesses. Dun and Bradstreet, Inc. Bethlehem, Pa.: Dun and Bradstreet, 1999–
380.1025   HF54.U5

Lists more than 50,000 companies by country, industry, and name, providing for each: sales volume, indication of whether it exports or imports, number of employees, SIC and DUNS numbers, description of field of activity, and name and title of senior operating officer.

653 The Directory of trade and professional associations in the European Union: = Répertoire de . . . associations professionnelles et commerciales dans l'Union européenne. Euroconfidential. London; New York: Europa/European Union, 1994– ISSN 1742-4011
HD2429.E88

Biennial. Gives contact information and publications for 750 associations in the European Union. Also gives contact information for 11,700 national member organizations and the Chambers of Commerce in Europe. Indexes for: acronyms and abbreviations, full names, keywords, and Standard Industrial Classification (SIC) codes.

654 Directory for doing business in Japan. http://www.jetro.go.jp/en/invest/directory/. Nihon Bo eki Shinko kai. Tokyo: Japan External Trade Organization (JETRO). 1998–
382.029452   HF3823

Lists Japanese companies and associations involved in international trade, as well as products. Gives contact information, representative, type of business, year established, capital, annual sales, number of employees, bank reference, product/service imported or exported. Searchable by business type and geograhic location. JETRO publishes in print *Japan trade directory (Nihon Bo eki Shinko kai)*.

655 Major companies of Europe. Graham & Whiteside. Farmington Hills, Mich.: Gale Cengage, 1982– ISSN 0266-934X
338.740254   HC241.2

Covers major companies and related service and professional organizations. Provides directory information, officers, products or services, parent company, number of employees, and summary financial information. Other similar titles from the same publisher: *Major companies of the Arab world*, *Major companies of central and eastern Europe and the commonwealth of independent states*, *Major companies of the Far East and Australasia*, *Major companies of Africa south of the Sahara*, *Major chemical and petrochemical companies of the world*, *Major energy companies of the world*, *Major financial institutions of the world*, *Major food and drink companies of the world*, *Major information technology companies of the world*, *Major pharmaceutical and biotechnology companies of the world*, and *Major telecommunications companies of the world*.

656 World chamber of commerce directory. Johnson Publishing Co. Loveland, Colo.: World Chamber of Commerce Directory, 1958– ISSN 1048-2849
380.106   HF294

Lists U.S. chambers of commerce by state and city, giving mailing address, telephone and fax numbers, name of president, number of members, and local population. Similar information is provided for state boards of tourism, convention and visitors bureaus, economic development organizations, Canadian chambers of commerce, American chambers of commerce abroad, foreign tourist information bureaus, and foreign chambers of commerce in the U.S. and abroad. Also lists key diplomats, U.S. and foreign embassy addresses.

657 World directory of trade and business journals. Euromonitor PLC. London: Euromonitor PLC, 1996–1998
ISSN 9780863386299
016.338   Z7164.C81
Lists some 2,000 magazines, newsletters, and journals. Gives language, frequency, content, country coverage, format, publisher and contact information. Arranged into 80 industry categories, beginning with advertising and ending with wholesaling. Two indexes: A-Z index by country and publisher with publications, and A-Z index of journals by country. Especially useful for finding a source for news, organizational information, trends or statistics on a company or industry that is not gathered in a reference resource. Published as recently as 1998 (3rd edition).

Statistics

658 Arab world competitiveness report.
World Economic Forum. Geneva, Switzerland: World Economic Forum, 2007– 320.9174927 1403948011
Annual, published in cooperation with OECD. Issue for 2011–2012 can be downloaded at http://www3.weforum.org/docs/WEF_AWC_Report_2011-12.pdf. Discusses issues of trade, investment and development. Older volumes contain country profiles for Algeria, Bahrain, Egypt, Jordan, Kuwait, Lebanon, Libya, Libyan Arab Jamahiriya, Morocco, Oman, Qatar, Saudi Arabia, Syria, Syrian Arab Republic, Tunisia, United Arab Emirates, and Yemen.

659 Consumer Europe. 26th ed.
Euromonitor PLC. London: Euromonitor International, 2011–
339.4/7   HD7022
Annual. Formed by the merger of *Consumer Western Europe* and *Consumer Eastern Europe*. Indicates relative size of market for hundreds of consumer products.

The current 2014 volume has data covering 2007–2012 and forecasts to 2017. Value figures in both local currency and U.S. dollars. Includes the following categories: alcoholic drinks, apparel, consumer appliances and electronics, consumer health products, eyewear, fresh food, home and garden products, hot drinks, packaged food, pet care, retail paper goods, soft drinks, tobacco, and toys and games. Provides the following national socio-economic indicators for context: population, health, foreign trade, household characteristics, income, and consumer expenditure. Covers 27 countries: Austria, Belgium, Bulgaria, Croatia, the Czech Republic, Denmark, Finland, France, Germany, Greece, Hungary, Ireland, Italy, Lithuania, the Netherlands, Norway, Poland, Portugal, Romania, Russia, Slovakia, Spain, Sweden, Switzerland, Turkey, Ukraine and the United Kingdom. Available in online format.

660 Datamyne. http://www.datamyne.com/. Datamyne, Inc. Miami: Datamyne, Inc. 2008–
                                     HF3000
Searchable source for import-export data for Latin American countries, the U.S., the European Union, China, Japan, South Korea and South Africa. Based on official government figures; frequently updated. Interactive tables and rankings drill down to specific cargos, ports of departure and destination, and names of importers and exporters. A comparable resource on import-export is *PIERS* (Port Import Export Reporting Service). The Foreign Trade Division of the U.S. Census Bureau markets an analytical tool called *USA trade online*.

661 Direction of trade statistics quarterly.
International Monetary Fund. Washington: International Monetary Fund, 1994–
ISSN 1017–2734
382   HF1016
Presents current values for import and export of merchandise among member states of the IMF, disaggregated to show important trading partners. About 160 countries are covered. Figures are also combined to show trade flow between world regions. Figures are combined annually in the *Direction of trade statistics year book*. Successor to the quarterly *Direction of trade statistics* (1981–1994).

662 Global market share planner. 6th ed. Euromonitor International. London;

Chicago: Euromonitor PLC, 2010. lxxxii, 834 p. ISBN 9781842645444

338.74021   HD2757.15

Tracks world-wide market size, market share, and key brands for companies producing consumer brands, across 52 national markets. Includes sections on market share tracker, world-leading multinationals, and major market share companies. Products analyzed include beauty and personal care products, and beer and wine. Index. Earlier editions are in multiple volumes, focused on world regions.

Internet Resources

663   Academy of international business.
http://aib.msu.edu/. Academy of International Business. East Lansing, Mich.: Eli Broad Graduate School of Management. 1995–

HD62.4

Home page for an internat. assoc., founded in 1959, to be the the "leading global community of scholars for the creation and dissemination of knowledge about international business and policy issues."—*About*

The website includes events, a career center, publications (*Journal of international business studies*, *AIB insights*, *AIB newsletter*, conference proceedings), and links to online resources (announcements, course content, academic publishers, paper depositories, journals, professional organizations, and mailing lists).

664   Deloitte international tax and business guides. http://www.deloitte .com/taxguides. Deloitte (Firm). New York: Deloitte Touche Tohmatsu Limited. 2007–

Information on laws and regulations for doing business in 50 countries, with coverage of investment climate (economic structure, banking and financing, foreign trade), business and regulatory environment (registration and licensing, price controls, monopolies and restraint of trade, intellectual property, mergers and acquisitions, accounting standards), foreign investment (foreign investment incentives and restrictions, exchange controls), choice of business entity (principal forms of doing business, establishing a branch, setting up a company), corporate and individual taxation (taxable income and rates, capital gains, foreign income and tax treaties, transfer

pricing, turnover and other indirect taxes and duties, tax compliance and administration), employment law (employees' rights and remuneration, wages and benefits, termination of employment), and entry requirements. Snapshots are available for 100 countries, giving country profiles, with economic indicators, tax rates, business forms, and labor environment.

665   Export.gov: helping U.S. companies export. http://export.gov/. United States. International Trade Administration. Washington: International Trade Administration, Dept. of Commerce. 2000–

HF1416.5

U.S. government source for information and assistance on exporting into global markets. Incorporates input from the U.S. Commercial Service, the Export-Import Bank, and the Small Business Administration. Sections address industries, countries, market research, trade events, free trade agreements, international sales and marketing, international financing, international logistics, overseas licenses & regulations, trade data and analysis, and trade problems. Lists U.S. Export Assistance Centers in the U.S. and U.S. Commercial Service offices abroad. Publishes guides to specific countries, such as Doing business in China (358).

666   Harmonized tariff schedule of the United States. http://www.usitc .gov/tata/hts/bychapter/index.htm. U.S. International Trade Commission. Washington: International Trade Commission. [1987–] ISSN 1066-0925

343.73056   KF6654.599

Approximately 5,000 six- to ten-digit product-based numbers arranged into 99 chapters, plus appendixes. The HTS classifies imported merchandise for rate of duty and for statistical purposes and is used by most countries. Three additional statistical annexes are Schedule C, Classification of Country and Territory Designations for U.S. Import Statistics; International Standard Country Codes; and Schedule D, Customs District and Port Codes.

667   ISI emerging markets. http://www .securities.com/. Internet Securities, Inc. New York: Internet Securities, Inc. 2001–

HG5993

EMIS (Emerging Markets Information Service) assembles reports for each country in Latin America and the Caribbean; Central and Southeast Europe; the Middle East, north Africa and sub-Saharan Africa; the Caucasus and Central Asia; and the Asia-Pacific region. Reporting covers general news; business, industry, and company news from sources in English and local languages; and company rankings by sales.

Management

Guides and Handbooks

668 The Blackwell handbook of cross-cultural management. Martin J. Gannon, Karen L. Newman. Oxford, U.K.; Malden, Mass.: Blackwell Business, 2002. xxiii, 509 p., ill. ISBN 9780631214304
658.049   HD62.4

Overview of theory and research findings. Organized into six sections: pt. 1: Frameworks for cross-cultural management; pt. 2: Strategy, structure, and inter-organizational relationships; pt 3: Managing human resources across cultures; pt. 4: Motivation, rewards, and leadership behavior; pt. 5: Interpersonal processes; and pt. 6: Corporate culture and values.

669 Business grammar, style, and usage: A desk reference for articulate and polished business writing and speaking. Alicia Abell. Boston: Aspatore, 2003 ISBN 9781587620263
808.06665   PE1115

General guidelines, rules for grammar and punctuation, guidelines for style, and information on avoiding common mistakes in business writing. Also offers tips for public speaking and effective meetings. Bibliography.

670 Handbook of organizational justice. Jerald Greenberg, Jason Colquitt. Mahwah, N.J.: Lawrence Erlbaum Associates, 2005. xxvi, 647 p., ill. ISBN 9780805842036
658.314   HD6971.3

Provides historical perspective and summary of current research. Articles cover consequences of treatment and justice in the workplace, cross-cultural differences, and the development of organizational justice. Looks at organizational justice from the

perspective of the public's perception of fairness in organizations. Author and subject indexes. Available as an e-book.

671 A primer on organizational behavior. 7th ed. James L. Bowditch, Anthony F. Buono, Marcus M. Stewart. Hoboken, N.J.: Wiley, 2008. xiv, 482 p., ill. ISBN 9780470086957
658.4   HD58.7

Provides an overview of topics and theories in organizational behavior, and serves as an introduction to basic terms and concepts. Covers the impact of management and leadership, attitudes, perception, motivation, communication including electronic communication, technology, and group dynamics including work in teams. Includes bibliographical references and indexes. Updated with new material on emotional intelligence, group dynamics, knowledge management, cultural change in organizations, and virtual teams. Appendixes on research and statistics. Author index. Subject index.

Encyclopedias

672 The Blackwell encyclopedia of management. 2nd ed. Cary L. Cooper, Chris Argyris, William H. Starbuck, Blackwell Publishing Ltd. Malden, Mass.: Blackwell, 2005. 13 v., ill. ISBN 9780631233176
658.003   HD30.15

Over 6,500 alphabetically arranged entries on the theory and practice of management. This 2nd ed. contains 30% new material. Twelve separate volumes deal with accounting, business ethics, entrepreneurship, finance, human resource management, international management, management information systems, managerial economics, marketing, operations management, organizational behavior, and strategic management. Vol. 13 is an index. Available as an e-book.

673 Encyclopedia of business and finance. 2nd ed. Burton S. Kaliski, Macmillan Reference. Detroit, Mich.: Macmillan Reference, 2007. 2 v. ISBN 0028660617
650.03   HF1001

Written for the novice but useful for anyone seeking background information on five key topics: accounting, finance and banking, management, management of information systems, and marketing. The 310 essays include graphs, tables, photographs, and recommended readings. Alphabetically arranged entries range from the history of computing to green marketing and the Sarbanes-Oxley Act. The 3rd ed. is projected for publication in 2014. Available as an e-book.

674 Encyclopedia of leadership. George R. Goethals, Georgia Jones Sorenson, James MacGregor Burns. Thousand Oaks, Calif.: SAGE Publications, 2004. 4 v., xlvi, 1927 p., ill., maps ISBN 9780761925972
658.409203   HD57.7

Contains 400 articles deal with biographical studies, case studies, gender issues, and leadership theories, concepts, and practices. Wide coverage of social science and historical themes. Well written by experts such as Warren Bennis. Four appendixes: bibliography of significant books on leadership, directory of leadership programs, primary sources: presidential speeches on foreign policy and war, and primary sources: sacred texts.

675 The encyclopedia of leadership: A practical guide to popular leadership theories and techniques. Murray Hiebert, Bruce Klatt. New York: McGraw-Hill, 2001. xxxi, 479 p., ill. ISBN 9780071363082
658.4092   HD57.7

Quick reference guide to over 200 business leadership principles, theories, tools, and techniques. Each explanation of a theory or tool is followed by an exercise or worksheet. Leadership concepts are grouped into 15 sections, such as leading change and critical thinking. Cross-references.

676 Encyclopedia of management. 7th ed. Sonya D. Hill. Detroit: Gale, Cengage Learning, 2012. xxx, 1133 p. ISBN 9781414459042
658.003   HD30.15

Covers functional areas such as corporate planning and strategic management, emerging topics in management, entrepreneurship, financial management and accounting, general management, human resources management, innovation and technology, international management, leadership, legal issues, management science and operations, management information systems, performance measures and assessment, personal growth and development for managers, production and operations management, quality management and

total quality management, supply chain management, and training and development. More than 300 essays in alphabetical order, written by academics and business professionals, with cross-references and recommended reading lists. New content reflects trends such as the use of handheld devices for Internet-based tools, social networking, network security, venture capital and entrepreneurship, and business in China. Includes a glossary of terms. Index. Available as an e-book.

677 International encyclopedia of business and management. 2nd ed. Malcolm Warner, John P. Kotter. London: Thomson Learning, 2002. 8 v., xvii, 7160 p., ill. ISBN 9781861521613
650.03   HF101

Contains 750 entries, intended to clarify international management and management education topics for students and faculty in higher education. Interdisciplinary in scope, including concepts from psychology, sociology, mathematics, computer engineering, political science, and economics.

678 Wiley encyclopedia of operations research and management science. James J. Cochran, Louis A. Cox. Hoboken, N.J.: Wiley, 2011. 8 v. (xliii, 6025 p.), ill. ISBN 9780470400630
658.003   T57.6

Covers theories, economics, and mathematics involved in ORMS. Signed articles, with bibliographical references, in alphabetical order. Suitable for researchers and graduate students: the approach is quantitative, with an emphasis on statistical and mathematical methodology. Introductory articles demand less background; advanced articles may include reviews of key research findings; and technical entries explore concepts in greater depth. Also includes case studies, and historical or biographical entries. Covers data mining, game theory, risk analysis, and supply chain management. Index. Available as an e-book.

Periodicals

679 Academy of Management journal. Academy of Management. Briarcliff Manor, N.Y.: Academy of Management, 1957– ISSN 0001-4273
658.05   HD28

Articles on management theory and practice, with empirical research results and theoretical considerations. Occasional thematic special issues. Topics include organizational behavior, human resources, strategy, and organizational theory. Recent articles are indexed on the Academy of Management website (http://www.aomonline.org/).

680 Administrative science quarterly.
Curtis Johnson Graduate School of Management, Cornell University.
Thousand Oaks, Calif.: SAGE, 1956–
ISSN 0001-8392
658.05   HD28
Includes reviews of new books on organizational studies and management. Theoretical and empirical articles from doctoral students and established scholars on organizational studies, including organizational behavior, sociology, psychology, strategic management, economics, public administration, and industrial relations.

681 International abstracts in operations research. International Federation of Operational Research Societies, Operations Research Society of America. Houndmills, Basingstoke, Hampshire, U.K.: Palgrave Press, 1961– ISSN 0020-580X
658.4034   HD20.5
Unique content with abstracts from over 180 journals covering operations and management science. Coverage begins in 1989. Also available as *IAOR Online*.

682 International journal of management reviews. British Academy of Management. Hoboken, N.J.: John Wiley & Sons, Inc., 1999– ISSN 1460-8545
658.0072   HD28
Provides literature surveys and reviews on accounting, entrepreneurship, management, marketing, strategy, and technology management. Issues have 3–4 articles, which range in length from 20 to 30 p.

683 MIT Sloan management review.
Sloan School of Management, Sloan Management Review Association.
Cambridge, Mass.: Sloan Management Review Association, MIT Sloan School of Management, 1998–. ill. ISSN 1532-9194
658.005   HD28

Articles written for business executives on all areas of management, with special attention to corporate strategy, leadership, management of technology, and innovation. Authors are academicians and practitioners. Available in online form: email alerts are available through the journal's web site, as are abstracts of recent articles.

Organizations and Associations

684 American management association.
http://www.amanet.org/. American Management Association. New York: American Management Association. 1997–
Home page for association founded in 1923 to provide "a full range of management development and educational services to individuals, companies and government agencies worldwide, including 486 of the Fortune 500 companies." —*About AMA*. The website has information on seminars, corporate solutions, government solutions, events, books and self-study, e-learning, and membership.

685 Professional ethics and insignia. 2nd ed. John P. Stierman, Jane Clapp. Lanham, Md.: Scarecrow Press, 2000. xii, 445 p., ill. ISBN 9780810836204
061.3   HD6504
An unusual collection of 222 statements for various occupations. Entries include address, telephone number, URL, insignia or emblem, and the full text of the association's code of ethics. In alphabetical order by association name. Index by profession.

Biographies

686 Biographical dictionary of management. Morgen Witzel. Bristol, U.K.: Thoemmes, 2001. 2 v. ISBN 9781855068711
658.00922   HD30.15
Contains 600 entries on leaders and scholars from around the world, who have made major contributions to business from the beginning of civilization to modern times. Written by some 50 international scholars, who note the work, scholarship, and contributions each individual has produced.

687 Encyclopedia of American women in business: from colonial times to the present. Carol Krismann. Westport, Conn.: Greenwood Press, 2005. 2 v., 692 p. ISBN 9780313327575

338.0922   HD6054.4.U6

Contains 327 brief entries on American businesswomen and nearly 100 entries on topics related to their lives, such as affirmative action, child care, and civil rights. Coverage begins in the 18th century. Appendixes for *Fortune* 50 most powerful women in American business, 1998–2003; *Working Woman* top thirty woman-owned businesses, 1997–2001; businesswomen by ethnic group; businesswomen by historical periods; businesswomen by profession; and women in Junior Achievement's national business hall of fame. Good cross-references, bibliography, and index.

688 The encyclopedia of the history of American management. Morgen Witzel. Bristol, U.K.: Thoemmes Continuum, 2005. xvii, 564 p. ISBN 9781843711315

338.092/273   HC102.5.A2

Contains 260 biographical entries, ranging from 600–2,500 words on business leaders and academicians. Entries include "work, writings, ideas, and contribution to the history of management." —*How to use*. Bibliographies are given for each entry. Especially useful for those who do not own *The biographical dictionary of management* (639), from which these entries are culled. Available as an e-book.

Management of Information Systems

Reviews of Research and Trends

689 FACCTS. http://www.faulkner.com/showcase/faccts.htm. Faulkner Information Services. Pennsauken, N.J.: Faulkner Information Services. 1995– ISSN 1082-7471

005   QA76.753

Over 1,200 reports on trends, issues, market conditions, implementation guides, companies, products, and services in information technology. Arranged into 14 categories: enterprise data networking, broadband, information security, electronic government, electronic business, content management, IT asset management, application development, Web site management, converging communications, telecom and global network services, mobile business strategies, wireless communications, and Internet strategies. Especially useful for the up-to-date technology trend reports. Also from this publisher: *Faulkner's advisory for IT studies (FAITS)*.

690 Forrester research. http://www.forrester.com/. Forrester Research. Cambridge, Mass.: Forrester. [1996–]

HF5548.32

Provides commercial-grade reports for paying clients. Nearly 17,000 original reports on technology's effect on business and the consumer in the United States, Canada, Europe, and Asia Pacific. Research is in two categories, technology and industry.

Topics in technology are application development, business intelligence, computing systems, consumer devices and access, content and collaboration, customer experience, enterprise applications, enterprise mobility, IT management, IT services, networking, portals and site technology, security, software infrastructure, and tech sector economics.

Topics in industry are brand strategy, brand tactics, consumer electronics, consumer products, customer insight, emerging marketing channels, energy and utilities, financial services, government, healthcare and life sciences, high tech, industry insight, manufacturing, marketing and advertising, marketing planning, media and entertainment, mobile services, professional services, relationship marketing, retail, telecommunications, television advertising, transportation and logistics, and travel.

Reports typically range from 3–20 pages, and some are available as videos.

691 Gartneradvisory intraweb. http://www.gartner.com/. Gartner Group. [Stamford, Conn.]: Gartner Group. 2000–

The database consists of content from Gartner Research and Advisory Services, Datapro, and Dataquest Research. Especially useful for reports that discuss strategy within the IT industry. Also has company profiles, trends, developments, and product reports.

692 Information systems: the state of the field. John Leslie King, Kalle Lyytinen.

Hoboken, N.J.: Wiley, 2006
ISBN 9780470017777
658.4038011   T58.6

Examines the evolution of the information systems discipline. The 11 essays and eight commentaries are well grounded, combining information from 30 yr. of literature from the field and the expertise of the authors. Available as an e-book.

Indexes; Abstract Journals

693 ACM Digital Library. http://dl.acm .org/dl.cfm. Association for Computing Machinery. New York: Association for Computing Machinery. 1998–

QA76

Provides free bibliographic access to the computing literature of the ACM (Association for Computing Machinery) and more than 6,000 other publishers. Contains more than 1,600,000 records describing books, journal articles, conference proceedings, doctoral dissertations, master's theses, and technical reports. Free access allows for use of the basic search and browse functions of the guide. Use of the advanced search function is restricted to ACM professionals, students, and Special Interest Group members. Subscribers to the ACM Digital Library also have access to the full text of the literature the ACM. Users can limit searches to full text content. Author Profiles are a welcome addition to the product with Institutional Profiles under development (beta). Includes a digital copy of the Encyclopedia of Computer Science, 4th edition by Ralston et al.

Formerly, the ACM Guide to Computing Literature and the ACM portal: The ACM Digital Library were separate products.

694 Internet and personal computing abstracts. http://www.ebscohost.com/ public/internet-personal-computing -abstracts. Ipswich, Mass.: EBSCO. 1980–
ISSN 1529-7705
016.00416   QA75.5

Abstracts and indexing for 400 trade journals, magazines, and a small number of journals. Titles include *CIO, Information resources management journal, IT professional, Linux journal, PC world, Social science computer review, Technology review,* and *Wired.* Coverage from 1980s to present. Includes product and vendor guides, software and hardware reviews, and developments in business and industry, education, and personal computing. Not all periodicals are indexed fully. Formerly *Microcomputer index* and *Microcomputer abstracts.*

695 Quality control and applied statistics. Executive Sciences Institute. Whippany, N.J.: ESI Publications, 1956–
ISSN 0033-5207
658.562015195   TS156.A1

Indexes and abstracts for selected articles. Useful for finding articles on quality management, risk and uncertainty, industrial management, computing, and information systems. International coverage.

Encyclopedias

696 Encyclopedia of business and finance. 2nd ed. Burton S. Kaliski, Macmillan Reference. Detroit, Mich.: Macmillan Reference, 2007. 2 v. ISBN 0028660617
650.03   HF1001

Written for the novice but useful for anyone seeking background information on five key topics: accounting, finance and banking, management, management of information systems, and marketing. The 310 essays include graphs, tables, photographs, and recommended readings. Alphabetically arranged entries range from the history of computing to green marketing and the Sarbanes-Oxley Act. The 3rd ed. is projected for publication in 2014. Available as an e-book.

697 Encyclopedia of information systems. Hossein Bidgoli. Amsterdam, The Netherlands; Boston: Academic Press, 2003. 4 v., ill. ISBN 9780122272400
004.03   QA76.15

Contains 200 peer-reviewed articles and 2,000 glossary entries on applications, artificial intelligence, data communications, database design and utilization, hardware and software, international issues, management support systems, office automation and end–user computing, social, legal, and organizational issues, systems analysis and design, and theories, methodologies, and foundations. Articles include an overview of the topic and further reading. Available as an e-book.

698 Encyclopedia of management.
7th ed. Sonya D. Hill. Detroit: Gale,
Cengage Learning, 2012. xxx, 1133 p.
ISBN 9781414459042
658.003   HD30.15

Covers functional areas such as corporate planning and strategic management, emerging topics in management, entrepreneurship, financial management and accounting, general management, human resources management, innovation and technology, international management, leadership, legal issues, management science and operations, management information systems, performance measures and assessment, personal growth and development for managers, production and operations management, quality management and total quality management, supply chain management, and training and development. More than 300 essays in alphabetical order, written by academics and business professionals, with cross-references and recommended reading lists. New content reflects trends such as the use of handheld devices for Internet-based tools, social networking, network security, venture capital and entrepreneurship, and business in China. Includes a glossary of terms. Index. Available as an e-book.

Dictionaries

**699 The call center dictionary: The complete
guide to call center and customer support
technology solutions. Rev. ed.** Madeline
Bodin, Keith Dawson. New York: CMP Books,
2002. 227 p., ill. ISBN 9781578200955
658.812   HF5548.2

Over 1,200 entries that explain the technology involved, and how the technology affects service. Includes some images. Available as an e-book.

Periodicals

700 AI magazine. American Association
for Artificial Intelligence. Palo Alto,
Calif.: American Association for Artificial
Intelligence, 1980–. ill. ISSN 0738-4602
001.53/5/05   Q334

Intended to provide current research and literature on artificial intelligence, this quarterly publication has book reviews, news, reports from conferences, articles, a calendar of events, and a regular column called

"AI in the News." Includes coverage of informatics, robotics, automation, innovation, and human cognition. Available in online form through aggregators.

**701 European journal of information
systems: An official journal of
the Operational Research Society.**
Operational Research Society. Houndmills,
Basingstoke, Hants, U.K.: Palgrave-
Macmillan, 1991–. ill. ISSN 0960-085X
658.4038011   T58.5

Articles, case studies, and book reviews on information systems from a European perspective. Some content is available for free at the publisher's website (http://www.palgrave-journals.com/ejis/index.html). The journal has a high impact factor and focuses on "technology, development, implementation, strategy, management and policy."—*About the journal*

702 Technology review. http://www
.technologyreview.com/. Massachusetts
Institute of Technology, MIT Alumni/
ae Association. Cambridge, Mass.:
Association of Alumni and Alumnae of
the Massachusetts Institute of Technology.
1998– ISSN 1099-274X
620   T171

Bimonthly periodical covering trends and developments in business technology, especially impact on the energy, nanotech, biotech, and infotech industries. Includes annual list of the top emerging technologies. For many years, it included an annual R&D Scorecard, published each fall, which now is useful for tracking historical research and development expenditures. Provides lists of innovators and entrepreneurs. Formerly *MIT's Technology Review* (1899–1997).

Marketing, Advertising, and Public Relations

Guides and Handbooks

**703 Advertising organizations and
publications: A resource guide.** John
Philip Jones. Thousand Oaks, Calif.:
SAGE Publications, 2000. xviii, 346 p., ill.
ISBN 9780761912361
659.1   HF5813.U6

Profiles 77 advertising and marketing communications organizations and publications, describing purpose and contact information. Primary focus is the U.S. Available as an e-book.

704 Exporters' encyclopaedia. Dun's Marketing Services. New York: Dun and Bradstreet International, 1982–2009. maps ISSN 8755-013X
382.602573 HF3011

Ceased in 2009. Comprehensive world marketing guide for 220 world markets. Designed as a guide to possible markets and also as an instructional manual for some practicalities (e.g. shipping and insurance). Country profiles include communications, key contracts, trade regulations, documentation, marketing data, transportation, and business travel. Other sections cover U.S. ports, U.S. foreign trade zones, World Trade Center Association members, U.S. government agencies providing assistance to exporters, foreign trade organizations, foreign communications, and general export and shipping information.

705 Handbook of marketing. Barton A. Weitz, Robin Wensley. London; Thousand Oaks, Calif.: SAGE, 2002. xix, 582 p., ill. ISBN 9780761956822
658.8 HF5415

Synthesizes the body of research relating to: the role of marketing in society, the history of research about marketing as a discipline, the role of marketing in the firm, marketing strategy, marketing activities, and marketing management. Includes chapters examining important special topics (e.g., global marketing, marketing in business markets, services marketing, the impact of the Internet on marketing). Written for graduate students in marketing. Available as an e-book.

706 Handbook of marketing scales: multi-item measures for marketing and consumer behavior research. 3rd ed. Richard G. Netemeyer, Kelly L. Haws, William O. Bearden. Los Angeles: SAGE, 2011. xiv, 603 p. ISBN 9781412980180
658.8/3 HF5415.3

Presents more than 150 marketing and consumer behavior scales with definitions, background on the scale's development, relevance to marketing, estimates of reliability and validity, and references to the scale in scholarly literature. Seventy scales are new since the second edition of 1999. Scales are grouped in chapters that deal with traits and individual difference variables; values and goals; involvement, information processing, and affect; reactions to marketing stimuli; attitudes about the performance of business firms, satisfaction and post-purchase behavior, social agencies, and the marketplace; and sales, sales management, organizational behavior, and inter-firm and intra-firm issues. Each entry speaks to construct, description, development, samples, validity and scores, and points to sources and references. Index. Available as an e-book.

707 Handbook of relationship marketing. Jagdish N. Sheth, Atul Parvatiyar. Thousand Oaks, Calif.: SAGE Publications, 2000. xvi, 660 p., ill. ISBN 9780761918103
658.8 HF5415.55

Collection of scholarly articles serves as a handbook on relationship marketing, so named because of its focus on the relationship between buyers, sellers, suppliers, and other key players in the marketing process. Since there are few textbooks solely on relationship marketing, this handbook serves as a core resource on the underlying theory and development of this subdiscipline. Each chapter contains extensive references making this a rich bibliographic resource on this topic. Thorough index enhances this work's value as a reference tool.

708 Handbook of services marketing and management. Teresa A. Swartz, Dawn Iacobucci. Thousand Oaks, Calif.: SAGE Publications, 2000. ix, 521 p., ill. ISBN 9780761916116
658 HD9980.5

Anthology introduces services marketing. This unique handbook meets the need for a comprehensive source providing theoretical and practical information on topics relating to the service economy. Useful to upper-level students, researchers, and managers in a myriad of service industries.

709 Marketing information: a strategic guide for business and finance libraries. Wendy Diamond, Michael R. Oppenheim. Binghamton, N.Y.: Haworth Information Press, 2004. xxvi, 342 p. ISBN 9780789021120
658.83 HF5415.2

Information about sources to use in marketing research. Use to discover where to look for: industry scans; companies, brands, and competitors; market research reports; demographic, geographic, and lifestyle sources; demographic niches; advertising and media planning; public relations; sales management, sales promotion, and retail; direct marketing and e-commerce; international marketing; product development, packaging, pricing, and place; social marketing; nonprofit organizations; services marketing; and legal/ethical issues. Available as an e-book.

710   Marketing metrics: the definitive guide to measuring marketing performance. 2nd ed. Paul W. Farris, Neil T. Bendle, Phillip E. Pfeifer, David J. Reibstein. Upper Saddle River, N.J.: FT Press, 2010. xv, 414 p., ill.
ISBN 9780137058297
658.8/3   HF5415.2
Particularly well-written guide to marketing metrics, from metrics for promotional strategy, advertising, customer perceptions and loyalty, market share, competitors' power, products, to metrics for portfolios, channels, and pricing strategies. A good source for definitions of metrics, such as share of wallet, as well as for coverage of why, when, and how to employ a metric. Updated since the first edition of 2006 with more information about social media and digital marketing. Available as an e-book.

711   Marketing scales handbook: a compilation of multi-item measures. Gordon C. Bruner, Paul J. Hensel, Karen E. James. Chicago: American Marketing Association, 1992–2013. 7 v.
ISBN 0877572267
658.83028   HF5415.3
Covers more than 2,000 multi-item measurement scales taken from seven leading marketing journals. Volumes include scales published in different years (1980–1989, 1990–1993, 1994–1997, 1998–2001, 2002–2005, 2006–2009, and 2010–2011). Describes origin of the scale, how the scale was measured, past results, psychometric characteristics, and possible research use. Volumes 6 and 7 have been published by GCBII Productions, in a downloadable online format. Gordon C. Bruner has also published *Marketing scales handbook: The top 20 multi-item measures used in consumer research* (2013).

712   The international handbook of market research techniques. 2nd ed. Robin Birn, Market Research Society. London: Kogan Page in association with MRS, 2002. xxvi, 594 p., ill. ISBN 9780749438654
658.83   HF5415.2
Essays on preparation, data collection, communications, advertising and media, analysis, and presentation of results. Intended for practitioners and students.

Reviews of Research and Trends

713   The bibliography of marketing research methods. 3rd ed. John R. Dickinson, Marketing Science Institute. Lexington, Mass.: Lexington Books, 1990. xi, 1025 p. ISBN 9780669216974
016.65883   Z7164.M18; HF5415.2
Contains 14,000 entries on market research, data collection, and data analysis drawn from marketing journals, handbooks, and conference proceedings, and from related disciplines. Entries are grouped by subject. Not annotated. Author and subject indexes.

714   Essential readings in marketing. Leigh McAlister, Ruth N. Bolton, Ross Rizley, Marketing Science Institute. Cambridge, Mass.: Marketing Science Institute, 2006. 196 p. ISBN 9780965711456
016.6588   HF5415
Abstracts of research articles in various areas of marketing, with brief essays at the beginning of each chapter explaining the topic. Chapters include: New products, growth, and innovation; Branding and brand equity; Metrics linking marketing to financial performance; Managing relationships with customers and organizations; The role of marketing; Research tools; Marketing mix; Customer insight; and Strategy. Supplemented in 2010 by *Essential readings in marketing: new advances in 2006–2010*.

Indexes; Abstract Journals

715   The bibliography of marketing research methods. 3rd ed. John R. Dickinson, Marketing Science Institute. Lexington, Mass.: Lexington Books, 1990. xi, 1025 p. ISBN 9780669216974
016.65883   Z7164.M18; HF5415.2

Contains 14,000 entries on market research, data collection, and data analysis drawn from marketing journals, handbooks, and conference proceedings, and from related disciplines. Entries are grouped by subject. Not annotated. Author and subject indexes.

716   Essential readings in marketing. Leigh McAlister, Ruth N. Bolton, Ross Rizley, Marketing Science Institute. Cambridge, Mass.: Marketing Science Institute, 2006. 196 p. ISBN 9780965711456
016.6588   HF5415

Abstracts of research articles in various areas of marketing, with brief essays at the beginning of each chapter explaining the topic. Chapters include: New products, growth, and innovation; Branding and brand equity; Metrics linking marketing to financial performance; Managing relationships with customers and organizations; The role of marketing; Research tools; Marketing mix; Customer insight; and Strategy. Supplemented in 2010 by *Essential readings in marketing: new advances in 2006–2010.*

Encyclopedias

717   The Advertising Age encyclopedia of advertising. John McDonough, Karen Egolf, Museum of Broadcast Communications. New York: Fitzroy Dearborn, 2003. 3 v., xxiii, 1873 p., 72 p. of plates, ill. ISBN 9781579581725
659.103   HF5803

The first comprehensive reference work on the history of advertising. A collaborative effort undertaken by Advertising Age (the profession's most important trade publication), the Museum of Broadcast Communications, and Duke University's Hartman Center for Sales, Advertising, and Marketing History. Profiles more than 120 advertising agencies, over 160 major advertisers, brands, and campaigns, and the lives of almost 50 prominent men and women. Includes thematic essays covering advertising theory, strategy, and practice (e.g., market research, psychographics, demographics, ethics, sex in advertising). Inclusion of more than 500 illustrations (including color reproductions of ads) makes this a visually appealing and fun resource. Exhaustive index and useful appendixes, including those providing chronological listings of top agencies and top advertisers.

718   All–American ads: 1900–1919. Jim Heimann. Koln, Germany; Los Angeles: Taschen, 2005. 638 p. ISBN 9783822825129
741.67097309041   HF5813.U6

The first in a series presenting reproductions of print advertising in the U.S. Each subsequent volume in the series covers a different decade: available volumes now cover every decade from the 1920s through the 1980s. Consumer market sectors include tobacco, automobiles, entertainment, fashion, beauty products, food and beverages, and travel.

719   Encyclopedia of business and finance. 2nd ed. Burton S. Kaliski, Macmillan Reference. Detroit, Mich.: Macmillan Reference, 2007. 2 v. ISBN 0028660617
650.03   HF1001

Written for the novice but useful for anyone seeking background information on five key topics: accounting, finance and banking, management, management of information systems, and marketing. The 310 essays include graphs, tables, photographs, and recommended readings. Alphabetically arranged entries range from the history of computing to green marketing and the Sarbanes-Oxley Act. The 3rd ed. is projected for publication in 2014. Available as an e-book.

720   Encyclopedia of major marketing campaigns. 2nd ed. Thomas Riggs. Detroit: Gale Group, 2006. xxii, 2063 p., ill. ISBN 9780787673567
659.1/0973   HF5837

Covers nearly 500 major campaigns from 1999–2005, in entries devoted to specific major companies. In 2–5 pages, gives an overview and historic context, information about the target market, expected outcomes, competition, marketing strategy and development hurdles, and the outcome of the campaign. Includes references to pertinent articles. Useful for learning why a campaign did, or did not, work. Arranged alphabetically by company name. The 1st ed. covered 500 major campaigns from the 20th century. Available as an e-book. Extended in 2013 by the related title *Encyclopedia of major marketing strategies.*

721   Encyclopedia of public relations. 2nd ed. Robert Lawrence Heath. Thousand Oaks, Calif.: SAGE Publ., 2013. 2 v. ISBN 9781452240794
659.203   HD59

Addresses topics in business, communications and journalism. Updated since the first edition of 2005 to reflect the role of the Internet and social media, greater attention to global trends, and the history of women in the field. Extensive themes include activism, advertising campaigns, blogs, branding and images, new technologies as a factor, social responsibility, ethics, crisis management, disclosure, fundraising, non-profit organizations, propaganda, opinion polls, government regulations, and the various print and broadcast media. Biographical content has been reduced. Signed entries in alphabetical order, with suggestions for further reading. Index. Available as an e-book.

722   The IEBM encyclopedia of marketing.
Michael John Baker. London: International Thomson Business, 1999. xiii, 865 p., ill.
ISBN 9781861523044
658.003   HF5415
Contains 63 articles by world renowned marketing experts like Philip Kotler, Gordon Foxall, and John O'Shaughnessy provide thorough explanations of selected marketing theories, techniques, and practices. Index.

723   The international encyclopedia of marketing. Michael Thomas, Stanley J. Paliwoda, European Marketing Confederation, NIMA (Organization). Oxford: Butterworth-Heinemann, 1997. 372 p., ill. ISBN 9780750635011
658.8/003   HF5415
Intended for practitioners. Mainly a European focus, but with terms and topics that apply internationally. Divided into 19 sections that cover the range of marketing areas (marketing research, business to business marketing, services marketing, retail marketing, etc.). References and index.

724   Wiley international encyclopedia of marketing. Jagdish N. Sheth, Naresh K. Malhotra. Chichester, West Sussex, U.K.: Wiley, 2011. 7 v., ill.
ISBN 9781405161787
658.8003   HF5415
Offers some 360 articles written by more than 500 contributing experts. Entries can be shorter summaries, or longer essays with extensive lists of references. Six individual volumes bring together content about marketing strategy, marketing research, consumer

behavior, advertising and integrated communication, product innovation and management, and international marketing; a seventh volume contains a cumulative index to the entire set, and contributor information. Attention is paid to current trends, such as globalization, the rise of Asian markets, and the impact of social media and the Internet. Also available as an e-book.

Dictionaries

725   Advertising slogans of America.
Harold S. Sharp. Metuchen, N.J.: Scarecrow Press, 1984. xi, 543 p.
ISBN 9780810816817
659.1322   HF6135
Fifteen thousand slogans used by 6,000 companies and organizations. Slogans, organizations, and products appear alphabetically.

726   The dictionary of marketing. Rona Ostrow, Sweetman R. Smith. New York: Fairchild Publications, 1988. 258 p., ill.
ISBN 9780870055737
380.10321   HF5415
Some 3,000 non-technical definitions, with etymologies, charts, graphs, and cross references.

727   Dictionary of marketing communications. Norman A. Govoni. Thousand Oaks, Calif.: SAGE, 2004. 249 p. ISBN 9780761927709
380.103   HF5412
Some 4,000 definitions of advertising, sales promotion, public relations, direct marketing, and e-marketing terms and concepts. Written by a business professor prompted by the needs of students in his marketing classes. Available as an e-book.

728   Dictionary of social and market research. Wolfgang J. Koschnick. Hampshire, U.K.; Brookfield, Vt.: Gower, 1996. 416 p., ill. ISBN 9780566076114
658.8303   HF5415.2
Contains 2,500 entries used to answer questions for students and practitioners as they conduct social and market research. Entries range from a brief sentence to two pages long, giving formulas, graphs, and explanations, rather than limiting all entries to terse definitions.

**729   Marketing: the encyclopedic
dictionary.** David Mercer. Oxford, U.K.;
Malden, Mass.: Blackwell, 1999. 422 p.,
ill. ISBN 9780631191070
658.8003   HF5412

Intended for practitioners, but useful for undergraduate and MBA students. Contains definitions for thousands of marketing terms, as well as longer discussions of topics. No index, but good cross-references.

730   Trade name origins. Adrian Room.
Lincolnwood, Ill.: NTC Pub. Group,
1997. 217 p. ISBN 9780844209043
929.9503   T324

A witty examination of the origin of some 700 well-known trade names, with an analysis of the process of choosing a new trade name. Prior editions had titles *Dictionary of trade name origins* and *NTC's dictionary of trade name origins*.

Periodicals

731   Advertising age. Advertising
Publications, Crain Communications Inc.
New York: Crain Communications, 1930–.
ill. ISSN 0001-8899
659.105   HF5801

Essential weekly trade publication tracking news and trends in advertising, marketing, brand management, and sales promotion, published also online. Articles on advertising campaigns often provide unique market share data. In addition to providing current industry news, this weekly is a rich source of statistical data, as it often includes reports on special markets. There are also special reports on leading marketers, technology, top agencies, and award winning campaigns. Partially available online at http://adage.com/ and available online through aggregators. Now also tracks blogs, and links to an online job-seeking service. Sometimes refered to as "Ad Age."

732   American demographics. American
Demographics, Inc., Dow Jones & Co.
Stamford, Conn.: Cowles Business Media,
1979–2004. ill. ISBN 01634089
301.32973   HB3505

This trade periodical has been an indispensable source for demographic and consumer trends, and corresponding market niches for products and services.

Issues often contain articles that do an excellent job of analyzing census data, especially for business implications. Ceased with 2004, but useful for finding historical information. Similar content has since appeared as a section within Advertising age (731).

733   JMR: Journal of marketing research.
American Marketing Association. Chicago:
American Marketing Association, 1964–.
ill. ISSN 0022-2437
658.8305   HF5415.2

As the title indicates, articles are on marketing research. The intended audience is technically oriented research analysts, educators, and statisticians. Available in online form. A regular "New books in review" column provides 1–3 book reviews in each issue, with texts of reviews freely available on the journal's website. Also available on the website are tables of contents back to 2002.

734   Journal of marketing. American
Marketing Association, American Marketing
Society, National Association of Marketing
Teachers. Chicago: American Marketing
Association, 1936–. ill. ISSN 0022-2429
658.8005   HF5415.A2

One of the top marketing journals, self-identified as being closely aligned with management practices. International in scope, with a focus on marketing practice and theory. Regular book reviews. Intended audience is marketing managers, consumers, or public policy makers. Tables of contents are available through the journal's website back to 2002. Also available online through aggregators.

**735   The journal of product innovation
management.** Product Development and
Management Association. Hoboken, N.J.:
John Wiley & Sons, 1984–. ill.
ISSN 0737-6782
658.57505   HF5415.153.J68

Articles on product innovation, development, and marketing. Occasional thematic issues on topics such as corporate entrepreneurship. Some issues review up to four books, with reviews ranging 2–3 pages in length. Available to PDMA members, and by subscription in print and online formats.

**736   Journal of the Academy of Marketing
Science.** Academy of Marketing Science.

Amsterdam, The Netherlands: Springer, 1973– ISSN 0092-0703

658.8005   HF5415

Articles, book and software reviews, and reports on legal decisions and regulatory actions affecting marketing internationally. Annual index in the last issue of each volume.

Directories

737 The advertising red books. LexisNexis. New Providence, N.J.: LexisNexis, 2003–

659.1125   HF5805

Covers 9,000 worldwide agency parent companies, 4,400 U.S. publicly traded companies, the top 2,000 global companies, and the 300 largest U.S. private companies. Use to find information on both advertisers and agencies, in separate volumes. Index and geographic index. Data for agencies includes contact information, year founded, number of employees, gross billings by media, NAICS and SIC codes, names of key personnel, and names of accounts. For advertisers, information includes contact information, year founded, number of employees, NAICS and SIC codes, month budget is set, media expenditures, and brands. Where possible, the name and email address for the Marketing Director for the advertiser is included. Available in online format.

738 The adweek directory. ASM Communications. New York: ASM Communications, 1998–2012 ISSN 1528-3291

659   HF6182.U5

Listing of ad agencies, public relations firms, media buying services, and specialized marketing companies. Entries include contact information, U.S. affiliates/branch offices, services offered, fields served, employees, year founded, key personnel, and major accounts. Also ranks agencies nationally and regionally, with revenue and percentage change from prior year, billings and percentage change from prior year. Ceased with 2012.

739 Brands and their companies. Donna J. Wood, Susan L. Stetler. Detroit: Gale Research, 1990– ISSN 1047-6407

602.75   T223.V4

Not sure what company is responsible for Night Owl? Don't even know what type of product it is? This

is the source for answers. Alphabetically lists brand names, even for discontinued brands, and then lists the manufacturer or distributor. Covers some U.S. 400,000 products and over 100,000 manufacturers. Brand names supplied by companies or found in print resources. Occasionally used by researchers interested in trademarks. Companion to *Companies and their brands* (741). Available as an e-book.

740 The brandweek directory. ASM Communications. New York: ASM Communications, 1998–2011. ill. ISSN 1530-616X

338.761659102573   HF6182.U5

Lists the top 2,000 brands by media spending, with contact information, ultimate parent organization, product/service category, media expenditures, lead advertising agency, additional agencies, and key personnel. Also provides the complete list of "superbrands" by industry category. Ceased with 2011.

741 Companies and their brands. Donna J. Wood. Detroit: Gale Research, 1990– ISSN 1047-6393

602.75   T223.V4

Alphabetical list of companies and the brand names attributed to them. Each entry is followed by the firm's address, telephone number, and list of trade names. Information is collected from print sources and from the individual companies. Companion to *Brands and their companies* (739).

742 The Direct marketing market place: the networking source of the direct marketing industry. National Register Publishing. Berkeley Heights, N.J.: National Register Publishing/Marquis Who's Who LLC, 1980– ISSN 0192-3137

381   HF5415.1

A source similar in purpose and format to *Literary market place* for the direct marketing field. Classified sections list 8,700 direct marketers of products and services (principally through mail order catalogs), service firms and suppliers, creative and consulting services, associations and events, awards, etc. Primarily U.S. listings, with a chapter on Canadian and foreign firms. Gives names, addresses, and telephone numbers for companies and individuals, number of employees, advertising budget related to direct marketing, and gross sales or billing. Also provides an overview of advertising expenditures by medium and market for four yr., with a forecast for future expenditures. Indexes of individuals and companies. Some issues have title: *Direct marketing marketplace.*

743 Editor and Publisher market guide.
The Editor and Publisher Company. New York: The Editor and Publisher, 1924–2010. maps, tables ISSN 0362-1200
658.8   PN4700

Individual market surveys of nearly 1,400 U.S. and Canadian cities where a daily newspaper is published. Arranged by state and city, with data in 16 categories such as population, households, climate, principal industries, military installations, and newspapers. Includes U.S. retail census data. *Better Living Index* ranks cities by cost of living, crime data, and education statistics. Ceased with 2010.

744 Green book. American Marketing Association. New York: New York Chapter, American Marketing Assoc., 1973–. ill.
ISSN 8756-534X
658.83025   HF5415.2

Useful for locating market research companies in the U.S. and abroad. V. 1 covers market research companies and services; v. 2 covers focus group companies, facilities, and services. *Green book* also publishes an online directory at http://www.greenbook.org/ with access to about 400 companies drawn from those in the print volumes. The print directory provides information on approximately 2,300 companies. Formerly *International directory of marketing research houses and services.*

745 Internet resources and services for international marketing and advertising: a global guide. James R. Coyle. Westport, Conn.: Oryx Press, 2002. xiii, 352 p. ISBN 9781573564076
658.848   HF1416

More than 2,000 commercial, organizational, and academic web sites (including e-journals) relating to marketing and advertising for more than 150 countries and regions, selected by a marketing and advertising professor at a leading U.S. business school. Priority is given to English-language sites that are free or that provide substantive free information in part. Strengths of this resource are rigor in identifying sites for inclusion, broad coverage, and availability

of multiple indexes by site title, Web site sponsor, country, and subject.

746 O'Dwyer's directory of public relations firms. J.R. O'Dwyer Co. New York: J.R. O'Dwyer, 1969–
ISSN 0078-3374
338.761659202573   HM263

Lists almost 3,000 U.S. and international public relations firms and public relations departments of advertising agencies. Entries generally include contact information, an indication of specialties, date founded, number of employees, list of major clients, name of the president/director, and list of other key staff. Multiple access points include a geographical index, a specialties index, and a cross-index to client companies of firms profiled. Rankings in this directory (such as ranking firms by net fees) are a popular feature.

747 SRDS business media advertising source. Standard Rate & Data Service. Des Plaines, Ill.: SRDS, 2009–
ISSN 2162-0202
659.13205   HF5905

Annual. Successor to SRDS business publication advertising source (748). Looks at 190 media markets, providing advertising rates, and contact information. Also available in online format.

748 SRDS business publication advertising source. Standard Rate and Data Service. Des Plaines, Ill.: SRDS, 1995–2009
ISSN 1529-6490
659   HF5905

Provides advertising rates for 9,000 trade publications, listed in 220 subject areas. Publication entries give total circulation; publisher's positioning statement; contact information; commission and cash discount; general rate policy; black/white rates; color rates; rates for covers and inserts; bleed information; special advertising positions; and classified, mail order, and specialty rates. Ceased with 2009, and succeeded by SRDS business media advertising source (747).

749 SRDS consumer magazine advertising source. Standard Rate and Data Service. Des Plaines, Ill.: SRDS, 1995–2009. ill.
ISSN 1086-8208
659.102573   HF5905

Lists 2,900 magazines, organized by interest (affluence, teen, gaming). Entries give publication frequency, contact information, editorial profile, executives, commission and cash discount, advertising rates, billed, special position, classified/mail order/specialty rates, special issue rates, general requirements, issue and closing dates, and circulation. Use for planning advertising costs and timing. Ceased with 2009, and succeeded by SRDS consumer media advertising source (750).

750 **SRDS consumer media advertising source.** Standard Rate & Data Service. Des Plains, Ill.: SRDS, 2009–
ISSN 2154-6401
659.1/025/73   HF5905

Annual. Successor to SRDS consumer magazine advertising source (749) with coverage expanded from print periodicals to include websites and direct marketing. Identifies some 2,800 listings for print media, 39,000 direct marketing lists, and over 700 media brands. Available online. Includes advertising rates and contact information.

751 **World directory of business information sources. 2nd ed.** Euromonitor. London: Euromonitor International Ltd., 2010. 2 v. (ccxxxviii, 1500 p.) ISBN 9781842645284
HF54.5

Identifies 22,000 publications and organizations, and covers information from 82 countries. Particularly strong on sources for tracking consumer goods, including market research, economic indicators, and specific products. Volume 1 lists professional associations, organizations, and similar groups, with contact information and some indication of their publications. Volume 2 lists publications, databases and websites. Replaces five previously published directories: *World directory of marketing information sources*; *World directory of business information websites*; *World directory of trade and business associations*; *World directory of trade and business journals*; and *World directory of business information libraries*. Detailed table of contents. Index.

Biographies

752 **The Ad men and women: A biographical dictionary of advertising.** Edd Applegate. Westport, Conn.:

Greenwood Press, 1994. xvii, 401 p.
ISBN 9780313278013
659.1092273   HF5810.A2

Provides difficult-to-find information on copywriters, art directors, and others. Biographical essays on more than 50 individuals who played a prominent role in advertising in 19th and 20th century America. Bibliographies accompanying entries are particularly rich sources of information, listing works by the individual, works about the individual, and notable clients and campaigns.

753 **Entrepreneurs, the men and women behind famous brand names and how they made it.** Joseph J. Fucini, Suzy Fucini. Boston: G.K. Hall, 1985. xviii, 297 p., ill., ports. ISBN 9780816187089
338.040922   HC29

Burpee's seeds, Gillette razors, Jacuzzi spas, Calvin Klein jeans, Phillip's Milk of Magnesia, and Reynold's Wrap are among 225 products bearing the names of their founders. Chronicles the history of these products and the individuals behind them. While some of these entrepreneurs have been forgotten, their stories remain fascinating reading. Provides substantive 3-4 p. biographical profiles for 50 individuals, and shorter biographical entries for 175 men and women. Well researched and includes an extensive bibliography.

754 **Made in America: the true stories behind the brand names that built a nation. Berkley ed.** John Gove. New York: Berkley Books, 2001. xiii, 303 p., ill., ports. ISBN 9780425178836
338.7092273   HC102.5.A2

Chef Boyardee, Dinty Moore, Uncle Ben's, and Welch's are all recognizable brand names, but few of us know the history behind these products. This engaging compendium brings together 74 biographical sketches (from 2 to 8 p. in length) of the individuals behind familiar brand names. A useful bibliography rounds out this compact work.

755 **So who the heck was Oscar Mayer?.** Doug Gelbert. New York: Barricade Books, 1996. 400 p., ill. ISBN 9781569800829
338.0092273B   HC102.5.A2

Gelbert reveals the person and story behind 200 well-known brand names such as Armour, Bacardi,

Marshall Field and Harley-Davidson. Brief biographical sketches (averaging one to two pages in length) are cleverly categorized under themes such as "In the Kitchen," "From the Bottle," "In the Closet," and "At the Game." Not only fun to read but thoroughly researched.

Statistics

756   Ad$pender. http://kantarmediana.com/intelligence/products/adspender. Kantar Media (Firm). London: Kantar Media. 2004–

HF5805

Adspender tracks spending on advertising for over three million brands, in a wide range of media: television (including network, Spanish-language network, cable, syndicated, and spot markets), radio (including network, national spot, and local markets), local and national magazines and newspapers, online ads, and outdoor displays. Top spenders are ranked by industry, brand, and parent company. Data time series covers up to 10 years.

757   Ad $ summary. TNS Media Intelligence, Media Watch, Competitive Media Reporting, Leading National Advertisers. New York: TNS Media Intelligence, 1973–. ill. ISSN 0190-7166

659   HF5801

Information on brands that spend over $250,000 annually in advertising; especially useful for finding information on the types of media spending on a brand. Ranks companies by media spending. Data found here are often used to calculate share of voice. Reports expenditures in various types of media: magazines, Sunday magazines, newspapers, national newspapers, network television, spot television, syndicated television, cable television, network radio, national spot radio, and outdoor. Known also as LNA (Leading National Advertisers) or CMR (after a previous publisher).

758   Advertising age. Advertising Publications, Crain Communications Inc. New York: Crain Communications, 1930–. ill. ISSN 0001-8899

659.105   HF5801

Essential weekly trade publication tracking news and trends in advertising, marketing, brand management, and sales promotion, published also online. Articles on advertising campaigns often provide unique market share data. In addition to providing current industry news, this weekly is a rich source of statistical data, as it often includes reports on special markets. There are also special reports on leading marketers, technology, top agencies, and award winning campaigns. Partially available online at http://adage.com/ and available online through aggregators. Now also tracks blogs, and links to an online job-seeking service. Sometimes refered to as "Ad Age."

759   Advertising ratios and budgets. Schonfeld and Associates. Lincolnshire, Ill.: Schonfeld and Associates, 1976–. v.

HF5801

Annual. Information for one year of advertising budgets for thousands of companies in hundreds of industries. Organized by SIC. Ratios include ad-to-sales and ad-to-gross margin. Also provides budget forecasts and growth rates. Useful for comparing ad spending, as well as for estimating advertising budgets.

760   The adweek directory. ASM Communications. New York: ASM Communications, 1998–2012 ISSN 1528-3291

659   HF6182.U5

Listing of ad agencies, public relations firms, media buying services, and specialized marketing companies. Entries include contact information, U.S. affiliates/branch offices, services offered, fields served, employees, year founded, key personnel, and major accounts. Also ranks agencies nationally and regionally, with revenue and percentage change from prior year, billings and percentage change from prior year. Ceased with 2012.

761   Best customers: demographics of consumer demand. 9th ed. New Strategist Publ. Amityville, N.Y.: New Strategist Publ., 2012. 795 p., ill. ISBN 9781937737108

339.470973   HC110.C6

Based on unpublished data from the Bureau of Labor Statistics' Consumer Expenditure Survey, this book is a useful tool for anyone interested in examining American spending patterns and how changing demographics affect the consumer marketplace. Chapters are arranged alphabetically by spending category and cover more than 300 products and services ranging from food and drink to utilities. For each product or service within the spending category, an overview identifies best customers and trends, followed by tables of statistics indicating the national average, best customers, and biggest customers (market share) by age, income, household type, race and Hispanic origin, region, and education. Appendixes include an explanation of the Consumer Expenditure Survey, percent reporting expenditure and amount spent, spending by product and service ranked by amount spent, and household spending trends over ten years. The index is fairly comprehensive and a good entry point for researchers looking for specific data. Also available as PDF with spreadsheets or as e-book.

762   ClickZ. http://www.clickz.com/. Incisive Interactive Marketing LLC (Firm). New York: Incisive Interactive Marketing LLC. [2006–]

HF5548.32

A treasure trove of statistics and trends about internet marketing, including advertising, business to business, broadband, demographics, education, e-mail and spam, entertainment, finance, geographics, government/politics, hardware, health care, professional, retailing, search tools, security, small/medium enterprises, software and IT, traffic patterns, and wireless. Some data back to 1999. Because ClickZ links to outside sources, some URLs can lead to broken links. Formerly called *CyberAtlas*, and *ClickZ Stats*.

763   Company/brand$. Leading National Advertisers, Inc., Media Watch (Organization), Competitive Media Reporting (Firm), TNS Media Intelligence (Firm). New York: Leading National Advertisers, 1974– ISSN 8756-1220

HF5801

Use to find the advertising expenditures in ten media formats (magazines, Sunday magazines, newspapers, outdoor, network TV, spot TV, syndicated TV, cable TV, network radio, and national spot radio) for U.S. companies. Similar to the *Advertising Age* occasional report (http://adage.com/images/random/lna2005.pdf).

764   Consumer Europe. 26th ed. Euromonitor PLC. London: Euromonitor International, 2011–

339.4/7   HD7022

Annual. Formed by the merger of *Consumer Western Europe* and *Consumer Eastern Europe*. Indicates relative size of market for hundreds of consumer products. The current 2014 volume has data covering 2007–2012 and forecasts to 2017. Value figures in both local currency and U.S. dollars. Includes the following categories: alcoholic drinks, apparel, consumer appliances and electronics, consumer health products, eyewear, fresh food, home and garden products, hot drinks, packaged food, pet care, retail paper goods, soft drinks, tobacco, and toys and games. Provides the following national socio-economic indicators for context: population, health, foreign trade, household characteristics, income, and consumer expenditure. Covers 27 countries: Austria, Belgium, Bulgaria, Croatia, the Czech Republic, Denmark, Finland, France, Germany, Greece, Hungary, Ireland, Italy, Lithuania, the Netherlands, Norway, Poland, Portugal, Romania, Russia, Slovakia, Spain, Sweden, Switzerland, Turkey, Ukraine and the United Kingdom. Available in online format.

765   Consumer Latin America. Euromonitor Publications Limited. London: Euromonitor Publications Limited, 1993–2010. ill. ISSN 1359-0979

330.98   HC130.C6

Market-size time series for last five yr. and forecasted time series for upcoming five yr. for over 330 consumer markets in six Latin American countries (Argentina, Brazil, Chile, Colombia, Mexico, and Venezuela), as well as economic, demographic, lifestyle, and purchasing data and analysis. Also lists manufacturer and brand shares for major consumer goods sectors. Print edition ceased with 2010, as Euromonitor moves to online products such as Passport GMID (804).

766   Consumer Middle East. Euromonitor PLC. London: Euromonitor PLC, 1998–2007

658.834C7583   HC415.15.Z9

Market-size time series for last five yr. and forecasted time series for upcoming five yr. for over 330 consumer markets, as well as economic, demographic, lifestyle, and purchasing data and analysis. Also lists manufacturer and brand shares for major consumer goods sectors. Covers Algeria, Egypt, Israel, Jordan, Kuwait, Morocco, Saudi Arabia, Tunisia, Turkey, United Arab Emirates, with information on political structure, main industries, and the economy. Tables rank per capita consumer market sizes by country. Print edition ceased with 2007, as Euromonitor moves to online products such as Passport GMID (804).

767   Consumer USA. Euromonitor Publications Limited. London: Euromonitor Publications Limited, 1988– 2010 ISSN 0952-9543
339.47097305   HC101
Market-size time series for last five yr. and forecasted time series for upcoming five yr. for over 330 consumer markets, as well as economic, demographic, lifestyle, and purchasing data and analysis. Also lists manufacturer and brand shares for major consumer goods sectors. Print edition ceased with 2010, as Euromonitor moves to online products such as Passport GMID (804).

768   Demographics USA. County ed. Market Statistics. New York: Market Statistics, 1993–2008. ill., maps
381.10973   HF5415.1
Demographic and economic data, consumer expenditure data, retail sales and number of establishments by store group, establishments and employment data, and occupation data. Projections for categories such as population, households, and retail sales. Especially useful for the *Effective Buying Income and Buying Power Index*. Also available in ZIP code ed. Ceased with edition of 2008.

769   The Direct marketing market place: the networking source of the direct marketing industry. National Register Publishing. Berkeley Heights, N.J.: National Register Publishing/Marquis Who's Who LLC, 1980– ISSN 0192-3137
381   HF5415.1
A source similar in purpose and format to *Literary market place* for the direct marketing field. Classified sections list 8,700 direct marketers of products and services (principally through mail order catalogs), service firms and suppliers, creative and consulting services, associations and events, awards, etc. Primarily U.S. listings, with a chapter on Canadian and foreign firms. Gives names, addresses, and telephone numbers for companies and individuals, number of

employees, advertising budget related to direct marketing, and gross sales or billing. Also provides an overview of advertising expenditures by medium and market for four yr., with a forecast for future expenditures. Indexes of individuals and companies. Some issues have title: *Direct marketing marketplace.*

770   Editor and Publisher market guide. The Editor and Publisher Company. New York: The Editor and Publisher, 1924– 2010. maps, tables ISSN 0362-1200
658.8   PN4700
Individual market surveys of nearly 1,400 U.S. and Canadian cities where a daily newspaper is published. Arranged by state and city, with data in 16 categories such as population, households, climate, principal industries, military installations, and newspapers. Includes U.S. retail census data. *Better Living Index* ranks cities by cost of living, crime data, and education statistics. Ceased with 2010.

771   European marketing data and statistics. Euromonitor. London; Chicago: Euromonitor International, 1962– ISSN 0071-2930
338.094   HA1107
Demographic trends and forecasts, and economic statistics for 45 European countries, including Russia and Turkey. Includes time series data on advertising, agricultural resources and output, automotives and transport, banking and finance, consumer expenditure, consumer market sizes, consumer prices and costs, economic indicators, education, energy resources and output, environmental data, external trade, health, home ownership, household profiles, income and deductions, industry, IT and telecommunications, labor, media and leisure, population, retailing, and travel and tourism. Sources include the International Monetary Fund, United Nations, national statistical offices, and national trade associations. Companion volume to *International marketing data and statistics* (219). Current edition also available as a PDF download.

772   Global market share planner. 6th ed. Euromonitor International. London; Chicago: Euromonitor PLC, 2010. lxxxii, 834 p. ISBN 9781842645444
338.74021   HD2757.15
Tracks world-wide market size, market share, and key brands for companies producing consumer

brands, across 52 national markets. Includes sections on market share tracker, world-leading multinationals, and major market share companies. Products analyzed include beauty and personal care products, and beer and wine. Index. Earlier editions are in multiple volumes, focused on world regions.

773 International marketing data and statistics. Euromonitor International. London: Euromonitor, 1975/76–
ISSN 0308-2938
382.09   HA42
Demographic trends and forecasts and economic statistics for 161 non-European countries. Includes up to 30 years of data on cultural indicators, consumer market sizes and expenditures, labor force, foreign trade, health, energy, environment, IT and telecommunications, literacy and education, crime, retailing, travel and tourism, and consumer prices. Sources include the International Monetary Fund, United Nations, national statistical offices and national trade associations. Companion volume to *European marketing data and statistics* (323).

774 Local market audience analyst. http://next.srds.com/media-data/consumer-demographics. Standard Rate & Data Service. Des Plaines, Ill.: SRDS. 2009–
HF5415.33.U6
Offers market profile reports, lifestyle analysis reports, demographics reports, and PRIZM reports. Marketing-oriented data includes age, gender, income and other demographic factors. Covers 210 Direct Market Areas (DMAs) and more than 3,000 counties in the U.S. Interactive map capability. Replaces *Lifestyle market analyst.*(ceased with 2008).

775 Marketer's guide to media. Adweek, Inc., Nielsen Business Media, ASM Communications, VNU Business Publications. New York: Adweek, Inc., 1978– ISBN 9781891204494
ISSN 1061-7159
338.4   HF5826.5
This annual neatly packages statistics for all the major types of media (including but not limited to television, radio, newspapers, magazines, online services, and outdoor advertising). Among the types of data collected are audience demographics, audience estimates, media rates, and data on

specific markets such as Hispanics and teens. Data are often used as the basis for projecting trends. Title varies.

776 Market research handbook: manuel statistique pour études de marché. Canada Statistics Canada. Ottawa, Canada: Dominion Bureau of Statistics, Merchandising and Services Division = Bureau fédéral de la statistique, Division du commerce et des services, 1969–2008. ill. ISSN 0590-9325
658.83971   HC111
Annual summary of Canadian national and international trade statistics. Includes data for national and 25 metropolitan markets, with demographic and economic projections. Organized into 11 sections: user's guide, population, labor market and income, consumer expenditures, housing and household characteristics, macroeconomic and financial statistics, international trade, business and industry statistics, census metropolitan areas and census agglomerations, glossary and alphabetic index. Ceased with the edition of 2008.

777 Market share reporter. Gale Research Inc., Gale Group. Detroit: Gale Research, 1991– ISSN 1052-9578
380.105   HF5410
Annual. Market share statistics for over 4,000 companies and 2,300 products and services. Compiled from periodicals and brokerage reports, and arranged by Standard Industrial Classification (SIC) code. Indexed by source, place name, product or service name, company, and brand name. Includes the information from what was *World Market Share Reporter*. Available as an e-book.

778 MRI+. http://www.mriplus.com/. Mediamark Research & Intelligence, LLC. [New York]: Mediamark Research, Inc. 1999–
HF5415.2
Mediamark reporter allows construction of detailed spreadsheets. Taps demographic information about users of consumer products and about the audiences of print and broadcast media. Includes age, household income, education, employment status/occupation, race within region, marital status, county size, marketing region, household size, and Hispanic

origin. Use to determine which consumers are most likely to use a product and what media those consumers read or watch. Reports can be exported to Excel. MRI+ has an interactive cost worksheet to help determine the price of an advertising campaign. Login necessary.

779 ProQuest statistical abstract of the United States. ProQuest. Lanham, Md.: Bernan Press, 2013. 1025 p.
ISBN 9781598885910
317.3   HA 202
Successor to the important federal publication. When the U.S. government cut funding for the Statistical Abstract of the United States (288) published by the Census Bureau, over the objections of librarians and researchers, ProQuest launched this replacement edition as an annual publication beginning with 2013. Intentionally mimics the format, scope and organization of the original resource. Remains an excellent source for the most current possible data on population, government finance, the economy, and even for some international statistics. Original source publications for figures in tables are indicated. Appendixes include a guide to sources of statistics, state statistical abstracts, and foreign statistical abstracts; discussion of metropolitan and micropolitan statistical areas; and a table of weights and measures. Index. Also available in an online edition, from which the data tables can be retrieved in PDF. http://proquest.libguides.com/statisticalabstract

780 Radio dimensions. Media Dynamics, Inc. New York: Media Dynamics, 2005–2013. ill. ISSN 1931-4795
659   HF6146.R3
Uses data from MRI, Simmons, Scarborough Research, and Radio Recall to show who listens to radio. Augmented by narratives that give context to the data. Chapters on: History of radio, Radio basics (trends in ownership, radio's penetration from 1925–present, ad revenue and profits from 1935–present), Radio audiences (Arbitron's PPM, average number of stations listened to per week, listening trends, daypart audiences, radio usage, internet radio, satellite radio), Reach and frequency patterns, SQAD's CPP estimates, and Qualitative factors. Ceased with edition of 2013; coverage of radio appears in the successor title The media book (801) from the same publisher.

781 Rand McNally commercial atlas and marketing guide. Rand McNally and Company. Skokie, Ill.: Rand McNally, 1983–2010. ill., maps
912   G1019
Annual economic and geographic information guide for the United States, including U.S. and metropolitan area maps, transportation and communications data, economic data, population data, state maps, and index of places and statistics by state. Useful for business planning: provides basic commercial data for counties, including figures for population, wholesale trade, and manufacturing. Ceased with the 2010 edition, but still widely held.

782 RDS tablebase. http://www.gale.cengage.com/rds/index.htm. Gale Cengage Learning (Firm). Farmington, Mich.: Gale Cengage Learning. 1996–
                                         HG4027
A terrific international statistical source for company, industry, and demographic information including market share, market size, market trends, price trends, rankings, sales forecasts, output and capacity, consumption, imports and exports, and shipments. Information comes from 900 trade publications, including *Accounting today*, *Adweek*, *Aftermarket business*, *Almanac of american employers*, *Beverage world*, *Chemical week*, *Datamonitor industry market research*, *Meed Middle East economic digest*, as well as reports, newsletters, and surveys. Sold as part of the *RDS business suite* which also includes *Business & industry*, and *Business and management practices*.

783 Research monitor. http://go.euromonitor.com/ResearchMonitor-Home.html. Euromonitor International. London: Euromonitor International. 2013–
                                         HF5415
Offers international marketing information on a smaller scale than Passport GMID (804): some eighty countries are covered, and 5,000 industries. Provides analysis of issues and trends, market forecasts, reports on industries and countries, and demographic and marketing statistics. Searchable by subject or geographic place.

**784 SRDS business media advertising
source.** Standard Rate & Data Service.
Des Plaines, Ill.: SRDS, 2009–
ISSN 2162-0202
659.13205   HF5905

Annual. Successor to SRDS business publication advertising source (748). Looks at 190 media markets, providing advertising rates, and contact information. Also available in online format.

**785 SRDS business publication advertising
source.** Standard Rate and Data Service.
Des Plaines, Ill.: SRDS, 1995–2009
ISSN 1529-6490
659   HF5905

Provides advertising rates for 9,000 trade publications, listed in 220 subject areas. Publication entries give total circulation; publisher's positioning statement; contact information; commission and cash discount; general rate policy; black/white rates; color rates; rates for covers and inserts; bleed information; special advertising positions; and classified, mail order, and specialty rates. Ceased with 2009, and succeeded by SRDS business media advertising source (747).

786 SRDS tv and cable source.
Standard Rate and Data Service (Firm).
Wilmette, Ill.: Standard Rate and
Data Service, 1994–. maps
ISSN 1071-4596
659.143   HF5905

Lists broadcast, cable, syndicated and alternative television outlets, organized by state. Entries give contact information, executives, corporate owner, system background, coverage, insertion networks, traffic specifications, and special features. Each market includes a profile, with sales rankings by merchandise, SQAD cost per point levels, top daily newspapers and newspaper groups, metro radio stations by county, and a demographic profile of the market. Also available online.

**787 The sourcebook of zip code
demographics. Census ed.** ESRI.
[Redlands, Calif.]: ESRI, 1991–
ISSN 2158-5164
317.305   HA203

Statistics on income, age, ethnicity, education, and employment for every zip code in the U.S. Includes

dominant lifestyle segmentation, dominant industry, as well as purchasing potential for selected products and services, such as apparel, footwear, groceries, furniture, and financial services. Useful for determining market potential and existing competition in an area. Published by ESRI beginning with 2009.

**788 Statistical abstract of the United
States.** U.S. Dept. of the Treasury, Bureau
of Statistics, U.S. Dept. of Commerce and
Labor, Bureau of Statistics, U.S. Bureau
of Foreign and Domestic Commerce,
U.S. Bureau of the Census, U.S. Census
Bureau. Washington: U.S. G.P.O., 1878–
2012. ill. ISSN 0081-4741
317.3   HA202

A single-volume work presenting quantitative summary statistics on the political, social, and economic organization of the United States. Statistics given in the tables cover a period of several years. Indispensable in any library: it serves not only as a first source for statistics of national importance but also as a guide to further information, as references are given to the sources of all tables. Includes a table of contents arranged by broad subject areas and a detailed alphabetical index. Also available online from the Census Bureau at http://www.census.gov/compendia/statab/.

In 2011, the Census Bureau announced that publication of the Statistical Abstract would cease after the 2012 edition due to federal budget cuts. In 2012, ProQuest announced plans to publish equivalent print and online versions. Under the title ProQuest Statistical Abstract of the United States (150), this new work began to appear with 2013.

Supplement: *County and city data book* (270).

789 TV dimensions. Media Dynamics, Inc.
New York: Media Dynamics, 1984–. ill.
ISSN 0884-1098
384.5443   HE8700.8

Analyzes television as an advertising medium. Accompanying articles give context to statistics. Contents include basics such as trends in household penetration and advertising since 1950; TV viewing patterns with demographics and impact of video recording, pay-per-view and mobile devices; programming appeal for types of shows and viewers; viewer attention and involvement patterns, comparing broadcast and cable; and commercial impact through measurement of viewer attitudes. Appendixes offer essays such as the state of the broadcast industry and the effectiveness of advertising.

790 Who buys what: identifying international spending patterns by lifestyle. 2nd ed. Euromonitor International. London: Euromonitor International, 2009. xlii, 1106 p., ill. ISBN 9781842644911

HF5415.32

Statistics cover trends in consumer expenditure, household characteristics, and disposable income for 52 countries. Expenditure is analyzed by size of household, household type, age of household head, economic status of household head, income decile, and region.

791 World consumer lifestyles databook. 12th ed. Euromonitor International. London: Euromonitor International, 2013. 708 p. ISBN 9781842645918

381.33 HF5415.3

Updated annually, this resource provides comparable lifestyle statistics for 76 countries going back 22 years where possible. Lifestyle areas include consumer segmentation by generation, population data, marriage/divorce rates, household ownership, income, consumer expenditure, employment and unemployment, education, eating, drinking, smoking, personal appearance, fashion, health and wellness, leisure and recreation, consumer technology, transport, and money. Available in print and as a downloadable PDF.

Market Research

792 Adforum. http://www.adforum.com/. AdForum (Firm). Hoboken, N.J.: AdForum MayDream. 2000–

HF6146.T42

Searchable database tracking worldwide advertising. Includes more than 70,000 ads that have appeared in print, radio, TV or other media. Information for more than 20,000 agencies, as well as news. Archive of award winners since 1999. Directories of consultants, trade fairs, and production firms.

793 Business insights. http://www.business -insights.com/. Datamonitor (Firm), Reuters. London: Reuters. 1998–2010

HF54.7

From 1998–2010, provided reports on energy, consumer goods, finance, health care, and technology. Reports, typically over 100 pages long, covered new product innovations, marketing strategies, market drivers, key players, trends, business opportunity forecasting, and industry interviews. International focus, especially strong for European coverage. Merged with Marketline (222) in 2010 to form Marketline Advantage (799).

794 Business insights. http://www .cengagesites.com/literature/782/gale -business-insights-global-essentials/. Gale (Firm). [Farmington Hills, Mich.]: Gale Cengage Learning. 2000–

HG4001

Until 2012, known as *Business and company resource center*. Redesigned at that time to support better searching across multiple kinds of content, manipulation of data to create custom charts, and advanced user tools such as text-to-speech and translation into more than 30 languages for the interface and some content. Web interface highlights company and industry information, comparison charts, and a glossary. Provides information about market share, market analysis and product trends, and allows comparison of companies. Content drawn from more than 3,900 periodicals (journals, newspapers, and trade publications); two million investment reports; 25,000 industry reports and 500 longer industry profiles with more detail; 2,500 market research reports; over 10,000 company histories from *International directory of company histories* (906) and more than 2,000 company chronologies; 500,000 shorter company profiles; 65,000 articles from *Business rankings annual* (909); and listings of 70,000 associations.

795 Emarketer. http://www.emarketer.com/. eMarketer (Organization). New York: eMarketer. 1996–

658.84 HF5548.32

Reports marketing information with an emphasis on online media, internet commerce and digital marketing. Reports are grouped by topic (such as advertising, B2B contacts, or mobile devices), by industry (such as consumer products, travel, or retail), and by geography (such as North America, Asia-Pacific, or Western Europe). Aggregates data from 2,800 sources, with summaries in reports and articles. Sources include Accenture, ACNielsen, *Advertising age* (731),

Harris Poll, Juniper Research, Jupitermedia, Media-mark Research Inc. (MRI), Rand Corporation, Pew Internet & American Life Project, Red Hat, Red Herring, as well as various advertising and marketing associations. The data is searchable, making this a good source for online marketing and e-commerce statistics.

796   Forrester research. http://www.forrester
.com/. Forrester Research. Cambridge,
Mass.: Forrester. [1996–]
                                          HF5548.32
Provides commercial-grade reports for paying clients. Nearly 17,000 original reports on technology's effect on business and the consumer in the United States, Canada, Europe, and Asia Pacific. Research is in two categories, technology and industry.

Topics in technology are application development, business intelligence, computing systems, consumer devices and access, content and collaboration, customer experience, enterprise applications, enterprise mobility, IT management, IT services, networking, portals and site technology, security, software infrastructure, and tech sector economics.

Topics in industry are brand strategy, brand tactics, consumer electronics, consumer products, customer insight, emerging marketing channels, energy and utilities, financial services, government, healthcare and life sciences, high tech, industry insight, manufacturing, marketing and advertising, marketing planning, media and entertainment, mobile services, professional services, relationship marketing, retail, telecommunications, television advertising, transportation and logistics, and travel.

Reports typically range from 3–20 pages, and some are available as videos.

797   ISI emerging markets. http://www
.securities.com/. Internet Securities, Inc.
New York: Internet Securities, Inc. 2001–
                                          HG5993
EMIS (Emerging Markets Information Service) assembles reports for each country in Latin America and the Caribbean; Central and Southeast Europe; the Middle East, north Africa and sub-Saharan Africa; the Caucasus and Central Asia; and the Asia-Pacific region. Reporting covers general news; business, industry, and company news from sources in English and local languages; and company rankings by sales.

798   Magazine dimensions. Media Dynamics,
Inc. New York: Media Dynamics, 1993–
2013 ISSN 1074-7419
659.132   HF6105.U5
Statistical information mixed with narrative, providing a picture of the magazine industry. Chapters include: General dimensions (history of magazines from 1740–2006, trends in magazines published and ad revenues, changing face of editorial content, magazine CPM's), magazine audiences (audience definitions, circulation trends, subscriber profiles, reader profiles by magazine, total audience by magazine, website audiences, reading diet by genre, median age and income trends, reader-per-copy, reach and frequency, and accumulation patterns), and qualitative factors (reader attitudes and intensity of exposure, location and timing of reading, advertising receptivity, comparison to TV), and Information sources (circulation audits, subscriber/panel studies, syndicated audience/marketing research). Ceased with 2013: replaced by Media book (801).

799   Marketline advantage. http://www
.marketline.com/overview/advantage/.
Datamonitor (Firm). London:
Datamonitor. 2010–
                                          HF54.7
Provides business intelligence for numerous products, with profiles for 30,000 companies worldwide, 4,000 industries, and 100 countries, in addition to relevant news and case studies. Sold as *Datamonitor 360* from 2010–2012, after the 2010 merger of the former Marketline (222) and Business insights (793) products. Note that comparable market research tools also exist aimed at the professional marketplace, not libraries: an example is *Frost & Sullivan market intelligence reports*.

800   Marketresearch.com academic.
http://www.marketresearch.com/.
Kalorama Information. Rockville, Md.:
Marketresearch.com. 1999–
                                          HF5415.2
Offers for sale the market research reports from over 700 sources (Icon Group, Kalorama, BizMiner, etc.). Browsable abstracts can be searched by publisher, country, and company name, and in industry categories: Consumer Goods (apparel, cosmetics and personal care, house and home, pet services and supplies, travel services), Food and Beverage (alcoholic

beverages, coffee and tea, soft drinks, confectionery, dairy products, food processing), Heavy Industry (energy, mining, utilities, construction, machines and parts, manufacturing, metals, paper and forest products, plastics, automotive, aviation & aerospace, logistics and shipping), Service Industries (accounting and finance, corporate services, banking and financial services, insurance), Public Sector (associations/non-profits, education, government), Life Science (biotechnology, agriculture, genomics, proteomics, medical imaging, healthcare facilities, managed care, regulation and policy, cardiovascular devices, equipment and supplies, wound care, pharmaceuticals, diseases and conditions, prescription drugs, therapeutic area), Technology & Media (computer equipment, electronics, networks, e-commerce and IT outsourcing, software, telecommunications, wireless), and Demographics (age, lifestyle and economics, multicultural).

Reports range in length, with some over 300 pages long, and give a variety of information (definition of industry, consumer demographics, consumer shopping habits, spending patterns, sales, establishments, employment, forecasts, trends, market size, market share, and market segmentation). Some company information is also included.

801 **The media book.** Media Dynamics (Firm). Nutley, N.J.: Media Dynamics, 2013–

Successor to Magazine dimensions (798) with first publication in the fall of 2013. Quantitative and qualitative data on the demographics of audiences reached by television, radio, magazines, the internet and newspapers, to support advertising and marketing needs.

802 **Mintel oxygen reports.** http://www .mintel.com/. Mintel Group, Ltd. (Firm). London; Chicago: Mintel Group, Ltd. 2003–

HC240.9

Full-text market research reports covering global consumer markets, with an emphasis on U.S. and European markets. Analyzes market share, segmentation, trends, and consumer demographics.

Access by subscription. Covers consumer goods and services, making this a good source of reports for market segments and consumer behavior, with reports like "Impact of celebrity chefs on cooking habits," "Nail color and care," and "MP3 players and other portable audio players," but not for business to business reports.

Market reports are available for automotive, beauty and personal, drink and tobacco, electronics, food and foodservice, health and medical, health and wellness, household, lifestyles, media, books and stationary, personal finances, retailing, technology, and travel. Reports include an executive summary, glossary, and sections on advertising and promotion, ownership and usage, attitudes and opinions, market drivers, market size and trends, market segmentation, future and forecast, and supply structure.

Consumer reports provide demographics, core needs and values, future trends, information on products currently targeted to the group, and advice on reaching and influencing the target audience. Consumer reports are available for financial lifestyles, general lifestyles, healthier lifestyles, and leisure lifestyles.

Marketing and promotion reports are for marketing and targeting, and promotions, incentives, and sponsorship. They include introduction and abbreviations, executive summary, background and market factors, challenges facing marketers, marketing segments, product development and pricing, and future trends.

Most data in Mintel can be downloaded into Excel. Reports cannot be viewed in their entirety and instead must be viewed in sections, making easy skimming or printing a report impossible.

803 **MRI+.** http://www.mriplus.com/. Mediamark Research & Intelligence, LLC. [New York]: Mediamark Research, Inc. 1999–

HF5415.2

Mediamark reporter allows construction of detailed spreadsheets. Taps demographic information about users of consumer products and about the audiences of print and broadcast media. Includes age, household income, education, employment status/occupation, race within region, marital status, county size, marketing region, household size, and Hispanic origin. Use to determine which consumers are most likely to use a product and what media those consumers read or watch. Reports can be exported to Excel. MRI+ has an interactive cost worksheet to help determine the price of an advertising campaign. Login necessary.

804 **Passport GMID.** http://www.euromonitor .com/. Euromonitor International. London, U.K.: Euromonitor International. [1999–]
658.8   HF5415.2

Also known under previous product names as *Global market information database*, *GMID*, or *Euromonitor GMID*. Market reports, company profiles, and demographic, economic, and marketing statistics for 205 countries. Market reports are for 16 consumer markets (food and drink, tobacco, toys, etc.) and 14 industrial and service markets (accountancy, broadcasting, chemicals, property services, etc.).

Reports have market size, market sectors, share of market, marketing activity, research and development, corporate overview, distribution, consumer profiles, market forecasts, sector forecasts, sources, and definitions. Additional reports are available for market segments, such as baby food. Company profiles have background, recent news, competitve environment, and outlook. Consumer lifestyle reports and very useful marketing background analyze the consumer by country, gender, age, marital status, educational attainment, ethnicity, religion, home ownership, household profile, employment, income, health, eating and personal grooming habits, leisure activities, personal finance, communication, transport, and travel.

Search for data, which can be exported into Excel or browse for reports. Data are available since 1977 and include inflation, exchange rates, GDP, GNI, government expenditures, government finance, income, labor, and money supply.

Similar information on a smaller scale is available in Research monitor (783) from the same publisher.

805 Policymap. http://www.policymap .com/. The Reinvestment Fund (TRF). Philadelphia: The Reinvestment Fund. 2008–

HA214

GIS-based mapping software that creates custom maps on demand, reflecting thousands of U.S. data points reflecting demographics, real estate and housing, mortgages, jobs and employment, public investment, crime, health, and education. Maps can cover small areas: not just states, counties, and cities or MSAs, but also ZIP codes, census tracts and block groups, or unusual boundaries such as school districts. Data comes from both public and proprietary sources. Originally crafted to support neighborhood redevelopment projects. Output can take the form of maps, tables or reports.

806 The retail market research yearbook. Richard K. Miller and Associates. Loganville, Ga.: Richard K. Miller and Associates, 2005– 381 p. ISSN 1930-966X

An overview of the retail market, with information on companies, consumers, and resources for each retail industry segment. Chapters include: Market summary; Current and future trends; Industry profile; Department stores; Discount stores and supercenters; Warehouse clubs; Supermarkets; Variety and dollar stores; Drug stores; Apparel; Footwear; Jewelry; Health, beauty, and cosmetics; Consumer electronics; Home decor and furnishings; Home centers and hardware; Housewares and home textiles; Book stores; Music and video; Office products; Sporting goods; Toys and video games; Pet supplies; Crafts and fabrics; Photography; Closeout and off-price chains; Convenience stores; Military post exchanges; Resale and thrift stores; E-commerce; Catalog and mail-order retail; Television home shopping; Christmas holiday shopping; Back-to-school; Holiday markets; and The bridal and wedding market.

807 Simmons oneview. http://www.experian .com/simmons-research/simmons-oneview .html. Simmons Market Research Bureau. Costa Mesa, Calif.: Experian Marketing Services. 1995–

658 HC110.C6

Survey-based data on household use of products and brands. Provides demographic reports on characteristics of product users and their choice of media, to develop advertising. Produced in print until 1994 as *Simmons study of media and markets*, then issued in CD-ROM, and now online. Formerly sold as *Choices 3*.

808 SimplyMap. http://www.simplymap.com. New York: Geographic Research, Inc. 2005–

G3701.A25

Produces on-the-fly data-based maps through selection of locations and variables for demographic or marketing information. Categories of variables include census data, consumer expenditure, market segments, and retail sales. Use of a filter allows combination of two variables. Maps can be exported as GIF or PDF files, and data reports can be exported as Excel, DBF, or CSV. Access requires a subscription for authentication and creation of an individual account.

809   SRDS tv and cable source. Standard Rate and Data Service (Firm). Wilmette, Ill.: Standard Rate and Data Service, 1994–. maps ISSN 1071-4596

659.143   HF5905

Lists broadcast, cable, syndicated and alternative television outlets, organized by state. Entries give contact information, executives, corporate owner, system background, coverage, insertion networks, traffic specifications, and special features. Each market includes a profile, with sales rankings by merchandise, SQAD cost per point levels, top daily newspapers and newspaper groups, metro radio stations by county, and a demographic profile of the market. Also available online.

810   Who's buying: executive summary of household spending. New Strategist. Ithaca, N.Y.: New Strategist, 2005– ISSN 1933-2009

658   HC110.C6

Based on data from the Bureau of Labor Statistics' *Consumer expenditure survey* (http://www.bls.gov/cex/). Tables show household spending trends over time, by age, income, marital status, size of household, U.S. region, ethnicity, and education. Glossary. Available as an e-book.

Internet Resources

811   Ad*Access. http://library.duke.edu/digitalcollections/adaccess/. John W. Hartman Center for Sales, Advertising, and Marketing History, Duke University Scriptorium, J. Walter Thompson Company. Durham, N.C.: Duke University Digital Collections. 1999

659.10285   HF5813.U6

Images of 7,000 advertisements printed in U.S. and Canadian newspapers and magazines between 1911 and 1955. Browse in five categories (beauty and hygiene, radio, television, transportation, and World War II) or search by words in the headline or in information about the ad, such as name of company, product, artist, program, or publication.

812   ClickZ. http://www.clickz.com/. Incisive Interactive Marketing LLC (Firm). New York: Incisive Interactive Marketing LLC. [2006–]

HF5548.32

A treasure trove of statistics and trends about internet marketing, including advertising, business to business, broadband, demographics, education, e-mail and spam, entertainment, finance, geographics, government/politics, hardware, health care, professional, retailing, search tools, security, small/medium enterprises, software and IT, traffic patterns, and wireless. Some data back to 1999. Because ClickZ links to outside sources, some URLs can lead to broken links. Formerly called *CyberAtlas*, and *ClickZ Stats*.

813   Emergence of advertising in America: 1850–1920. http://library.duke.edu/digitalcollections/eaa/. Duke University Rare Book, Manuscript, and Special Collections Library, Library of Congress. Durham, N.C.: Duke University Libraries Digital Collections. 2001–

659.109   HF5813.U6

Searchable database with access to more than 3,300 advertisements, photographs, and images of advertising-related artifacts and consumer goods from the U.S. Many images in color.

814   Knowthis.com. http://www.knowthis.com/. Paul Christ. [West Chester, Pa.]: KnowThis.com. 1998–

658.8   HF5415

Online portal for marketing resources. 135 categories and content including tutorials, articles, forums, links to associations, online groups, and research reports, make finding information and reading about marketing easy. A great first stop for background information. Editor Paul Christ is an MBA/PhD professor at West Chester Universityof Pennsylvania. Also publishes *KnowThis: Marketing basics*.

815   Web marketing today. http://www.wilsonweb.com/wmt/. Wilson Internet Services. Rocklin, Calif.: Wilson Internet Services. 1995– 384 p. ISSN 1094-8112

Links to articles and other resources for web marketing and e-commerce. Categories for Industry Case Studies, Business to Business (B2B), Online Transactions, E-Commerce Environmental Design, Store-Building "Cart" Software, Website Promotion, Business Site Environmental Design, Paid Advertising, E-Mail Marketing, Miscellaneous Web Marketing, and Local Web Marketing. Access is a mix of fee and free.

Organizations and Associations

816 Marketing power. http://www
.marketingpower.com/. American
Marketing Association. Chicago: American
Marketing Association. [2001–]
658.806   HF5410
Home page for AMA. The assoc. supports marketing
professionals in the U.S. and Canada. The website
has membership information, resources for members, AMA publications (*Marketing News*, *Journal of
Public Policy & Marketing*, *Marketing Management*,
Marketing Research, *Marketing Health Services*, *Journal
of Marketing*, *Journal of Marketing Research*, *Journal of
International Marketing*), best practices, case studies,
webcasts, hot topics, dictionary of marketing terms,
careers, and tools (marketing templates, project
management, statistics resources, ROI enhancers).

Operations Management

Guides and Handbooks

**817 Handbook of quantitative supply
chain analysis: modeling in the
e-business era.** David Simchi-Levi,
S. David Wu, Zuo-Jun Shen. Boston:
Kluwer, 2004. xiii, 817 p., ill.
ISBN 9781402079528
658.70151   HD38.5
Includes trends, theory, and practice. Organized
into five parts: emerging paradigms for supply chain
analysis; auctions and bidding; supply chain coordinations in e-business; multi-channel coordination; and network design, IT, and financial services.
Strong coverage of game theory as it applies to supply chains.

**818 Operations research calculations
handbook. 2nd ed.** Dennis Blumenfeld.
Boca Raton, Fla.: CRC Press, 2009. xvii,
238 p., ill. ISBN 9781420052404
658.4034   T57.6
Updates the first edition of 2001. Results and formulas used in systems modeling and systems behavior.
Adds newly derived formulas and new content on
topics such as order statistics, traffic flow and delay,
heuristic search methods, hyper-exponential and

hypo-exponential distributions, and distance norms.
Chapters on means and variances, discrete probability
distributions, continuous probability distributions,
probability relationships, stochastic processes, queu-
ing theory results, production systems modeling,
inventory control, distance formulas for logistics analysis, linear programming formulations, mathematical
functions, calculus results, matrices, and combinator-
ics. Bibliography. Index. Available as an e-book.

**819 The supply management handbook.
7th ed.** Joseph L. Cavinato, Anna E.
Flynn, Ralph G. Kauffman. New York:
McGraw-Hill, 2006. xiv, 945 p., ill.
ISBN 9780071445139
658.7   HD39.5
Formerly *The purchasing handbook* and written by
three business professors, discusses topics like: next-
generation supply methodologies, social responsibility, logistics, and supply management. Includes
impact of technology on supply management.

Indexes; Abstract Journals

820 Inspec. http://www.theiet.org/resources/
inspec/. Institution of Engineering and
Technology. London: Institution of
Engineering and Technology. 1969–
621.05   T45
Index to the literature on physics, electrical engineering, electronics, control theory and technology, computing, and control engineering. Made up
of four subfiles: *Series A, Physics Abstracts*; *Series B,
Electrical and Electronics Abstracts*; *Series C, Computer
and Control Abstracts*; *Series D, Information Technology*. This database is available online from several
vendors. Coverage starts in 1898 (when it was called
Science Abstracts), and database contains over 9 million records. Can be accessed via Elsevier's Engineering Village platform.

821 MathSciNet. http://www.ams.org/
mathscinet/. American Mathematical
Society. Providence, R.I.: American
Mathematical Society. [1990?]–
                                               QA1
Subscription/fee-based database is the online ver-
sion of the print resources *Mathematical reviews* and
Current mathematical publications. MathSciNet is a

comprehensive, searchable index of mathematics literature from 1940 to the present. Includes a few bibliographic entries for retrodigitized items back to the 1800s. Updated continuously. Contains reference lists, bibliographic citations, and mathematical reviews to over 2 million items. The full text of the *review* is available, even the very short ones, from the MathSciNet entry. Mathematical formulae are displayed using MathJax, an open source tool for displaying mathematics in any web browser. If the review or bibliography refers to other items in the database, they are also linked. Full text of the articles still needs to be accessed through link resolvers and your subscriptions (either personal or institutional). Reviewers are members of the research mathematics community and make this a vital resource for mathematics. MathSciNet overlaps a great deal with Zentralblatt MATH, and despite changes to both, MathSciNet is still easier to use.

One of the greatest strengths of MathSciNet is a sophisticated and highly reliable author name authority control.

Access to either MathSciNet or Zentralblatt MATH is essential for any library serving a university-level mathematics department or a sizeable group of research mathematicians. Heavily used as well by statisticians, engineers, physicists, and others doing research involving advanced mathematics. Like many online databases, MathSciNet allows the pairing of mobile devices to institutional users so they can access it off-site.

822 Operations research/management science. Executive Sciences Institute. Whippany, N.J.: Executive Sciences Institute, [1961]– ISSN 0030-3658
001   HD28
Abstracts for 150 journals, arranged by subject, with an annual index in the December issue. Particularly useful, as lengthy summaries contain research results. Coverage from 1961.

823 Quality control and applied statistics. Executive Sciences Institute. Whippany, N.J.: ESI Publications, 1956–
ISSN 0033-5207
658.562015195   TS156.A1
Indexes and abstracts for selected articles. Useful for finding articles on quality management, risk and

uncertainty, industrial management, computing, and information systems. International coverage.

Encyclopedias

824 Encyclopedia of management.
7th ed. Sonya D. Hill. Detroit: Gale, Cengage Learning, 2012. xxx, 1133 p. ISBN 9781414459042
658.003   HD30.15
Covers functional areas such as corporate planning and strategic management, emerging topics in management, entrepreneurship, financial management and accounting, general management, human resources management, innovation and technology, international management, leadership, legal issues, management science and operations, management information systems, performance measures and assessment, personal growth and development for managers, production and operations management, quality management and total quality management, supply chain management, and training and development. More than 300 essays in alphabetical order, written by academics and business professionals, with cross-references and recommended reading lists. New content reflects trends such as the use of handheld devices for Internet-based tools, social networking, network security, venture capital and entrepreneurship, and business in China. Includes a glossary of terms. Index. Available as an e-book.

825 Encyclopedia of optimization. 2nd ed.
Christodoulos A. Floudas, P. M. Pardalos. New York: Springer, 2009. 7 v., ill. ISBN 9780387747583
519.603   QA402.5
Updates the first edition of 2001, with 150 new entries on topics in areas such as health care and transportation. Coverage of operations research, mathematical programming, algorithms, calculus of variations and optimal control, mathematical modeling, and industrial mathematics. Written by numerous experts from around the world, with entries ranging from 4–10 p. in length. Name index. Subject index. Available as an e-book.

826 Encyclopedia of supply chain management. James B. Ayers. Boca Raton, Fla.: CRC Press, 2012. 2 v. (xlvii, 1364, I-28 p.), ill. ISBN 9781439861486
658.003   HD38.5

Includes some 300 entries on topics such as project management, the use of modeling, retail supply chains, the impact of globalization, and the influence of techniques such as Six Sigma and LEAN principles. Index.

827   Wiley encyclopedia of operations research and management science. James J. Cochran, Louis A. Cox. Hoboken, N.J.: Wiley, 2011. 8 v. (xliii, 6025 p.), ill. ISBN 9780470400630
658.003   T57.6

Covers theories, economics, and mathematics involved in ORMS. Signed articles, with bibliographical references, in alphabetical order. Suitable for researchers and graduate students: the approach is quantitative, with an emphasis on statistical and mathematical methodology. Introductory articles demand less background; advanced articles may include reviews of key research findings; and technical entries explore concepts in greater depth. Also includes case studies, and historical or biographical entries. Covers data mining, game theory, risk analysis, and supply chain management. Index. Available as an e-book.

Periodicals

828   European journal of operational research. Association of European Operational Research Societies. Amsterdam, The Netherlands: Elsevier Science, 1977–. ill. ISSN 0377-2217
001.424   T57.6

Articles, editorials, case studies, and book reviews on operations management and research. Organized into eight sections: continuous optimization; discrete optimization; production, manufacturing, and logistics; stochastics and statistics; decision support; computing, artificial intelligence, and information management; O.R. applications; and interfaces with other disciplines. Subscriptions available in online form.

829   International abstracts in operations research. International Federation of Operational Research Societies, Operations Research Society of America. Houndmills, Basingstoke, Hampshire, U.K.: Palgrave Press, 1961– ISSN 0020-580X
658.4034   HD20.5

Unique content with abstracts from over 180 journals covering operations and management science. Coverage begins in 1989. Also available as *IAOR Online*.

830   The journal of product innovation management. Product Development and Management Association. Hoboken, N.J.: John Wiley & Sons, 1984–. ill. ISSN 0737-6782
658.57505   HF5415.153.J68

Articles on product innovation, development, and marketing. Occasional thematic issues on topics such as corporate entrepreneurship. Some issues review up to four books, with reviews ranging 2–3 pages in length. Available to PDMA members, and by subscription in print and online formats.

831   SIAM review. Society for Industrial and Applied Mathematics. Philadelphia: Society for Industrial and Applied Mathematics, [1959–]. ill. ISSN 0036-1445
519   QA1

One of the leading journals in the field, *SIAM review* is presented in five sections: Survey and Review, Problems and Techniques, SIGEST, Education, and Book Reviews. The book review section is quite lengthy, with up to 25 reviews. Reviews are signed and have references.

Organizations and Associations

832   American productivity and quality center. http://www.apqc.org/. APQC. Houston, Tex.: APQC. 2003– 658.47

Home page for an organization devoted to benchmarking and best-practice research. The website includes case studies, professional development, survey hosting, success profiles, and a knowledge base. The knowledge base is for finding best practices, books, case studies, measures and metrics, newsletters, presentations, surveys/questionnaires, and white papers. Many services are for members only.

833   INFORMS online. http://www .informs.org/. Institute for Operations Research and the Management Sciences. Catonsville, Md.: Institute for Operations Research and the Management Sciences. 1996–
658   HD30.25

Home page for an institute that serves professionals, students, and academics interested in operations research, and is the publisher of two of the top journals in the field, *Operations Research* and *Management Science*. The website includes INFORMS Meetings Database (conference presentations), Member Directory, Press Releases, Expert List, Publications, Awards, Scholarships, Education, Careers, and Resources (including a comprehensive list of operations research resources).

834   Production and operations management. http://www.poms.org/. Production and Operations Management Society. Baltimore: Production and Operations Management Society. 1992–
TS155.A1

Home page for POMS, an organization promoting information in the field. Has information on society membership, its publications (*Production and operations management* and *POMS chronicle*), meetings, research, education, placement, and colleges.

5 *Company Information*

Directories

835 American wholesalers and distributors directory. Gale Research Inc., Gale Group. Detroit: Gale Research, 1992– ISSN 1061-2114

381.2029473   HF5421

Annual. Lists 27,000 companies in the U.S. and Puerto Rico. Includes name and address, fax number, Standard Industrial Classification (SIC) code, principal product lines, total number of employees, estimated annual sales volume, and principal officers. Indexed by SIC code, state and city, and company name. Information can be hard to find for many of these privately held companies, making this a handy source. Available as an e-book.

836 America's corporate families: the billion dollar directory. Dun's Marketing Services. Parsippany, N.J.: Dun & Bradstreet, 1987– ISSN 0890-6645

338.8202573   HG4057.A147

Vol. 1 lists more than 12,000 U.S. parent companies in alphabetical order, together with some 74,000 domestic branches, subsidiaries, and divisions. Each parent entry provides directory information, total number of company locations, total employees, sales and net worth, officers, SIC codes, stock ticker and exchange, date founded, board of directors, product line, and DUNS number. For dependent firms, gives directory information, percent of ownership, sales at that location, products, SIC codes, number of local employees, and officers. Vol. 2 lists all companies in alphabetical order, by state and city, and by SIC code (in numerical order, then by state and city). Includes index of SIC codes. Vol. 3, *America's corporate families and international affiliates*, lists approximately 1,500 U.S. parent companies with 12,000 foreign subsidiaries, as sell as foreign ultimate parents and their U.S. subsidiaries.

837 America's corporate finance directory. LexisNexis Group (Firm). Atlanta, Ga.: LexisNexis Group, 1994– ISSN 1080-1227

338.7402573   HG4057

Annual. Covers major publicly and privately owned companies, with contact information, financial data, and lists of key company officers. Indexes of individuals by financial responsibility and all personnel, and of companies by SIC code and geographical location, and as parent companies and subsidiaries.

838 Asia's 10,000 largest companies: marketing and financial information on Asia's top companies. Oxford, U.K.: ELC International, 2006– ISBN 9781907128127

338.74095   HG4234.85

Lists leading companies in banking, agriculture, mining, construction, business and personal services, electronics manufacturing, industrial manufacturing,

154

food, beverage, tobacco, chemicals, petroleum, pharmaceuticals, wholesale, retail, transportation and oil, publishing, communications, hotels and restaurants, insurance, investment, real estate, and utilities. Entries give SIC code, sales, profit, employees, sales per employee, assets, equity, equity as a percentage of assets, and year established. Ranks Asia's 500 most profitable companies, 500 biggest money losers, and 100 largest companies by industry sector.

839 BioScan. BioWorld. Atlanta, Ga.: BioWorld; Thomson Reuters, 1987–
ISSN 0887-6207
338.76208/025   HD9999.B44
Information on some 2,200 U.S. and foreign companies in the biotechnology and biopharmaceutical sectors, giving contact information, company history, number of employees, facilities, very brief financial highlights (sales, net income, earnings per share, shares outstanding, total assets), business strategy, alliances, mergers and acquisitions, principal investors, and products in development, and products on the market. Available online through *BioWorld*.

840 Brands and their companies. Donna J. Wood, Susan L. Stetler. Detroit: Gale Research, 1990– ISSN 1047-6407
602.75   T223.V4
Not sure what company is responsible for Night Owl? Don't even know what type of product it is? This is the source for answers. Alphabetically lists brand names, even for discontinued brands, and then lists the manufacturer or distributor. Covers some U.S. 400,000 products and over 100,000 manufacturers. Brand names supplied by companies or found in print resources. Occasionally used by researchers interested in trademarks. Companion to *Companies and their brands* (741). Available as an e-book.

841 Business and company ASAP. http:// www.gale.cengage.com/pdf/facts/bcprof .pdf. Gale Cengage (Firm). Farmington Hills, Mich.: Gale Cengage. 1999–
HF5030
Combines company data, a corporate directory, and business news with backfiles extending back to 1980. Searchable by keyword, subjects, or SIC codes.

For more information, such as industry reports and profiles in greater depth, and information on a larger number of companies, consider Business insights: essentials (581).

842 Companies and their brands. Donna J. Wood. Detroit: Gale Research, 1990–
ISSN 1047-6393
602.75   T223.V4
Alphabetical list of companies and the brand names attributed to them. Each entry is followed by the firm's address, telephone number, and list of trade names. Information is collected from print sources and from the individual companies. Companion to *Brands and their companies* (739).

843 Corporate affiliations. http://www .corporateaffiliations.com/. LexisNexis Group. New Providence, N.J.: LexisNexis Group. 2001– ISBN 9781573872737
HG4057
Profiles some one million public and private companies, with information on affiliates, subsidiaries, and divisions. Search by company type, location, title of executive, NAICS or SIC code, number of employees, sales revenue, ownership, fiscal year, stock exchange, earnings, assets, net worth, and liabilities. Profiles include contact information, very brief business description, year founded, number of employees, NAICS and SIC codes, names of top executives, outside service firms, and top competitors. Most useful for visual who-owns-whom hierarchies, linking to profiles for all companies in the hierarchy. While international in scope, coverage is best for the United States. Historical backfile is available, with coverage from 1993. Also available in print as the *Directory of corporate affiliations*.

844 Corporate giving directory. 29th ed. Information Today Inc. Medford, N.J.: Information Today, 1991–. 1578 p.
361.765
Profiles of over 1,000 corporate charitable giving programs in the United States. Entries include cash, nonmonetary, and corporate sponsorship giving; matching gift and company-sponsored volunteer programs; corporate operating locations; geographic preferences; officers and directors; application procedures; and recently awarded grants data.

"Approximately 21 percent of the companies featured in this edition cover difficult-to-research direct giving programs, which are often untapped sources of support"—*Introd.*

Fourteen indexes.

845 D and B million dollar directory: America's leading public and private companies. Dun and Bradstreet, Inc. Bethlehem, Pa.: Dun and Bradstreet, 1997– ISSN 1093-4812

338.740973 HC102.D8

The first three volumes contain company entries. The fourth volume indexes companies by geography, and the fifth volume by industrial classification. Covers U.S. and Canadian public and private companies with sales of $1,000,000 or more. Entries include address and telephone number for headquarters, annual sales, number of employees, Standard Industrial Classification (SIC) codes, names and titles for top executives, and year established.

Also available as an online database, adding capabilities to search by executive name and to export records.

846 D and B principal international businesses. Dun and Bradstreet, Inc. Bethlehem, Pa.: Dun and Bradstreet, 1999–

380.1025 HF54.U5

Lists more than 50,000 companies by country, industry, and name, providing for each: sales volume, indication of whether it exports or imports, number of employees, SIC and DUNS numbers, description of field of activity, and name and title of senior operating officer.

847 Directory for doing business in Japan. http://www.jetro.go.jp/en/invest/directory/. Nihon Bo eki Shinko kai. Tokyo: Japan External Trade Organization (JETRO). 1998–

382.029452 HF3823

Lists Japanese companies and associations involved in international trade, as well as products. Gives contact information, representative, type of business, year established, capital, annual sales, number of employees, bank reference, product/service imported or exported. Searchable by business type and geographic location. JETRO publishes in print *Japan trade directory (Nihon Bo eki Shinko kai)*.

848 Directory of American firms operating in foreign countries. Juvenal L. Angel. New York: Uniworld Business Publications, 1955/56–2009 ISSN 0070-5071

338.88025 HG4538.A1D5

Lists over 3,000 U.S. firms with more than 36,000 branches, subsidiaries, and affiliates in 196 countries. Pt. 1 is an alphabetical list of companies and lists by country foreign operations. Entries contain basic directory information, as well as names of key personnel, product information, and location of foreign branches, subsidiaries, and affiliates. Pt. 2 contains the directory information for the parent organizations with names and addresses for foreign branches, subsidiaries, and affiliates. Print version ceased with 2009; available in online format as *UniWorld*. Companion to *Directory of foreign firms operating in the United States* (850).

849 Directory of corporate archives in the United States and Canada. http://www2.archivists.org/groups/business-archives-section/directory-of-corporate-archives-in-the-united-states-and-canada-indexed-by-location. Gregory S. Hunter. Chicago: Business Archives Section, Society of American Archivists. 1997–

Entries for locations of corporate historical records, with contact information, type of organization, hours of service, conditions of access, holdings, and total number of volumes. Some professional associations are included.

850 Directory of foreign firms operating in the United States. New York: Simon and Schuster, 1969–2010 ISSN 0070-5543

338.88873025 HG4057

Lists some 3,500 foreign firms from 86 countries that own nearly 10,000 businesses in the U.S. Gives locations for the American headquarters and selected branches, subsidiaries or affiliates. Includes contact information. Pt. 1 is an alphabetical listing by American affiliate country, pt. 2 is an alphabetical listing by foreign firm, and pt. 3 is an alphabetical listing by American affiliate. Ceased in paper with the 15th edition of 2010. Available online through *UniWorld*. Companion to the *Directory of American firms operating in foreign countries* (848).

851 Directory of United States exporters.
New York: Journal of Commerce, 1990–
2010 ISSN 1057-6878

HF3011.D63

Describes U.S. cargo shippers and the products they export. Gives contact information, SIC code, top executives, TEU's (twenty-foot equivalent unit container size) and metric tonnage, estimated value, ports of exit, and products. Arranged by state and indexed by company and product (uses Harmonized Commodity Codes). Also provides contact information for: export assistance centers, U.S. and foreign commercial service international posts, trade commissions, foreign embassies and consulates, U.S. foreign trade zones, world ports, and banks and other financial services. Companion to *Directory of United States importers* (852). Ceased with edition of 2010.

852 Directory of United States importers.
Journal of Commerce, Inc. New York: Journal of Commerce, 1991–2010. ill. ISSN 1057-5111

382.502573   HF3012.D53

A geographical listing of importers to the U.S., indexed by products (Harmonized Commodity Codes) and industry [Standard Industrial Classification (SIC) codes]. Gives contact information, SIC code, top executives, TEU's (Twenty-foot Equivalent Unit container size) and metric tonnage, estimated value, ports of exit, and products. Also provides contact information for: trade commissions, foreign embassies and consulates in the U.S., U.S. foreign trade zones, world ports, and banks and other financial services. Companion to the *Directory of United States exporters* (851). Ceased with the edition of 2010.

**853 Harris U.S. manufacturers directory.
National ed.** Harris InfoSource, National Association of Manufacturers (U.S.). Twinsburg, Ohio: Harris InfoSource, 2000– ISSN 1531-8273

338   HF5035

Entries for U.S. companies include location, contact information, industry descriptions, Standard Industrial Classification (SIC) or NAICS codes, executive names, and size. Indexed by company name, geography, product or service category, and SIC code. Libraries receiving questions about local companies may want to invest in the regional and state directories also published by Harris. Regional editions are

published for the Northeast, Southeast, Midwest, and West. Available in an online version.

854 Headquarters USA: A directory of contact information for headquarters and other central offices of major businesses and organizations nationwide. Omnigraphics (Firm). Detroit: Omnigraphics, 1977–
ISSN 1531-2909

384.602573   HF5035

Annual. Contains over 100,000 entries listing central offices for businesses, professional organizations, government agencies, non-profits, military bases, sports teams, associations, industries, and political organizations. Minimal listings: name, mailing address, Web address, ZIP Code, fax, stock exchange information, and phone or toll-free numbers. Useful conglomerate and subsidiaries section. Separate volumes with listings alphabetically and by subject. Also available electronically as *HQ Online*. Formerly *Business phone book USA*.

855 Hoover's handbook of private companies. Hoover's. Austin, Tex.: Hoover's Business Press, 1997–
ISSN 1555-3744

338.7402573   HG4057

Covers 900 of the largest and most important private enterprises, including corporations, hospitals and health care organizations, charitable and membership organizations, mutual and cooperative organizations, joint ventures, government-owned corporations, and some major university systems. Information includes "A List-Lover's Compendium" with lists of the largest and fastest-growing companies; company profiles; and indexes: companies by industry, by headquarters, and by executive. Company profiles list top executives, locations, competitors, very brief historical financials covering 10 yr. (revenue, net income, net profit, number of employees, annual growth), current business profile and company history. Given how difficult basic financial information can be to find on private organizations, even the little information provided here can be useful.

856 Major chemical and petrochemical companies of the world. Graham & Whiteside. London: Graham & Whiteside, 2000– ISSN 1369-5444

661.804   HD9650.3 658.0029;

Lists over 7,000 companies, giving contact information, executive names, business description, brand names and trademarks, subsidiaries, principal bank, principal law firm, ticker symbol, date established, number of employees, auditors, and two years of very brief financial information (sales turnover, profit before tax, profit after tax, dividend per share, earnings per share, share capital, shareholders' equity).

857 Major companies of Europe. Graham & Whiteside. Farmington Hills, Mich.: Gale Cengage, 1982– ISSN 0266-934X
338.740254   HC241.2

Covers major companies and related service and professional organizations. Provides directory information, officers, products or services, parent company, number of employees, and summary financial information. Other similar titles from the same publisher: *Major companies of the Arab world, Major companies of central and eastern Europe and the commonwealth of independent states, Major companies of the Far East and Australasia, Major companies of Africa south of the Sahara, Major chemical and petrochemical companies of the world, Major energy companies of the world, Major financial institutions of the world, Major food and drink companies of the world, Major information technology companies of the world, Major pharmaceutical and biotechnology companies of the world,* and *Major telecommunications companies of the world.*

858 Major telecommunications companies of the world. Graham & Whiteside Ltd. Farmington Hills, Mich.: Gale Cengage, 1998– ISSN 1369-5460
384.043025   HE7621

Annual. Entries for 3,500 companies from around the world, giving contact information, executives' names, principal activities, parent company, subsidiaries, status (public/private), number of employees, and principal shareholders. Includes companies in the cellular and interneet markets. Useful for libraries that do not have good international business directories.

859 National directory of corporate giving. Foundation Center. New York: The Center, 1989– ISSN 1050-9852
361.76502573   HV89

Describes more than 4,300 companies, 1,600 corporate giving programs and 3,300 company-sponsored foundations, based on information provided to the Foundation Center or whose gift-giving activities were verified through public records. Entries, arranged alphabetically by company include general descriptions of the firms and their "giving mechanisms," types of programs funded, limitations (e.g., geographic, type of recipient), and relevant publications. Seven indexes: officers, donors, trustees, and administrators; geographic; international giving; type of support; subject; types of business; and corporation, foundation, and giving programs by name.

860 National directory of corporate public affairs. Columbia Books. Bethesda, Md.: Columbia Books, 1983– ISSN 0749-9736
659.28502573   HD59

Lists more than 2,600 companies that maintain public affairs or government affairs programs, with entries for 14,000 executives. Includes home address and Washington, D.C. address, associated political action committees, contributions to candidates, corporate foundations and corporate giving programs (with annual grant total, geographic preference, primary interests), public affairs personnel, and publications. Personnel directory, indexes by geography and by industry.

861 National directory of minority-owned business firms. Thomas D. Johnson, Business Research Services. Lombard, Ill.: Business Research Services, 1986– ISSN 0886-3881
338.642202573   HD2346.U5

Includes complete address, contact name, minority type, date founded, trading area, business description, number of employees, and sales volume for 47,000 businesses.

862 National minority and women-owned business directory. Diversity Information Resources, Inc. Minneapolis, Minn.: Diversity Information Resources, 2004–. ill. ISSN 1553-6025
338   HD2358.5.U6

Annual. Contains 9,000 entries in 84 industries with contact information, URL, products/services, year established, minority type, number of employees, annual sales, and certification. Indexed by company.

863 ReferenceUSA. http://www.referenceusa
.com/. infoUSA (Firm). Omaha, Neb.:
infoUSA Inc. 1999–

HF5035

Business directory covers 24 million U.S. businesses, 4 million new business, and 1.5 million
Canadian businesses. White pages cover 89 million
U.S. residents, and 12 million Canadian residential
households. Identifies over 800,000 U.S. health
care providers. Most used for the ability to download customized lists of companies from searches by
geography, size of business, sales volume, number of
employees, and executive gender.

864 Standard & Poor's netAdvantage.
http://www.netadvantage
.standardandpoors.com/. Standard and
Poor's Corporation. New York: Standard &
Poor's. 2001–

332.67   HG4515.95

Provides current market news, reports on stocks
and mutual funds, company profiles, corporation
records, and a biographical register of corporate
executives. Includes information on 85,000 privately held companies. Information from the S&P
500, S&P MidCap 400, and S&P SmallCap 600
indexes. Reprints text from recent issues of *The Outlook* and *Industry Surveys*. Searches allow screening
of stocks and bonds by industry, value, earnings.
Search by NAICS, or within 50 industries or 115
sub-industries.

**865 Standard and Poor's register
of corporations, directors, and
executives.** Standard and Poor's. New
York: Standard and Poor's. ill.
ISSN 0361-3623

332.67   HG4057

Annual. Information on public and private corporations, with current address, financial and marketing
information, and biographies for corporate executives and directors. Useful for identifying corporate
relationships and executive's business connections.
Vol. 1 lists firms, v. 2 lists executives, v. 3 provides
indexes including Standard Industrial Classification
(SIC) codes and geography. Available online as part
of *NetAdvantage*.

**866 Ward's business directory of U.S.
private and public companies.** Gale

Research Inc. Detroit: Gale Research,
1990– ISSN 1048-8707
338.7402573   HG4057

Vol. 1–3 list alphabetically over 110,000 public and
private companies, describing type of company,
number of employees, sales, officers, Standard Industrial Classification (SIC) codes, imports/exports, and
parent/subsidiary information. Vol.4 lists companies
by zip code within states and ranks the top 1,000
private and top 1,000 public companies, including tabular analysis by state, revenue per employee,
and SIC. Vol. 5 ranks companies by sales within SIC
codes and contains names of chief executive officers.
Most of the companies listed are privately held, making this source invaluable. Available in online format.

**867 World directory of trade and business
journals.** Euromonitor PLC. London:
Euromonitor PLC, 1996–1998
ISBN 9780863386299
016.338   Z7164.C81

Lists some 2,000 magazines, newsletters, and journals. Gives language, frequency, content, country
coverage, format, publisher and contact information. Arranged into 80 industry categories, beginning with advertising and ending with wholesaling.
Two indexes: A–Z index by country and publisher
with publications, and A–Z index of journals by
country. Especially useful for finding a source for
news, organizational information, trends or statistics
on a company or industry that is not gathered in a
reference resource. Published as recently as 1998
(3rd edition).

Corporate Profiles

**868 The almanac of American employers:
market research, statistics and trends
pertaining to the leading corporate
employers in America.** Jack W. Plunkett.
Houston, Tex.: Plunkett Research, 1985–
ISSN 1088-3150
338.7/4/02573   HF5382.75.U6

A comprehensive guide to the labor market in the
U.S., with profiles of more than 500 major companies, both private and public. Unique features
include information on companies most likely to
hire women and minorities, company hiring patterns
(will hire MBA's, engineers, liberal arts majors, etc.),

and company profiles that give textual information including corporate culture and plans for growth. Historical and projected statistics are updated in each edition, and include a U.S. Employment Overview; Total Employees, All Nonfarm Payrolls, Private Industry & Government; U.S. Civilian Labor Force; Number of People Employed and Unemployed, U.S.; Unemployed Jobseekers by Sex, Reason for Unemployment & Active Job Search Methods Used; U.S. Labor Force Ages 16 to 24 Years Old by School Enrollment, Educational Attainment, Sex, Race & Ethnicity; Medical Care Benefits in the U.S.: Access; Participation and Take-Up Rates; Retirement Benefits in the U.S.: Access, Participation and Take-Up Rates; Top 30 U.S. Occupations by Numerical Change in Job Growth; Top 30 U.S. Occupations by Percent Change in Job Growth; Occupations with the Largest Expected Employment Increases, U.S.; and Occupations with the Fastest Expected Decline. For the top "American Employers 500" list of firms, shows lists by Number of Employees, By Revenues, and By Profits; and organized by Industry List With Codes, Index of Companies Within Industry Groups, Alphabetical Index, Index of U.S. Headquarters Location by State, Index by Regions of the U.S. Where the Firms Have Locations, Index of Firms with International Operations, and Index of Firms Noted as Hot Spots for Advancement for Women & Minorities. Suggests Seven Keys for Job Seekers (Financial Stability, Growth Plan, Research and Development Programs, Product Launch and Production, Marketing and Distribution Methods, Employee Benefits, Quality of Work Factors, Other Considerations).

869 BigCharts. http://bigcharts.marketwatch .com/. MarketWatch, Inc. San Francisco: MarketWatch, Inc. 1998–

HG4638

Best known for historic stock quotes, BigCharts has information on over 50,000 symbols, including current information on all NYSE, Nasdaq, AMEX, and OTC stocks, all NASDAQ quoted mutual funds, as well as leading financial indexes and international exchanges. The current information includes company profiles, company financials, news, charts, analyst estimates, analysis, and intraday stock screeners. Historic quotes include open, closing, high and low prices, volume traded, split adjusted price, and adjustment factor since 1970.

870 Biznar. http://biznar.com/. Deep Web Technologies, Inc. Santa Fe, N.M.: Deep Web Technologies, Inc. 2008–

HF1

Federated search engine retrieving business-related information from more than 60 sites including government agencies and NGOs, blogs, and business and general news sources. An alternative to conventional search engines, with results that tend to show fewer advertisements, job postings, and Wikipedia entries. Other emerging alternative search engines for business research include *Enigma.io* which collates results from public data sets, and RankAndFiled .com which indexes and displays SEC filings by drawing on the EDGAR system.

871 Business insights. http://www .cengagesites.com/literature/782/gale -business-insights-global-essentials/. Gale (Firm). [Farmington Hills, Mich.]: Gale Cengage Learning. 2000–

HG4001

Until 2012, known as *Business and company resource center*. Redesigned at that time to support better searching across multiple kinds of content, manipulation of data to create custom charts, and advanced user tools such as text-to-speech and translation into more than 30 languages for the interface and some content. Web interface highlights company and industry information, comparison charts, and a glossary. Provides information about market share, market analysis and product trends, and allows comparison of companies. Content drawn from more than 3,900 periodicals (journals, newspapers, and trade publications); two million investment reports; 25,000 industry reports and 500 longer industry profiles with more detail; 2,500 market research reports; over 10,000 company histories from *International directory of company histories* (906) and more than 2,000 company chronologies; 500,000 shorter company profiles; 65,000 articles from *Business rankings annual* (909); and listings of 70,000 associations.

872 Corporate affiliations. http://www .corporateaffiliations.com/. LexisNexis Group. New Providence, N.J.: LexisNexis Group. 2001–

HG4057

Profiles some one million public and private companies, with information on affiliates, subsidiaries, and divisions. Search by company type, location, title of executive, NAICS or SIC code, number of employees, sales revenue, ownership, fiscal year, stock exchange, earnings, assets, net worth, and liabilities. Profiles include contact information, very brief business description, year founded, number of employees, NAICS and SIC codes, names of top executives, outside service firms, and top competitors. Most useful for visual who-owns-whom hierarchies, linking to profiles for all companies in the hierarchy. While international in scope, coverage is best for the United States. Historical backfile is available, with coverage from 1993. Also available in print as the *Directory of corporate affiliations*.

873 Factiva. http://www.dowjones.com/ factiva/. Dow Jones & Co. New York: Dow Jones and Reuters. [2001–]

HG4515.9

Full-text articles from wire services such as Dow Jones and Reuters, major American and world newspapers such as the *New York Times*, leading business newspapers such as the *Wall Street Journal*, and a wide range of periodicals including *Barron's* and *Forbes*. Provides industry snapshots for more than 100 categories such as insurance, steel production, or alternative fuels; current and recent stock and currency price quotes (with graphing capability); and company snapshots for tens of thousands of worldwide firms. Content is in 28 languages.

874 General businessfile ASAP. http://www .gale.cengage.com/customer_service/ sample_searches/gbfasap.htm. Gale Group (Firm). Farmington Hills, Mich.: Gale Cengage. 1999–

016.07   HF5030

Includes a variety of business research sources in one product: full text of selected newspaper and journal articles, indexing of other periodicals, directory information for 200,000 companies, and Investext investment reports. Some content extends back to 1980. Rolling coverage of one year of the *Wall Street Journal*. Searchable by keywords in abstracts or full text, author name, or subject term.

875 Hoovers. http://www.hoovers.com/. Reference Press, Hoover's, Inc. Short Hills, N.J.: Dun & Bradstreet. 1996–

338.7   HG4057

More than 60 million records describe public and private companies primarily in the United States, but including Canada, United Kingdom, Europe, and Asia/Pacific. Profiles have an overview, history, family tree, industry information, products/operations, top competitors, competitive landscape, top executives with biographies, news, significant developments, and financial data. Financial summaries may include an income statement; balance sheet; cash flow; historical financials such as five years of P/E and per share; stock quotes; interactive stock charts; market data; earnings estimates; this year's ratios for the company, industry, and market; SEC filings; and industry watch for trends.

Content is tracked for 900 industries, organized into numerous larger categories: Agriculture & Forestry; Arts, Entertainment & Recreation; Beverage Manufacturing; Biotechnology Product Manufacturing; Business Services; Chemical Manufacturing; Commercial Equipment Repair & Maintenance; Commercial Printing; Computer Hardware Manufacturing; Computer Software; Construction; Consumer Products Manufacturing; Consumer Services; Contract Electronics Manufacturing; Education; Electric Power Generation; Electric Power Transmission, Distribution & Marketing; Electric Utilities; Electrical Products Manufacturing; Fabricated Metal Product Manufacturing; Financial Services; Food Manufacturing; Government; Health Care Products Manufacturing; Health Care; HVAC Equipment Manufacturing; Industrial Manufacturing; Insurance; Leasing of Intangible Assets; Lodging; Machinery Manufacturing; Magnetic & Optical Media; Manufacturing & Reproduction; Managed Application & Network Services; Management of Companies & Enterprises; Media; Membership Organizations; Mining; Miscellaneous Manufacturing; Natural Gas Distribution & Marketing; Nonclassifiable establishments; Nonmetallic Mineral Product Manufacturing; Nonprofit Institutions; Oil & Gas Exploration & Production; Oil & Gas Field Services; Oil & Gas Well Drilling; Petroleum & Coal Products Manufacturing; Pharmaceutical Manufacturing; Primary Metals Manufacturing; Private Households; Professional Services; Real Estate; Religious Organizations; Rental & Leasing; Restaurants, Bars & Food Services; Retail; Security Products Manufacturing; Semiconductor & Other Electronic Component Manufacturing; Telecommunications Equipment Manufacturing; Telecommunications Services; Transportation Equipment Manufacturing; Transportation

Services; Water & Sewer Utilities; Wholesale; and Wood Product Manufacturing.

Coverage can be brief, but generally includes a fact sheet, overview, selected companies, industry watch with video interviews, news from the last 90 days, and web resources for terminology, associations, and organizations, and online publications. Hoover's print publications include (*Hoover's handbook of American business* (876), *Hoover's handbook of private companies* (855)).

876 Hoover's handbook of American business. Gary Hoover. Austin, Tex.: Hoovers Inc., 1992–. ill. ISSN 1055-7202

338.7402573   HG4057

Annual. Profiles 750 U.S. companies, about 50 of which are privately owned. In one to two pages, profiles discuss company history, major events, current strategy, and place in the industry. Lists top executives, contact information, domestic locations, number and type of international locations, products or services as a percentage of sales, competitors, and a brief snapshot of historical financials, with three financial ratios (debt ratio, return on equity, and current ratio). Indexed by industry, location of headquarters, and executive name. Available online through Hoovers Online (875).

877 Hoover's handbook of private companies. Hoover's. Austin, Tex.: Hoover's Business Press, 1997–

ISSN 1555-3744

338.7402573   HG4057

Covers 900 of the largest and most important private enterprises, including corporations, hospitals and health care organizations, charitable and membership organizations, mutual and cooperative organizations, joint ventures, government-owned corporations, and some major university systems. Information includes "A List-Lover's Compendium" with lists of the largest and fastest-growing companies; company profiles; and indexes: companies by industry, by headquarters, and by executive. Company profiles list top executives, locations, competitors, very brief historical financials covering 10 yr. (revenue, net income, net profit, number of employees, annual growth), current business profile and company history. Given how difficult basic financial information can be to find on private organizations, even the little information provided here can be useful.

878 Investext plus. http://research.thomsonib.com/. Thomson Financial (Firm). Boston: Thomson Reuters. [1998–]

HG4001

Company news and industry reports written by analysts in some 500 investment banks in North America, Europe, Asia/Pacific, Latin America, Africa, and the Middle East. Also contains research reports on 190 trade associations. Reports range from 1–100 pages long. Covers 10,000 publicly traded U.S. companies. Reports give earnings estimates, financials, business ratios, trends, forecasts, credit ratings, analysis, text of conference calls, and stock prices. Industry reports give background, financials, business ratios, trends, forecasts, analysis, and some brief company profiles. Formerly Research Bank Web. Coverage is global and dates from 1980 to the present.

879 MarketLine business information centre. http://www.marketline.com/. MarketLine. London; New York: MarketLine. 1994–2010

HD2709

Merged with Business insights (793) in 2010 to form Marketline advantage (799).

Provided profiles of about large companies, industry segments, and countries, with an international scope. Company profile information included business descriptions and histories, major products and services, revenue analysis, key employees and biographies, locations and subsidiaries, company view (often taken from an annual report), SWOT analysis, and list of top competitors. Industry profiles were Datamonitor reports, with an executive summary, market overview, market value, market segmentation, competitve landscape, leading companies, and market forecast. Country profiles offered information on the economy, politics and government. Valued for international coverage of industry segments, with reports like "Beer in China." Shares of company profiles were 45 percent United States, 35 percent European, 15 percent Asian, and 5 percent from the rest of world.

880 Marketresearch.com academic. http://www.marketresearch.com/. Kalorama Information. Rockville, Md.: Marketresearch.com. 1999–

HF5415.2

Offers for sale the market research reports from over 700 sources (Icon Group, Kalorama, BizMiner, etc.). Browsable abstracts can be searched by publisher, country, and company name, and in industry categories: Consumer Goods (apparel, cosmetics and personal care, house and home, pet services and supplies, travel services), Food and Beverage (alcoholic beverages, coffee and tea, soft drinks, confectionery, dairy products, food processing), Heavy Industry (energy, mining, utilities, construction, machines and parts, manufacturing, metals, paper and forest products, plastics, automotive, aviation & aerospace, logistics and shipping), Service Industries (accounting and finance, corporate services, banking and financial services, insurance), Public Sector (associations/nonprofits, education, government), Life Science (biotechnology, agriculture, genomics, proteomics, medical imaging, healthcare facilities, managed care, regulation and policy, cardiovascular devices, equipment and supplies, wound care, pharmaceuticals, diseases and conditions, prescription drugs, therapeutic area), Technology & Media (computer equipment, electronics, networks, e-commerce and IT outsourcing, software, telecommunications, wireless), and Demographics (age, lifestyle and economics, multicultural).

Reports range in length, with some over 300 pages long, and give a variety of information (definition of industry, consumer demographics, consumer shopping habits, spending patterns, sales, establishments, employment, forecasts, trends, market size, market share, and market segmentation). Some company information is also included.

881   Orbis: a world of company information. http://orbis.bvdinfo .com/. Bureau van Dijk (Firm). Amsterdam: Bureau van Dijk Electronic Pub. 2002–

HD2731

Detailed hard-to-find company information for 65,000 private firms, with less complete coverage for up to 100 million companies in the Asia-Pacific region, Europe and the Americas. Includes news, financial profiles, contact names, documents, and stock data if applicable. Also tracks related patent information. *Zephyr* is a related tool for mergers and acquisitions, IPOs and venture capital deals.

882   Organization charts: structures of 230 businesses, government agencies, and non-profit organizations. 3rd ed. Nick Sternberg, Scott Heil. Detroit: Gale Research, 2000. xi, 353 p., ill. ISBN 0787624527

658.402   HD38

A unique collection of over 200 organization charts, showing how corporations are structured. "Organizations of many types, sizes, and from a variety of industries have been included: large and small, public and private, profit and non-profit, international and local."—*Pref.* This 3rd ed. contains some of the same corporations as the earlier editions, allowing comparison over time.

883   Passport GMID. http://www.euromonitor .com/. Euromonitor International. London, U.K.: Euromonitor International. [1999–]

658.8   HF5415.2

Also known under previous product names as *Global market information database*, *GMID*, or *Euromonitor GMID*. Market reports, company profiles, and demographic, economic, and marketing statistics for 205 countries. Market reports are for 16 consumer markets (food and drink, tobacco, toys, etc.) and 14 industrial and service markets (accountancy, broadcasting, chemicals, property services, etc.).

Reports have market size, market sectors, share of market, marketing activity, research and development, corporate overview, distribution, consumer profiles, market forecasts, sector forecasts, sources, and definitions. Additional reports are available for market segments, such as baby food. Company profiles have background, recent news, competitve environment, and outlook. Consumer lifestyle reports and very useful marketing background analyze the consumer by country, gender, age, marital status, educational attainment, ethnicity, religion, home ownership, household profile, employment, income, health, eating and personal grooming habits, leisure activities, personal finance, communication, transport, and travel.

Search for data, which can be exported into Excel or browse for reports. Data are available since 1977 and include inflation, exchange rates, GDP, GNI, government expenditures, government finance, income, labor, and money supply.

Similar information on a smaller scale is available in Research monitor (783) from the same publisher.

884 PrivCo: private company financial intelligence. http://www.privco.com/. PrivCo (Firm). New York: PrivCo. 2009–

HG4057

Covers private companies, private investors, venture capital funding, private merger and acquisition deals, and private equity deals. Profiles and financial information for more than 200,000 companies, primarily in the U.S., Canada, and the U.K. Searchable by location, industry sector, SIC/NAICS code, and annual revenue, or by company or investor name.

885 The value line investment survey.
U.S. ed. Value Line. New York: Value Line, 1936–. diagrs. ISSN 0042-2401

332.6305   HG4501.V26

In three parts: ratings and reports, selection and opinion, and summary and index. Ratings and reports provides stock analysis for some 1,700 stocks and is a good source for betas, quarterly dividends, earnings per share, and other ratios. Also includes 90 short industry reviews. Selection and opinion analyzes the economy and stock markets, providing stock picks. Summary and index provides screening data on stocks and industries. Available also in online format.

886 The value line investment survey: small and mid-cap. Expanded ed.
Value Line. New York: Value Line, 1995–ISSN 1080-7705

332.605   HG4501.V262

Reports on 1,800 small and mid-cap stocks, with consensus earning estimates and basic financials. Each issue profiles 130–140 companies, with business descriptions, corporate developments, betas, total shareholder return, four years of quarterly sales, quarterly dividends, and quarterly earnings per share data, as well as other ratio and financial data. In two parts: ratings and reports, and summary and index. Used primarily for investing, as well as by researchers for gathering financial data. The expanded edition is now called *Small/mid-cap edition*. Available in an online version.

Financial Filings

887 Accounting research manager. http://www.accountingresearchmanager.com/.

CCH Incorporated. Riverwoods, Ill.: Wolters Kluwer. 2004–

HF5626

Includes a dizzying array of authoritative and interpretive financial reporting literature. Divided into accounting, SEC, auditing, and government sections, each with standards, interpretations, and examples. The acccounting section has documents from the Financial Accounting Standards Board (FASB), Emerging Issues Task Force (EITF), and International Accounting Standards Board (IASB). The SEC section includes Regulations S-X and S-K, Forms 10-K and 10-Q, SABs, Sarbanes-Oxley, Public Company Accounting Oversight Board (PCAOB), and Regulation S-B. The audit section includes AICPA, Public Company Accounting Oversight Board (PCAOB), U.S. Department of Housing and Urban Development, Office of Management and Budgets (OMB), and American Institute of Certified Public Accountants (AICPA). The government section includes GASB, GAO, and OMB.

Documents are color coded: white for authoritative, beige for interpretation, blue for proposed, and green for SEC. They also show amendments, deletions, or suspensions. SEC filings since 1994, available in Word, Adobe Acrobat, and Excel. Highlights current developments and events on the home page. An online tutorial and regularly scheduled live tutorials are available and recommended to master the database. Updated five times a day.

888 Bankscope. http://www.bvdinfo.com/en-us/products/company-information/international/bankscope. Bureau van Dijk Electronic Publishing. Brussels, Belgium: Bureau van Dijk Electronic Publishing. 1998–

HG1501

Financial information on more than 11,000 public and private banks worldwide. Provides standardized reports, ratings, ownership data, financial analysis, security and price information, scanned images of the bank's annual or interim accounts, and country risk reports. Most data goes back eight years. Data sources include Fitch Ratings. Standardized reports contain detailed consolidated and/or unconsolidated balance sheet and income statement, as well as 36 pre-calculated ratios. Data can be downloaded to Excel. Also available through WRDS (235).

889 EDGAR database of corporate information. http://www.sec.gov/edgar
.shtml. U.S. Securities and Exchange
Commission. Washington: U.S. Securities
and Exchange Commission. 1994–
338.6 HF5035

U.S. public company filings from 1993 through
the present, from the SEC. Mutual fund filings
since Feb. 6, 2006. Search by company name, fund
name, ticker symbol, filing number, state, NAICS
or Standard Industrial Classification (SIC) code,
and Ownership Forms. Mutual fund prospectuses,
also known as 484 filings, also available. Useful for
researchers interested in more than the numbers in
a financial filing. *WordsAnalytics* and RankAndFiled
.com are alternative interfaces to EDGAR content.

890 Foundation center 990 finder. http://
foundationcenter.org/findfunders/
990finder/. Foundation Center. New York:
Foundation Center. 2006–
AS911

Gives completed IRS forms 990 (Return of Organization Exempt from Income Tax) and 990PF (Return
of Private Foundation) from 1993 to the present. The
forms give revenue and expenses; information about
officers, directors, trustees, foundation managers,
highly paid employees, and contractors; summary of
direct charitable activities; private operating foundations; and grants and contributions paid. Search by
organization name, state, ZIP code, employer identification number (EIN), and year.

891 Mergent online. http://www.mergent
.com/. Moody's Investors Service,
Financial Information Services. New York:
Moody's Investors Service. 1997–
338.74 HG4061

Provides a full source of information on company
details, equity pricing, company financials, indus-
try reports, news, and 58,000 annual reports. Cov-
ers U.S. and international public and private firms.
Reports can be created by searching company details
(Synopsis, Financial Highlights, History, Joint Ven-
tures, Business, Property, Subsidiary, Long Term
Debt, and Capital Structure); research and news
(Historic News, Institutional Holdings, and Insider
Holdings); and financial statements (Income State-
ment, Balance Sheet, Cash Flows, and Profitability
Ratios). Financials can be exported into Excel. More

than 1,500 one-page equity reports for NYSE, NAS-
DAQ, and AMEX companies, with quarterly financial
results, analyses of future prospects, and operating
ratios. Access to SEC EDGAR filings from 1993 to
present and data on 20,000 non-U.S.-based corporations. Industry reports, while brief, are international
in scope. Includes content formerly found in the
Mergent manuals (*Mergent industrial manual, Mergent
international manual, Mergent bank & finance manual,
Mergent OTC industrial manual, Mergent OTC unlisted
manual,* and *Mergent public utility & transportation
manual*) once known as Moody's, except for the
Municipal and government manual.

892 ProQuest historical annual reports.
http://www.proquest.com/en-US/catalogs/
databases/detail/pq_hist_annual_repts
.shtml. ProQuest Information and
Learning Company. Ann Arbor, Mich.:
ProQuest Information and Learning.
2006–
HG4028.B2

PDF copies of annual reports from 1884 to the present
for nearly 850 U.S. companies. Most coverage begins
before 1950. From the 222-page long report for Union
Pacific Railway Company in 1884 to the 28-page long
Dell Annual Report from 2005, this is a unique collection. Not all company coverage is complete, as reports
for some years have not yet been located. In addition to
the standard ProQuest search capabilities, companies
can be browsed by year, name, or industry.

893 Research insight. https://www.capitaliq
.com/home.aspx. Capital IQ (Firm). New
York: Standard and Poor's. 1998–
657.3 HG4001

Research Insight is the new interface to Compustat.
An essential resource with the most recent 20 years
of U.S. and Canadian financial statement data and
monthly closing stock price data, six months of daily
stock prices, and GlobalVantage, the most recent
10 years of financial data for companies in 80 countries. Not an easy database to use; complex screening
is possible, which becomes easier from within Excel.
Screening can be done for data items in financial
reports. Choose from quarterly or annual financials,
and from nearly every data item within a financial
report. Over 100 preformatted reports are available
(EVAntage, company highlights, cash flow statements, combined reports, common size statements,

institutional holdings). Data is also available for geographic areas, industry composites, aggregates, and stock indexes, and about 7,000 inactive companies.

894   Thomson one banker. http://banker
.thomsonone.com/. Thomson Financial
(Firm). New York: Thomson Reuters.
2003–

HG4057.A1

65,000 active and inactive global companies, with company financials, earnings estimates, analyst forecasts, market indices data, mergers and acquisitions, and corporate transaction data from 1998, and near real-time market data and stock quotes from Thomson Financial, Datastream advance (207), Extel, First Call, Worldscope, and Disclosure. Most data is a rolling ten years. Allows advanced screening and use of Excel to download and analyize data.

Indexes; Abstract Journals

895   ABI/Inform global. http://www.il
.proquest.com/products_pq/descriptions/
abi_inform_global.shtml. ProQuest. Ann
Arbor, Mich.: ProQuest. 1971–

HF54.7.A25

ABI/Inform, an early and important entrant in the bibliographic database marketplace, has expanded coverage and changed platforms over the years: access today of course is via the Web. Indexing and abstracting of business periodicals, some economics periodicals, as well as other periodicals related to business. Periodical coverage extends back as far as 1923 in some cases. Sold in several versions: extent of content varies with price.

ABI/Inform global covers more than 3,700 publications, with more than 2,600 available in full text. Includes 18,000 business-related dissertations, some 5,000 business case studies, the *Wall Street Journal* since 1984, and *EIU ViewsWire*.

ABI/Inform complete includes more than 6,000 periodicals, 30,000 business-related dissertations, the *Economist* and *Wall Street Journal*, 100,000 working papers from sources like OECD, and analysis of industries, markets and countries.

ABI/Inform research covers over 1,800 journals, with more than 1,200 available in full text.

ABI/Inform dateline offers some 280 periodicals, with more than 230 available in full text. These

include journals, newspapers, trade magazines and regional sources.

A comparable and competing product is Business source elite (34).

896   Business insights. http://www
.cengagesites.com/literature/782/gale
-business-insights-global-essentials/. Gale
(Firm). [Farmington Hills, Mich.]: Gale
Cengage Learning. 2000–

HG4001

Until 2012, known as *Business and company resource center*. Redesigned at that time to support better searching across multiple kinds of content, manipulation of data to create custom charts, and advanced user tools such as text-to-speech and translation into more than 30 languages for the interface and some content. Web interface highlights company and industry information, comparison charts, and a glossary. Provides information about market share, market analysis and product trends, and allows comparison of companies. Content drawn from more than 3,900 periodicals (journals, newspapers, and trade publications); two million investment reports; 25,000 industry reports and 500 longer industry profiles with more detail; 2,500 market research reports; over 10,000 company histories from *International directory of company histories* (906) and more than 2,000 company chronologies; 500,000 shorter company profiles; 65,000 articles from *Business rankings annual* (909); and listings of 70,000 associations.

897   Business source elite. http://www
.ebscohost.com/academic/business-source
-elite. EBSCO Publishing. Ipswich, Mass.:
EBSCO. 1997– ISSN 1092-9754

338   HF5001

Comprehensive indexing of a wide range of business-related periodicals, reports and news sources. EBSCO publishes several versions of its business database product, with content that varies in extent and pricing. All include access to a *Regional business news* collection. All resources are delivered over the Web.

Business Source elite covers more than 1,100 business periodicals, including Harvard Business Review (47), and more than 10,000 Datamonitor company profiles. Over 1,000 journals are full text. Backfiles from 1985.

Business Source complete indexes some 2,000 peer-reviewed business journals and over 1,800 trade periodicals, many in full text, with some coverage from as early as 1886; over a million company profiles; market reports, industry reports and economic reports on individual countries; and 9,000 case studies.

Business Source premier covers some 2,200 periodicals, with some full text going back to 1965, and a smaller array of marketing, industry, company and country reports.

Business source corporate is a similar product marketed to companies, with full text from 2,700 periodicals, and numerous company, industry and country profiles and reports.

Successor to the print-format *Business periodicals index* (1959–) and online *Business abstracts* (1991–), published until 2011 by the H. W. Wilson Company. Incorporates older content formerly found in *Business periodicals index retrospective* (1913–1982).

A similar and competing product is ABI/Inform global (31).

898 LexisNexis academic. http://www .lexisnexis.com/en-us/products/lexisnexis -academic.page. LexisNexis (Firm). Bethesda, Md.: LexisNexis. 1984–
KF242.A1
Searchable full-text subscription database that includes full text of articles from more than 2,500 newspapers, news from more than 300 local and regional newspapers, blogs and other web sources via WebNews, broadcast transcripts from the major radio and TV networks; national and international wire services; campus newspapers; polls and surveys; and over 600 newsletters. Non-English language news sources available in Spanish, French, German, Italian, and Dutch. Dates of coverage vary by individual source, with newspapers updated daily. Legal content includes federal and U.S. state statutes and cases, including Supreme Court decisions since 1790; some 800 law reviews; federal regulations; Shepherd's citations; and selective international coverage. Business content includes company information for 80 million public, private and international firms; profiles of 58 million executives; SEC filings; and industry profiles. A comparable resource for legal, news and business content is Westlaw (43).

899 Westlaw. http://legalsolutions .thomsonreuters.com/law-products/. West Publishing. Eagan, Minn.: West Publishing/Thomson Reuters. 1975–

One of the major online platforms for U.S. legal research, combined with full text searching of news, and business research content. Searchable full text of federal and state statutes, case law including Supreme Court opinions, administrative codes, and specialized legal content including some international coverage. Also includes periodical literature, from legal journals and law reviews to newspapers and magazines. This is the online equivalent of print format West legal volumes, and incorporates the West Key Number System which groups entries by topic. Available only to subscribers, including working professional attorneys, courts, and law schools with their libraries. News content benefits from the connection to Reuters. WestlawNext offers "Company Investigator" searching and report-making based on 30 million company profiles. A comparable resource is LexisNexis (39).

Histories

900 A bibliography of British business histories. Francis Goodall. Aldershot, U.K.; Brookfield, Vt.: Gower, 1987. 638 p. ISBN 0566053071
016.338740941   Z7165.G8; HC253
The main section lists works alphabetically by author, giving full bibliographic information for each title and noting the presence of indexes or illustrations, the name of the firm described, its primary SIC, and a code for the source library. Preliminary pages include an essay on the nature, new directions, and methodology of business history, the British standard industrial classification, a bibliography of business history bibliographies, libraries with business history collections, and a list of abbreviations. Company name and SIC indexes.

901 Encyclopedia of American business history. Charles R. Geisst. New York: Facts On File, 2005
ISBN 9780816043507
338.097303   HF3021
Contains 400 entries on businesses and industries, business events, and leaders, as well as business and economic topics from 1776 to the present. Entries are cross-referenced and include recommended readings. Writing is accessible for students in high school, but coverage is complete enough to be useful to a much wider audience. Includes a chronology and

15 primary documents, including essays, legislative acts, and court judgments. Available as an e-book.

902 Encyclopedia of American business history and biography. Facts On File. New York: Facts On File, 1988–1994. ill.
0816013713   HC102

Combines biographical entries with articles discussing major companies, government and labor organizations, inventions, and legal decisions for various industries. The signed entries range in length from one-half to ten or more pages; most include photographs or other illustrations, and list publications and references, archives, and unpublished documents. Each volume is available separately. Ten volumes were published up to 1994, including *The airline industry*; *The automobile industry, 1896–1920*; *The automobile industry, 1920–1980*; *Banking and finance to 1913*; *Banking and finance, 1913–1989*; *Iron and steel in the nineteenth century*; *Iron and steel in the twentieth century*; *Railroads in the nineteenth century*; and *Railroads in the age of regulation, 1900–1980*.

903 Directory of corporate archives in the United States and Canada. http://www2.archivists.org/groups/business-archives-section/directory-of-corporate-archives-in-the-united-states-and-canada-indexed-by-location. Gregory S. Hunter. Chicago: Business Archives Section, Society of American Archivists. 1997–

Entries for locations of corporate historical records, with contact information, type of organization, hours of service, conditions of access, holdings, and total number of volumes. Some professional associations are included.

904 Global companies in the twentieth century: selected archival histories. Malcolm McIntosh, Ruth Thomas. London; New York: Routledge, 2001. 9 v., ill., maps ISBN 0415181100
338.88   HD2755.5

While *Global Companies* examines a select set of companies (BBC, Levi Strauss and Co., Broken Hill Proprietary Company, Barclays, BP Amoco, Rio Tinto, Cable and Wireless, Marks and Spencer, and Royal Dutch/Shell), it does so thoroughly. Uses company archival documents to analyze how the companies have changed and adapted over time.

905 International bibliography of business history. Francis Goodall, T. R. Gourvish, Steven Tolliday. London; New York: Routledge, 1997. xvi, 668 p. ISBN 9780415086417
016.3387   HF1008

Selective bibliography of business history in the U.S., Europe, Japan, and the "rest of the world." Annotations are critical and explain the nature and content of each work. Arranged by industry, with an index for authors and for firms mentioned in each work.

906 International directory of company histories. Jay P. Pederson, Tina Grant, St. James Press. Farmington Hills, Mich.: Gale Cengage, 1988– ISSN 1557-0126
338.7   HD2721

Perhaps the best known source of company histories, each volume covers about 250 companies. Entries are 3–5 p. long, with information on founding, major corporate events, management, key dates, principal subsidiaries, divisions and units, and main competitors. Volumes include a cumulative index to companies and personal names. Beginning with v. 7, volumes contain a cumulative index to industries, and beginning with v. 37, a geographical index to companies. Also available online in Business insights: essentials. (581).

907 United States business history, 1602–1988: a chronology. Richard Robinson. New York: Greenwood Press, 1990. xii, 643 p. ISBN 9780313260957
338.0973   HC103

"Designed to provide a basic calendar of representative events . . . in the evolution of U.S. business."—*Pref.* Contains descriptive historical data, arranged by year, then under categories of general news and business news. Significant individuals, specific companies, inventions, trade unions, and key business, economic, and social developments are included. Brief bibliography; detailed index. Complemented by *Robinson's business history of the world: a chronology*.

Statistics

908 Bizminer. http://www.bizminer.com/. Brandow Company (Firm). Camp Hill, Pa.: Brandow Company. 2002–
     HF1416

Provides financial analysis of U.S. industries and their markets. Covers some 9,000 sectors. Includes recent sales figures, balance sheet summaries, and financial ratios for companies; and survey of firms, market volume, annual sales, and startup activity for industries. Searchable by NAICS, keyword, and names of companies.

909 Business rankings annual. Business Library (Brooklyn Public Library). Detroit: Gale Research, 1989– ISSN 1043-7908
338.74097305   HG4050
Collects together some 5,000 business ranking lists from newspapers, periodicals, directories, statistical annuals, and other publications, arranged alphabetically by subject. The "top ten" entries from each list are reprinted here. International in scope, content covers companies, products, services, and activities ranked by factors including assets, sales, revenue, production, employees, and market value. Each entry provides ranking criteria, first ten items in the original list, and source information including publication frequency. Available as an e-book.

910 Daily stock price record. Standard and Poor's Corporation. New York: Standard and Poor's, 1993–2011 ISSN 1072-3846
332.632220973   HG4915
Pt. 1 includes Standard and Poor's Indexes and the Dow Jones Averages. Pt. 2 includes information on daily volume, high, low, and closing prices for New York Stock Exchange, NASDAQ, Over the Counter, and American Stock Exchange stocks. Very useful as a historical source, especially for defunct stocks whose symbols and prices are difficult to find in other sources. Ceased in print format in mid-2011: later daily prices can be found in online sources such as BigCharts (557).

911 D and B business rankings. Dun and Bradstreet, Inc. Bethlehem, Pa.: Dun & Bradstreet, 1997–
338.7402573   HG4057
Ranks leading U.S. public and private businesses by annual sales volume and number of employees in five separate sections: alphabetically by company name, by state, by industry category, public businesses, and private businesses. Concluding sections cross-index division names with headquarter companies and list chief executives and other officers by function.

912 Estimates. http://thomsonreuters.com/estimates/. Thomson Reuters. New York: Thomson Reuters. 2008–
332.6   HG4501
Provides historical broker analyst information for more than 20,000 companies, as far back as 1976 for U.S. firms, since 1985 for Canada; since 1987 for Europe, the Middle East, Africa and the Asia/Pacific region; and since 1992 for Latin America. Forecasts include sales, revenue, net income, earnings, and dividends. Includes content from the Institutional Brokers Estimate System or I/B/E/S.

913 Market share reporter. Gale Research Inc., Gale Group. Detroit: Gale Research, 1991– ISSN 1052-9578
380.105   HF5410
Annual. Market share statistics for over 4,000 companies and 2,300 products and services. Compiled from periodicals and brokerage reports, and arranged by Standard Industrial Classification (SIC) code. Indexed by source, place name, product or service name, company, and brand name. Includes the information from what was *World Market Share Reporter*. Available as an e-book.

914 Mergerstat review. Merrill Lynch Business Brokerage and Valuation, W.T. Grimm and Co., Houlihan, Lokey, Howard, and Zukin. Chicago: The Company, 1982–. ill. ISSN 1071-4065
338.830973   HD2746.5
Annual review of mergers and acquisitions. Pt. 1 is statistical analysis with aggregate announcements, composition of aggregate net merger and acquisition announcements, method of payment, P/E offered, divestitures, publicly traded sellers, privately owned sellers, foreign sellers, aggressive buyers, financial advisor ranking, legal advisor ranking, top managers, and termination fees. Pt. 2 is industry analysis with highlights, industry groups, spotlights giving industry activity for the two most active industries by Standard Industrial Classification (SIC) code, multiples (TIC/EBITDA, P/E), premiums, composition, and cross-border activity. Pt. 3 is a geographical analysis with U.S. buyers and sellers by state, and foreign buyers and sellers. Pt. 4 is current year rosters with completed and pending transactions with pricing disclosed, canceled transactions with pricing disclosed, transactions with termination fees disclosed, and the

composition of the Mergerstat $1 billion club. Pt. 5 is a historical review with a 25-year statistical review, record holders, 100 largest announcements in history, and largest announcements by industry. Pt. 6 lists transactions by seller SIC code. There is also a glossary of terms. Available as an e-book, as *Mergerstat M&A Database*.

915 **RDS tablebase.** http://www.gale.cengage .com/rds/index.htm. Gale Cengage Learning (Firm). Farmington, Mich.: Gale Cengage Learning. 1996–

HG4027

A terrific international statistical source for company, industry, and demographic information including market share, market size, market trends, price trends, rankings, sales forecasts, output and capacity, consumption, imports and exports, and shipments. Information comes from 900 trade publications, including *Accounting today*, *Adweek*, *Aftermarket business*, *Almanac of american employers*, *Beverage world*, *Chemical week*, *Datamonitor industry market research*, *Meed Middle East economic digest*, as well as reports, newsletters, and surveys. Sold as part of the *RDS business suite* which also includes *Business & industry*, and *Business and management practices*.

916 **Research insight.** https://www.capitaliq .com/home.aspx. Capital IQ (Firm). New York: Standard and Poor's. 1998–

657.3 HG4001

Research Insight is the new interface to Compustat. An essential resource with the most recent 20 years of U.S. and Canadian financial statement data and monthly closing stock price data, six months of daily stock prices, and GlobalVantage, the most recent 10 years of financial data for companies in 80 countries. Not an easy database to use; complex screening is possible, which becomes easier from within Excel. Screening can be done for data items in financial reports. Choose from quarterly or annual financials, and from nearly every data item within a financial report. Over 100 preformatted reports are available (EVAntage, company highlights, cash flow statements, combined reports, common size statements, institutional holdings). Data is also available for geographic areas, industry composites, aggregates, and stock indexes, and about 7,000 inactive companies.

917 **Standard and Poor's industry surveys.** Standard and Poor's. New York: Standard and Poor's, 1973–2012 ISSN 0196-4666

332.67 HC106.6

Detailed analyses of 22 industry categories and the major companies in each category. Contains a basic analysis and a comprehensive source of information, updated by a current analysis. The analysis includes trends, information on how the industry operates, key ratios and statistics (revenues, net income, profit ratios, balance sheet ratios, equity ratios, per-share data, company and product rankings), information on how to analyze a company in that industry, and a glossary. Company and industry indexes. Ceased with edition of 2012.

918 **WRDS.** https://wrds-web.wharton.upenn .edu/wrds/. Wharton School. Philadelphia: The Wharton School, University of Pennsylvania. 1993–

HG4026

Wharton research data services supports quantitative data research through web access to a hosting service, for a number of financial databases, including Compustat (now *Research insight*) (573), CRSP (Center for Research in Securities Prices), Dow Jones Averages, FDIC, Philadelphia Stock Exchange, Institutional Brokers Estimate System (IBES), BankScope (888) from Bureau van Dijk, CSMAR China Stock Market databases, Eventus, Global Insight, NYSE-TAQ, and OptionMetrics.

6 Basic Industry Information

Overviews

919 Business monitor online. http://www
.businessmonitor.com/. Business Monitor
International (Firm). London: Business
Monitor International. 2004–
382.02   HF1379
Subscription service with reports on industry sectors,
countries including risk factors, and financial markets. News and analysis for specific world nations,
and industries including agribusiness, autos, commercial banking, consumer electronics, defense &
security, food & drink, freight transport, information technology, infrastructure, insurance, metals,
mining, oil & gas, petrochemicals, pharmaceuticals,
medical devices, power, real estate, renewables,
retail, shipping, telecommunications, tourism, and
water. Profiles for 500 multinational companies.
Includes coverage of emerging markets.

920 Encyclopedia of American industries.
6th ed. Gale/Cengage Learning.
Farmington Hills, Mich.: Gale Research,
2011. 3 v., ill. ISBN 9781414486833
ISSN 1941-2428
338/.0973/03   HC102
Sixth edition of 2011, in a series that began in 1994.
Volume 1 covers manufacturing industries; v. 2 covers agriculture, mining, construction, wholesale, &
retail industries; v. 3 covers finance, service & public administration industries. Articles are grouped

by product areas, such as furniture manufacturing
or retail services, and then by four-digit SIC codes.
Entries deal with industries as a whole, rather than
specific companies (for which see International
Directory of Company Histories (906)). Index. Also
available as an e-book.

921 Factiva. http://www.dowjones.com/
factiva/. Dow Jones & Co. New York: Dow
Jones and Reuters. [2001–]
                                          HG4515.9
Full-text articles from wire services such as Dow
Jones and Reuters, major American and world newspapers such as the *New York Times*, leading business newspapers such as the *Wall Street Journal*, and
a wide range of periodicals including *Barron's* and
Forbes. Provides industry snapshots for more than
100 categories such as insurance, steel production,
or alternative fuels; current and recent stock and currency price quotes (with graphing capability); and
company snapshots for tens of thousands of worldwide firms. Content is in 28 languages.

922 Hoovers. http://www.hoovers.com/.
Reference Press, Hoover's, Inc. Short Hills,
N.J.: Dun & Bradstreet. 1996–
338.7   HG4057
More than 60 million records describe public and
private companies primarily in the United States,
but including Canada, United Kingdom, Europe,
and Asia/Pacific. Profiles have an overview, history,

171

family tree, industry information, products/operations, top competitors, competitive landscape, top executives with biographies, news, significant developments, and financial data. Financial summaries may include an income statement; balance sheet; cash flow; historical financials such as five years of P/E and per share; stock quotes; interactive stock charts; market data; earnings estimates; this year's ratios for the company, industry, and market; SEC filings; and industry watch for trends.

Content is tracked for 900 industries, organized into numerous larger categories: Agriculture & Forestry; Arts, Entertainment & Recreation; Beverage Manufacturing; Biotechnology Product Manufacturing; Business Services; Chemical Manufacturing; Commercial Equipment Repair & Maintenance; Commercial Printing; Computer Hardware Manufacturing; Computer Software; Construction; Consumer Products Manufacturing; Consumer Services; Contract Electronics Manufacturing; Education; Electric Power Generation; Electric Power Transmission, Distribution & Marketing; Electric Utilities; Electrical Products Manufacturing; Fabricated Metal Product Manufacturing; Financial Services; Food Manufacturing; Government; Health Care Products Manufacturing; Health Care; HVAC Equipment Manufacturing; Industrial Manufacturing; Insurance; Leasing of Intangible Assets; Lodging; Machinery Manufacturing; Magnetic & Optical Media; Manufacturing & Reproduction; Managed Application & Network Services; Management of Companies & Enterprises; Media; Membership Organizations; Mining; Miscellaneous Manufacturing; Natural Gas Distribution & Marketing; Nonclassifiable establishments; Nonmetallic Mineral Product Manufacturing; Nonprofit Institutions; Oil & Gas Exploration & Production; Oil & Gas Field Services; Oil & Gas Well Drilling; Petroleum & Coal Products Manufacturing; Pharmaceutical Manufacturing; Primary Metals Manufacturing; Private Households; Professional Services; Real Estate; Religious Organizations; Rental & Leasing; Restaurants, Bars & Food Services; Retail; Security Products Manufacturing; Semiconductor & Other Electronic Component Manufacturing; Telecommunications Equipment Manufacturing; Telecommunications Services; Transportation Equipment Manufacturing; Transportation Services; Water & Sewer Utilities; Wholesale; and Wood Product Manufacturing.

Coverage can be brief, but generally includes a fact sheet, overview, selected companies, industry watch with video interviews, news from the last 90 days, and web resources for terminology, associations, and organizations, and online publications. Hoover's print publications include (*Hoover's handbook of American business* (876), *Hoover's handbook of private companies* (855)).

923 IBISWorld United States. http://www .ibisworld.com/. IBISWorld. New York: IBISWorld. 1999–

HC103

700 reports on American industries. Industry reports can be located using NAICS numbers. Major categories include: Accommodation & Food Services; Administration, Business Support & Waste Management Services; Agriculture, Forestry, Fishing & Hunting; Arts, Entertainment & Recreation; Construction; Educational Services; Finance & Insurance; Healthcare & Social Assistance; Information; Manufacturing; Mining; Other Services (except Public Administration); Professional, Scientific & Technical Services; Real Estate & Rental and Leasing; Retail Trade; Transportation & Warehousing; Utilities; and Wholesale Trade.

Reports include industry definition; information about the supply chain; key statistics; segmentations (products and services segmentation, major market segments, industry concentration, geographic spread); market characteristics (market size, demand determinants, domestic and international markets, basis of competition, life cycle); industry conditions (barriers to entry, taxation, industry assistance, regulation and deregulation, cost structure, capital and labor intensity, technology and systems, industry volatility, globalization); key factors (sensitivities and success factors); key competitors; and industry performance (current and historical). Glossaries and guides to jargon. Setting this database apart are reports on small industries, such as parking lots and garages.

924 Industry research using the economic census: how to find it, how to use it. Jennifer C. Boettcher, Leonard M. Gaines. Westport, Conn.: Greenwood Press, 2004. xv, 305 p., ill., 1 map ISBN 157356351X
338.097300727   HC101

Very useful guide to U.S. census concepts, methodology, terminology, and data sources, location of economic census resources. Appendixes for acronyms and initials, sample questionnaires, government print office, regional depository libraries, and state data centers. Available as an e-book.

925 Investext plus. http://research.thomsonib.com/. Thomson Financial (Firm). Boston: Thomson Reuters. [1998–]

HG4001

Company news and industry reports written by analysts in some 500 investment banks in North America, Europe, Asia/Pacific, Latin America, Africa, and the Middle East. Also contains research reports on 190 trade associations. Reports range from 1–100 pages long. Covers 10,000 publicly traded U.S. companies. Reports give earnings estimates, financials, business ratios, trends, forecasts, credit ratings, analysis, text of conference calls, and stock prices. Industry reports give background, financials, business ratios, trends, forecasts, analysis, and some brief company profiles. Formerly Research Bank Web. Coverage is global and dates from 1980 to the present.

926 Manufacturing and distribution USA: industry analyses, statistics, and leading companies. Gale Group. Detroit: Gale Group, 2000–. ill. ISSN 1529-7659

338   HD9721

Industry analyses, statistics, and contact information for U.S. companies in the manufacturing, wholesaling, and retail industries. National and state profiles give leading establishments, employment, payroll, inputs, and outputs. Includes public and private companies. Regularly updated: 7th edition published in 2013. Also available as an e-book.

927 Marketresearch.com academic. http://www.marketresearch.com/. Kalorama Information. Rockville, Md.: Marketresearch.com. 1999–

HF5415.2

Offers for sale the market research reports from over 700 sources (Icon Group, Kalorama, BizMiner, etc.). Browsable abstracts can be searched by publisher, country, and company name, and in industry categories: Consumer Goods (apparel, cosmetics and personal care, house and home, pet services and supplies, travel services), Food and Beverage (alcoholic beverages, coffee and tea, soft drinks, confectionery, dairy products, food processing), Heavy

Industry (energy, mining, utilities, construction, machines and parts, manufacturing, metals, paper and forest products, plastics, automotive, aviation & aerospace, logistics and shipping), Service Industries (accounting and finance, corporate services, banking and financial services, insurance), Public Sector (associations/nonprofits, education, government), Life Science (biotechnology, agriculture, genomics, proteomics, medical imaging, healthcare facilities, managed care, regulation and policy, cardiovascular devices, equipment and supplies, wound care, pharmaceuticals, diseases and conditions, prescription drugs, therapeutic area), Technology & Media (computer equipment, electronics, networks, e-commerce and IT outsourcing, software, telecommunications, wireless), and Demographics (age, lifestyle and economics, multicultural).

Reports range in length, with some over 300 pages long, and give a variety of information (definition of industry, consumer demographics, consumer shopping habits, spending patterns, sales, establishments, employment, forecasts, trends, market size, market share, and market segmentation). Some company information is also included.

928 Mergent online. http://www.mergent.com/. Moody's Investors Service, Financial Information Services. New York: Moody's Investors Service. 1997–

338.74   HG4061

Provides a full source of information on company details, equity pricing, company financials, industry reports, news, and 58,000 annual reports. Covers U.S. and international public and private firms. Reports can be created by searching company details (Synopsis, Financial Highlights, History, Joint Ventures, Business, Property, Subsidiary, Long Term Debt, and Capital Structure); research and news (Historic News, Institutional Holdings, and Insider Holdings); and financial statements (Income Statement, Balance Sheet, Cash Flows, and Profitability Ratios). Financials can be exported into Excel. More than 1,500 one-page equity reports for NYSE, NASDAQ, and AMEX companies, with quarterly financial results, analyses of future prospects, and operating ratios. Access to SEC EDGAR filings from 1993 to present and data on 20,000 non-U.S.-based corporations. Industry reports, while brief, are international in scope. Includes content formerly found in the Mergent manuals (*Mergent industrial manual, Mergent* international manual, *Mergent bank & finance manual, Mergent OTC industrial manual, Mergent OTC unlisted manual,* and *Mergent public utility & transportation manual*) once known as Moody's, except for the *Municipal and government manual.*

929 Mintel oxygen reports. http://www
.mintel.com/. Mintel Group, Ltd. (Firm). London; Chicago: Mintel Group, Ltd. 2003–

HC240.9

Full-text market research reports covering global consumer markets, with an emphasis on U.S. and European markets. Analyzes market share, segmentation, trends, and consumer demographics.

Access by subscription. Covers consumer goods and services, making this a good source of reports for market segments and consumer behavior, with reports like "Impact of celebrity chefs on cooking habits," "Nail color and care," and "MP3 players and other portable audio players," but not for business to business reports.

Market reports are available for automotive, beauty and personal, drink and tobacco, electronics, food and foodservice, health and medical, health and wellness, household, lifestyles, media, books and stationary, personal finances, retailing, technology, and travel. Reports include an executive summary, glossary, and sections on advertising and promotion, ownership and usage, attitudes and opinions, market drivers, market size and trends, market segmentation, future and forecast, and supply structure.

Consumer reports provide demographics, core needs and values, future trends, information on products currently targeted to the group, and advice on reaching and influencing the target audience. Consumer reports are available for financial lifestyles, general lifestyles, healthier lifestyles, and leisure lifestyles.

Marketing and promotion reports are for marketing and targeting, and promotions, incentives, and sponsorship. They include introduction and abbreviations, executive summary, background and market factors, challenges facing marketers, marketing segments, product development and pricing, and future trends.

Most data in Mintel can be downloaded into Excel. Reports cannot be viewed in their entirety and instead must be viewed in sections, making easy skimming or printing a report impossible.

930 North American industry classification system: United States, 2012. United States. Office of Management and Budget. Lanham, Md.; Springfield, Va.: Bernan; National Technical Information Service, 2012. 1470 p. ISBN 9781598885491
330   HF1042

The North American Industry Classification System (NAICS) is the replacement for Standard Industrial Classification (935) (SIC) codes. This manual has been issued in versions for 2002, 2007 and 2012. Presents NAICS codes, industry definitions, and tables linking NAICS and SIC. NAICS uses a "2- through 6-digit hierarchical classification system" to analyze sectors such as manufacturing, mining, retail and agriculture. Available on the web at http://www.census.gov/eos/www/naics/.

931 Occupational outlook handbook. http://www.bls.gov/ooh/. United States Bureau of Labor Statistics. Washington: U.S. Department of Labor. 1998–
331   HD8051

Biennial official government estimate of trends and potential employment in 800 occupations. Browsable by major Occupation Groups (such as Healthcare or Media & Communication), by rate of pay, by projected rate of job growth, by projected absolute number of new jobs, or alphabetically. Searchable by rate of pay, level of required education, and anticipated numbers of new openings. Entries for each occupation indicate median pay, required education or credentials, number of jobs nationally, and anticipated growth. Launched in print in 1949, and available on the Web since 1998. Reprints (932) are sold by private publishers as well.

932 Occupational outlook handbook. JIST Works, Inc. Indianapolis, Ind.: JIST Works, 1987–. ill. ISSN 0082-9072
331   HF5381.U62

Reprint of the original U.S. government publication: current information is freely available online (629). Gives information on employment trends and outlook in more than 800 occupations. Indicates nature of work, qualifications, earnings and working conditions, entry level jobs, information on the job market in each state, where to go for more information, etc. The similar *Career guide to industries* ceased in 2012.

933 Passport GMID. http://www.euromonitor
.com/. Euromonitor International.
London, U.K.: Euromonitor International.
[1999–]
658.8   HF5415.2

Also known under previous product names as *Global
market information database*, *GMID*, or *Euromonitor GMID*. Market reports, company profiles, and
demographic, economic, and marketing statistics for
205 countries. Market reports are for 16 consumer
markets (food and drink, tobacco, toys, etc.) and 14
industrial and service markets (accountancy, broadcasting, chemicals, property services, etc.).

Reports have market size, market sectors, share of
market, marketing activity, research and development,
corporate overview, distribution, consumer profiles,
market forecasts, sector forecasts, sources, and definitions. Additional reports are available for market segments, such as baby food. Company profiles have
background, recent news, competitve environment,
and outlook. Consumer lifestyle reports and very useful marketing background analyze the consumer by
country, gender, age, marital status, educational attainment, ethnicity, religion, home ownership, household profile, employment, income, health, eating and
personal grooming habits, leisure activities, personal
finance, communication, transport, and travel.

Search for data, which can be exported into Excel
or browse for reports. Data are available since 1977
and include inflation, exchange rates, GDP, GNI,
government expenditures, government finance,
income, labor, and money supply.

Similar information on a smaller scale is available
in Research monitor (783) from the same publisher.

934 Standard and Poor's industry surveys.
Standard and Poor's. New York: Standard
and Poor's, 1973–2012 ISSN 0196-4666
332.67   HC106.6

Detailed analyses of 22 industry categories and the
major companies in each category. Contains a basic
analysis and a comprehensive source of information,
updated by a current analysis. The analysis includes
trends, information on how the industry operates,
key ratios and statistics (revenues, net income, profit
ratios, balance sheet ratios, equity ratios, per-share
data, company and product rankings), information
on how to analyze a company in that industry, and
a glossary. Company and industry indexes. Ceased
with edition of 2012.

**935 Standard industrial classification
manual: 1987.** United States Office of
Management and Budget. Springfield, Va.:
National Technical Information Service,
1987. 705 p.
338/.02/0973   HF1042

Although the NAICS (930) code system has replaced
SIC since 1997, these four-digit hierarchical codes
are still cited in some reference tools, and the published manuals are still widely held. Businesses are
classified by divisions (such as agriculture, manufacturing or services) and subsections reflecting their
activities. Established by the U.S. government in
1937 to improve information-gathering.

**936 The value line investment survey:
small and mid-cap. Expanded ed.**
Value Line. New York: Value Line, 1995–
ISSN 1080-7705
332.605   HG4501.V262

Reports on 1,800 small and mid-cap stocks, with
consensus earning estimates and basic financials.
Each issue profiles 130–140 companies, with business descriptions, corporate developments, betas,
total shareholder return, four years of quarterly sales,
quarterly dividends, and quarterly earnings per share
data, as well as other ratio and financial data. In two
parts: ratings and reports, and summary and index.
Used primarily for investing, as well as by researchers for gathering financial data. The expanded edition is now called *Small/mid-cap edition*. Available in
an online version.

Indexes; Abstract Journals

937 ABI/Inform global. http://www.il
.proquest.com/products_pq/descriptions/
abi_inform_global.shtml. ProQuest. Ann
Arbor, Mich.: ProQuest. 1971–
                                      HF54.7.A25

ABI/Inform, an early and important entrant in the
bibliographic database marketplace, has expanded
coverage and changed platforms over the years:
access today of course is via the Web. Indexing and
abstracting of business periodicals, some economics periodicals, as well as other periodicals related to
business. Periodical coverage extends back as far as
1923 in some cases. Sold in several versions: extent
of content varies with price.

ABI/Inform global covers more than 3,700 publications, with more than 2,600 available in full text. Includes 18,000 business-related dissertations, some 5,000 business case studies, the *Wall Street Journal* since 1984, and *EIU ViewsWire*.

ABI/Inform complete includes more than 6,000 periodicals, 30,000 business-related dissertations, the *Economist* and *Wall Street Journal*, 100,000 working papers from sources like OECD, and analysis of industries, markets and countries.

ABI/Inform research covers over 1,800 journals, with more than 1,200 available in full text.

ABI/Inform dateline offers some 280 periodicals, with more than 230 available in full text. These include journals, newspapers, trade magazines and regional sources.

A comparable and competing product is Business source elite (34).

938   Business source elite. http://www
.ebscohost.com/academic/business-source
-elite. EBSCO Publishing. Ipswich, Mass.:
EBSCO. 1997– ISSN 1092-9754

338   HF5001

Comprehensive indexing of a wide range of business-related periodicals, reports and news sources. EBSCO publishes several versions of its business database product, with content that varies in extent and pricing. All include access to a *Regional business news* collection. All resources are delivered over the Web.

Business Source elite covers more than 1,100 business periodicals, including Harvard Business Review (47), and more than 10,000 Datamonitor company profiles. Over 1,000 journals are full text. Backfiles from 1985.

Business Source complete indexes some 2,000 peer-reviewed business journals and over 1,800 trade periodicals, many in full text, with some coverage from as early as 1886; over a million company profiles; market reports, industry reports and economic reports on individual countries; and 9,000 case studies.

Business Source premier covers some 2,200 periodicals, with some full text going back to 1965, and a smaller array of marketing, industry, company and country reports.

Business source corporate is a similar product marketed to companies, with full text from 2,700 periodicals, and numerous company, industry and country profiles and reports.

Successor to the print-format *Business periodicals index* (1959–) and online *Business abstracts* (1991–), published until 2011 by the H. W. Wilson Company. Incorporates older content formerly found in *Business periodicals index retrospective* (1913–1982).

A similar and competing product is ABI/Inform global (31).

939   LexisNexis academic. http://www
.lexisnexis.com/en-us/products/lexisnexis
-academic.page. LexisNexis (Firm).
Bethesda, Md.: LexisNexis. 1984–

KF242.A1

Searchable full-text subscription database that includes full text of articles from more than 2,500 newspapers, news from more than 300 local and regional newspapers, blogs and other web sources via WebNews, broadcast transcripts from the major radio and TV networks; national and international wire services; campus newspapers; polls and surveys; and over 600 newsletters. Non-English language news sources available in Spanish, French, German, Italian, and Dutch. Dates of coverage vary by individual source, with newspapers updated daily. Legal content includes federal and U.S. state statutes and cases, including Supreme Court decisions since 1790; some 800 law reviews; federal regulations; Shepherd's citations; and selective international coverage. Business content includes company information for 80 million public, private and international firms; profiles of 58 million executives; SEC filings; and industry profiles. A comparable resource for legal, news and business content is Westlaw (43).

940   Westlaw. http://legalsolutions
.thomsonreuters.com/law-products/.
West Publishing. Eagan, Minn.: West
Publishing/Thomson Reuters. 1975–

One of the major online platforms for U.S. legal research, combined with full text searching of news, and business research content. Searchable full text of federal and state statutes, case law including Supreme Court opinions, administrative codes, and specialized legal content including some international coverage. Also includes periodical literature, from legal journals and law reviews to newspapers and magazines. This is the online equivalent of print format West legal volumes, and incorporates the West Key Number System which groups entries by topic. Available only to subscribers, including working professional attorneys, courts, and law schools with their libraries. News content benefits from the connection to Reuters. WestlawNext offers "Company Investigator" searching and report-making based on 30 million company profiles. A comparable resource is LexisNexis (39).

Financial Ratios

941 Almanac of business and industrial financial ratios. Leo Troy. Englewood Cliffs, N.J.: Prentice-Hall, 1997–
ISSN 0747-9107
338.740973   HF5681.R25
Annual. Data come from nearly 5 million IRS tax returns. Table 1 reports operating and financial information for all corporations. Table 2 reports operating and financial information for all corporations with a net income. Also includes 50 performance indicators. Covers 179 industries, arranged by Standard Industrial Classification (SIC) code. The easiest ratio source to use.

942 Business ratios and formulas: a comprehensive guide. 3rd ed. Steven M. Bragg. Hoboken, N.J.: Wiley, 2012. xvii, 355 p., ill. ISBN 9781118169964
650.01/513   HF5691
Covers some 250 operational criteria available to managers: these are numerical analytical tools useful for founding or running a business. Definitions for ratios and formulas that look at asset utilization, operating performance, cash flow, liquidity, capital structure, return on investment, market performance, finance and accounting matters, engineering of parts and products, human resources, logistics and supply chain, production, and sales and marketing. Measures are explained, with illustrative examples. "Cautions" explain when another measure would be better suited, as well as how a measure can be misunderstood. Appendix lists all measures. Glossary of terms in finance and accounting. Designed for managers, but useful for anyone who must calculate and understand business ratios. Available as an e-book.

943 Industry norms and key business ratios, one year. Dun & Bradstreet Credit Services. Murray Hill, N.J.: Dun and Bradstreet Information Services,

1989– ISSN 1534-391X
338.0973   HF5681.R25
Reports 14 business ratios for some 800 industries. Includes balance sheet data. Arranged by Standard Industrial Classification (SIC) code. Data is from public and private companies listed in D&B's Financial Information Database. Also available online as *Key Business Ratios*.

944 IRS corporate financial ratios. United States Internal Revenue Service, Schonfeld & Associates. Evanston, Ill.: Schonfeld & Associates, 1982– ISSN 1938-548X
338   HG4050
Ratios based on IRS corporate filings for over 250 industries, arranged by NAICS codes. There are 76 ratios for turnover, expenses, cost of operating, bad debt and allowable debt, employment, profitability, taxes, investment, fixed assets, debt, net worth, coverage, and working capital. Ratios are presented by firm size, as well as those with and without a profit.

945 RMA annual statement studies. Robert Morris Associates, Risk Management Association. Philadelphia: Robert Morris Associates, 1977–. ill. ISSN 1545-7699
338   HF5681.B2
Annual. Using 190,000 statements from member institutions, RMA presents 19 financial ratios (current, quick, times interest earned, etc.), with common-size balance sheet and income statement items sorted by asset and sales size. Five years of data. Contains 700 industries, arranged by NAICS code. Has useful definitions in the front, often necessary as formulas for ratios can vary.

946 Standard and Poor's analysts' handbook. Standard and Poor's. New York: Standard and Poor's, 1964–
                           HG4905
The best source for historic data (contains 30 years worth). Provides income and balance sheet data for 80 industries represented by the S&P 500 Index. Contains basic ratios (current, quick, debt to total assets, debt to total equity, debt to total capital, inventory turnover, total assets turnover, profit margin, return on total assets), but is especially useful for the per share calculations and data (net sales, EBITDA, EBITDA margin, depreciation and amortization, operating income after depreciation, diluted

earnings per share, dividends per share, price to book value ratio, book value per share). Updated monthly, with data on the most recent 16 quarters (price, sales, diluted earnings, basic earnings, diluted P/E ratio, dividends, yield, total return index, current and future earnings estimates).

947   Standard and Poor's industry surveys.
Standard and Poor's. New York: Standard and Poor's, 1973–2012 ISSN 0196-4666
332.67   HC106.6
Detailed analyses of 22 industry categories and the major companies in each category. Contains a basic analysis and a comprehensive source of information, updated by a current analysis. The analysis includes trends, information on how the industry operates, key ratios and statistics (revenues, net income, profit ratios, balance sheet ratios, equity ratios, per-share data, company and product rankings), information on how to analyze a company in that industry, and a glossary. Company and industry indexes. Ceased with edition of 2012.

Statistics

948   Bizminer. http://www.bizminer.com/.
Brandow Company (Firm). Camp Hill, Pa.: Brandow Company. 2002–
                               HF1416
Provides financial analysis of U.S. industries and their markets. Covers some 9,000 sectors. Includes recent sales figures, balance sheet summaries, and financial ratios for companies; and survey of firms, market volume, annual sales, and startup activity for industries. Searchable by NAICS, keyword, and names of companies.

949   County business patterns. http:// www.census.gov/econ/cbp/. U.S. Census Bureau. Washington: U.S. Dept. of Commerce, Economics and Statistics Administration, U.S. Census Bureau. [1999]–
330.973   HC106.82.C68

Provides a searchable database for business establishments and their numbers of employees for all counties and zip codes. Organizes data for 1998 to recent by NAICS codes, and data for 1994 to 1997 by SIC codes.

Print editions of older *County business patterns* publications available in larger depository libraries.

950   RDS tablebase. http://www.gale.cengage .com/rds/index.htm. Gale Cengage Learning (Firm). Farmington, Mich.: Gale Cengage Learning. 1996–
                               HG4027
A terrific international statistical source for company, industry, and demographic information including market share, market size, market trends, price trends, rankings, sales forecasts, output and capacity, consumption, imports and exports, and shipments. Information comes from 900 trade publications, including *Accounting today*, *Adweek*, *Aftermarket business*, *Almanac of american employers*, *Beverage world*, *Chemical week*, *Datamonitor industry market research*, *Meed Middle East economic digest*, as well as reports, newsletters, and surveys. Sold as part of the *RDS business suite* which also includes *Business & industry*, and *Business and management practices*.

951   World industry and market outlook.
Barnes Reports Division. Bath, Maine: C. Barnes & Co., 2006–
338.0021   HC10
Published annually, this report provides worldwide data on major and minor manufacturing, retail, wholesale and services industries. Arranged by industry with tables covering current and forecasted estimates for establishments, employment and sales by country. Beginning in 2014, reports will also include a worldwide economic forecast with establishment and sales changes plus projected changes in gross domestic product (GDP), population, inflation, unemployment, poverty, country debt and deficits, and imports and exports. Available as PDF, spreadsheet (Excel), or print format edition. Also available in EBSCO Business Source (34) from 2011 to present.

7 Specialized Industry Information

Agribusiness

Specialized Sources of Industry Data

952 Agletter. http://www.chicagofed.org/
webpages/publications/Agletter/. Federal
Reserve Bank of Chicago. Chicago: Federal
Reserve Bank of Chicago. 1995–
ISSN 1080-8639
338 S21

Information on credit conditions at Seventh Federal
Reserve District agricultural banks, agricultural economic indicators (prices received by farmers, consumer prices, exports, farm machinery, production, or stocks), and farmland value. Called *Agricultural letter* up to 1994.

953 Agricultural prices. U.S. Dept. of
Agriculture, Crop Reporting Board,
U.S. Dept. of Agriculture, Bureau of
Agricultural Economics, U.S. Dept. of
Agriculture, Agricultural Marketing Service,
U.S. Dept. of Agriculture, Agricultural
Statistics Board. Washington: U.S. Dept. of
Agriculture, National Agricultural Statistics
Service, 1942– ISSN 0002-1601
338.130973 HD9004.U523a

The annual summary of indexes of prices received
and paid by U.S. farmers: prices received for farm
commodities by states and prices paid for production
items by region and the U.S. over the past year and

earlier years. As of 2010, the online *Agricultural prices summary* has been replaced by the searchable *Quick stats* database at http://quickstats.nass.usda.gov/.

**954 Agricultural prices: Price indices and
absolute prices, quarterly statistics =
Prix agricoles: Indices de prix et prix
absolus, statistiques trimestrielles.**
Statistical Office of the European
Communities. Luxembourg: Office des
publications officielles des Communautés
européennes, 1990– ISSN 1015-9924
338.13094021 HD1920.5.A17

An annual compilation of both price indexes and
absolute prices during the ten-year span 1989–99
for all member states of the European Union. Explanations and tables are in English, French, and German. Recent figures are available in the 'Agriculture and fisheries' theme area of the 'Statistics' tab on the Eurostat web site.

955 Freedonia focus reports. http://www
.freedoniagroup.com/FocusReports.aspx.
Freedonia Group. Cleveland, Ohio:
Freedonia Group. 2001–
HC106.82

Industry outlook information on a subscription
basis. More than 600 reports cover eighteen industry categories: automotive, chemicals, construction, consumer goods, electronics, energy, food and agriculture (including tobacco), industrial components,

life sciences (both medical and pharmaceutical), machinery, metals and minerals, miscellaneous and service industries, packaging, paper and printing (including publishing), plastics, rubber, textiles and leather (including apparel), and wood (including furniture and fixtures). Provides market size, historical demand, forecasts of demand, and profiles of leading companies. Browsable by major regions: Australia, Brazil, Canada, China, France, Germany, India, Italy, Japan, Mexico, Russia, South Korea, Spain, the U.K., and the U.S.

956 Hoovers. http://www.hoovers.com/.
Reference Press, Hoover's, Inc. Short Hills, N.J.: Dun & Bradstreet. 1996–

338.7   HG4057

More than 60 million records describe public and private companies primarily in the United States, but including Canada, United Kingdom, Europe, and Asia/Pacific. Profiles have an overview, history, family tree, industry information, products/operations, top competitors, competitive landscape, top executives with biographies, news, significant developments, and financial data. Financial summaries may include an income statement; balance sheet; cash flow; historical financials such as five years of P/E and per share; stock quotes; interactive stock charts; market data; earnings estimates; this year's ratios for the company, industry, and market; SEC filings; and industry watch for trends.

Content is tracked for 900 industries, organized into numerous larger categories: Agriculture & Forestry; Arts, Entertainment & Recreation; Beverage Manufacturing; Biotechnology Product Manufacturing; Business Services; Chemical Manufacturing; Commercial Equipment Repair & Maintenance; Commercial Printing; Computer Hardware Manufacturing; Computer Software; Construction; Consumer Products Manufacturing; Consumer Services; Contract Electronics Manufacturing; Education; Electric Power Generation; Electric Power Transmission, Distribution & Marketing; Electric Utilities; Electrical Products Manufacturing; Fabricated Metal Product Manufacturing; Financial Services; Food Manufacturing; Government; Health Care Products Manufacturing; Health Care; HVAC Equipment Manufacturing; Industrial Manufacturing; Insurance; Leasing of Intangible Assets; Lodging; Machinery Manufacturing; Magnetic & Optical Media; Manufacturing & Reproduction; Managed Application & Network Services; Management of Companies & Enterprises; Media; Membership Organizations; Mining; Miscellaneous Manufacturing; Natural Gas Distribution & Marketing; Nonclassifiable establishments; Nonmetallic Mineral Product Manufacturing; Nonprofit Institutions; Oil & Gas Exploration & Production; Oil & Gas Field Services; Oil & Gas Well Drilling; Petroleum & Coal Products Manufacturing; Pharmaceutical Manufacturing; Primary Metals Manufacturing; Private Households; Professional Services; Real Estate; Religious Organizations; Rental & Leasing; Restaurants, Bars & Food Services; Retail; Security Products Manufacturing; Semiconductor & Other Electronic Component Manufacturing; Telecommunications Equipment Manufacturing; Telecommunications Services; Transportation Equipment Manufacturing; Transportation Services; Water & Sewer Utilities; Wholesale; and Wood Product Manufacturing.

Coverage can be brief, but generally includes a fact sheet, overview, selected companies, industry watch with video interviews, news from the last 90 days, and web resources for terminology, associations, and organizations, and online publications. Hoover's print publications include (*Hoover's handbook of American business* (876), *Hoover's handbook of private companies* (855)).

957 IBISWorld United States. http://www .ibisworld.com/. IBISWorld. New York: IBISWorld. 1999–

HC103

700 reports on American industries. Industry reports can be located using NAICS numbers. Major categories include: Accommodation & Food Services; Administration, Business Support & Waste Management Services; Agriculture, Forestry, Fishing & Hunting; Arts, Entertainment & Recreation; Construction; Educational Services; Finance & Insurance; Healthcare & Social Assistance; Information; Manufacturing; Mining; Other Services (except Public Administration); Professional, Scientific & Technical Services; Real Estate & Rental and Leasing; Retail Trade; Transportation & Warehousing; Utilities; and Wholesale Trade.

Reports include industry definition; information about the supply chain; key statistics; segmentations (products and services segmentation, major market segments, industry concentration, geographic spread); market characteristics (market size, demand determinants, domestic and international markets, basis of competition, life cycle); industry conditions (barriers to entry, taxation, industry assistance, regulation and deregulation, cost structure, capital and labor intensity, technology and systems, industry volatility, globalization); key factors (sensitivities and success factors); key competitors; and industry performance (current and historical). Glossaries and guides to jargon. Setting this database apart are reports on small industries, such as parking lots and garages.

958 Standard and Poor's industry surveys.
Standard and Poor's. New York: Standard and Poor's, 1973–2012 ISSN 0196-4666
332.67   HC106.6

Detailed analyses of 22 industry categories and the major companies in each category. Contains a basic analysis and a comprehensive source of information, updated by a current analysis. The analysis includes trends, information on how the industry operates, key ratios and statistics (revenues, net income, profit ratios, balance sheet ratios, equity ratios, per-share data, company and product rankings), information on how to analyze a company in that industry, and a glossary. Company and industry indexes. Ceased with edition of 2012.

959 Statistical highlights of U.S. agriculture. U.S. Dept. of Agriculture, National Agricultural Statistics Service, U.S. Dept. of Agriculture, Economic Research Service, U.S. Dept. of Agriculture, World Agricultural Outlook Board. Washington: U.S. Dept. of Agriculture, National Agricultural Statistics Service, 1996–. ill.
S411.S714

"[B]rings together the most important economic and statistical information in agriculture in a single summary report."—*Opening letter*

Provides a timely snapshot of American agricultural production and consumption. Each basic measured segment of the agricultural sector receives a brief descriptive summary followed by a set of data tables. Geographic scope is state and national level. Chronological span is the most recent five years. Not indexed.

Aggregated data used in the publication are collected by the USDA Economic Research Service,

National Agricultural Statistics Service, and World Agricultural Outlook Board. Missing from this report is data from the Agricultural Marketing Service and Foreign Agricultural Service.

Published as part of the USDA Statistical Bulletin series. 2004/2005, no. 1003; 2002/2003, no. 1000; 2001/2002, no. 976; 2000/2001, no. 971; 1999/2000, 967; 1996/1997, no. 936.

For a wide range of agricultural statistics, see the NASS site at http://www.nass.usda.gov/.

960 USDA economics, statistics and market information system. http://usda.mannlib.cornell.edu/MannUsda/homepage.do. U.S. Dept. of Agriculture, Agricultural Marketing Service, U.S. Dept. of Agriculture, Economic Research Service, U.S. Dept. of Agriculture, National Agricultural Statistics Service, U.S. Dept. of Agriculture, World Agricultural Outlook Board. Washington; Ithaca, N.Y.: U.S. Dept. of Agriculture; Albert R. Mann Library, Cornell University. 1994–
S21

Aggregates most of the major agricultural production, consumption, and market periodicals produced by the four USDA economic agencies: Agricultural Marketing Service, Economic Research Service, National Agricultural Statistics Service, and the World Agricultural Outlook Board. These publications report on U.S. and international agriculture and related topics. Some publications contain time-sensitive information. The system contains nearly 2,500 report and dataset titles and is updated daily.

Organizations and Associations

961 AAEA. http://www.aaea.org/. Agricultural and Applied Economics Association. Milwaukee, Wis.: Agricultural and Applied Economics Association. 2001–
338   HD1415

Home page for a group supporting study of the economics of agriculture, rural communities, and natural resources. The website leads to information about AAEA, membership and meetings, publications, the AAEA Trust, job postings, an FAQ, and a link to the online magazine *Choices: The magazine of food, farm, and resource issues.* AAEA also publishes *American journal of agricultural economics*, *Review of agricultural economics*, and *AAEA newsletter*. Formerly the American Agricultural Economics Association.

962 Agricultural retailers association.
http://www.aradc.org/. Agricultural Retailers Association. Washington: Agricultural Retailers Association. 2000–
338   S631

Home page connects to issue briefs (Agricultural Business Security Tax Credit, Chemical Site Security, Natural Gas, etc.), a newsletter, and annual reports, as well as links to state associations, Congress, government offices, and the media. This advocacy group's site is useful for news, some statistics, and for viewing what is important to agribusiness retailers and distributors.

963 National agri-marketing association.
http://www.nama.org/. National Agri-Marketing Association. Overland Park, Kans.: National Agri-Marketing Association. 1996–
HD9001

Organization home page focuses on the marketing of agribusiness and its associated products. It holds an annual conference and an annual forum. The website has a calendar of events, a membership directory (accessible to members only), links to member company websites, and industry news from their publication *AgriMarketing*.

964 National grain and feed association.
http://www.ngfa.org/. National Grain and Feed Association. Washington: National Grain and Feed Association. 1998–
338.17310973   SB189

Trade association home page links to news, a calendar of events, trade rules and arbitration, facts, career information, and history. Covers corn, wheat, soybeans, sunflower, barley, rye, oats, and flaxseed.

965 USDA. http://www.usda.gov/. U.S. Dept. of Agriculture. Washington: U.S. Dept. of Agriculture. 1996–
S21

Among the duties of the USDA is monitoring agribusiness. The agribusiness portion of the website covers biotechnology; commodity standards and grades; data and statistics; exporting goods; food distribution; food labeling and packaging; food quality; food safety; importing goods; marketing assistance; organic certification; price support; quality assurance; safety inspections; trade policy and procedures; and transportation and distribution.

Internet Resources

966 AgNIC home: agriculture network information collaborative. http://www.agnic.org/. AgNIC. Beltsville, Md.: Agriculture Network Information Collaborative. 2000–
630.028553   S493

Formerly Agriculture Network Information Center. Provides access to agricultural information, including information about commercial agriculture and farming of specific crops. The Search box can be used to reach numerous citations and full text resources. Developed by AgNIC member libraries, extension services, and non-profit institutes in cooperation with the National Agricultural Library and the USDA Agricultural Research Service.

967 Technical conversion factors for agricultural commodities. http://www.fao.org/economic/the-statistics-division-ess/methodology/methodology-systems/technical-conversion-factors-for-agricultural-commodities/en/. Rome, Italy: Food and Agricultural Organization of the United Nations. 2000
630.212   S413

First ed., 1960; 2nd draft ed., 1972.

"This latest electronic publication updates two earlier printed versions of the publication produced in 1960 and revised in 1972, by the Statistics Division of FAO. It is an extremely useful and necessary compendium for both statisticians and economists to follow the commodity product sequence (referred to as 'the commodity tree') and allows one the possibility of using the information presented to convert product data from primary equivalent to secondary equivalent and/or vice versa. Also, it is an essential tool in building up supply utilization accounts, food balance sheets and calculating derived agricultural statistics. The document shows, inter alia, data per country for crop seeding rates, waste rates, extraction rates, the average live weight of animals, birth rates, take-off rates, as well as yield per animal for a number of major livestock products."—*Introd.*

The current digital edition is published as a PDF file. Released in 2000, the site description indicates that the content is continuously updated. Searchable by keyword. Also, the information is organized by continent and country, and a clickable world map speeds navigation through the file. Ends with 61 commodity tree graphics that illustrate the commodity product extraction sequence. This digital edition does not include the data collection forms found in the 1972 edition. Also missing are simple conversion factors, such as bushel into kilograms.

Published in English, French, and Spanish. A majority of the country descriptions are written in English, with less frequent French and Spanish descriptions associated with Francophone and Hispanophone nations.

Additional Reference Sources

968 AgEcon search. http://ageconsearch.umn
.edu/. University of Minnesota. St. Paul,
Minn.: University of Minnesota. [1997?]–
630.072   HD1415 005.74; 630;
Contains the full text of working papers, conference papers and journal articles in applied economics, including the subtopics of agricultural, consumer, energy, environmental, and resource economics. Contributors include academic institutions, government agencies, professional associations, and nongovernment organizations. AgEcon Search is maintained at the University of Minnesota by the Dept. of Applied Economics and University Libraries. The American Agricultural Economics Association is a primary sponsor.

**969 Elsevier's dictionary of agriculture, in
English, German, French, Russian and
Latin.** T. Tosheva, M. Djarova, Boria na
Delii ska. New York: Elsevier Science B.V.,
2000. 777, [1] p. ISBN 0444500057
630.3   S411.T64
Contains 9,389 terms "commonly used in agriculture science, practice and education" covering "all fields related to agriculture."—*Pref.* The first part lists English terms followed by their German, French, and Russian equivalents. Latin names are also provided

for plants, animals, epizootic diseases, and pests. Chemical formulas are given where appropriate. The second section includes separate indexes for the French, German, Russian, and Latin terms, referring back to the first part.

970 Encyclopedia of agricultural science.
Charles J. Arntzen, Ellen M. Ritter. San
Diego, Calif.: Academic Press, 1994. 4 v.,
ill. ISBN 0122266706
630.3   S411.E713
"Intended for a broad international audience of . . . students, . . . faculty, . . . research scientists, extension specialists and development workers; agricultural producers, . . . as well as advanced high school students and the general reader with a background in science."—*Pref.*

This four-volume encyclopedia covers plant, animal, forest, soil, and range sciences; entomology; horticulture; natural resources; agricultural engineering; agricultural economics; food and fiber processing and industries; agricultural organizations; and social issues in agriculture. Two hundred ten articles averaging ten pages each are arranged alphabetically. Each article is organized with an outline, glossary, essay, and bibliography. Numerous illustrations, charts, and tables. Index. Appendixes list U.S. colleges and universities granting degrees in agriculture and U.N. organizations concerned with agriculture.

**971 Urner Barry's meat and poultry
directory.** Urner Barry Publications. Tom's
River, N.J.: Urner Barry Publications,
1983– ISSN 0738-6745
381.456649202573   HD9413.U76
"[O]ver 10,000 listings of producers, processors, distributors, further processors, HRI suppliers, importers, exporters, slaughterers and renderers in the meat and poultry industries."—*2007 Urner Barry advertisement.*

For more than a century, Urner Barry publications have helped set benchmarks in domestic agricultural prices. This 800-page annual directory for the U.S. meat and poultry industry, first published in 1983, is comprehensive and authoritative. It provides specific company data in four categories: an alphageographical listing of companies, a brand name index, a plant number index, and key personnel information index.

Biotechnology

Specialized Sources of Industry Data

972   BioScan. BioWorld. Atlanta, Ga.:
BioWorld; Thomson Reuters, 1987–
ISSN 0887-6207
338.76208/025   HD9999.B44

Information on some 2,200 U.S. and foreign companies in the biotechnology and biopharmaceutical sectors, giving contact information, company history, number of employees, facilities, very brief financial highlights (sales, net income, earnings per share, shares outstanding, total assets), business strategy, alliances, mergers and acquisitions, principal investors, and products in development, and products on the market. Available online through *BioWorld*.

973   Hoovers. http://www.hoovers.com/.
Reference Press, Hoover's, Inc. Short Hills,
N.J.: Dun & Bradstreet. 1996–
338.7   HG4057

More than 60 million records describe public and private companies primarily in the United States, but including Canada, United Kingdom, Europe, and Asia/Pacific. Profiles have an overview, history, family tree, industry information, products/operations, top competitors, competitive landscape, top executives with biographies, news, significant developments, and financial data. Financial summaries may include an income statement; balance sheet; cash flow; historical financials such as five years of P/E and per share; stock quotes; interactive stock charts; market data; earnings estimates; this year's ratios for the company, industry, and market; SEC filings; and industry watch for trends.

Content is tracked for 900 industries, organized into numerous larger categories: Agriculture & Forestry; Arts, Entertainment & Recreation; Beverage Manufacturing; Biotechnology Product Manufacturing; Business Services; Chemical Manufacturing; Commercial Equipment Repair & Maintenance; Commercial Printing; Computer Hardware Manufacturing; Computer Software; Construction; Consumer Products Manufacturing; Consumer Services; Contract Electronics Manufacturing; Education; Electric Power Generation; Electric Power Transmission, Distribution & Marketing; Electric Utilities; Electrical Products Manufacturing; Fabricated Metal Product Manufacturing; Financial Services; Food Manufacturing; Government; Health Care Products Manufacturing; Health Care; HVAC Equipment Manufacturing; Industrial Manufacturing; Insurance; Leasing of Intangible Assets; Lodging; Machinery Manufacturing; Magnetic & Optical Media; Manufacturing & Reproduction; Managed Application & Network Services; Management of Companies & Enterprises; Media; Membership Organizations; Mining; Miscellaneous Manufacturing; Natural Gas Distribution & Marketing; Nonclassifiable establishments; Nonmetallic Mineral Product Manufacturing; Nonprofit Institutions; Oil & Gas Exploration & Production; Oil & Gas Field Services; Oil & Gas Well Drilling; Petroleum & Coal Products Manufacturing; Pharmaceutical Manufacturing; Primary Metals Manufacturing; Private Households; Professional Services; Real Estate; Religious Organizations; Rental & Leasing; Restaurants, Bars & Food Services; Retail; Security Products Manufacturing; Semiconductor & Other Electronic Component Manufacturing; Telecommunications Equipment Manufacturing; Telecommunications Services; Transportation Equipment Manufacturing; Transportation Services; Water & Sewer Utilities; Wholesale; and Wood Product Manufacturing.

Coverage can be brief, but generally includes a fact sheet, overview, selected companies, industry watch with video interviews, news from the last 90 days, and web resources for terminology, associations, and organizations, and online publications. Hoover's print publications include (*Hoover's handbook of American business* (876), *Hoover's handbook of private companies* [855]).

**974   Plunkett's biotech and genetics
industry almanac.** Jack W. Plunkett.
Houston, Tex.: Plunkett Research, 2001–
ISSN 1546-5756
338   HD9999.B44

Data on over 400 leading companies, both public and private, in biotechnology, genetics, and pharmaceuticals. Company profiles include types of business, brands and affiliates, contacts, employee benefits and top salaries, sales and profit numbers, growth plans, and competitive advantage. Especially useful for the industry background and trends, statistics and rankings at the front of the volume (U.S. biotech industry financing 1997–2005, U.S. health expenditure amounts 1980–2015, global

R&D investments by research-based pharmaceutical companies 1970–2005, R&D spending by function, U.S. FDA approval times for new drugs 1993–2005, etc.), and information on the main associations and organizations in the back of the volume. Most information is for the U.S., but some international coverage is provided. Available as an e-book.

975   Standard and Poor's industry surveys.
Standard and Poor's. New York: Standard and Poor's, 1973–2012 ISSN 0196-4666
332.67   HC106.6
Detailed analyses of 22 industry categories and the major companies in each category. Contains a basic analysis and a comprehensive source of information, updated by a current analysis. The analysis includes trends, information on how the industry operates, key ratios and statistics (revenues, net income, profit ratios, balance sheet ratios, equity ratios, per-share data, company and product rankings), information on how to analyze a company in that industry, and a glossary. Company and industry indexes. Ceased with edition of 2012.

Organizations and Associations

976   BIO. http://www.bio.org/. Biotechnology Industry Organization. Washington: Biotechnology Industry Organization. 1996–
338   TP248.2
Home page of a relatively new advocacy association: BIO was founded in 1993. Its website has news and media, coverage of national issues (health care, food and agriculture, industrial and environmental, bioethics, intellectual property, regulatory, tax and financial), state and local initiatives, letters, testimony and comments, speeches and publications, industry at a glance (statistics, guide, timeline, reports), events and conferences, and business and finance.

977   USDA. http://www.usda.gov/. U.S. Dept. of Agriculture. Washington: U.S. Dept. of Agriculture. 1996–
S21
Among the duties of the USDA is monitoring agribusiness. The agribusiness portion of the website covers biotechnology; commodity standards and grades; data and statistics; exporting goods; food

distribution; food labeling and packaging; food quality; food safety; importing goods; marketing assistance; organic certification; price support; quality assurance; safety inspections; trade policy and procedures; and transportation and distribution.

Chemical

Specialized Sources of Industry Data

978   Chemical economics handbook.
Stanford Research Institute. Stanford, Calif.: Stanford Research Institute, 1951–. loose-leaf, charts
HD9651
Reports on 300 chemical products (such as acetaldehyde) or product groups (acrylic resins and plastics), with information on manufacturing processes, environmental issues, and supply and demand by region (producing companies, statistics, consumption, price and trade). Coverage is for the United States, Western Europe, and Japan. For sale in digital format from IHS/SRI.

979   Freedonia focus reports. http://www .freedoniagroup.com/FocusReports.aspx. Freedonia Group. Cleveland, Ohio: Freedonia Group. 2001–
HC106.82
Industry outlook information on a subscription basis. More than 600 reports cover eighteen industry categories: automotive, chemicals, construction, consumer goods, electronics, energy, food and agriculture (including tobacco), industrial components, life sciences (both medical and pharmaceutical), machinery, metals and minerals, miscellaneous and service industries, packaging, paper and printing (including publishing), plastics, rubber, textiles and leather (including apparel), and wood (including furniture and fixtures). Provides market size, historical demand, forecasts of demand, and profiles of leading companies. Browsable by major regions: Australia, Brazil, Canada, China, France, Germany, India, Italy, Japan, Mexico, Russia, South Korea, Spain, the U.K., and the U.S.

980   Hoovers. http://www.hoovers.com/. Reference Press, Hoover's, Inc. Short Hills, N.J.: Dun & Bradstreet. 1996–
338.7   HG4057

More than 60 million records describe public and private companies primarily in the United States, but including Canada, United Kingdom, Europe, and Asia/Pacific. Profiles have an overview, history, family tree, industry information, products/operations, top competitors, competitive landscape, top executives with biographies, news, significant developments, and financial data. Financial summaries may include an income statement; balance sheet; cash flow; historical financials such as five years of P/E and per share; stock quotes; interactive stock charts; market data; earnings estimates; this year's ratios for the company, industry, and market; SEC filings; and industry watch for trends.

Content is tracked for 900 industries, organized into numerous larger categories: Agriculture & Forestry; Arts, Entertainment & Recreation; Beverage Manufacturing; Biotechnology Product Manufacturing; Business Services; Chemical Manufacturing; Commercial Equipment Repair & Maintenance; Commercial Printing; Computer Hardware Manufacturing; Computer Software; Construction; Consumer Products Manufacturing; Consumer Services; Contract Electronics Manufacturing; Education; Electric Power Generation; Electric Power Transmission, Distribution & Marketing; Electric Utilities; Electrical Products Manufacturing; Fabricated Metal Product Manufacturing; Financial Services; Food Manufacturing; Government; Health Care Products Manufacturing; Health Care; HVAC Equipment Manufacturing; Industrial Manufacturing; Insurance; Leasing of Intangible Assets; Lodging; Machinery Manufacturing; Magnetic & Optical Media; Manufacturing & Reproduction; Managed Application & Network Services; Management of Companies & Enterprises; Media; Membership Organizations; Mining; Miscellaneous Manufacturing; Natural Gas Distribution & Marketing; Nonclassifiable establishments; Nonmetallic Mineral Product Manufacturing; Nonprofit Institutions; Oil & Gas Exploration & Production; Oil & Gas Field Services; Oil & Gas Well Drilling; Petroleum & Coal Products Manufacturing; Pharmaceutical Manufacturing; Primary Metals Manufacturing; Private Households; Professional Services; Real Estate; Religious Organizations; Rental & Leasing; Restaurants, Bars & Food Services; Retail; Security Products Manufacturing; Semiconductor & Other Electronic Component Manufacturing; Telecommunications Equipment Manufacturing; Telecommunications

Services; Transportation Equipment Manufacturing; Transportation Services; Water & Sewer Utilities; Wholesale; and Wood Product Manufacturing.

Coverage can be brief, but generally includes a fact sheet, overview, selected companies, industry watch with video interviews, news from the last 90 days, and web resources for terminology, associations, and organizations, and online publications. Hoover's print publications include (*Hoover's handbook of American business* (876), *Hoover's handbook of private companies* (855)).

981 Plunkett's chemicals, coatings, and plastics industry almanac. Jack W. Plunkett. Houston, Tex.: Plunkett Research, 2005– ISSN 1935-8563
540   HD9650.3

Data on nearly 400 major companies, both public and private. Company profiles include types of business, brands and affiliates, contacts, employee benefits and top salaries, sales and profit numbers, growth plans, and competitive advantage. Especially useful for the industry trends, statistics and rankings at the front of the volume (World consumption of plastic materials: 1990, 2003, and 2015; U.S. exports and imports of plastics and plastic articles: 2000–2005; U.S. exports and imports of organic chemicals: 2000–2005; Summary of U.S. primary production of specified inorganic chemicals: 2000–2005; Total U.S. primary production of specified industrial gases: 2000–2004; etc.), and information on the main associations and organizations in the back of the volume. Most information is for the U.S., but some international coverage is provided. Available as an e-book.

982 Standard and Poor's industry surveys. Standard and Poor's. New York: Standard and Poor's, 1973–2012 ISSN 0196-4666
332.67   HC106.6

Detailed analyses of 22 industry categories and the major companies in each category. Contains a basic analysis and a comprehensive source of information, updated by a current analysis. The analysis includes trends, information on how the industry operates, key ratios and statistics (revenues, net income, profit ratios, balance sheet ratios, equity ratios, per-share data, company and product rankings), information on how to analyze a company in that industry, and a glossary. Company and industry indexes. Ceased with edition of 2012.

Organizations and Associations

983 AmericanChemistry.com. http://www
.americanchemistry.com/. American
Chemistry Council. [Arlington, Va.]:
American Chemistry Council.
2000–
540.9   QD18.U6
Home page for the American Chemistry Council,
founded in 1872 to represent chemical companies, and now including chlorine and plastics companies. The site includes policy issues, security,
environment, product stewardship, tax and trade,
news, initiatives, and industry statistics (chemistry in economy, chemistry-dependent economy,
chemistry-dependent jobs, consumer chemFactor, industrial chemFactor, packaging chemFactor,
economic impact, industry profile, industry facts,
business of chemistry, jobs and wages). Additional
advocacy associations exist for various segments of
the chemical industry, including the National Paint
& Coatings Association, the Adhesive and Sealant
Council, and the Synthetic Organic Chemical Manufacturers Association.

Additional Reference Sources

**984 Harris U.S. manufacturers
directory. National ed.** Harris
InfoSource, National Association of
Manufacturers (U.S.). Twinsburg,
Ohio: Harris InfoSource, 2000–
ISSN 1531-8273
338   HF5035
Entries for U.S. companies include location, contact information, industry descriptions, Standard
Industrial Classification (SIC) or NAICS codes,
executive names, and size. Indexed by company
name, geography, product or service category, and
SIC code. Libraries receiving questions about local
companies may want to invest in the regional and
state directories also published by Harris. Regional
editions are published for the Northeast, Southeast, Midwest, and West. Available in an online
version.

**985 Major chemical and petrochemical
companies of the world.** Graham &

Whiteside. London: Graham & Whiteside,
2000– ISSN 1369-5444
661.804   HD9650.3 658.0029;
Lists over 7,000 companies, giving contact information, executive names, business description,
brand names and trademarks, subsidiaries, principal bank, principal law firm, ticker symbol, date
established, number of employees, auditors, and
two years of very brief financial information (sales
turnover, profit before tax, profit after tax, dividend
per share, earnings per share, share capital, shareholders' equity).

986 Passport GMID. http://www.euromonitor
.com/. Euromonitor International.
London, U.K.: Euromonitor International.
[1999–]
658.8   HF5415.2
Also known under previous product names as
Global market information database, GMID, or *Euromonitor GMID.* Market reports, company profiles,
and demographic, economic, and marketing statistics for 205 countries. Market reports are for
16 consumer markets (food and drink, tobacco,
toys, etc.) and 14 industrial and service markets
(accountancy, broadcasting, chemicals, property
services, etc.).

Reports have market size, market sectors, share
of market, marketing activity, research and development, corporate overview, distribution, consumer profiles, market forecasts, sector forecasts,
sources, and definitions. Additional reports are
available for market segments, such as baby food.
Company profiles have background, recent news,
competitve environment, and outlook. Consumer
lifestyle reports and very useful marketing background analyze the consumer by country, gender, age, marital status, educational attainment,
ethnicity, religion, home ownership, household
profile, employment, income, health, eating
and personal grooming habits, leisure activities,
personal finance, communication, transport,
and travel.

Search for data, which can be exported into Excel
or browse for reports. Data are available since 1977
and include inflation, exchange rates, GDP, GNI,
government expenditures, government finance,
income, labor, and money supply.

Similar information on a smaller scale is available
in *Research monitor* (783) from the same publisher.

Computers

Specialized Sources of Industry Data

987 Directory of top computer executives.
East ed. Applied Computer Research.
Phoenix: Applied Computer Research Inc.,
1972– ISSN 1936-4202
338.4.7004/02574   HD9696.C63
Lists information technology information for companies with minimum gross revenues of $50 million or a minimum of 250 employees in manufacturing and service, banking, diversified finance, insurance, retail, transportation, utilities, education, health service, federal government, state government, and local government. Entries give company name, contact information, top computer executive names, subsidiary divisions, type of industry, second level manager names, major computer systems used, number of PCs deployed throughout the organization, and number of information system employees. Arranged geographically and indexed by company name and industry classification. Available in print and pdf editions for the Eastern U.S., Western U.S., and Canada. Also available online.

988 FACCTS. http://www.faulkner.com/
showcase/faccts.htm. Faulkner
Information Services. Pennsauken, N.J.:
Faulkner Information Services. 1995–
ISSN 1082-7471
005   QA76.753
Over 1,200 reports on trends, issues, market conditions, implementation guides, companies, products, and services in information technology. Arranged into 14 categories: enterprise data networking, broadband, information security, electronic government, electronic business, content management, IT asset management, application development, Web site management, converging communications, telecom and global network services, mobile business strategies, wireless communications, and Internet strategies. Especially useful for the up-to-date technology trend reports. Also from this publisher: *Faulkner's advisory for IT studies (FAITS)*.

989 Gartneradvisory intraweb. http://www
.gartner.com/. Gartner Group. [Stamford,
Conn.]: Gartner Group. 2000–

The database consists of content from Gartner Research and Advisory Services, Datapro, and Dataquest Research. Especially useful for reports that discuss strategy within the IT industry. Also has company profiles, trends, developments, and product reports.

990 Hoovers. http://www.hoovers.com/.
Reference Press, Hoover's, Inc. Short Hills,
N.J.: Dun & Bradstreet. 1996–
338.7   HG4057
More than 60 million records describe public and private companies primarily in the United States, but including Canada, United Kingdom, Europe, and Asia/Pacific. Profiles have an overview, history, family tree, industry information, products/operations, top competitors, competitive landscape, top executives with biographies, news, significant developments, and financial data. Financial summaries may include an income statement; balance sheet; cash flow; historical financials such as five years of P/E and per share; stock quotes; interactive stock charts; market data; earnings estimates; this year's ratios for the company, industry, and market; SEC filings; and industry watch for trends.

Content is tracked for 900 industries, organized into numerous larger categories: Agriculture & Forestry; Arts, Entertainment & Recreation; Beverage Manufacturing; Biotechnology Product Manufacturing; Business Services; Chemical Manufacturing; Commercial Equipment Repair & Maintenance; Commercial Printing; Computer Hardware Manufacturing; Computer Software; Construction; Consumer Products Manufacturing; Consumer Services; Contract Electronics Manufacturing; Education; Electric Power Generation; Electric Power Transmission, Distribution & Marketing; Electric Utilities; Electrical Products Manufacturing; Fabricated Metal Product Manufacturing; Financial Services; Food Manufacturing; Government; Health Care Products Manufacturing; Health Care; HVAC Equipment Manufacturing; Industrial Manufacturing; Insurance; Leasing of Intangible Assets; Lodging; Machinery Manufacturing; Magnetic & Optical Media; Manufacturing & Reproduction; Managed Application & Network Services; Management of Companies & Enterprises; Media; Membership Organizations; Mining; Miscellaneous Manufacturing; Natural Gas Distribution & Marketing; Nonclassifiable establishments; Nonmetallic Mineral

Product Manufacturing; Nonprofit Institutions; Oil & Gas Exploration & Production; Oil & Gas Field Services; Oil & Gas Well Drilling; Petroleum & Coal Products Manufacturing; Pharmaceutical Manufacturing; Primary Metals Manufacturing; Private Households; Professional Services; Real Estate; Religious Organizations; Rental & Leasing; Restaurants, Bars & Food Services; Retail; Security Products Manufacturing; Semiconductor & Other Electronic Component Manufacturing; Telecommunications Equipment Manufacturing; Telecommunications Services; Transportation Equipment Manufacturing; Transportation Services; Water & Sewer Utilities; Wholesale; and Wood Product Manufacturing.

Coverage can be brief, but generally includes a fact sheet, overview, selected companies, industry watch with video interviews, news from the last 90 days, and web resources for terminology, associations, and organizations, and online publications. Hoover's print publications include (*Hoover's handbook of American business* (876), *Hoover's handbook of private companies* (855)).

991   Plunkett's e-commerce and internet business almanac. Jack W. Plunkett. Houston, Tex.: Plunkett Research, 2001–. ill. ISSN 1548-5447
338.7   HF5548.32

Annual. Like all the Plunkett almanacs, contains data on 300 major companies. Company profiles include types of business, brands and affiliates, contacts, employee benefits and top salaries, sales and profit numbers, growth plans, and competitive advantage. Especially useful for the industry statistics and rankings at the front of the volume. Also contains a glossary of key words and phrases. Available as an e-book.

992   Plunkett's infotech industry almanac. Jack W. Plunkett. Galveston, Tex.: Plunkett Research, 1996–
025.025   HD9696.C63

Covers the hardware, software, entertainment, and telecommunications industries, as well as 500 major companies both public and private in those industries. Company profiles include types of business, brands and affiliates, contacts, employee benefits and top salaries, sales and profit numbers, growth plans, and competitive advantage. Especially useful for the industry trends, statistics and rankings (number of high speed internet lines; U.S. infotech industry

quarterly revenue; U.S. data processing, hosting, and related services industry estimated revenue, and expenses; value of computers and electronic products manufacturers' shipments, inventories, and orders by industry, U.S, 1992–present, etc.), and information on the main associations and organizations. Most information is for the U.S., but some international coverage is provided. Available as an e-book.

993   Standard and Poor's industry surveys. Standard and Poor's. New York: Standard and Poor's, 1973–2012 ISSN 0196-4666
332.67   HC106.6

Detailed analyses of 22 industry categories and the major companies in each category. Contains a basic analysis and a comprehensive source of information, updated by a current analysis. The analysis includes trends, information on how the industry operates, key ratios and statistics (revenues, net income, profit ratios, balance sheet ratios, equity ratios, per-share data, company and product rankings), information on how to analyze a company in that industry, and a glossary. Company and industry indexes. Ceased with edition of 2012.

Organizations and Associations

994   IEEE computer society. http://www.computer.org/. IEEE Computer Society. Washington: IEEE Computer Society. 1997–
QA75.5

Home page for the society, founded in 1946 to serve computer professionals. Its website has publications (technical magazines, journals, letters, tutorials, books), abstracts and tables of contents of the conference publications, career development and educational activities, communities, and a volunteer center.

Construction and Real Estate

Specialized Sources of Industry Data

995   Freedonia focus reports. http://www.freedoniagroup.com/FocusReports.aspx. Freedonia Group. Cleveland, Ohio: Freedonia Group. 2001–
HC106.82

Industry outlook information on a subscription basis. More than 600 reports cover eighteen industry categories: automotive, chemicals, construction, consumer goods, electronics, energy, food and agriculture (including tobacco), industrial components, life sciences (both medical and pharmaceutical), machinery, metals and minerals, miscellaneous and service industries, packaging, paper and printing (including publishing), plastics, rubber, textiles and leather (including apparel), and wood (including furniture and fixtures). Provides market size, historical demand, forecasts of demand, and profiles of leading companies. Browsable by major regions: Australia, Brazil, Canada, China, France, Germany, India, Italy, Japan, Mexico, Russia, South Korea, Spain, the U.K., and the U.S.

996 Hoovers. http://www.hoovers.com/.
Reference Press, Hoover's, Inc. Short Hills, N.J.: Dun & Bradstreet. 1996–
338.7   HG4057
More than 60 million records describe public and private companies primarily in the United States, but including Canada, United Kingdom, Europe, and Asia/Pacific. Profiles have an overview, history, family tree, industry information, products/operations, top competitors, competitive landscape, top executives with biographies, news, significant developments, and financial data. Financial summaries may include an income statement; balance sheet; cash flow; historical financials such as five years of P/E and per share; stock quotes; interactive stock charts; market data; earnings estimates; this year's ratios for the company, industry, and market; SEC filings; and industry watch for trends.

Content is tracked for 900 industries, organized into numerous larger categories: Agriculture & Forestry; Arts, Entertainment & Recreation; Beverage Manufacturing; Biotechnology Product Manufacturing; Business Services; Chemical Manufacturing; Commercial Equipment Repair & Maintenance; Commercial Printing; Computer Hardware Manufacturing; Computer Software; Construction; Consumer Products Manufacturing; Consumer Services; Contract Electronics Manufacturing; Education; Electric Power Generation; Electric Power Transmission, Distribution & Marketing; Electric Utilities; Electrical Products Manufacturing; Fabricated Metal Product Manufacturing; Financial Services; Food Manufacturing; Government; Health Care Products Manufacturing; Health Care; HVAC Equipment Manufacturing; Industrial Manufacturing; Insurance; Leasing of Intangible Assets; Lodging; Machinery Manufacturing; Magnetic & Optical Media; Manufacturing & Reproduction; Managed Application & Network Services; Management of Companies & Enterprises; Media; Membership Organizations; Mining; Miscellaneous Manufacturing; Natural Gas Distribution & Marketing; Nonclassifiable establishments; Nonmetallic Mineral Product Manufacturing; Nonprofit Institutions; Oil & Gas Exploration & Production; Oil & Gas Field Services; Oil & Gas Well Drilling; Petroleum & Coal Products Manufacturing; Pharmaceutical Manufacturing; Primary Metals Manufacturing; Private Households; Professional Services; Real Estate; Religious Organizations; Rental & Leasing; Restaurants, Bars & Food Services; Retail; Security Products Manufacturing; Semiconductor & Other Electronic Component Manufacturing; Telecommunications Equipment Manufacturing; Telecommunications Services; Transportation Equipment Manufacturing; Transportation Services; Water & Sewer Utilities; Wholesale; and Wood Product Manufacturing.

Coverage can be brief, but generally includes a fact sheet, overview, selected companies, industry watch with video interviews, news from the last 90 days, and web resources for terminology, associations, and organizations, and online publications. Hoover's print publications include (*Hoover's handbook of American business* (876), *Hoover's handbook of private companies* (855)).

997 IBISWorld United States. http://www.ibisworld.com/. IBISWorld. New York: IBISWorld. 1999–
                                                   HC103
700 reports on American industries. Industry reports can be located using NAICS numbers. Major categories include: Accommodation & Food Services; Administration, Business Support & Waste Management Services; Agriculture, Forestry, Fishing & Hunting; Arts, Entertainment & Recreation; Construction; Educational Services; Finance & Insurance; Healthcare & Social Assistance; Information; Manufacturing; Mining; Other Services (except Public Administration); Professional, Scientific & Technical Services; Real Estate & Rental and Leasing; Retail Trade; Transportation & Warehousing; Utilities; and Wholesale Trade.

Reports include industry definition; information about the supply chain; key statistics; segmentations (products and services segmentation, major market segments, industry concentration, geographic spread); market characteristics (market size, demand determinants, domestic and international markets, basis of competition, life cycle); industry conditions (barriers to entry, taxation, industry assistance, regulation and deregulation, cost structure, capital and labor intensity, technology and systems, industry volatility, globalization); key factors (sensitivities and success factors); key competitors; and industry performance (current and historical). Glossaries and guides to jargon. Setting this database apart are reports on small industries, such as parking lots and garages.

998 Plunkett's real estate and construction industry almanac. Jack W. Plunkett. Houston, Tex.: Plunkett Research, 2003–
ISSN 1553-3557
333.3   HD1361

Data on nearly 400 leading companies, both public and private. Company profiles include types of business, brands and affiliates, contacts, employee benefits and top salaries, sales and profit numbers, growth plans, and competitive advantage. Especially useful for the industry background, trends, statistics and rankings at the front of the volume (average U.S. employment in the construction industry: 1995–2005; U.S. commercial, residential, and farm mortgages by holder: 2000–2005; U.S. home mortgages by holder: 2000–2005; financial assets and liabilities of U.S. real estate investment trusts (REITs): 2001–2005; home equity loans by holder, U.S.: 2000–2005; estimates of the total housing inventory for the U.S.: 2004–2005; new privately-owned housing starts, U.S.: 1980–2005; U.S. residential rental vacancy rates by region: selected years 1995–2005; absorption rates of U.S. rental apartments: 2000–March 2005), and information on the main associations and organizations in the back of the volume. Most information is for the U.S., but some international coverage is provided. Available as an e-book.

Organizations and Associations

999 Associated general contractors of America. http://www.agc.org/.
Associated General Contractors of

America. Washington: Associated General Contractors of America. 1996–
                                         TA201

Home page for an advocacy group promoting commercial construction. Founded in 1918 as a trade association. The site has information on safety and risk management, contract documents, supervisory training, labor and human resources, the environment, construction economics, marketing, careers, legislative and public affairs, and news.

1000 National association of realtors.
http://www.realtor.org/. National Association of Realtors. Chicago: National Association of Realtors. 2002–
                                         HD1361

Home page of the second highest-spending lobbying organization in the U.S. Advocates around issues in real estate, and regulation of financial and lending services. Reports housing statistics; issues research reports such as surveys of commercial and residential real estate, or housing price indices. Some content restricted to association members.

Internet Resources

1001 Bankrate.com. http://www.bankrate .com/. Intelligent Life Corp. North Palm Beach, Fla.: Intelligent Life Corp. 1995–

Previously known as *Bank rate monitor.* Reports current rates for U.S. mortgages, the prime rate based on *Wall Street Journal* surveys, and the London Interbank Offered Rate (LIBOR). Provides credit- and loan-related news, and calculators for determining loan payments.

1002 The blue book building and construction network. http://www .thebluebook.com/. Contractors Register. Jefferson Valley, N.Y.: Contractors Register, Inc. 1996–
624/.029/4747   TH13.N4

Searchable online directory to locate contractors, manufacturers and suppliers. Search by state to find companies, contact information, geographical area served, year established, types of projects, typical project size, labor affiliation, license number, recent projects completed, manufacturers certifications, and brands used. Available for selected states and regions in print as *Blue book of building and construction.*

1003 Zillow. www.Zillow.com. Seattle, Wash.: Zillow.com. 2005–

HD7293

Database of 110,000,000 U.S. residential properties, searchable by address, ZIP code or from maps. When available, includes descriptions, photographs, and recent price and property tax figures. Estimates home values, rental rates, and mortgage costs. Intended for buyers, sellers, renters and real estate professionals. Comparable competing web sites include *Yahoo! Homes* and *Trulia*.

Additional Reference Sources

1004 Barron's real estate handbook.
7th ed. Jack P. Friedman, Jack C. Harris, Barry A. Diskin. Hauppauge, N.Y.: Barron's Educational Series, 2009. iv, 777 p., ill. ISBN 9780764161100
333.33   HD1375

Intended as a practical guide to the terminology and methods used in American home real estate. Most of the book is a glossary in which examples clarify the definitions. Includes separate guides for buyers and sellers, summaries of federal regulations, a discussion of appraisers, tables related to mortgage payments, and appendices including formulas and sample forms. Updated to reflect changes in real estate conditions since the beginning of the Great Recession. Index.

1005 The complete real estate encyclopedia: from AAA tenant to zoning variance and everything in between. Denise L. Evans, O. William Evans. New York: McGraw-Hill, 2007. xiii, 479 p., ill., maps
333.33003   HD1365

Defines more than 3,000 terms, covering construction, renting and leasing, taxes, developers, loans and mortgages, investment topics, and legal issues. Explanatory illustrations and charts. Sample forms. URLs for important websites. Appendixes include abbreviations, and glossaries of technical terms and jargon.

1006 The dictionary of real estate appraisal. 5th ed. Appraisal Institute (U.S.). Chicago: Appraisal Institute, 2010. xii, 403 p., ill. ISBN 9781935328070
333.33/203   HD1387

Combines 5,000 definitions of terms with examples of usage and advice to investors. Specific glossaries cover business valuation, statistics, architecture, construction, agriculture, and the environment. Contains useful formulas, charts, and figures. Also deals with property types and subtypes; real estate organizations and professional designations; federal agencies, legislation, court cases, and programs; and tables for measures and conversions. Bibliography. Contains cross-references.

1007 Dictionary of real estate terms. 8th ed. Jack P. Friedman, Jack C. Harris, J. Bruce Lindeman. Hauppauge, N.Y.: Barron's, 2013. xi, 560 p., ill.
333.3303   HD1365

Over 3,000 brief entries in alphabetical order defining terms related to architecture and construction, loans and mortgages, zoning, property appraisal, and more. Many entries conclude with explanatory examples, and there are helpful illustrations, graphs and charts. Intended for buyers and sellers, real estate professionals, and attorneys. Gives addresses of important organizations and associations. Appendix with abbreviations, formulas and diagrams. Bibliography. Index.

1008 The encyclopedia of housing.
2nd ed. Andrew T. Carswell. Thousand Oaks, Calif.: SAGE Publ., 2012. 2 v. (xxxii, 872 p.), ill. ISBN 9781412989572
363.503   HD7287

Some 300 signed articles, in alphabetical order with suggestions for further reading, address topics ranging from affordability and discrimination to sustainability and urban redevelopment. Updated since the first edition of 2001, to reflect developments in the housing industry and the impact of the mortgage crisis of 2008 on the market and regulations. Attention is paid to zoning, the influence of HUD, suburbs and urban sprawl, public housing, significant government agencies, and private associations. Relies on perspectives from sociology, anthropology, law, political science, and urban planning. Index. Available as an e-book.

1009 Sustainable development policy directory. W. Alan Strong, Lesley A. Hemphill. Oxford; Malden, Mass.: Blackwell, 2006. xi, 659 p. ISBN 9781405121507
338.927025   HC79.E5

Provides background information on sustainable development policy and actions in the "built environment" for industry and communities. Brings a European and international perspective, with a focus on the United Kingdom and Ireland. Each chapter gives the main challenges of that topic, and lists policy documents from the 1970s to the present (with the objectives of the policy, the contents of the document, and where available, the URLs for the documents). Chapters include: Biodiversity, Climate change, Construction, Energy, Environment, Planning, Pollution, Social issues, Sustainable development policy and practice, Transport, Urban development, Waste management, and Water. Available as an e-book.

Consulting

Specialized Sources of Industry Data

1010 Hoovers. http://www.hoovers.com/.
Reference Press, Hoover's, Inc. Short Hills, N.J.: Dun & Bradstreet. 1996–
338.7   HG4057
More than 60 million records describe public and private companies primarily in the United States, but including Canada, United Kingdom, Europe, and Asia/Pacific. Profiles have an overview, history, family tree, industry information, products/operations, top competitors, competitive landscape, top executives with biographies, news, significant developments, and financial data. Financial summaries may include an income statement; balance sheet; cash flow; historical financials such as five years of P/E and per share; stock quotes; interactive stock charts; market data; earnings estimates; this year's ratios for the company, industry, and market; SEC filings; and industry watch for trends.

Content is tracked for 900 industries, organized into numerous larger categories: Agriculture & Forestry; Arts, Entertainment & Recreation; Beverage Manufacturing; Biotechnology Product Manufacturing; Business Services; Chemical Manufacturing; Commercial Equipment Repair & Maintenance; Commercial Printing; Computer Hardware Manufacturing; Computer Software; Construction; Consumer Products Manufacturing; Consumer Services; Contract Electronics Manufacturing; Education; Electric Power Generation; Electric Power Transmission, Distribution & Marketing; Electric Utilities; Electrical Products Manufacturing; Fabricated Metal Product Manufacturing; Financial Services; Food Manufacturing; Government; Health Care Products Manufacturing; Health Care; HVAC Equipment Manufacturing; Industrial Manufacturing; Insurance; Leasing of Intangible Assets; Lodging; Machinery Manufacturing; Magnetic & Optical Media; Manufacturing & Reproduction; Managed Application & Network Services; Management of Companies & Enterprises; Media; Membership Organizations; Mining; Miscellaneous Manufacturing; Natural Gas Distribution & Marketing; Nonclassifiable establishments; Nonmetallic Mineral Product Manufacturing; Nonprofit Institutions; Oil & Gas Exploration & Production; Oil & Gas Field Services; Oil & Gas Well Drilling; Petroleum & Coal Products Manufacturing; Pharmaceutical Manufacturing; Primary Metals Manufacturing; Private Households; Professional Services; Real Estate; Religious Organizations; Rental & Leasing; Restaurants, Bars & Food Services; Retail; Security Products Manufacturing; Semiconductor & Other Electronic Component Manufacturing; Telecommunications Equipment Manufacturing; Telecommunications Services; Transportation Equipment Manufacturing; Transportation Services; Water & Sewer Utilities; Wholesale; and Wood Product Manufacturing.

Coverage can be brief, but generally includes a fact sheet, overview, selected companies, industry watch with video interviews, news from the last 90 days, and web resources for terminology, associations, and organizations, and online publications. Hoover's print publications include (*Hoover's handbook of American business* (876), *Hoover's handbook of private companies* (855)).

1011 IBISWorld United States. http://www .ibisworld.com/. IBISWorld. New York: IBISWorld. 1999–

HC103
700 reports on American industries. Industry reports can be located using NAICS numbers. Major categories include: Accommodation & Food Services; Administration, Business Support & Waste Management Services; Agriculture, Forestry, Fishing & Hunting; Arts, Entertainment & Recreation; Construction; Educational Services; Finance & Insurance; Healthcare & Social Assistance; Information; Manufacturing; Mining; Other Services (except

Public Administration); Professional, Scientific & Technical Services; Real Estate & Rental and Leasing; Retail Trade; Transportation & Warehousing; Utilities; and Wholesale Trade.

Reports include industry definition; information about the supply chain; key statistics; segmentations (products and services segmentation, major market segments, industry concentration, geographic spread); market characteristics (market size, demand determinants, domestic and international markets, basis of competition, life cycle); industry conditions (barriers to entry, taxation, industry assistance, regulation and deregulation, cost structure, capital and labor intensity, technology and systems, industry volatility, globalization); key factors (sensitivities and success factors); key competitors; and industry performance (current and historical). Glossaries and guides to jargon. Setting this database apart are reports on small industries, such as parking lots and garages.

1012 Plunkett's consulting industry almanac. Jack W. Plunkett. Houston, Tex.: Plunkett Research, 2003–
ISSN 1552-2288
331   HD69.C6P58

Data on more than 250 leading public and private companies. Company profiles include types of business, brands and affiliates, contacts, employee benefits and top salaries, sales and profit numbers, growth plans, and competitive advantage. Especially useful for the industry trends, statistics and rankings at the front of the volume (Employment in management and technical consulting services, U.S. 1995–2005; Largest computer and internet consulting companies 2004–2005; Largest human resources consulting companies 2004–2005; Largest management consulting companies 2004–2005), and information on the main associations and organizations in the back of the volume. Available as an e-book.

Organizations and Associations

1013 Association of management consulting firms. http://www.amcf.org/. Association of Management Consulting Firms. New York: Association of Management Consulting Firms. 1998–
Home page for an association for consultants, founded in 1929. The AMCF site provides benchmarking data, member polls, annual operating survey (reports on annual billing revenues, size of professional staff, typical project size, number of domestic offices), news, and an event calendar, mostly available to members. There are similar associations for different types of consultants (Independent Computer Consultants Association, Association of Consultants to Nonprofits, Association of Consulting Foresters, etc.).

Additional Reference Sources

1014 Consultants and consulting organizations directory. Gale Research (Firm). Detroit: Gale Group, 1973–. 7 v.
ISSN 0196-1292
658.4/6/025   HD 69.C6

Organized into 14 general fields of consulting. Entries give contact information, brief description of activities, mergers and former names, geographic area served, and where possible, annual consulting revenue. Published annually since 1988, triennially since 1973. 2013 will see the 38th edition.

1015 D and B consultants directory. Dun and Bradstreet Corporation. Bethlehem, Pa.: Dun and Bradstreet, 1998–
ISSN 1524-9743
658.4602573   HD69.C6

Annual. Provides information on more than 30,000 of the largest consulting firms in the U.S, with profiles arranged alphabetically. Companies are cross-referenced geographically and by consulting activity.

Financial Services and Insurance

Specialized Sources of Industry Data

1016 The Bankers' almanac. Reed Information Services Ltd. West Sussex, England: Reed Information Services, 1993– ISSN 1462-4125
                                     HG2984

International coverage of over 4,000 banks, with information on executives, bank owners and their percentage of shares, bank correspondents, bank name changes, liquidations, balance sheet figures, profits and loss statements, world and country rankings, credit ratings, national bank and SWIFT codes. Available as an e-book.

1017 Banking and monetary statistics, 1941–1970. Board of Governors of the Federal Reserve System. Washington: Board of Governors of the Federal Reserve System, 1976. vii, 1168 p.

332.0973   HG2493

Includes "data on the condition and operation of all banks . . . statistics of bank debits, bank earnings, bank suspensions, branch, group, and chain banking, currency, money rates, security markets, Treasury finance, production and movement of gold, and international financial developments." *Pref.* Full text is available online at http://fraser.stlouisfed.org .proxy1.cl.msu.edu/publication/?pid=41. The preceding volume, *Banking and monetary statistics, 1914– 1941*, is online at http://fraser.stlouisfed.org.proxy1 .cl.msu.edu/publication/?pid=38.

1018 Bankscope. http://www.bvdinfo.com/ en-us/products/company-information/ international/bankscope. Bureau van Dijk Electronic Publishing. Brussels, Belgium: Bureau van Dijk Electronic Publishing. 1998–

      HG1501

Financial information on more than 11,000 public and private banks worldwide. Provides standardized reports, ratings, ownership data, financial analysis, security and price information, scanned images of the bank's annual or interim accounts, and country risk reports. Most data goes back eight years. Data sources include Fitch Ratings. Standardized reports contain detailed consolidated and/or unconsolidated balance sheet and income statement, as well as 36 pre-calculated ratios. Data can be downloaded to Excel. Also available through WRDS (235).

1019 Best's aggregates and averages: life/ health, United States and Canada. A.M. Best Company. Oldwick, N.J.: A.M. Best Company, 1986– ISSN 1551–8302

368   HG8941

Summary data on the insurance industry. Includes balance sheet and summary of operations, annual statements, quantitative analysis, insurance expenses,

time series, premiums written, industry underwriting, leading companies and groups (with assets, policy-holders surplus, reserves, premiums written, underwriting gain/loss, net investment income, realized capital gains, underwriting expense ratio, etc.), rankings, and composite listings. Coverage is for Canada and the United States. Also available for Property/ Casualty (1020). Formerly *Best's insurance reports.*

1020 Best's aggregates and averages: property/casualty, United States and Canada. A. M. Best Company. Oldwick, N.J.: A. M. Best Company, 1976– ISSN 1933-4621

368.09   HG8945

Summary data on the insurance industry. Includes balance sheet and summary of operations, annual statements, quantitative analysis, insurance expenses, time series, premiums written, industry underwriting, leading companies and groups (with assets, policyholders surplus, reserves, premiums written, underwriting gain/loss, net investment income, realized capital gains, underwriting expense ratio, etc.), rankings, and composite listings. Coverage is for Canada and the United States. Also available for Life/Health (1019). Formerly *Best's insurance reports.*

1021 Credit union directory. http://purl .access.gpo.gov/GPO/LPS208. National Credit Union Administration. Alexandria, Va.: National Credit Union Administration. 1996– ISSN 0196-3678

334/.22/02573   HG2037

Information from NCUA on U.S. credit unions, except "state-chartered natural person credit unions that are either uninsured or covered by private insurance corporations." —*Pref.* Gives charter number, address, name of CEO/manager, telephone number, assets, loans, net worth ratio, percent share growth, percent loan growth, loans/assets ratio, investments/ assets ratio, number of members, and number of full-time employees. Also includes national statistics.

1022 Fact book. Securities Industry and Financial Markets Association. New York: Securities Industry and Financial Markets Association, 2007– ISSN 1945-4449

332.6   HG4910

Annual. Provides information on capital markets, the securities industry, market activity, investor participation, global markets, savings, and investment. Good for finding statistics on corporate underwriting and private placements, capital raised for U.S. business, initial public offerings by state, total U.S. mergers and acquisitions, securities industry employment by firm category, securities industry profitability, pre-tax profit margins and return on equity, stock market capitalization, stock exchange activity, compound annual rates of return by decade for stocks, bonds and treasuries, and value of international securities offerings. Some data goes back to 1965. Successor to *Securities industry fact book*.

1023 The financial services fact book.
Insurance Information Institute, Financial Services Roundtable. New York: Insurance Information Institute [and] Financial Services Roundtable, 2002–. ill.
ISSN 1537-6257
658   HG181
Current information on insurance, banking, securities, and the financial services industry as a whole. Includes statistics on U.S. savings, investment and debt ownership, consumer fraud and identity theft, convergence of financial services companies, IT spending, and the growth of online commerce. The most current Fact book is available at http://www2 .iii.org/financial/.

1024 Freedonia focus reports. http://www
.freedoniagroup.com/FocusReports.aspx.
Freedonia Group. Cleveland, Ohio:
Freedonia Group. 2001–
                                       HC106.82
Industry outlook information on a subscription basis. More than 600 reports cover eighteen industry categories: automotive, chemicals, construction, consumer goods, electronics, energy, food and agriculture (including tobacco), industrial components, life sciences (both medical and pharmaceutical), machinery, metals and minerals, miscellaneous and service industries, packaging, paper and printing (including publishing), plastics, rubber, textiles and leather (including apparel), and wood (including furniture and fixtures). Provides market size, historical demand, forecasts of demand, and profiles of leading companies. Browsable by major regions: Australia, Brazil, Canada, China, France, Germany, India, Italy, Japan, Mexico, Russia, South Korea, Spain, the U.K., and the U.S.

1025 Hoovers. http://www.hoovers.com/.
Reference Press, Hoover's, Inc. Short Hills, N.J.: Dun & Bradstreet. 1996–
338.7   HG4057
More than 60 million records describe public and private companies primarily in the United States, but including Canada, United Kingdom, Europe, and Asia/Pacific. Profiles have an overview, history, family tree, industry information, products/operations, top competitors, competitive landscape, top executives with biographies, news, significant developments, and financial data. Financial summaries may include an income statement; balance sheet; cash flow; historical financials such as five years of P/E and per share; stock quotes; interactive stock charts; market data; earnings estimates; this year's ratios for the company, industry, and market; SEC filings; and industry watch for trends.

Content is tracked for 900 industries, organized into numerous larger categories: Agriculture & Forestry; Arts, Entertainment & Recreation; Beverage Manufacturing; Biotechnology Product Manufacturing; Business Services; Chemical Manufacturing; Commercial Equipment Repair & Maintenance; Commercial Printing; Computer Hardware Manufacturing; Computer Software; Construction; Consumer Products Manufacturing; Consumer Services; Contract Electronics Manufacturing; Education; Electric Power Generation; Electric Power Transmission, Distribution & Marketing; Electric Utilities; Electrical Products Manufacturing; Fabricated Metal Product Manufacturing; Financial Services; Food Manufacturing; Government; Health Care Products Manufacturing; Health Care; HVAC Equipment Manufacturing; Industrial Manufacturing; Insurance; Leasing of Intangible Assets; Lodging; Machinery Manufacturing; Magnetic & Optical Media; Manufacturing & Reproduction; Managed Application & Network Services; Management of Companies & Enterprises; Media; Membership Organizations; Mining; Miscellaneous Manufacturing; Natural Gas Distribution & Marketing; Nonclassifiable establishments; Nonmetallic Mineral Product Manufacturing; Nonprofit Institutions; Oil & Gas Exploration & Production; Oil & Gas Field Services; Oil & Gas Well Drilling; Petroleum & Coal Products Manufacturing; Pharmaceutical Manufacturing; Primary Metals Manufacturing; Private Households; Professional Services; Real Estate;

Religious Organizations; Rental & Leasing; Restaurants, Bars & Food Services; Retail; Security Products Manufacturing; Semiconductor & Other Electronic Component Manufacturing; Telecommunications Equipment Manufacturing; Telecommunications Services; Transportation Equipment Manufacturing; Transportation Services; Water & Sewer Utilities; Wholesale; and Wood Product Manufacturing.

Coverage can be brief, but generally includes a fact sheet, overview, selected companies, industry watch with video interviews, news from the last 90 days, and web resources for terminology, associations, and organizations, and online publications. Hoover's print publications include (*Hoover's handbook of American business* [876], *Hoover's handbook of private companies* [855]).

1026 IBISWorld United States. http://www
.ibisworld.com/. IBISWorld. New York: IBISWorld. 1999–

HC103

700 reports on American industries. Industry reports can be located using NAICS numbers. Major categories include: Accommodation & Food Services; Administration, Business Support & Waste Management Services; Agriculture, Forestry, Fishing & Hunting; Arts, Entertainment & Recreation; Construction; Educational Services; Finance & Insurance; Healthcare & Social Assistance; Information; Manufacturing; Mining; Other Services (except Public Administration); Professional, Scientific & Technical Services; Real Estate & Rental and Leasing; Retail Trade; Transportation & Warehousing; Utilities; and Wholesale Trade.

Reports include industry definition; information about the supply chain; key statistics; segmentations (products and services segmentation, major market segments, industry concentration, geographic spread); market characteristics (market size, demand determinants, domestic and international markets, basis of competition, life cycle); industry conditions (barriers to entry, taxation, industry assistance, regulation and deregulation, cost structure, capital and labor intensity, technology and systems, industry volatility, globalization); key factors (sensitivities and success factors); key competitors; and industry performance (current and historical). Glossaries and guides to jargon. Setting this database apart are reports on small industries, such as parking lots and garages.

1027 Plunkett's banking, mortgages, and credit industry almanac. Jack W. Plunkett. Houston, Tex.: Plunkett Research, 2004–. ill.

HG2441

Data on over 300 major companies, both public and private. Company profiles include types of business, brands and affiliates, contacts, employee benefits and top salaries, sales and profit numbers, growth plans, and competitive advantage. Especially useful for the industry trends, statistics, and rankings at the front of the volume (top banks, main mergers and acquisitions, home ownership rates, consumer credit outstanding, etc.), and information on the main associations and organizations in the back of the volume. Most information is for the U.S., but some international coverage is provided (U.K., China, India, and Japan). Available as an e-book.

1028 Standard and Poor's industry surveys. Standard and Poor's. New York: Standard and Poor's, 1973–2012
ISSN 0196-4666
332.67   HC106.6

Detailed analyses of 22 industry categories and the major companies in each category. Contains a basic analysis and a comprehensive source of information, updated by a current analysis. The analysis includes trends, information on how the industry operates, key ratios and statistics (revenues, net income, profit ratios, balance sheet ratios, equity ratios, per-share data, company and product rankings), information on how to analyze a company in that industry, and a glossary. Company and industry indexes. Ceased with edition of 2012.

Organizations and Associations

1029 American bankers association.
http://www.aba.com/. American Bankers Association. Washington: American Bankers Association. 1996–
332   HG4501

Home page for the advocacy group for U.S. banks. Organized into areas such as policy statements; letters to Congress; a job bank; conference information; a list of experts; and reports. Includes member services. Some content limited to members.

1030 FDIC. http://www.fdic.gov/. Federal
Deposit Insurance Corporation.
Washington: Federal Deposit Insurance
Corporation. [1996–]
                HG1662.U5
Home page for the Federal Deposit Insurance Cor-
poration, which insures deposits, examines financial
institutions for soundness and consumer protection,
and manages receiverships. Website is organized into:
Deposit Insurance, Consumer Protection, Industry
Analysis, Regulation & Examinations, Asset Sales,
and News & Events. Includes Call Reports and Thrift
Financial Reports from 1998 to the present; an institution directory for federally insured institutions;
Summary of Deposits; Quarterly Banking Profile with
figures since December 31, 1994; statistics on banking
and depository institutions; and laws and regulations.

**1031 National association of mutual
insurance companies.** http://www
.namic.org/. National Association
of Mutual Insurance Companies.
Indianapolis, Ind.: National Association of
Mutual Insurance Companies. 1997–
                HG8057
Home page of an advocacy group founded in 1895
to serve mutual (non–publicly traded) insurance
companies. The site has a registered user access
member directory, news, discussion forums, pod-
casts, *IN magazine*, seminars, event calendar, and
government affairs (includes reports and policy statements). Some content limited to members.

Additional Reference Sources

1032 The bank directory. Accuity (Firm).
Skokie, Ill.: Accuity, 2005–. 5 v.
ISSN 1941-6369
332.1/025/73   HG2441
Annual. Successor to *Thomson bank directory*. Provides information for U.S. and international banks,
including national routing codes, personnel, basic
financials, credit ratings, standard settlement instructions, and industry statistics and rankings. Also available through various aggregator databases.

1033 Banking information source. http://
www.proquest.com/en-US/catalogs/
databases/detail/pq_banking_info.shtml.

ProQuest Information and Learning
Company. Ann Arbor, Mich.: ProQuest
Information and Learning
                HG181
Indexes some 690 periodicals, including scholarly
journals and trade publications, with full text of
recent years for more than 500 titles. Information
about automation, marketing, credit unions, international banking, investment banking, pension funds,
private banking, savings and loan institutions, and
women and minorities in banking. Also available
through Dialog.

1034 Bankrate.com. http://www.bankrate.com/.
Intelligent Life Corp. North Palm Beach,
Fla.: Intelligent Life Corp. 1995–
Previously known as *Bank rate monitor*. Reports current rates for U.S. mortgages, the prime rate based
on *Wall Street Journal* surveys, and the London Interbank Offered Rate (LIBOR). Provides credit- and
loan-related news, and calculators for determining
loan payments.

1035 The Corporate finance sourcebook.
National Register Publishing (Firm).
Berkeley Heights, N.J.: National Register
Publishing, 1979– ISSN 0163-3031
332.02573   HG4057
Annual directory of firms involved in capital investments and financial services (e.g., venture capital,
private lenders, commercial and financial factors,
business intermediaries, leasing companies and corporate real estate, commercial, U.S.-based foreign,
and investments banks and trusts, securities analysts
and CPA/auditing firms). Entries include personnel,
financial information, type of investor or service, minimum investment, funds available, average number
of deals completed annually, industry preferences,
and exit criteria. Indexed by name of company, personnel, and geography.

1036 The credit union directory. Accuity,
Credit Union National Association.
Duluth, Ga.: Accuity, 2006–
334   HG2037
Organized by state and then by city, the Directory
gives contact information, date founded, number of
employees, charter, CUNA ID, route number, Fed-
wire status, one year of financial information (asset
rank, assets, shares, loans), number of members,

ROA, executive names, and branches. Published in cooperation with the Credit Union National Association. Formerly *Credit union journal registry of credit unions*.

1037 Dictionary of banking terms. 6th ed.
Thomas P. Fitch. Hauppauge, N.Y.: Barrons Educational Series, 2012. viii, 519 p.
ISBN 9780764147562
332.103   HG151
Contains more than 3,000 brief definitions for terms used in banking practices, laws, and regulations, including investment and commercial banking, finance and money management. Good cross-references. Includes diagrams and charts. Intended for business persons, students and consumers.

1038 Elsevier's banking dictionary in seven languages: English, American, French, Italian, Spanish, Portuguese, Dutch, and German. 3rd rev. and enl. ed.
Julio Ricci. Amsterdam, The Netherlands; New York: Elsevier, 1990. 359 p.
ISBN 9780444880673
332.1/03   HG151
A polyglot dictionary for banking and finance arranged on an English-language base with equivalent terms in the other languages. The third revision of Elsevier's banking dictionary in seven languages, adding Portuguese to the list of languages. More than 2,400 terms; indexed by terms in the other languages.

1039 Encyclopedia of American business history and biography. Facts On File.
New York: Facts On File, 1988–1994. ill.
0816013713   HC102
Combines biographical entries with articles discussing major companies, government and labor organizations, inventions, and legal decisions for various industries. The signed entries range in length from one-half to ten or more pages; most include photographs or other illustrations, and list publications and references, archives, and unpublished documents. Each volume is available separately. Ten volumes were published up to 1994, including *The airline industry*; *The automobile industry, 1896–1920*; *The automobile industry, 1920–1980*; *Banking and finance to 1913*; *Banking and finance, 1913–1989*; *Iron and steel in the nineteenth century*; *Iron and steel in the twentieth century*; *Railroads in the nineteenth century*; and *Railroads in the age of regulation, 1900–1980*.

1040 Mergent bank and finance manual.
Mergent, Inc. New York: Mergent, Inc., 2001– ISSN 1539-6444
332.13   HG4961
Covers banks, insurance companies, investment trusts, and financial institutions. Has basic company financials, company description, list of properties and subsidiaries, report of independent auditors, annual meeting date, capital stock, dividends and long-term debt information, and contact information. Included in Mergent Online (891).

1041 North American financial institutions directory. North American ed ed.
Thomson Financial Publishing, Accuity (Firm). Skokie, Ill.: Thomson Financial, 2000–. maps ISSN 1529-1367
332.10257   HG1536
Covers Canada, the U.S., Central America, the Caribbean, and Mexico. Entries vary in length from very brief to extensive, the latter providing information about branches and corporate and financial structure. A separate section lists banks by name and gives ranked lists of banks, commercial banks, savings and loan banks, and credit unions. Includes directories of associations, the Federal Reserve System, pertinent government organizations (e.g., the Secret Service), and a limited directory of the largest international banks.

1042 Obamacare survival guide: the Affordable Care Act and what it means for you and your healthcare.
First ed. Nick J. Tate. West Palm Beach, Fla.: Humanix Books, 2013. xxi, 241 pages ISBN 9780893348625
362.10973   RA395.D44
Written as implementation of the Affordable Care Act (Obamacare) remains in flux, this is an early entry in the ranks of reference sources. Like most writing on the topic, this work has a point of view, but is one of the most widely owned publications on the topic in libraries, attempting an overview and summary. Includes information about timetables; projected impact on health insurance and Medicaid; the new health insurance exchanges; cost and cost control issues; and implications for small businesses.

1043 Passport GMID. http://www.euromonitor
.com/. Euromonitor International.
London, U.K.: Euromonitor International.
[1999–]
658.8   HF5415.2

Also known under previous product names as
Global market information database, *GMID*, or *Euromonitor GMID*. Market reports, company profiles,
and demographic, economic, and marketing statistics for 205 countries. Market reports are for
16 consumer markets (food and drink, tobacco,
toys, etc.) and 14 industrial and service markets
(accountancy, broadcasting, chemicals, property
services, etc.).

Reports have market size, market sectors, share
of market, marketing activity, research and development, corporate overview, distribution, consumer
profiles, market forecasts, sector forecasts, sources,
and definitions. Additional reports are available for
market segments, such as baby food. Company profiles have background, recent news, competitve environment, and outlook. Consumer lifestyle reports
and very useful marketing background analyze the
consumer by country, gender, age, marital status,
educational attainment, ethnicity, religion, home
ownership, household profile, employment, income,
health, eating and personal grooming habits, leisure
activities, personal finance, communication, transport, and travel.

Search for data, which can be exported into Excel
or browse for reports. Data are available since 1977
and include inflation, exchange rates, GDP, GNI,
government expenditures, government finance,
income, labor, and money supply.

Similar information on a smaller scale is available
in Research monitor (783) from the same publisher.

**1044 The Thorndike encyclopedia of
banking and financial tables:
yearbook.** Boston: Warren, Gorham, and
Lamont, 1975–2010 ISSN 0196-7762
332.8/2/0212   HG1626

Tables for loan payment and amortization, compound interest and annuity, simple interest, savings
and withdrawals, installment loans, and investment. Narrative materials reflecting new developments in finance, investment, laws and regulations,
etc. Updates *Thorndike encyclopedia of banking
and financial tables* (1987). Ceased with edition
of 2010.

Food and Beverage

**1045 The business of wine: an
encyclopedia.** Geralyn Brostrom, Jack
Brostrom. Westport, Conn.: Greenwood
Press, 2009. xxi, 304 p.
ISBN 9780313354007
338.4/7663203   HD9370.5

Includes 140 articles on the production, packaging, retail sale and consumption of wine, including
summaries of the industry in major countries, notes
about major varieties, and biographies of industry leaders. There is some emphasis on the United
States. Appendix includes statistical data about production and the market in major wine-producing
and wine-consuming countries. Bibliography. Index.
Also available as an e-book.

1046 Plunkett's food industry almanac.
Jack W. Plunkett. Houston, Tex.: Plunkett
Research, 2003– ISSN 1547-6308
338.1   HD9003

Data on 300 major companies including in retail, distribution, and specialty products. Company profiles
include types of business, brands and affiliates, contacts, employee benefits and top salaries, sales and profit numbers, growth plans, and competitive advantage.
Especially useful for the industry statistics and rankings
at the front of the volume. Available as an e-book.

Specialized Sources of Industry Data

1047 Beverage industry annual manual.
BNP Media. Troy, Mich.: BNP Media,
1972/3–. ill., some col. ISSN 8755-0717
338.476630973   HD9348.U5

Entries for over 750 companies, nearly 1,200 products, and 750 resources, such as industry associations. Also has information on marketing, distribution,
trends, consumption, and production.

1048 Food and beverage market place. Grey
House Publishing, Inc. Millerton, N.Y.:
Grey House, 2001– ISSN 1936-2501
381   HD9003

Annual. Formerly *Thomas food and beverage market
place*. Combines *Food and beverage market place*, *Food
and beverage market place—suppliers guide*, and *Thomas*

food industry register, to form a comprehensive directory for companies in the industry. 40,000 company profiles include contact information, executive titles, company description, parent company name, company divisions, number of employees, size of facility, sales volume, Standard Industrial Classification (SIC) codes, company type, and other locations. Published in three volumes. Vol. 1 lists food and beverage manufacturers and has indexes for brand names and ethnic foods. Vol. 2, products, equipment, and services, is arranged alphabetically by product or service. Indexes for brand name, transportation region, transportation type, and wholesale product type. Vol. 3, brokers, importers, exporters, consumer catalogs, and industry resources, with indexes for each. Also available online.

1049 Freedonia focus reports. http://www
.freedoniagroup.com/FocusReports.aspx.
Freedonia Group. Cleveland, Ohio:
Freedonia Group. 2001–

HC106.82

Industry outlook information on a subscription basis. More than 600 reports cover eighteen industry categories: automotive, chemicals, construction, consumer goods, electronics, energy, food and agriculture (including tobacco), industrial components, life sciences (both medical and pharmaceutical), machinery, metals and minerals, miscellaneous and service industries, packaging, paper and printing (including publishing), plastics, rubber, textiles and leather (including apparel), and wood (including furniture and fixtures). Provides market size, historical demand, forecasts of demand, and profiles of leading companies. Browsable by major regions: Australia, Brazil, Canada, China, France, Germany, India, Italy, Japan, Mexico, Russia, South Korea, Spain, the U.K., and the U.S.

1050 Hoovers. http://www.hoovers.com/.
Reference Press, Hoover's, Inc. Short Hills,
N.J.: Dun & Bradstreet. 1996–

338.7 HG4057

More than 60 million records describe public and private companies primarily in the United States, but including Canada, United Kingdom, Europe, and Asia/Pacific. Profiles have an overview, history, family tree, industry information, products/operations, top competitors, competitive landscape, top executives with biographies, news, significant developments,

and financial data. Financial summaries may include an income statement; balance sheet; cash flow; historical financials such as five years of P/E and per share; stock quotes; interactive stock charts; market data; earnings estimates; this year's ratios for the company, industry, and market; SEC filings; and industry watch for trends.

Content is tracked for 900 industries, organized into numerous larger categories: Agriculture & Forestry; Arts, Entertainment & Recreation; Beverage Manufacturing; Biotechnology Product Manufacturing; Business Services; Chemical Manufacturing; Commercial Equipment Repair & Maintenance; Commercial Printing; Computer Hardware Manufacturing; Computer Software; Construction; Consumer Products Manufacturing; Consumer Services; Contract Electronics Manufacturing; Education; Electric Power Generation; Electric Power Transmission, Distribution & Marketing; Electric Utilities; Electrical Products Manufacturing; Fabricated Metal Product Manufacturing; Financial Services; Food Manufacturing; Government; Health Care Products Manufacturing; Health Care; HVAC Equipment Manufacturing; Industrial Manufacturing; Insurance; Leasing of Intangible Assets; Lodging; Machinery Manufacturing; Magnetic & Optical Media; Manufacturing & Reproduction; Managed Application & Network Services; Management of Companies & Enterprises; Media; Membership Organizations; Mining; Miscellaneous Manufacturing; Natural Gas Distribution & Marketing; Nonclassifiable establishments; Nonmetallic Mineral Product Manufacturing; Nonprofit Institutions; Oil & Gas Exploration & Production; Oil & Gas Field Services; Oil & Gas Well Drilling; Petroleum & Coal Products Manufacturing; Pharmaceutical Manufacturing; Primary Metals Manufacturing; Private Households; Professional Services; Real Estate; Religious Organizations; Rental & Leasing; Restaurants, Bars & Food Services; Retail; Security Products Manufacturing; Semiconductor & Other Electronic Component Manufacturing; Telecommunications Equipment Manufacturing; Telecommunications Services; Transportation Equipment Manufacturing; Transportation Services; Water & Sewer Utilities; Wholesale; and Wood Product Manufacturing.

Coverage can be brief, but generally includes a fact sheet, overview, selected companies, industry watch with video interviews, news from the last 90 days, and web resources for terminology, associations, and organizations, and online publications. Hoover's print publications include (*Hoover's handbook of American business* [876], *Hoover's handbook of private companies* [855]).

1051 Hospitality and tourism index. http://www.ebscohost.com/academic/hospitality-tourism-index. EBSCO Publishing. Ipswich, Mass.: EBSCO Publishing. 2003–
TX911.3.M27

Indexes scholarly research and industry news relating to all areas of hospitality and tourism, including culinary arts, hotel management, and travel. Formed from the now ceased Cornell University's hospitality database, the Universities of Surrey and Oxford Brookes Articles in Hospitality and Tourism, and Purdue University's Lodging, Restaurant, and Tourism Index. Coverage as early as 1965, with depth increasing in the 1980s.

1052 Standard and Poor's industry surveys. Standard and Poor's. New York: Standard and Poor's, 1973–2012 ISSN 0196-4666
332.67
HC106.6

Detailed analyses of 22 industry categories and the major companies in each category. Contains a basic analysis and a comprehensive source of information, updated by a current analysis. The analysis includes trends, information on how the industry operates, key ratios and statistics (revenues, net income, profit ratios, balance sheet ratios, equity ratios, per-share data, company and product rankings), information on how to analyze a company in that industry, and a glossary. Company and industry indexes. Ceased with edition of 2012.

1053 Technomic top 500 chain restaurant report. Technomic Information Services. Chicago: Technomic Information Services, 1999–
TX945

Often cited in trade publications, this report analyzes trends and offers forecasts for the restaurant business. Review of outlets and sales by menu category (pizza, Asian, seafood, etc.) and service segment (limited service, casual dining, midscale, fine dining). Tracks mergers, acquisitions, bankruptcies and IPO activity. Identifies emerging leaders. Appendixes include alphabetical listing; chains ranked by U.S. systemwide sales; chains ranked by U.S. systemwide

units; average unit volume by chain; international sales and units; and chains indexed by menu category and ranked by share of sales.

Organizations and Associations

1054 American beverage association. http://www.ameribev.org/. American Beverage Association. Washington: American Beverage Association. 1999–
338
HD9349.S633

Home page for the advocacy group for the U.S. non-alcoholic beverage industry, including sports and energy drinks and bottled water. Offers useful statistics and background. Sections include a directory of "Who Makes What" drink products, calorie and nutrition information, statements on recycling and water use, news, and a directory of suppliers for ingredients, services and equipment. Some content limited to members. Formerly the National Soft Drink Association.

1055 Food and drug administration. http://www.fda.gov/. Food and drug administration. Washington: U.S. Department of Health and Human Services. 1996–
353.0077/8
RA395.A3

Home page for the FDA, with a wide range of information for the consumer and the researcher, including: Enforcement Activities (clinical trials, enforcement report, product recalls and alerts); Products Regulated by FDA (animal drugs and food, aquaculture, bioengineered food, biologics, gene therapy, mobile phones, sunlamps, tattoos, food, drugs, xenotransplantation); news; hot topics; publications; major initiatives/activities (advisory committees, bar coding, buying medical products online, Data Council, Facts@FDA) and Food Industry (Prior Notice of Imports, Registration of Food Facilities).

1056 International dairy foods association. http://www.idfa.org/. International Dairy Foods Association. Washington: International Dairy Foods Association. 1998–
630
HD9275

Home page for the advocacy group representing the U.S. dairy industry, including milk, cheese, and ice cream. The site has industry facts, regulations, legislation, economic analysis, product marketing, meetings and training, and products and publications. Most useful for the statistics on the industry, links to butter and cheese cash prices, butter and milk futures and options, and federal milk marketing order data/prices. There are similar associations for various areas of the food industry, including the Chocolate Manufacturers Association, Natural Products Association, and the Foodservice and Packaging Institute.

1057 National restaurant association.
http://www.restaurant.org/. National Restaurant Association. Washington: National Restaurant Association. 2007

Home page for association, founded in 1919, representing 935,000 restaurant and foodservice companies. The website has news, community outreach, food safety and nutrition, careers and education, policy and politics, events, tips for running a business, and industry research. The industry research portion of the site has Industry Overviews (at a glance, forecast, state and local statistics), Research by Topic (H/R, operations, consumer, economy), links to resources for company research, and current industry trends. A great resource for locating demographic trends, consumer food-and-beverage preferences, cost of sales, gross profits, and employee turnover. Some data is available for free.

1058 Snack food association. http://www.sfa .org/. Snack Food Association. Alexandria, Va.: Snack Food Association. 1998–
664   TX803.P8

Home page for the advocacy group for "convenience foods" such as potato chips and popcorn. The association was founded in 1937 and is international in scope. The SFA website has information for consumers and the press, policy statements, a calendar of events, and lists of published guides and manuals.

Additional Reference Sources

1059 The Oxford encyclopedia of food and drink in America. 2nd ed. Andrew F. Smith. New York: Oxford University Press, 2013. 3 v., ill. ISBN 9780199734962
641.597303   TX349

Contains 1,400 signed articles in alphabetical order on the social and economic history of food

and beverages in the U.S., from 350 contributors. Entries cover food-related events (Thanksgiving), personalities (Julia Child), restaurant and franchise companies (A&W or Burger King), advertising and branding figures (Aunt Jemima), issues (biotechnology), and food types (sushi or biscuits). Enlarged to three volumes since the 1st ed. of 2004. New are culinary profiles of major cities, more biographies, more histories of brands, and coverage of ethnic food cultures. Appendixes provide lists of food-related websites, libraries, museums, and organizations. Bibliography. Index. Available as an e-book.

1060 Passport GMID. http://www.euromonitor .com/. Euromonitor International. London, U.K.: Euromonitor International. [1999–]
658.8   HF5415.2

Also known under previous product names as *Global market information database*, *GMID*, or *Euromonitor GMID*. Market reports, company profiles, and demographic, economic, and marketing statistics for 205 countries. Market reports are for 16 consumer markets (food and drink, tobacco, toys, etc.) and 14 industrial and service markets (accountancy, broadcasting, chemicals, property services, etc.).

Reports have market size, market sectors, share of market, marketing activity, research and development, corporate overview, distribution, consumer profiles, market forecasts, sector forecasts, sources, and definitions. Additional reports are available for market segments, such as baby food. Company profiles have background, recent news, competitve environment, and outlook. Consumer lifestyle reports and very useful marketing background analyze the consumer by country, gender, age, marital status, educational attainment, ethnicity, religion, home ownership, household profile, employment, income, health, eating and personal grooming habits, leisure activities, personal finance, communication, transport, and travel.

Search for data, which can be exported into Excel or browse for reports. Data are available since 1977 and include inflation, exchange rates, GDP, GNI, government expenditures, government finance, income, labor, and money supply.

Similar information on a smaller scale is available in Research monitor (783) from the same publisher.

Health Care

Specialized Sources of Industry Data

1061 The Dartmouth atlas of health care.
http://www.dartmouthatlas.org/atlases
.shtm. Dartmouth Institute for Health
Policy and Clinical Practice, Dartmouth
Medical School, American Hospital
Association. Lebanon, N.H.: Dartmouth
Institute for Health Policy and Clinical
Practice

The Dartmouth Atlas Project started as a series of
books and is now accessible via a web-based resource,
providing access to the *Dartmouth atlas of health care*
series (national editions, specialty-specific editions,
state editions, and regional editions). Describes and
illustrates quality, cost, and delivery of healthcare
services in the U.S. and geographic variations in
practice patterns, with description of the physician
workforce and distribution of resources. Written for
health policy analysts and other health professionals.
The home page at http://www.dartmouthatlas.org/
index.shtm provides additional information.

**1062 Department of health and human
services.** http://www.hhs.gov/. U.S.
Department of Health and Human
Services. Washington: U.S. Department of
Health and Human Services. 1997–

HV85

Home page for the U.S. Department of Health and
Human Services (HHS), responsible for "protecting
the health of all Americans and providing essential
human services, especially for those who are least
able to help themselves." —*HHS What We Do*. To
that end, their website provides a rich source of
information on aging, disasters and emergencies,
diseases and conditions, drug and food information,
families and children, grants and funding, policies
and regulations, reference collections (dictionaries
and glossaries, various indexes, clinical trials database, food additive database, statistics, reports),
resource locators, safety and wellness, and specific
populations. Includes information on the economic and business impact of the Affordable Care Act
(Obamacare). Formerly the Department of Health,
Education and Welfare (HEW), until separated from
the Department of Education in 1979.

1063 Faststats A to Z. http://www.cdc.gov/
nchs/fastats/Default.htm. National Center
for Health Statistics (NCHS). Hyattsville,
Md.: U.S. Dept. of Health and Human
Services, Centers for Disease Control and
Prevention, National Center for Health
Statistics

Provides topic-appropriate public health statistics
(e.g., birth data, morbidity and mortality statistics,
and health care use) and relevant links to further
information and publications. Includes state and territorial data, with clickable map for individual state
data. Also includes data derived from the "Behavioral Risk Factor Surveillance System (BRFSS)," which
compiles data for 16 negative behaviors.

1064 Freedonia focus reports. http://www
.freedoniagroup.com/FocusReports.aspx.
Freedonia Group. Cleveland, Ohio:
Freedonia Group. 2001–

HC106.82

Industry outlook information on a subscription
basis. More than 600 reports cover eighteen industry categories: automotive, chemicals, construction,
consumer goods, electronics, energy, food and agriculture (including tobacco), industrial components,
life sciences (both medical and pharmaceutical),
machinery, metals and minerals, miscellaneous and
service industries, packaging, paper and printing
(including publishing), plastics, rubber, textiles and
leather (including apparel), and wood (including furniture and fixtures). Provides market size, historical
demand, forecasts of demand, and profiles of leading
companies. Browsable by major regions: Australia,
Brazil, Canada, China, France, Germany, India, Italy,
Japan, Mexico, Russia, South Korea, Spain, the U.K.,
and the U.S.

**1065 Health and healthcare in the United
States: County and metro area data.**
Richard K. Thomas, NationsHealth
Corporation. Lanham, Md.: Bernan Press,
c1999–c2001. 2 v., maps ISSN 1526-1573
362   RA407.3.H415

First ed., 1999–2nd ed., 2000; 2nd ed. technical consultant, Russell G. Bruce. Compendium
of health-related statistics and reference maps for
each of the 3,000 counties and the 80 metropolitan areas in the U.S.—demographics, vital statistics,
healthcare resources, and Medicare data. Based on

information from the National Center for Health Statistics and the U.S. Bureau of the Census. Accompanying CD-ROMs make it possible to manipulate the data. Also available as an e-book.

1066 Health care state rankings. Morgan
   Quitno Corporation. Lawrence, Kans.:
   Morgan Quitno Corp., 1993–
   ISSN 1065-1403
   362.10973   RA407.3.H423

Description based on 2011 ed. Subtitle: *Health care across America.* Contains data relating to medical care, delivery of health care, and health status indicators, which are derived from federal and state government sources, and from professional and private organizations. Presented in tabular form, with tables arranged in seven categories: Birth and reproductive health; Deaths; Facilities (hospitals, nursing homes, etc.); Finance; Incidence of disease; Providers; Physical fitness. Appendix (with 2008 and 2009 charts), sources, and index. Another title, *Health care state perspectives,* includes state-specific reports for each of the 50 states.

1067 Health in the Americas. Pan American
   Sanitary Bureau. Washington: Pan
   American Health Organization, Pan
   American Sanitary Bureau, Regional Office
   of the World Health Organization, 1998–.
   v., ill.
   362.1/09181/2   RA10.P252 610/.8s;

Published by Pan American Health Organization (PAHO); "Salud en las Américas."

Title varies: Previously had title *Summary of reports on the health conditions in the Americas* and *Health conditions in the Americas.* Description based on 2007 ed. (2 v.): v. 1, Regional analysis; v. 2, Country-by-country assessment.

Health data, facts, health trends, and related information for Central and South America, with emphasis on health disparities. Provides a vision for the future of health and health challenges in the Americas. Also available online through netLibrary; both print and online versions in English or Spanish.

A complement to this publication is *Health statistics from the Americas,* publ. in print format 1991–98, and now online (2003 ed. http://www.paho.org/english/dd/pub/SP_591.htm and 2006 ed. http://www.paho.org/English/DD/AIS/HSA2006.htm).

1068 Hoovers. http://www.hoovers.com/.
   Reference Press, Hoover's, Inc. Short Hills,
   N.J.: Dun & Bradstreet. 1996–
   338.7   HG4057

More than 60 million records describe public and private companies primarily in the United States, but including Canada, United Kingdom, Europe, and Asia/Pacific. Profiles have an overview, history, family tree, industry information, products/operations, top competitors, competitive landscape, top executives with biographies, news, significant developments, and financial data. Financial summaries may include an income statement; balance sheet; cash flow; historical financials such as five years of P/E and per share; stock quotes; interactive stock charts; market data; earnings estimates; this year's ratios for the company, industry, and market; SEC filings; and industry watch for trends.

Content is tracked for 900 industries, organized into numerous larger categories: Agriculture & Forestry; Arts, Entertainment & Recreation; Beverage Manufacturing; Biotechnology Product Manufacturing; Business Services; Chemical Manufacturing; Commercial Equipment Repair & Maintenance; Commercial Printing; Computer Hardware Manufacturing; Computer Software; Construction; Consumer Products Manufacturing; Consumer Services; Contract Electronics Manufacturing; Education; Electric Power Generation; Electric Power Transmission, Distribution & Marketing; Electric Utilities; Electrical Products Manufacturing; Fabricated Metal Product Manufacturing; Financial Services; Food Manufacturing; Government; Health Care Products Manufacturing; Health Care; HVAC Equipment Manufacturing; Industrial Manufacturing; Insurance; Leasing of Intangible Assets; Lodging; Machinery Manufacturing; Magnetic & Optical Media; Manufacturing & Reproduction; Managed Application & Network Services; Management of Companies & Enterprises; Media; Membership Organizations; Mining; Miscellaneous Manufacturing; Natural Gas Distribution & Marketing; Nonclassifiable establishments; Nonmetallic Mineral Product Manufacturing; Nonprofit Institutions; Oil & Gas Exploration & Production; Oil & Gas Field Services; Oil & Gas Well Drilling; Petroleum & Coal Products Manufacturing; Pharmaceutical Manufacturing; Primary Metals Manufacturing; Private Households; Professional Services; Real Estate; Religious Organizations; Rental & Leasing; Restaurants, Bars & Food Services; Retail; Security Products Manufacturing;

Semiconductor & Other Electronic Component Manufacturing; Telecommunications Equipment Manufacturing; Telecommunications Services; Transportation Equipment Manufacturing; Transportation Services; Water & Sewer Utilities; Wholesale; and Wood Product Manufacturing.

Coverage can be brief, but generally includes a fact sheet, overview, selected companies, industry watch with video interviews, news from the last 90 days, and web resources for terminology, associations, and organizations, and online publications. Hoover's print publications include (*Hoover's handbook of American business* (876), *Hoover's handbook of private companies* (855)).

1069 MEPS Medical Expenditure Panel Survey. http://www.meps.ahrq.gov/mepsweb/. U.S. Agency for Healthcare Research and Quality. Bethesda, Md.: Agency for Healthcare Research and Quality. 1996–

RA408.5

Produced by Agency for Health Care Research and Quality (AHRQ) (1074).

"Set of large-scale surveys of families and individuals, their medical providers (doctors, hospitals, pharmacies, etc.), and employers across the United States. MEPS collects data on the specific health services that Americans use, how frequently they use them, the cost of these services, and how they are paid for, as well as data on the cost, scope, and breadth of health insurance held by and available to U.S. workers" (*Website*). Provides information on health expenditures, utilization of health services, health insurance, and nursing homes, and reimbursement mechanisms. MEPS topics include access to health care, children's health, children's insurance coverage, health care disparities, mental health, minority health, the uninsured, and other topics. Further details concerning the survey background, data overview, and frequently asked questions are provided at the website. Provides fulltext access to MEPS publications: highlights, research findings, statistical briefs, etc. MEPS publications can be searched at http://meps.ahrq.gov/mepsweb/data _stats/publications.jsp

1070 Partners in information access for the public health workforce. http://phpartners.org/. U.S. National Library of Medicine. Bethesda, Md.: U.S. National

Library of Medicine, National Institutes of Health, Dept. of Health and Human Services. 2003–

"Collaboration of U.S. government agencies, public health organizations, and health sciences libraries which provides timely, convenient access to selected public health resources on the Internet . . . [with the mission of] helping the public health workforce find and use information effectively to improve and protect the public's health."—*Website*

Provides links to the individual partner websites, such as Agency for Healthcare Research and Quality (AHRQ) (1074), American Public Health Association (APHA), Association of Schools of Public Health (ASPH), Association of State and Territorial Health Officials (ASTHO), Centers for Disease Control and Prevention (CDC), MLANET: Medical Library Association's network of health information professionals, National Library of Medicine, and several other organizations. Provides extensive information on several public health topics (currently to bioterrorism, environmental health, and HIV/AIDS). For additional information and links see the Partners in Information Access for the Public Health Workforce fact sheet at http://www.nlm.nih.gov/nno/partners.html.

1071 Standard and Poor's industry surveys. Standard and Poor's. New York: Standard and Poor's, 1973–2012 ISSN 0196-4666

332.67   HC106.6

Detailed analyses of 22 industry categories and the major companies in each category. Contains a basic analysis and a comprehensive source of information, updated by a current analysis. The analysis includes trends, information on how the industry operates, key ratios and statistics (revenues, net income, profit ratios, balance sheet ratios, equity ratios, per-share data, company and product rankings), information on how to analyze a company in that industry, and a glossary. Company and industry indexes. Ceased with edition of 2012.

1072 WHOSIS. http://www.who.int/whosis/. World Health Organization. Geneva, Switzerland: World Health Organization. [1994]–

Published by World Health Organization (WHO).

Provides description and online access to statistical and epidemiological information, data, and tools available from WHO and other sites: mortality and health status, disease statistics, health systems statistics, risk factors and health services, and inequities in health. Provides links to several databases: WHOSIS database, with the latest "core health indicators" from WHO sources (including *The world health report* and *World health statistics* (1073)), which make it possible to construct tables for any combination of countries, indicators and years, Causes of death database, WHO global infobase online, Global health atlas, and Reproductive health indicators database.

As of 2011, WHOSIS has been incorporated into WHO's Global health observatory (GHO) which provides additional data & tools, and also more analysis and reports.

1073 World health statistics. http://www
.who.int/gho/publications/world_health
_statistics/en/index.html. World Health
Organization. Geneva, Switzerland: World
Health Organization. 2005–

RA407.A1

1939/46–96 publ. as *World health statistics annual = Annuaire de statistiques sanitaires mondiales* (print version).

Part of WHOSIS: WHO statistical information system (1072).

Provides online access to the 2005–2013 reports. Description based on 2013 online edition (http://www.who.int/whosis/whostat/EN_WHS2011_Full.pdf).

Contents: pt. I, "Health-related millennium development goals"; pt. II, "Global health indicators"; tables: 1. "Life expectancy and mortality"; 2. "Cause-specific mortality and morbidity"; 3. "Selected infectious diseases"; 4. "Health service coverage"; 5. "Risk factors"; 6. "Health systems"; 7. "Health expenditure"; 8. "Health inequities"; 9. "Demographic and socioeconomic statistics."

"Annual compilation of health-related data for its 193 Member States . . . includes a summary of the progress made towards achieving the health-related Millennium Development Goals (MDGs) and associated targets . . . using publications and databases produced and maintained by the technical programmes and regional offices of WHO. Indicators have been included on the basis of their relevance to global public health; the availability and quality of the data; and the reliability and comparability of the resulting estimates. Taken together, these indicators provide a comprehensive summary of the

current status of national health and health systems." —*Introd.* Derived from multiple sources, depending on each indicator and the availability and quality of data. Every effort has been made to ensure the best use of country-reported data – adjusted where necessary to deal with missing values, to correct for known biases, and to maximize the comparability of the statistics across countries and over time (cf. Introd.) A print version is also available.

Organizations and Associations

1074 Agency for Healthcare Research and
Quality (AHRQ). http://www.ahrq
.gov. Agency for Healthcare Research and
Quality (U.S.). Rockville, Md.: Agency for
Healthcare Research and Quality. 1997–

Searchable website ("search AHRQ" and "A–Z Quick Menu") provides access to a variety of resources, with links to clinical and consumer health information, research findings, funding opportunities, data and surveys, quality assessment, specific populations (minorities, women, elderly, and others), and public health preparedness (bioterrorism and response). Links to a large number of full-text documents, including links to the tools, literature, and news in patient safety (e.g., *AHRQ patient safety network*) and tips on how to prevent medical errors.

1075 American hospital association. http://
www.aha.org/aha_app/index.jsp. American
Hospital Association. Chicago: American
Hospital Association. 1998–

Home page for association, founded in 1898, to represent hospitals, health care networks, and their consumers. The website provides "Fast Facts on U.S. Hospitals," reports and studies, trends, testimony, regulations, and a section for members only. Some information is only available for a fee.

1076 American Public Health Association
(APHA). http://www.apha.org/. American
Public Health Association. Washington:
American Public Health Association.
1998–

RA421

Searchable website of the American Public Health Association (APHA), an organization representing public health professionals, with the mission to protect Americans and their communities from health threats. Provides links to 29 sections (http://www .apha.org/membergroups/sections/aphasections/) representing major public health disciplines or public health programs and selected links to a wide variety of public health topics and resources (e.g., A–Z Health Topics at http://www.apha.org/advocacy/ and Public Health Links at http://www.apha.org/ about/Public+Health+Links/). APHA participates in Partners in Information Access for the Public Health Workforce (1070), a collaborative project to provide public health professionals with access to information resources to help them improve the health of the American public.

1077 Department of health and human services. http://www.hhs.gov/. U.S. Department of Health and Human Services. Washington: U.S. Department of Health and Human Services. 1997–

HV85

Home page for the U.S. Department of Health and Human Services (HHS), responsible for "protecting the health of all Americans and providing essential human services, especially for those who are least able to help themselves." —*HHS What We Do.* To that end, their website provides a rich source of information on aging, disasters and emergencies, diseases and conditions, drug and food information, families and children, grants and funding, policies and regulations, reference collections (dictionaries and glossaries, various indexes, clinical trials database, food additive database, statistics, reports), resource locators, safety and wellness, and specific populations. Includes information on the economic and business impact of the Affordable Care Act (Obamacare). Formerly the Department of Health, Education and Welfare (HEW), until separated from the Department of Education in 1979.

1078 Federation of American hospitals. http://www.fah.org/. Federation of American Hospitals. Washington: Federation of American Hospitals. 2003–
Home page for an advocacy group representing privately-owned and managed community hospitals and health systems. The website has testimony, congressional communications, health and economic statistics, list of member facilities, information on the annual meeting, and a members only section. Formerly the Federation of American Health Systems (FAHS).

Internet Resources

1079 Agency for Healthcare Research and Quality (AHRQ). http://www.ahrq .gov. Agency for Healthcare Research and Quality (U.S.). Rockville, Md.: Agency for Healthcare Research and Quality. 1997–
Searchable website ("search AHRQ" and "A–Z Quick Menu") provides access to a variety of resources, with links to clinical and consumer health information, research findings, funding opportunities, data and surveys, quality assessment, specific populations (minorities, women, elderly, and others), and public health preparedness (bioterrorism and response). Links to a large number of full-text documents, including links to the tools, literature, and news in patient safety (e.g., *AHRQ patient safety network*) and tips on how to prevent medical errors.

1080 Centers for Medicare and Medicaid services (U.S.). http://cms.hhs.gov/. Centers for Medicare and Medicaid Services (U.S.), U.S. Health Care Financing Administration. Baltimore: Centers for Medicare and Medicaid Services, U.S. Dept. of Health and Human Services. 2001–

RA395.A3

Centers for Medicare and Medicaid Services (CMS), formerly Health Care Financing Administration.

Detailed information on Medicare, the federal health insurance program for people 65 years and older and for younger people with certain disabilities, providing details on enrollment, benefits, and other data; Medicaid, a joint federal and state program (state programs vary from state to state) that helps with medical costs for people with low income and limited means; SCHIP (State Children's Health Insurance Program); regulation and guidance manuals and Health Insurance Portability and Accountability Act (HIPAA), research, statistics, data and systems. Also provides various tools and resources helpful in navigating this website, for example a "glossary tool," an "acronym lookup tool," "FAQs," and others.

Includes information on the electronic health record (EHR) (http://www.cms.gov/Medicare/E-Health/ EHealthRecords/index.html), sometimes also called electronic medical record (EMR) which "allows healthcare providers to record patient information electronically instead of using paper records" and furthermore "the ability to support other care-related activities directly or indirectly through various interfaces, including evidence-based decision support, quality management, and outcomes reporting."—*Website*. Also provides related links, for example, to the "EHR Incentive Program" and "Health Level Seven International (HL7)" standards for interoperability.

1081 The Dartmouth atlas of health care.
http://www.dartmouthatlas.org/atlases .shtm. Dartmouth Institute for Health Policy and Clinical Practice, Dartmouth Medical School, American Hospital Association. Lebanon, N.H.: Dartmouth Institute for Health Policy and Clinical Practice

The Dartmouth Atlas Project started as a series of books and is now accessible via a web-based resource, providing access to the *Dartmouth atlas of health care* series (national editions, specialty-specific editions, state editions, and regional editions). Describes and illustrates quality, cost, and delivery of healthcare services in the U.S. and geographic variations in practice patterns, with description of the physician workforce and distribution of resources. Written for health policy analysts and other health professionals. The home page at http://www.dartmouthatlas.org/index.shtm provides additional information.

1082 European health for all database (HFA-DB). http://data.euro.who.int/hfadb/. World Health Organization Regional Office for Europe. Copenhagen, Denmark: World Health Organization Regional Office for Europe. 2000s–
Description based on Jan. 2013 version.

Provides basic health statistics and health trends for the member states of the WHO European Region, with approximately 600 health indicators, including basic demographic and socioeconomic indicators; some lifestyle- and environment-related indicators; mortality, morbidity, and disability; hospital discharges; and health care resources, utilization, and expenditures. Can be used as a tool for international comparison and for assessing the health situation and trends in any European country. Help available at https://euro.sharefile.com/d-sb7422ab51e54f20b.

1083 Faststats A to Z. http://www.cdc.gov/nchs/fastats/Default.htm. National Center for Health Statistics (NCHS). Hyattsville, Md.: U.S. Dept. of Health and Human Services, Centers for Disease Control and Prevention, National Center for Health Statistics

Provides topic-appropriate public health statistics (e.g., birth data, morbidity and mortality statistics, and health care use) and relevant links to further information and publications. Includes state and territorial data, with clickable map for individual state data. Also includes data derived from the "Behavioral Risk Factor Surveillance System (BRFSS)," which compiles data for 16 negative behaviors.

1084 HealthCare.gov. http://www.healthcare .gov. United States.; Department of Health and Human Services., U.S. Centers for Medicare & Medicaid Services. Baltimore: U.S. Centers for Medicare & Medicaid Services. 2010–

RA395.A3

Also available in Spanish at http://www.CuidadoDe Salud.gov; other language resources available at https://www.healthcare.gov/language-resource/

The new health care law, the Patient Protection and Affordable Care Act (also referred to as Affordable Care Act, ACA, and "Obamacare"), changes the American health care system in many ways, with significant impact on individuals and families, and on small businesses. ACA is designed to expand access to more affordable health insurance, to improve quality of healthcare services, to increase consumer protection, to emphasize prevention and wellness, to improve healthcare system performance, to curb healthcare costs, etc. Guaranteed coverage, individual mandate, and financial assistance are important features of ACA. The law is administered by the Center for Consumer Information & Insurance Oversight, and creates public health insurance exchanges, i.e., online marketplaces in all U.S. states. Different levels of plans are available as well as cost assistance for qualified persons. U.S. citizens and legal residents are eligible to apply for coverage. Starting 1 Oct 2013, Americans who don't have insurance can choose from quality, affordable health insurance plans in the Marketplace for coverage that begins 1 Jan 2014. Open enrollment starts 1 Oct 2013 and closes on 31 Mar 2014. Applicants must have enrolled by 15 Dec 2013 for coverage effective 1 Jan 2014.

HealthCare.gov tabs: Learn; Get insurance; Individuals & families; Small businesses; All topics: Health insurance marketplace; Using the marketplace; Getting lower costs on coverage; Young adults; Businesses; Health insurance basics; Other health insurance programs; If you have health insurance; Rights, protections, and the law; Prevention.

The federal website for the new health law information, managed by the Centers for Medicare & Medicaid Services (U.S.) (1080). Provides access to official resources to help health consumers learn about and get ready for changes, with information about ACA and the opening of the new health insurance Marketplace in every state. These resources provide answers to questions about health coverage options, private health plans and comparison of private health plans, status of a particular state's Marketplace, how to get help enrolling in the Marketplace, pre-existing conditions, how to get an estimate of costs and savings on Marketplace insurance, etc.

Selected links to ACA resources from government/organizations websites:

Healthcare.gov

"Contact us (Affordable Care Act)"—https://www.healthcare.gov/contact-us/

"Find local help (Affordable Care Act)"—https://localhelp.healthcare.gov/

"Read the law" http://www.hhs.gov/healthcare/rights/law/index.html

"What's the marketplace in my state"? http://www.healthcare.gov/what-is-the-marketplace-in-my-state

Finder.HealthCare.gov http://finder.healthcare.gov/: This tool can help with finding health insurance coverage needed before 2014.

HealthCare.gov Archive https://www.healthcare.gov/archive/: Includes all material formerly found on HealthCare.gov, captured at weekly intervals.

Marketplace social media channels to share stories: http://Facebook.com/HealthCare.gov; http://Facebook.com/CuidadoDeSalud.gov; @HealthCareGov; @CuidadoDeSalud

Centers for Medicare & Medicaid Services CMS .gov selected links

Affordable Care Act in Action at CMS http://cms.gov/about-cms/aca/affordable-care-act-in-action-at-cms.html

Marketplace.CMS.gov http://marketplace.cms.gov/

Marketplace.CMS.gov "Get official resources" http://marketplace.cms.gov/getofficialresources/get-official-resources.html

"Champion for coverage" http://marketplace.cms.gov/help-us/champion.html

Glossary https://www.healthcare.gov/glossary/

HHS (U.S. Dept. of Health and Human Services) selected links

Healthcare.gov sitemap https://www.healthcare.gov/sitemap/

HHS gov/HealthCare http://www.hhs.gov/healthcare/

Affordable Care Act http://www.hhs.gov/opa/affordable-care-act/index.html

Affordable Care Act fact sheets http://www.hhs.gov/healthcare/facts/factsheets/index.html

Key features of the health care law http://www.hhs.gov/healthcare/facts/timeline/index.html

Key features of the Affordable Care Act by year http://www.hhs.gov/healthcare/facts/timeline/timeline-text.html

State by state: "Click on your state to learn about health care where you live" http://www.hhs.gov/healthcare/facts/bystate/statebystate.html

Blog: Join social media channels to keep up with the latest developments http://www.hhs.gov/healthcare/facts/blog/index.html

National Library of Medicine (NLM)

Health insurance (MedlinePlus) http://www.nlm.nih.gov/medlineplus/healthinsurance.html

National Network of Libraries of Medicine (NN/LM)

Greater Midwest Region http://nnlm.gov/gmr/outreach/aca.html

MidContinental Region http://nnlm.gov/mcr/resources/aca.html

Middle Atlantic Region http://guides.nnlm.gov/mar_aca

New England Region http://nnlm.gov/ner/training/aca.html

Pacific Northwest Region http://nnlm.gov/pnr/ACA.html

Pacific Southwest Region http://guides.nnlm.gov/psr/aca

South Central Region http://nnlm.gov/scr/outreach/aca.html

Southeastern/Atlantic Region http://guides.nnlm.gov/sea/ACA

Substance Abuse and Mental Health Services Administration (SAMHSA)

"Getting ready for the health insurance marketplace toolkits" for various user groups (e.g., general audience, community-based prevention, consumer, family, peer & recovery community organizations, and others) http://marketplace.cms.gov/getofficialresources/other-partner-resources/other-partner-resources.html

Related websites

AARP http://www.aarp.org/

American Library Association (ALA) http://www.ala.org/tools/affordable-care-act

American Medical Association (AMA) "Some facts about ACA implementation" http://www.ama-assn.org/resources/doc/washington/aca-implementation-fa cts.pdf

Enroll America webinar series http://www.enroll america.org/resources/webinars/the-road-to-march-31-effective-outreach-and-enrollment-strategies-to-use-now/?source=hp

Kaiser Family Foundation

"Understanding health reform: Resources for consumers" http://kff.org/health-reform/

"State health insurance marketplace profiles" http://kff.org/state-health-marketplace-profiles/

"Summary of the Affordable Care Act" http://kff.org/health-reform/fact-sheet/summary-of-new-health-reform-l aw/

OCLC WebJunction (Partnership between Web Junction and ZeroDivide, funded by the Institute of Museum and Library Services [IMLS] to provide the library community with training and information about patron requests for health insurance-related resources, with the "mission to promote learning for all library staff providing an open, affordable online learning community" (*Website*):

"Health happens in libraries" http://www.web junction.org/explore-topics/ehealth.html

"Preparing libraries for the Affordable Care Act" http://www.webjunction.org/news/webjunction/preparing-libraries-affordable-care-act .html

Rural Assistance Center (RAC) http://www.raconline.org/topics/health-insurance-outreach-and-enrollment?utm_source=racupdate&utm_medium=email&utm_campaign=update022014

1085 Partners in information access for the public health workforce. http://phpartners.org/. U.S. National Library of Medicine. Bethesda, Md.: U.S. National Library of Medicine, National Institutes of Health, Dept. of Health and Human Services. 2003–

"Collaboration of U.S. government agencies, public health organizations, and health sciences libraries which provides timely, convenient access to selected public health resources on the Internet . . . [with the mission of] helping the public health workforce find and use information effectively to improve and protect the public's health."—*Website*

Provides links to the individual partner websites, such as Agency for Healthcare Research and Quality (AHRQ) (1074), American Public Health Association (APHA), Association of Schools of Public Health (ASPH), Association of State and Territorial Health Officials (ASTHO), Centers for Disease Control and Prevention (CDC), MLANET: Medical Library Association's network of health information professionals, National Library of Medicine, and several other organizations. Provides extensive information on several public health topics (currently to bioterrorism, environmental health, and HIV/AIDS). For additional information and links see the Partners in Information Access for the Public Health Workforce fact sheet at http://www.nlm.nih.gov/nno/partners.html.

1086 State snapshots. http://statesnapshots.ahrq.gov/snaps11/. Agency for Healthcare Research and Quality. Rockville, Md.: Agency for Healthcare Research and Quality. 2007–

Based on data collected from the *National health-care quality report* (http://purl.access.gpo.gov/GPO/LPS62498). Also called *NHRQ state snapshots*. Linked Agency for Healthcare Research and Quality (1074) Web site.

Provides "state-specific health care quality information including strengths, weaknesses, and opportunity for improvement . . . [to] better understand healthcare quality and disparities" (*Website*). A "state selection map" (http://nhqrnet.ahrq.gov/inhqrdr/state/select) allows users to choose a particular state and compare it to other states in terms of healthcare quality, types of care (preventive, acute, and chronic), settings of care (hospitals, ambulatory care, nursing home, and home health), several specific conditions, and clinical preventive services.

Provides help with interpretation of results and a methods section.

The Kaiser Family Foundation makes a comparable website available: "State Health Facts" (http://www.statehealthfacts.org). Provides statistical data and health policy information on various health topics, with a standardized menu for information about each state ("individual state profiles" tab) and to find out how it compares to the U.S. overall ("50 state comparisons" tab). Categories include demography and the economy, health status, health coverage and the uninsured, Medicaid and SCHIP, health costs and budgets, Medicare, managed care and health insurance, providers and service use, minority health, women's health, and HIV/AIDS.

Additional Reference Sources

1087 AHA guide to the health care field.
American Hospital Association. Chicago: Healthcare Infosource, Inc., 1997–98 –

RA977.A1

Title varies: 1949–71, pt. 2 of Aug. issue (called "Guide issue," 1956–70) of *Hospitals*, which superseded *American hospital directory* (1945–48); 1972–73, *The AHA guide to the health care field*; 1974–96, *American Hospital Association guide to the health care field*.

Description based on 2011–2012 ed.; 2014 ed. available.

"Provides basic data reflecting the delivery of health care in the United States and associated areas, and is not to serve as an official and all-inclusive list of services offered by individual hospitals."—*Acknowledgements and Advisements*. Four major sections, each with table of contents and explanatory information: (A) Hospitals, institutional, and associate members; (B) networks, health care systems, and alliances; (C) lists of health organizations, agencies, and providers; and (D) indexes. Also available in CD-ROM format. Additional information about this resource is available at http://www.AHAdata.com. Statistical information concerning hospitals is published in AHA hospital statistics.

A web-based resource, American hospital directory® (AHD®) http://www.ahd.com/ (by a Kentucky Company) provides data for over 6,000 hospitals, with data derived from Medicare claims, hospital cost reports, Centers for Medicare and Medicaid Services, and other sources (further details at http://www.ahd.com/data_sources.html). While most features of this website are only available to subscribers, free access is provided to "hospital profiles."

1088 The dictionary of health economics.
2nd ed. A. J. Culyer. Chelthenham, U.K.; Northampton, Mass.: Edward Elgar, 2010. xix, 694 p., ill. ISBN 9781849800419
362.103   RA410.A3C85

Concise definitions of terms, concepts, and methods from the field of health economics and related fields, such as epidemiology, pharmacoeconomics, medical sociology, medical statistics, and others. Expanded number of words and phrases relating to health economics of poor and middle-income countries (cf. *Pref.*). Increased number of entries in this edition (from 1,586 in the previous edition to 2,130). Many cross-references. An appendix contains "100 economic studies of health interventions." For health services researchers and professionals. Also available as an e-book. A similar title is *Dictionary of health economics and finance* (1089).

1089 Dictionary of health economics and finance. David E. Marcinko, Hope R. Hetico. New York: Springer Publ., 2006. 436 p. ISBN 0826102549
338.47362103   RA410.A3D53

Definitions, abbreviations and acronyms, and eponyms of medical economics and health care sector terminology. Bibliography. A similar title is *The dictionary of health economics* (1088).

1090 Dictionary of health insurance and managed care. David Edward Marcinko. New York: Springer Publ. Co., 2006 ISBN 0826149944
368.382003   RA413.D53

Health insurance, managed care plans and programs, health care industry terminology and definitions, abbreviatons, and acronyms. Also available as e-book.

1091 Encyclopedia of biostatistics. 2nd ed.
P. Armitage, Theodore Colton. Chichester, U.K.; West Sussex, U.K.: John Wiley, 2005. 8 v. ISBN 047084907X
610.21   RA409.E53

First edition, 1998 (6 v.). Description based on rev. and enl. ed., 2005 (8 v.).

Contents: v. 1, A–Chap; v. 2, Char–Dos; v. 3, Dou–Gre; v. 4, Gro–Mar; v. 5, Mas–Nui; v. 6, Nul–Ran; v. 7, Rao–Str; v. 8, Stu–Z, index.

Biostatistics can be defined as the application of statistical methods to the life sciences, medicine, and the health sciences. Clinical epidemiology, clinical trials, disease modeling, epidemiology, statistical computing, and vital and health statistics are some examples of the areas covered. This edition contains more than 1,300 articles, with approximately 300 revised and 182 new entries. New topics include, for example, applications of biostatistics to bioinformatics, study of the human genome, and outbreaks of infectious-disease epidemics. Bibliographies, many cross-references, author index, and a selected list of review articles. Also available as an e-book.

1092 Encyclopedia of health care management. Michael J. Stahl. Thousand Oaks, Calif.: Sage, 2004. xxxvii, 621 p., ill. ISBN 0761926747

362.1068   RA971.E52

Alphabetical list of entries at the beginning of the book provides an overview of the terminology and variety of subject areas covered in this resource including business and economics, statistics, law, clinical research, informatics, and others. A reader's guide with the following major headings is provided: Accounting and activity-based costing, Economics, Finance, Health policy, Human resources, Information technology, Institutions and organizations, International health care issues, Legal and regulatory issues, Managed care, Marketing and customer value, Operations and decision making, Pharmaceuticals and clinical trials, Quality, Statistics and data mining, and Strategy. The main section, consisting of approximately 650 entries, is alphabetically arranged. Each entry contains the term's definition, background, and other relevant information. Includes tables on health care acronyms, medical degrees, medical legislation, and others. Cross-references, list of further readings, and websites. Index. Also available as an e-book.

1093 Essentials of managed health care. 6th ed. Peter R. Kongstvedt. Burlington, Mass.: Jones and Bartlett Learning, 2013. xxv, 688 p., ill. ISBN 9781449653316

RA413.E87

First ed., 1989; 4th ed., 2001 had title *The managed health care handbook.* 5th ed., 2007 is the rev. ed. of two different titles by the same author: *The managed health care handbook*, 4th ed., 2001, and rev. ed. of *Essentials of managed health care*, 4th ed., 2001.

Contents: Pt I, Introduction to health insurance and managed health care (ch. 1–3); pt. II, Network contracting and provider payment (ch. 4-6); pt. III, Management of utilization and quality (ch. 7–15); pt. IV, Sales, finance, and administration (ch. 16–23); pt. V, Special markets (ch. 24–27); pt. VI, Laws and regulations (ch. 28–30); glossary; index.

Intended as a guide and a resource to the managed health care system, with information on types of managed care plans and integrated healthcare delivery systems, physician networks in managed health care, prescription drug benefits in managed health care, etc.

Handbook of health delivery systems by Yih, available in print and also as an e-book, provides related information.

1094 Health care reform around the world. Andrew C. Twaddle. Westport, Conn.: Auburn House, 2002. xiii, 419 p., ill. ISBN 0865692882

362.1   RA394.H4145

Describes health care reform efforts and trends in different countries, with roughly comparable information for the countries included. Ch. 1 is an international comparison of health care system reforms—United Kingdom, Eastern and Western Europe, United States, the Middle East, Latin America, Asia, and Oceania. Also available as an e-book.

1095 Health care systems around the world: Characteristics, issues, reforms. Marie L. Lassey, William R. Lassey, Martin J. Jinks. Upper Saddle River, N.J.: Prentice Hall, 1997. xiii, 370 p., ill., maps ISBN 0131042335

362.1   RA393.L328

Contents: Introduction, basic issues and concepts; The countries and their characteristics; The United States, high-technology and limited access; Canada, challenges to public payment for universal care; Japan, preventive health care as cultural norm; Germany, a tradition of universal health care; France, centrally controlled and locally managed; The Netherlands, gradual adaptation; Sweden, decentralized comprehensive care; The United Kingdom, the economy model; The Czech Republic, a new mixture of public and private services; Hungary, creating a remodeled system; Russia, transition to market and consumer orientation; China, privatizing socialist health care; Mexico, modernizing structure and expanded rural services; Organization variations and reforms; Economic organization of health care, comparative perspectives; Expectations for reform, a glimpse at the future. Description and analysis of health care systems in different countries, addressing demographic, social, and economic characteristics, also health promotion, prevention of disease, and health care. Includes bibliographical references and index.

A 2013 publication, *Health care systems around the world: A comparative guide* by Boslaugh, describes health care systems for a large number of countries. Arranged in alphabetical order by country, with content for each country presented in a standardized format, allowing for comparison from country to country.

1096 Health care systems of the developed world: How the United States' system remains an outlier. Duane A. Matcha. Westport, Conn.: Praeger, 2003. x, 198 p., ill. ISBN 027597992X

362.1/0973   RA441.M38

Contents: ch. 1, Introduction; ch. 2, The United States; ch. 3, Canada; ch. 4, United Kingdom; ch. 5, Germany; ch. 6, Sweden; ch. 7, Japan; ch. 8, Conclusion. Provides an introduction to selected major healthcare systems, with consideration of their historical and political basis. Provides a framework for analysis and comparison of the different systems. Various tables and figures related to health insurance, personal health care expenditures, self-rated health status, future concerns, and others. Includes bibliographical references and index. Also available as an e-book.

World health systems: challenges and perspectives by Fried et al. presents profiles of health systems in 28 countries. *Health care systems around the world: Characteristics, issues, reforms* (1095), provides additional information in this area. Milton I Roemer's *National health systems of the world* remains an important title. It consists of a comprehensive study and analysis of national health systems in 68 industrialized, middle-income, and very poor countries, with a cross-national analysis of the major health care issues within different systems.

1097 HealthSTAR (Ovid). http://www.ovid .com/site/products/ovidguide/hstrdb .htm. National Library of Medicine (U.S.). Sandy, Utah: Ovid Technologies. 2000–

Ovid HealthSTAR (HSTR); HealthSTAR (Health Services Technology, Administration, and Research).

"Comprised of data from the National Library of Medicine's (NLM) MEDLINE and former Health-STAR databases . . . contains citations to the published literature on health services, technology, administration, and research. It focuses on both the clinical and non-clinical aspects of health care delivery. . . . Offered by Ovid as a continuation of NLM's now-defunct HealthSTAR database. Retains all existing backfile citations and is updated with new journal citations culled from MEDLINE. Contains citations and abstracts (when available) to journal articles, monographs, technical reports, meeting abstracts and papers, book chapters, government documents, and newspaper articles from 1975 to the present." —*Publ. notes.* A list of NLM's retired databases, including the original HealthSTAR database, can be found at http://www.nlm.nih.gov/services/pastdatabases.html.

Relevant content on health services research, health technology, health administration, health policy, health economics, etc., can also be found in MEDLINE® (1099)/PubMed®, NLM® Gateway, and also CINAHL®.

1098 Hospital and health administration index. American Hospital Association., American Hospital Association.; Resource Center., National Library of Medicine (U.S.). Chicago: American Hospital Association, 1995–1999 ISSN 1077-1719

016.36211   Z6675.H75H67; RA963

1945–54, *Index of current hospital literature;* 1955–57, *Hospital periodical literature index;* 1957–94, *Hospital literature index,* cumulated at five-year intervals for the 1945–77 volumes as *Cumulative index of hospital literature.* Discontinued; last published in 1999. Described as a "primary guide to literature on hospital and other health care facility administration, including multi-institutional systems, health policy and planning, and the administrative aspects of health care delivery . . . Special emphasis is given to the theory of health care systems in general; health care in industrialized countries, primarily in the United States; and provision of health care both inside and outside of health care facilities" (*Introd.*). A separate online database, HealthSTAR (Health Services Technology, Administration, and Research) for this literature, previously maintained by NLM, is no longer available (cf. list of NLM's retired databases at http://www.nlm.nih .gov/services/pastdatabases.html). Relevant content is available via MEDLINE (1099)/PubMed or Health-STAR (Ovid) (1097), and also CINAHL

1099 MEDLINE. http://purl.access.gpo.gov/ GPO/LPS4708. National Library of Medicine (U.S.). Bethesda, Md.: National Library of Medicine (U.S.). 1971–
                                          Z6660
MEDLINE®—Medical literature analysis and retrieval system online (National Library of Medicine®—NLM), primary subset of PubMed® and part of the databases provided by the National Center for Biotechnology Information (NCBI). Coverage extends back to 1946, with some older material.

Bibliographic database, providing comprehensive access to the international biomedical literature from the fields of medicine, nursing, dentistry, veterinary medicine, allied health, and the preclinical sciences. It is also a primary source of information from the international literature on biomedicine, including the following topics as they relate to biomedicine and health care: Biology, environmental science, marine biology, plant and animal science, biophysics, and chemistry. For indexing articles, NLM uses MeSH: Medical subject headings®, a controlled vocabulary of biomedical terms. An increasing number of MEDLINE citations contain a link to the free full-text articles.

The MEDLINE database is the electronic counterpart of *Index medicus*®, *Index to dental literature*, and the *International nursing index*. The databases is offered at no additional cost on a variety of indexing platforms.

For detailed information, see the MEDLINE fact sheet at http://www.nlm.nih.gov/pubs/factsheets/ medline.html, which also includes a list of related fact sheets (e.g., "MEDLINE, PubMed, and PMC (PubMed Centeral): How are they different?").

1100 Obamacare survival guide: the Affordable Care Act and what it means for you and your healthcare. First ed. Nick J. Tate. West Palm Beach, Fla.: Humanix Books, 2013. xxi, 241 pages ISBN 9780893348625
362.10973   RA395.D44
Written as implementation of the Affordable Care Act (Obamacare) remains in flux, this is an early

entry in the ranks of reference sources. Like most writing on the topic, this work has a point of view, but is one of the most widely owned publications on the topic in libraries, attempting an overview and summary. Includes information about timetables; projected impact on health insurance and Medicaid; the new health insurance exchanges; cost and cost control issues; and implications for small businesses.

1101 Passport GMID. http://www.euromonitor .com/. Euromonitor International. London, U.K.: Euromonitor International. [1999–]
658.8   HF5415.2
Also known under previous product names as *Global market information database*, *GMID*, or *Euromonitor GMID*. Market reports, company profiles, and demographic, economic, and marketing statistics for 205 countries. Market reports are for 16 consumer markets (food and drink, tobacco, toys, etc.) and 14 industrial and service markets (accountancy, broadcasting, chemicals, property services, etc.).

Reports have market size, market sectors, share of market, marketing activity, research and development, corporate overview, distribution, consumer profiles, market forecasts, sector forecasts, sources, and definitions. Additional reports are available for market segments, such as baby food. Company profiles have background, recent news, competitve environment, and outlook. Consumer lifestyle reports and very useful marketing background analyze the consumer by country, gender, age, marital status, educational attainment, ethnicity, religion, home ownership, household profile, employment, income, health, eating and personal grooming habits, leisure activities, personal finance, communication, transport, and travel.

Search for data, which can be exported into Excel or browse for reports. Data are available since 1977 and include inflation, exchange rates, GDP, GNI, government expenditures, government finance, income, labor, and money supply.

Similar information on a smaller scale is available in Research monitor (783) from the same publisher.

1102 World health systems: Challenges and perspectives. 2nd ed. Bruce Fried, Laura M. Gaydos. Chicago: Health Administration Press, 2012. xxx, 780 p. ISBN 9781567934205
362.1   RA441.W676

215

Contents: Pt. I, Current issues facing global health systems; pt. II, Profiled countries: The low income countries (ch. 7-11); The middle-income countries (ch. 12–18); The high-income countries (ch. 19-31); glossary; index.

This revised edition presents new introductory chapters on health systems (e.g., defining a health system, health system strengthening, health system regulation, and the politics of health system reform) and profiles of 26 health systems from around the world. Organized in three categories by the wealth of each nation: low-, middle-, and high-income countries. Addresses the various challenges health services face, how they are organized, and how they are financed. Each chapter includes disease patterns and health system financing, also past, present status, and future health policy issues and various challenges of the individual health systems.

Leisure

1103 **Encyclopedia of sports management and marketing.** Linda E. Swayne, Mark Dodds. Thousand Oaks, Calif.: SAGE Publications, 2011. 4 v. (xxxvi, 1858 p.), ill. (some col.) ISBN 9781412973823
796.06/9   GV713
More than 800 signed articles in alphabetical order on the business of sports in the United States, including topics such as sponsorship and branding, marketing, fan behavior, the role of the media and the Internet, contracts and salaries, labor issues, event and venue management, and ticket pricing. Provides articles about American professional teams (NFL, NHL, MLB, NBA and others) that briefly trace franchise histories, including ownership, stadium locations, and marketing highlights. Appendix of legislative texts, such as Title IX. Chronology. Bibliography. Glossary. Also available as an e-book.

1104 **Music business: the key concepts.** Richard Strasser. London; New York: Routledge, 2010. xiv, 194 p. ISBN 9780415995344
338.4/778   ML102.M85
Defines and discusses 175 core business concepts for the recording, publishing and live performance of music. Covers music publishing, recording services and record production, artist management and concert promotion, and online music services. Includes the impact of the Internet, current intellectual property law, and the regulatory environment. Suggestions for further reading. Bibliography. Index.

Specialized Sources of Industry Data

1105 **Hospitality and tourism index.** http://www.ebscohost.com/academic/hospitality-tourism-index. EBSCO Publishing. Ipswich, Mass.: EBSCO Publishing. 2003–
TX911.3.M27
Indexes scholarly research and industry news relating to all areas of hospitality and tourism, including culinary arts, hotel management, and travel. Formed from the now ceased Cornell University's hospitality database, the Universities of Surrey and Oxford Brookes Articles in Hospitality and Tourism, and Purdue University's Lodging, Restaurant, and Tourism Index. Coverage as early as 1965, with depth increasing in the 1980s.

1106 **IBISWorld United States.** http://www.ibisworld.com/. IBISWorld. New York: IBISWorld. 1999–
HC103
700 reports on American industries. Industry reports can be located using NAICS numbers. Major categories include: Accommodation & Food Services; Administration, Business Support & Waste Management Services; Agriculture, Forestry, Fishing & Hunting; Arts, Entertainment & Recreation; Construction; Educational Services; Finance & Insurance; Healthcare & Social Assistance; Information; Manufacturing; Mining; Other Services (except Public Administration); Professional, Scientific & Technical Services; Real Estate & Rental and Leasing; Retail Trade; Transportation & Warehousing; Utilities; and Wholesale Trade.

Reports include industry definition; information about the supply chain; key statistics; segmentations (products and services segmentation, major market segments, industry concentration, geographic spread); market characteristics (market size, demand determinants, domestic and international markets, basis of competition, life cycle); industry conditions (barriers to entry, taxation, industry assistance, regulation and deregulation, cost structure, capital and labor intensity, technology and systems, industry volatility, globalization); key factors (sensitivities and success factors); key competitors; and industry performance (current and historical). Glossaries and guides to jargon. Setting this database apart are reports on small industries, such as parking lots and garages.

1107 Plunkett's airline, hotel, and travel industry almanac. Jack W. Plunkett.
Houston, Tex.: Plunkett Research, 2002–. ill. ISSN 1554-1215
387.7   HE9803.A2
Data on more than 300 major companies, both public and private: airlines, bus companies, resort chains, car rentals and more. Company profiles include types of business, brands and affiliates, contacts, employee benefits and top salaries, sales and profit numbers, growth plans, and competitive advantage. Especially useful for the industry trends, statistics and rankings (forecasts to 2032, top destinations worldwide, top airlines, top tourism nations, etc.) at the front of the volume and information on the main associations and organizations in the back of the volume. Most information is for the U.S., but some international coverage is provided. Available as an e-book.

1108 Plunkett's entertainment and media industry almanac. Jack W. Plunkett.
Houston, Tex.: Plunkett Research, 1998–
ISSN 1521-6160
302.23/025/73   P88.8
Data on nearly 400 leading companies, both public and private. Company profiles include types of business, brands and affiliates, contacts, employee benefits and top salaries, sales and profit numbers, growth plans, and competitive advantage. Especially useful for the industry background, trends, statistics and rankings at the front of the volume (estimated revenue in the U.S. information and entertainment sector by NAICS Code, U.S. magazine advertising revenue and pages for PIB measured magazines: 1960–2005, number of U.S. magazines: 1988–2005, U.S. periodical publishing revenues 2001–2005, annual U.S. newspaper advertising expenditures, 1990–2006, percent of U.S. households with alternative broadcast delivery systems: 1997–2006, U.S. personal consumption expenditures for recreation by product or service: 1990–2005), and information on the main associations and organizations in the back of the volume. Most information is for the U.S., but

some international coverage is provided. Available as an e-book.

1109 Plunkett's sports industry almanac: the only comprehensive guide to the sports industry. Jack W. Plunkett.
Houston, Tex.: Plunkett Research, 2005–
ISSN 1937-0997
796   GV716
Data on some 350 leading companies, both public and private, including manufacturers, professional sports teams, and fitness clubs. Company profiles include types of business, brands and affiliates, contacts, employee benefits and top salaries, sales and profit numbers, growth plans, and competitive advantage. Especially useful for the industry trends, statistics and rankings (top 30 U.S. recreational sports/activities ranked by participation, U.S. sports league summary, annual revenues from sports broadcast rights fees, overview of the media contracts of the big four sports, U.S. sporting goods exports: 1995–2005), and information on the main associations and organizations. Most information is for the U.S., but some international coverage is provided. Available as an e-book.

1110 Standard and Poor's industry surveys.
Standard and Poor's. New York: Standard and Poor's, 1973–2012 ISSN 0196-4666
332.67   HC106.6
Detailed analyses of 22 industry categories and the major companies in each category. Contains a basic analysis and a comprehensive source of information, updated by a current analysis. The analysis includes trends, information on how the industry operates, key ratios and statistics (revenues, net income, profit ratios, balance sheet ratios, equity ratios, per-share data, company and product rankings), information on how to analyze a company in that industry, and a glossary. Company and industry indexes. Ceased with edition of 2012.

1111 Technomic top 500 chain restaurant report. Technomic Information Services.
Chicago: Technomic Information Services, 1999–
                          TX945
Often cited in trade publications, this report analyzes trends and offers forecasts for the restaurant business. Review of outlets and sales by menu category (pizza, Asian, seafood, etc.) and service segment

(limited service, casual dining, midscale, fine dining). Tracks mergers, acquisitions, bankruptcies and IPO activity. Identifies emerging leaders. Appendixes include alphabetical listing; chains ranked by U.S. systemwide sales; chains ranked by U.S. systemwide units; average unit volume by chain; international sales and units; and chains indexed by menu category and ranked by share of sales.

1112 Trends in the hotel industry. U.S. ed.
Pannell, Kerr, Forster, PKF Consulting.
New York: Pannell, Kerr, Forster, 1980–. ill.
ISSN 0276-5357
338.47647947301   TX909.A1
Gives trends and financial performance (revenue, expense, and profit information) for U.S. hotels. Arranged by property type, location, rate, and size. Also lists franchise fees, payroll costs by dollars per available room, percentage of occupancy, utility costs, marketing, and departmental costs and expenses (rooms, food, beverage, telecommunications). Also available in online format.

1113 Welcome to Office of Travel and Tourism Industries. http://travel.trade .gov/. International Trade Administration (ITA), Office of Travel & Tourism Industries. Washington: U.S. Department of Commerce. 1997–

G155.U6
Home page for OTTI, the Office of Travel & Tourism Industries, charged to be "the sole source for characteristic statistics on international travel to and from the United States" —About the OTTI. The site bears this out, with historical tables counting inbound and outbound travelers to the United States (data beginning in 1994), as well as current statistics, divided into national (visitors to the United States and U.S. travelers abroad), state/city/territory (visitors to U.S. states, territories, and cities), and country (country and region level data for visitors to the United States and U.S. travel abroad).

Organizations and Associations

1114 American hotel and lodging association. http://www.ahla.com/. American Hotel and Lodging Association. Washington: American Hotel and Lodging Association. 2002–
647.947   TX911

Home page for the advocacy group for representing "individual hotel property members, hotel companies, student and faculty members, and industry suppliers." —About. The AHLA site is organized into Membership; Hotel Hospitality News; Governmental Affairs; Hotel Meetings and Events; Hotel Hospitality Products; Hospitality Sponsorships; AH&LA Information Center; Hospitality Publications; Careers in Hospitality; Hotel Press Room; AH&LA Membership; Feature Hospitality Program; and Insurance Center. Free highlights on the site include a history of lodging, Lodging Industry Profile, Top 50 Hotel Companies (gives number of domestic and international rooms and properties for each company), and industry links.

1115 Entertainment software association: home page. http://www.theesa.com/. Entertainment Software Association. Washington: Entertainment Software Association. 2003–

GV1469.15
Home page for trade association serving the U.S. computer and video game industry. "Annual Report" summarizes convention news and updates on legislative and regulatory matters. "Industry Facts" reports on state-by-state employment levels and summary sales figures. Tracks public policy, copyright, and legal trends. Posts available jobs from sponsoring companies such as Nintendo and Sony.

1116 National restaurant association. http://www.restaurant.org/. National Restaurant Association. Washington: National Restaurant Association. 2007
Home page for association, founded in 1919, representing 935,000 restaurant and foodservice companies. The website has news, community outreach, food safety and nutrition, careers and education, policy and politics, events, tips for running a business, and industry research. The industry research portion of the site has Industry Overviews (at a glance, forecast, state and local statistics), Research by Topic (H/R, operations, consumer, economy), links to resources for company research, and current industry trends. A great resource for locating demographic trends, consumer food-and-beverage preferences, cost of sales, gross profits, and employee turnover. Some data is available for free.

Internet Resources

1117 Fantini's gaming report. http://www
.fantiniresearch.com/. Frank Fantini.
Dover, Del.: Fantini Research. 2000–
HV6721

Online subscription resource. Tracks the gambling
industry worldwide, including conference information, revenue and earnings figures, sale of major
properties, performance of stock of gaming-related
companies, betting over the Internet, and Native
American casinos.

1118 SBRnet. http://www.sbrnet.com/. SBRnet.
Princeton, N.J.: SBRnet. 1996–
HD9992.A1

Presents articles and consumer statistics for commerce related to sports apparel, baseball/softball,
basketball, billiards/bowling, boxing, camping,
cheerleading, climbing, equestrian, exercise/fitness,
eyewear, field hockey, fishing, football, footwear,
golf, gymnastics, hunting/target shooting, ice hockey,
lacrosse, martial arts, motorsports, paintball, rac-
quet sports, running/track and field, soccer, sports
medicine, volleyball, water sports, wheel sports, win-
ter sports, wrestling, broadcasting, careers, college
sports, disabled, endorsement, facilities, financial,
licensing, new media, the Olympics, sponsorship,
sport management education, total sporting goods
market, women's sports, and youth/amateur.
Includes directories to professional and college sports
teams in the U.S. and Canada, 10,000 other sports
organizations, employment and marketing agencies,
and trade shows and meetings with a calendar.

Additional Reference Sources

**1119 The American beauty industry
encyclopedia.** Julie A. Willett. Santa
Barbara, Calif.: Greenwood, 2010. xxv,
338 p., ill. ISBN 9780313359491
338.4/76467203   TT958

More than 100 signed articles in alphabetical order
deal with the business and culture of personal beauty.
Emphasis on the U.S. in the 19th and 20th centuries. Covers topics related to hair and clothing styles,
key entrepreneurs, major companies and products,
advertising, the print and broadcast media, and

issues of race and gender. Reflects perspectives from
sociology, history, anthropology, popular culture,
art, cultural studies, gender studies, fashion, marketing, and media studies. Illustrated with black and
white photographs. Chronology from ancient times
to 2009. Bibliography. Index. Available as an e-book.

1120 A companion to tourism. Alan A. Lew,
Colin Michael Hall, Allan M. Williams.
Malden, Mass.: Blackwell, 2004. xviii,
622 p., ill. ISBN 0631235647
910.01   G155.A1

Contains 48 chapters divided into six parts focused
on "the major research and theoretical subject areas
of tourism studies."—*Pref.* Each chapter is signed
and has a list of references. Index. Available as
an e-book.

**1121 The complete 21st century travel and
hospitality marketing handbook.**
Bob Dickinson, Andrew Vladimir. Upper
Saddle River, N.J.: Pearson Prentice Hall,
2004. xxi, 627 p., ill., ports. 0131133144

A handbook of essays on current marketing issues
and trends, by leaders in the tourism and travel
industry.

1122 Dictionary of travel and tourism.
http://www.oxfordreference.com/view/
10.1093/acref/ISBN9780191733987
.001.0001/acref-ISBN9780191733987.
Allen Beaver. Oxford; New York: Oxford
University Press. 2012
ISBN 9780191733987
910/.3   G155.A1

6,500 entries identify and define industry terms, the
names of technical practices, acronyms and abbreviations, and association names. Revises and updates
the 2005 CABI edition, *Dictionary of travel and tourism
terminology*, with additional information about topics
such as procedures of the TSA, branding and social
media, and Web-based developments such as Expe-
dia Travel Agents Affiliate Program (TAAP). Written
from a British perspective, but global in coverage.

**1123 Dictionary of travel, tourism and
hospitality. 3rd ed.** S. Medlik. Oxford,
U.K.; Boston: Butterworth-Heinemann,
2003. ix, 273 p., maps ISBN 0750656506
338.479103   G155.A1

Divided into seven parts. The largest (Pt. 1) is a dictionary of over 4,000 terms. Pts. 2 and 3 are definitions of international and national organizations. Pt. 4 is a biographical dictionary of people associated with the travel industry. Pt. 5 is a list of abbreviations. Pt. 6 is a table giving information on countries of the world. Pt. 7 is a bibliography of dictionaries, journals, directories, manuals, sources of statistics, and other books. Available as an e-book.

1124 Hoovers. http://www.hoovers.com/.
Reference Press, Hoover's, Inc. Short Hills, N.J.: Dun & Bradstreet. 1996–
338.7   HG4057
More than 60 million records describe public and private companies primarily in the United States, but including Canada, United Kingdom, Europe, and Asia/Pacific. Profiles have an overview, history, family tree, industry information, products/operations, top competitors, competitive landscape, top executives with biographies, news, significant developments, and financial data. Financial summaries may include an income statement; balance sheet; cash flow; historical financials such as five years of P/E and per share; stock quotes; interactive stock charts; market data; earnings estimates; this year's ratios for the company, industry, and market; SEC filings; and industry watch for trends.

Content is tracked for 900 industries, organized into numerous larger categories: Agriculture & Forestry; Arts, Entertainment & Recreation; Beverage Manufacturing; Biotechnology Product Manufacturing; Business Services; Chemical Manufacturing; Commercial Equipment Repair & Maintenance; Commercial Printing; Computer Hardware Manufacturing; Computer Software; Construction; Consumer Products Manufacturing; Consumer Services; Contract Electronics Manufacturing; Education; Electric Power Generation; Electric Power Transmission, Distribution & Marketing; Electric Utilities; Electrical Products Manufacturing; Fabricated Metal Product Manufacturing; Financial Services; Food Manufacturing; Government; Health Care Products Manufacturing; Health Care; HVAC Equipment Manufacturing; Industrial Manufacturing; Insurance; Leasing of Intangible Assets; Lodging; Machinery Manufacturing; Magnetic & Optical Media; Manufacturing & Reproduction; Managed Application & Network Services; Management of Companies & Enterprises; Media; Membership

Organizations; Mining; Miscellaneous Manufacturing; Natural Gas Distribution & Marketing; Nonclassifiable establishments; Nonmetallic Mineral Product Manufacturing; Nonprofit Institutions; Oil & Gas Exploration & Production; Oil & Gas Field Services; Oil & Gas Well Drilling; Petroleum & Coal Products Manufacturing; Pharmaceutical Manufacturing; Primary Metals Manufacturing; Private Households; Professional Services; Real Estate; Religious Organizations; Rental & Leasing; Restaurants, Bars & Food Services; Retail; Security Products Manufacturing; Semiconductor & Other Electronic Component Manufacturing; Telecommunications Equipment Manufacturing; Telecommunications Services; Transportation Equipment Manufacturing; Transportation Services; Water & Sewer Utilities; Wholesale; and Wood Product Manufacturing.

Coverage can be brief, but generally includes a fact sheet, overview, selected companies, industry watch with video interviews, news from the last 90 days, and web resources for terminology, associations, and organizations, and online publications. Hoover's print publications include (*Hoover's handbook of American business* (876), *Hoover's handbook of private companies* (855)).

1125 Legalized gambling: a reference handbook. 2nd ed. William N. Thompson. Santa Barbara, Calif.: ABC-CLIO, 1997. xxvi, 297 p., ill. ISBN 9780585101408
795   HV6710
Covers economic, legislative and ethical aspects, including casinos, state lotteries, charity bingo games, pari-mutuel betting, video poker, and history of the gaming industry. Discusses government regulatory bodies, and the most prominent venues. Chronology. Biographical sketches. Directory of organizations. Bibliography. Glossary. Index.

1126 The SAGE handbook of tourism studies. Tazim Jamal, Mike Robinson. Los Angeles; London: SAGE, 2009. xix, 716 p., ill., maps ISBN 9781412923972
338.4791   G155.7
Almost 40 essays covering the current state of scholarship on the evolution of global tourism, and issues in tourism studies such as conservation, ethics, security and management challenges. Employs the perspectives of anthropology, sociology, economics,

hospitality management, civil rights, and transport studies. Available as an e-book.

1127 Tourism and the travel industry: An information sourcebook. Peter M. Enggass. Phoenix: Oryx Press, 1988. viii, 152 p. ISBN 0897742672
016.3801459104   Z6004.T6E3; G155.A1

Somewhat dated, yet still useful. Contains 846 entries. The aim of the book is "to provide a comprehensive and easily searched source of reference on tourism and the travel industry."—*Introd.* Author, title, and subject indexes.

1128 Travel, tourism, and hospitality research: A handbook for managers and researchers. 2nd ed. J. R. Brent Ritchie, Charles R. Goeldner. New York: Wiley, 1994. xxiv, 614 p., ill. ISBN 9780471582489
338.479104072   G155.A1

Intended to be "a major reference book which will be of use to: 1. managers in tourism . . . [and] 2. beginning researchers who require an overview of available research methods, in a single source combined with an associated basic bibliography, which will permit them to pursue more in-depth work when required."—*Introd.* Contains 52 chapters organized into seven parts. Each chapter is signed and contains references. Index.

Media

Specialized Sources of Industry Data

1129 Broadcasting and cable yearbook. R. R. Bowker. New Providence, N.J.: R. R. Bowker, 1993–2010. ill. ISSN 0000-1511
384.540973   HE8689

Profiles of 4,825 AM radio stations, 9,000 FM radio stations, and 2,180 television stations in the U.S., and 1,100 Canadian TV and radio stations. Includes call letters, frequency or channel, contact information, ownership, programming information, and key personnel. Industry overview has market rankings, business rankings, television advertising shares, history of broadcasting and cable, chronology of electronic media, and FCC's rules of broadcasting. Also contains directory information for over 5,100 service

companies, such as law firms, engineers, marketing consultants, and industry associations. Ceased with edition of 2010: succeeded by Complete television, radio & cable industry directory (1130).

1130 Complete television, radio and cable industry directory. Grey House Publ. Amenia, N.Y.: Grey House Pub., 2013–
384.54/097   HE8689

Covers over 22,000 company or station listings for the U.S. and Canada. Identifies more than 72,000 executives and contacts in the fields of television, cable, radio, satellite carriers, programming services, technology and equipment, and professional services. Current notes about associations, events, educational opportunities, awards, and relevant news about legal, regulatory and government agency changes. Entries for stations include station format, call letters, frequency, antenna and transmitter data, contact information (including telephone, fax, URL, and address), hours of operation, special programming, affiliates, advertising rates, ownership, and national and regional network affiliations. Also available in online form. Successor to Broadcasting and cable yearbook (1129).

1131 Editor and publisher newspaper data book. Editor & Publisher Co. New York: Editor & Publisher Co., 2013–. maps
PN4700

Annual. Information about some 25,000 companies, including newspapers of all kinds, syndicates and news services, equipment suppliers, and related entities such as schools of journalism. Vol. 1 covers daily newpapers, Vol. 2 covers weeklies. Contact information, names of key personnel, circulation figures, advertising rates. Successor to Editor and publisher international year book.

1132 Freedonia focus reports. http://www.freedoniagroup.com/FocusReports.aspx. Freedonia Group. Cleveland, Ohio: Freedonia Group. 2001–
HC106.82

Industry outlook information on a subscription basis. More than 600 reports cover eighteen industry categories: automotive, chemicals, construction, consumer goods, electronics, energy, food and agriculture (including tobacco), industrial components, life sciences (both medical and pharmaceutical), machinery, metals and minerals, miscellaneous and service industries, packaging, paper and printing (including publishing), plastics, rubber, textiles and leather (including apparel), and wood (including furniture and fixtures). Provides market size, historical demand, forecasts of demand, and profiles of leading companies. Browsable by major regions: Australia, Brazil, Canada, China, France, Germany, India, Italy, Japan, Mexico, Russia, South Korea, Spain, the U.K., and the U.S.

1133 IBISWorld United States. http://www
.ibisworld.com/. IBISWorld. New York:
IBISWorld. 1999–

HC103

700 reports on American industries. Industry reports can be located using NAICS numbers. Major categories include: Accommodation & Food Services; Administration, Business Support & Waste Management Services; Agriculture, Forestry, Fishing & Hunting; Arts, Entertainment & Recreation; Construction; Educational Services; Finance & Insurance; Healthcare & Social Assistance; Information; Manufacturing; Mining; Other Services (except Public Administration); Professional, Scientific & Technical Services; Real Estate & Rental and Leasing; Retail Trade; Transportation & Warehousing; Utilities; and Wholesale Trade.

Reports include industry definition; information about the supply chain; key statistics; segmentations (products and services segmentation, major market segments, industry concentration, geographic spread); market characteristics (market size, demand determinants, domestic and international markets, basis of competition, life cycle); industry conditions (barriers to entry, taxation, industry assistance, regulation and deregulation, cost structure, capital and labor intensity, technology and systems, industry volatility, globalization); key factors (sensitivities and success factors); key competitors; and industry performance (current and historical). Glossaries and guides to jargon. Setting this database apart are reports on small industries, such as parking lots and garages.

**1134 International television and video
almanac.** Quigley Publishing Company.
New York: Quigley Pub. Co., 1987–. ill.
ISSN 0895-2213
384.5505 HE8700

Provides brief factual and contact information for stations and ownership; networks and distributors; cable, satellite and wireless providers; production services; video and DVD distributors; professional organizations; and government offices. Review of the year's awards, television series, miniseries and movies. Short biographies of 5,000 individuals.

1135 Library and book trade almanac.
[Information Today, Inc.]. Medford, N.J.:
Information Today, Inc., 2009–
ISSN 2150-5446
020.5 Z731.A47

Title varies: 1956–58, American library annual [new series]; 1959–61, American library and book trade annual; 1962–88, The Bowker annual of library and book trade information; 1989–2008, The Bowker annual: Library and book trade almanac. Includes reviews of the year's events, trends, and legislation relevant to librarianship and publishing; reports from federal agencies and key organizations; statistics on placement and salaries of beginning librarians; scholarship and award winners; statistics on library expenditures, facilities, and rankings; statistics on publishing output and average prices of books; bibliographies of recent books in librarianship, bestsellers, and award-winning books; directories of library consortia and associations; and a calendar of conferences and book fairs. Indexes: organizations; subjects.

1136 The media book. Media Dynamics
(Firm). Nutley, N.J.: Media Dynamics,
2013–

Successor to Magazine dimensions (798) with first publication in the fall of 2013. Quantitative and qualitative data on the demographics of audiences reached by television, radio, magazines, the internet and newspapers, to support advertising and marketing needs.

**1137 Plunkett's entertainment and media
industry almanac.** Jack W. Plunkett.
Houston, Tex.: Plunkett Research, 1998–
ISSN 1521-6160
302.23/025/73 P88.8

Data on nearly 400 leading companies, both public and private. Company profiles include types of business, brands and affiliates, contacts, employee benefits and top salaries, sales and profit numbers, growth plans, and competitive advantage. Especially useful for the industry background, trends, statistics and rankings at the front of the volume (estimated revenue in the U.S. information and entertainment sector by NAICS Code, U.S. magazine advertising revenue and pages for PIB measured magazines: 1960–2005, number of U.S. magazines: 1988–2005, U.S. periodical publishing revenues 2001–2005, annual U.S. newspaper advertising expenditures, 1990–2006, percent of U.S. households with alternative broadcast delivery systems: 1997–2006, U.S. personal consumption expenditures for recreation by product or service: 1990–2005), and information on the main associations and organizations in the back of the volume. Most information is for the U.S., but some international coverage is provided. Available as an e-book.

1138 Radio dimensions. Media Dynamics, Inc. New York: Media Dynamics, 2005–2013. ill. ISSN 1931-4795
659   HF6146.R3
Uses data from MRI, Simmons, Scarborough Research, and Radio Recall to show who listens to radio. Augmented by narratives that give context to the data. Chapters on: History of radio, Radio basics (trends in ownership, radio's penetration from 1925–present, ad revenue and profits from 1935–present), Radio audiences (Arbitron's PPM, average number of stations listened to per week, listening trends, daypart audiences, radio usage, internet radio, satellite radio), Reach and frequency patterns, SQAD's CPP estimates, and Qualitative factors. Ceased with edition of 2013; coverage of radio appears in the successor title The media book (801) from the same publisher.

1139 SRDS tv and cable source. Standard Rate and Data Service (Firm). Wilmette, Ill.: Standard Rate and Data Service, 1994–. maps ISSN 1071-4596
659.143   HF5905
Lists broadcast, cable, syndicated and alternative television outlets, organized by state. Entries give contact information, executives, corporate owner, system background, coverage, insertion networks, traffic specifications, and special features. Each market includes a profile, with sales rankings by merchandise, SQAD cost per point levels, top daily newspapers and newspaper groups, metro radio stations by county, and a demographic profile of the market. Also available online.

1140 Standard and Poor's industry surveys. Standard and Poor's. New York: Standard and Poor's, 1973–2012 ISSN 0196-4666
332.67   HC106.6
Detailed analyses of 22 industry categories and the major companies in each category. Contains a basic analysis and a comprehensive source of information, updated by a current analysis. The analysis includes trends, information on how the industry operates, key ratios and statistics (revenues, net income, profit ratios, balance sheet ratios, equity ratios, per-share data, company and product rankings), information on how to analyze a company in that industry, and a glossary. Company and industry indexes. Ceased with edition of 2012.

1141 Television and cable factbook. Warren Communications News. Washington: Warren Communications News, Inc., 1982–. ill. ISSN 0732-8648
384.5502573   TK6540
Contains 930,000 entries, organized into four parts: cable systems, television stations, media ownership, and media services. Covers the U.S. and Canada. Geographic listings describe basic equipment, services and costs, ownership history and personnel, market rankings, sales and transfers, etc. Includes suppliers, associations, network services, regulations and their agencies, plus advertising and marketing services and statistics. Published from 1946–50 as *TV directory*; from 1951–81 as *Television factbook*. Available as an e-book.

1142 TV dimensions. Media Dynamics, Inc. New York: Media Dynamics, 1984–. ill. ISSN 0884-1098
384.5443   HE8700.8
Analyzes television as an advertising medium. Accompanying articles give context to statistics. Contents include basics such as trends in household penetration and advertising since 1950; TV viewing patterns with demographics and impact of video recording, pay-per-view and mobile devices; programming appeal for types of shows and viewers; viewer attention and involvement patterns, comparing broadcast and cable; and commercial impact through measurement of viewer attitudes. Appendixes offer essays such as the state of the broadcast industry and the effectiveness of advertising.

Organizations and Associations

1143 Association of American Publishers.
http://www.publishers.org/. Association
of American Publishers. Washington:
Association of American Publishers. 1996–
070.5/381.45002   Z284
Home page for the advocacy group for U.S. trade and
academic publishers, including numerous scholarly
societies. Website provides policy statements, links
to reports, and other resources. Some content such
as statistical and industry reports is limited to members, but summaries may be public.

1144 FCC.gov. http://www.fcc.gov/. Federal
Communications Commission.
Washington: Federal Communications
Commission. 2007
Home page for the Federal Communications Commission, founded in 1923 to regulate interstate
and international communications, now including
radio, television, wire, satellite and cable. The website contains a treasure trove of information, including reports, statistics, trends, rules and regulations,
and more. Examples include annual reports on cable
industry prices, periodic reviews of the radio industry,
the statistics of communications common carriers,
statistical trends in telephony, local and long distance
telephone industries, local telephone competition
and broadband deployment, telephone industry infrastructure and service quality, federal-state joint board
monitoring reports, telephone numbering facts, and
international traffic data. The "FCC Consumer Publications Library" on the Web site provides printable
articles about broadcasting, telephone service, privacy
issues and other consumer-oriented topics.

**1145 STM: International Association of
Scientific, Technical, and Medical
Publishers.** http://www.stm-assoc.org/.
International Association of Scientific,
Technical & Medical Publ. Oxford: STM.
1999–
                                   Z286.S4
Home page of the largest trade association for the
academic and professional publishing market,
including publishers of scientific journals, with over
120 member organizations worldwide. Source for
policy statements on issues such as copyright and

interlibrary loan; recorded presentations on issues
and trends; and information about initiatives for low-
cost access in developing countries, such as HINARI
for health content and AGORA for agriculture. Some
content limited to members.

Additional Reference Sources

1146 Hoovers. http://www.hoovers.com/.
Reference Press, Hoover's, Inc. Short Hills,
N.J.: Dun & Bradstreet. 1996–
338.7   HG4057
More than 60 million records describe public and
private companies primarily in the United States, but
including Canada, United Kingdom, Europe, and
Asia/Pacific. Profiles have an overview, history, family
tree, industry information, products/operations, top
competitors, competitive landscape, top executives
with biographies, news, significant developments, and
financial data. Financial summaries may include an
income statement; balance sheet; cash flow; historical
financials such as five years of P/E and per share; stock
quotes; interactive stock charts; market data; earnings
estimates; this year's ratios for the company, industry,
and market; SEC filings; and industry watch for trends.

Content is tracked for 900 industries, organized
into numerous larger categories: Agriculture & Forestry; Arts, Entertainment & Recreation; Beverage
Manufacturing; Biotechnology Product Manufacturing; Business Services; Chemical Manufacturing;
Commercial Equipment Repair & Maintenance;
Commercial Printing; Computer Hardware Manufacturing; Computer Software; Construction; Consumer Products Manufacturing; Consumer Services;
Contract Electronics Manufacturing; Education; Electric Power Generation; Electric Power Transmission,
Distribution & Marketing; Electric Utilities; Electrical
Products Manufacturing; Fabricated Metal Product
Manufacturing; Financial Services; Food Manufactur-
ing; Government; Health Care Products Manufactur-
ing; Health Care; HVAC Equipment Manufacturing;
Industrial Manufacturing; Insurance; Leasing of Intan-
gible Assets; Lodging; Machinery Manufacturing;
Magnetic & Optical Media; Manufacturing & Repro-
duction; Managed Application & Network Services;
Management of Companies & Enterprises; Media;
Membership Organizations; Mining; Miscellaneous
Manufacturing; Natural Gas Distribution & Market-
ing; Nonclassifiable establishments; Nonmetallic

Mineral Product Manufacturing; Nonprofit Institutions; Oil & Gas Exploration & Production; Oil & Gas Field Services; Oil & Gas Well Drilling; Petroleum & Coal Products Manufacturing; Pharmaceutical Manufacturing; Primary Metals Manufacturing; Private Households; Professional Services; Real Estate; Religious Organizations; Rental & Leasing; Restaurants, Bars & Food Services; Retail; Security Products Manufacturing; Semiconductor & Other Electronic Component Manufacturing; Telecommunications Equipment Manufacturing; Telecommunications Services; Transportation Equipment Manufacturing; Transportation Services; Water & Sewer Utilities; Wholesale; and Wood Product Manufacturing.

Coverage can be brief, but generally includes a fact sheet, overview, selected companies, industry watch with video interviews, news from the last 90 days, and web resources for terminology, associations, and organizations, and online publications. Hoover's print publications include (*Hoover's handbook of American business* (876), *Hoover's handbook of private companies* (855)).

1147 Magazine dimensions. Media Dynamics, Inc. New York: Media Dynamics, 1993–2013 ISSN 1074-7419

659.132   HF6105.U5

Statistical information mixed with narrative, providing a picture of the magazine industry. Chapters include: General dimensions (history of magazines from 1740–2006, trends in magazines published and ad revenues, changing face of editorial content, magazine CPM's), magazine audiences (audience definitions, circulation trends, subscriber profiles, reader profiles by magazine, total audience by magazine, website audiences, reading diet by genre, median age and income trends, reader-per-copy, reach and frequency, and accumulation patterns), and qualitative factors (reader attitudes and intensity of exposure, location and timing of reading, advertising receptivity, comparison to TV), and Information sources (circulation audits, subscriber/panel studies, syndicated audience/marketing research). Ceased with 2013: replaced by Media book (801).

1148 Passport GMID. http://www.euromonitor .com/. Euromonitor International. London, U.K.: Euromonitor International. [1999–]

658.8   HF5415.2

Also known under previous product names as *Global market information database*, *GMID*, or *Euromonitor GMID*. Market reports, company profiles, and demographic, economic, and marketing statistics for 205 countries. Market reports are for 16 consumer markets (food and drink, tobacco, toys, etc.) and 14 industrial and service markets (accountancy, broadcasting, chemicals, property services, etc.).

Reports have market size, market sectors, share of market, marketing activity, research and development, corporate overview, distribution, consumer profiles, market forecasts, sector forecasts, sources, and definitions. Additional reports are available for market segments, such as baby food. Company profiles have background, recent news, competitve environment, and outlook. Consumer lifestyle reports and very useful marketing background analyze the consumer by country, gender, age, marital status, educational attainment, ethnicity, religion, home ownership, household profile, employment, income, health, eating and personal grooming habits, leisure activities, personal finance, communication, transport, and travel.

Search for data, which can be exported into Excel or browse for reports. Data are available since 1977 and include inflation, exchange rates, GDP, GNI, government expenditures, government finance, income, labor, and money supply.

Similar information on a smaller scale is available in Research monitor (783) from the same publisher.

1149 This business of television. Rev. and updated 3rd ed. Howard J. Blumenthal, Oliver R. Goodenough. New York: BillBoard Books, 2006. xxiv, 568 p. ISBN 9780823077632

384.554   HE8700.8

In 11 sections this comprehensive updated edition covers the basics of television (broadcast, cable, satellite, and home video), such as marketing, distribution, and production. Sections include: Distribution, Regulation of distribution, Audience measurement and advertising, Programming business (market segments, economics of production, sales), Big media, Broader definition of television (public television, home shopping, religious television), Programming and program development, Regulation of programming, Production, Legal and business affairs, and Television outside the U.S. Appendixes provide various contract forms.

1150 World radio TV handbook: The directory of global broadcasting. WRTH. Oxford, U.K.: WRTH Publications, Ltd., 1947–. ill., maps, music, ports. ISSN 0144-7750

621.384   TK6540

"A complete directory of international radio and television" including short wave. Published by various hands: Copenhagen, Denmark: O. Lund Johansen, 1961–82; New York: Billboard Publications, 1982–2007. Continues *World radio handbook for listeners including world-wide radio who's who*, *World-radio-television handbook*, and *World radio handbook*. WRTH is currently divided into the following sections: Features (product reviews, articles, interviews), National radio, International radio, Frequency lists, Television, and Reference. Listing of worldwide radio and TV services; world satellite broadcasts; short, medium, and long wave frequency tables; list of official international broadcasting organizations; internet resources; and users clubs. Available in online form.

Motor Vehicles

Specialized Sources of Industry Data

1151 Census of transportation. United States Dept. of Commerce, Bureau of the Census. Washington: U.S. Dept. of Commerce, Bureau of the Census, 1963–2003. 54 v.

380.50973   HE203.C44

Includes the results of the truck inventory and use survey, commodity transportation survey, vehicle inventory and use survey, and national travel survey. Begun in 1963 and continued through data of 1997 (published in 2003). Information is now part of the *Economic Census*. The Economic Census from 1977 to 2007 is available online at http://www.census.gov/prod/www/economic_census.html.

1152 Freedonia focus reports. http://www.freedoniagroup.com/FocusReports.aspx. Freedonia Group. Cleveland, Ohio: Freedonia Group. 2001–

HC106.82

Industry outlook information on a subscription basis. More than 600 reports cover eighteen industry categories: automotive, chemicals, construction,

consumer goods, electronics, energy, food and agriculture (including tobacco), industrial components, life sciences (both medical and pharmaceutical), machinery, metals and minerals, miscellaneous and service industries, packaging, paper and printing (including publishing), plastics, rubber, textiles and leather (including apparel), and wood (including furniture and fixtures). Provides market size, historical demand, forecasts of demand, and profiles of leading companies. Browsable by major regions: Australia, Brazil, Canada, China, France, Germany, India, Italy, Japan, Mexico, Russia, South Korea, Spain, the U.K., and the U.S.

1153 Global market data book. Crain Communications. Detroit: Crain Communications, 2007–

HD9710.A1

Published as the annual reference issue of *Automotive news* (1158). Formerly *Market data book*. Covers information on production (car and truck production history and forecasts, five-year histories by country, production by assembly plant, car and light-truck production by platform, car and truck production by model and by month), dealers (J.D. Power and Assoc. data, dealer census data, financial data, ad spending data, used-car prices and volumes), and sales data (light-vehicle sales history and forecasts, light-vehicle sales summaries by make, car and truck sales, five-year history by make, car and light-truck sales by model and by month).

1154 Plunkett's automobile industry almanac. Jack W. Plunkett. Houston, Tex.: Plunkett Research, 2003–. ill. ISSN 1552-3004

381   HD9710.U5

Data on 300 major companies including manufacturing, retailing and financial services. Company profiles include types of business, brands and affiliates, contacts, employee benefits and top salaries, sales and profit numbers, growth plans, and competitive advantage. Especially useful for the industry trends, statistics, and rankings at the front of the volume. Available as an e-book.

1155 Ward's motor vehicle facts and figures. Ward's Communications Inc. Southfield, Mich.: Ward's Communications, 1999–. ill. ISSN 1553-8184

629.222   HD9710.U5

Annual data for the U.S. automotive industry. The data are presented in the following categories: production/factory sales, retail sales, registrations, automotive trade, materials, transportation expenditures, travel trends, automotive businesses (including corporate profits, R&D, and expenditures), environment/regulations, and traffic fatalities. Includes international data. Online as WardsAuto.com.

1156 Ward's world motor vehicle data.
Ward's Communications Inc. Southfield, Mich.: Ward's Communications, 2000–. ill. ISSN 1553-8176
629.222   HD9710.A1
Contains 30 yrs. of data on production and sales for passenger cars and commercial vehicles for 47 countries. Also has production by manufacturer, sales by manufacturer, total vehicles in operation by country and vehicle type, and assembly plant locations by manufacturer and region. Information derived from government agencies, trade associations, and private sources. Online as WardsAuto.com.

1157 World automotive market report.
Educational and Research Foundation of MEMA, Inc. Des Plaines, Ill.: Auto and Truck International, 1993–2007. ill., maps ISSN 1080-1987
380.1456292021   HD9710.A1
Cesaed with edition of 2007 but still useful for finding historical statistics. Contents: world motor vehicle production/assembly, world vehicle census summary, vehicles on the road throughout the world, United States automotive parts trade, world trade in new motor vehicles, world motor vehicle markets. Lists organizations that supply data.

Periodicals

1158 Automotive news. Crain Automotive Group. Detroit: Crain Automotive Group, 1938–. ill. ISSN 0005-1551
338.4762922205   TL1
Weekly. Reports trends, developments, and economic impacts for the automotive industry. An annual supplement to *Automotive News* is the Global market data book (1153), with information on production, dealers, and sales.

Organizations and Associations

1159 Automotive aftermarket industry association (AAIA). http://www .aftermarket.org/. Automotive Aftermarket Industry Association. Bethesda, Md.: Automotive Aftermarket Industry Association. 1997– 380.106
Home page for trade association representing manufacturers, distributors and retailers for "motor vehicle parts, accessories, service, tools, equipment, materials and supplies." —*About.* The site includes *Aftermarket insider magazine*, newsletters, press releases, and information about events, education, government affairs, international trade, market research, member services, and standards and technology. AAIA annually publishes a digital *Aftermarket factbook*.

Internet Resources

1160 New car prices and used car book values—NADAguides. http://www .nadaguides.com/. National Automobile Dealers Association. Costa Mesa, Calif.: NADAguides. 1997–
629.222   TL162
Information for automobiles (including SUVs and light trucks), motorcycles, boats and recreational vehicles. Browsable and searchable lists by make and model. FAQs. Comparable resources are Kelley (1162) and Edmunds (1161).

1161 New cars, used cars, car reviews and pricing—Edmunds.com. http://www .edmunds.com/. Edmund Publications Corporation. Santa Monica, Calif.: Edmunds.com, Inc. 1996–
629.222   TL162
Searchable database identifies automobiles (including SUVs and light trucks) and prices. Directory of car dealers. Reviews, advice for buying, insuring and maintaining new or used vehicles. FAQs. List of recalls. Comparable resources include Kelley (1162) and NADA (1160).

1162 Official Kelley blue book new car and used car prices and values.

http://www.kbb.com/. Kelley Blue Book
Co. Irvine, Calif.: Kelley Blue Book. 1996–
629.222   TL162

Provides lists, rankings and reviews of automobiles,
including SUVs and light trucks. Interactive features
for vehicle comparison, calculation of payments, and
projected cost to operate and maintain. Directory of
car dealerships. Comparable sources are Edmunds
(1161) or NADA (1160).

Additional Reference Sources

**1163 Encyclopedia of American business
history and biography.** Facts On File.
New York: Facts On File, 1988–1994. ill.
0816013713   HC102

Combines biographical entries with articles discussing major companies, government and labor organizations, inventions, and legal decisions for various
industries. The signed entries range in length from
one-half to ten or more pages; most include photographs or other illustrations, and list publications
and references, archives, and unpublished documents. Each volume is available separately. Ten volumes were published up to 1994, including *The
airline industry*; *The automobile industry, 1896–1920*;
The automobile industry, 1920–1980; *Banking and
finance to 1913*; *Banking and finance, 1913–1989*;
Iron and steel in the nineteenth century; *Iron and
steel in the twentieth century*; *Railroads in the nineteenth century*; and *Railroads in the age of regulation,
1900–1980*.

1164 Hoovers. http://www.hoovers.com/.
Reference Press, Hoover's, Inc. Short Hills,
N.J.: Dun & Bradstreet. 1996–
338.7   HG4057

More than 60 million records describe public and
private companies primarily in the United States, but
including Canada, United Kingdom, Europe, and
Asia/Pacific. Profiles have an overview, history, family tree, industry information, products/operations,
top competitors, competitive landscape, top executives with biographies, news, significant developments, and financial data. Financial summaries may
include an income statement; balance sheet; cash
flow; historical financials such as five years of P/E
and per share; stock quotes; interactive stock charts;
market data; earnings estimates; this year's ratios for
the company, industry, and market; SEC filings; and
industry watch for trends.

Content is tracked for 900 industries, organized
into numerous larger categories: Agriculture & For-
estry; Arts, Entertainment & Recreation; Beverage
Manufacturing; Biotechnology Product Manufacturing; Business Services; Chemical Manufacturing;
Commercial Equipment Repair & Maintenance;
Commercial Printing; Computer Hardware Man-
ufacturing; Computer Software; Construction;
Consumer Products Manufacturing; Consumer
Services; Contract Electronics Manufacturing; Edu-
cation; Electric Power Generation; Electric Power
Transmission, Distribution & Marketing; Electric
Utilities; Electrical Products Manufacturing; Fabri-
cated Metal Product Manufacturing; Financial Ser-
vices; Food Manufacturing; Government; Health
Care Products Manufacturing; Health Care; HVAC
Equipment Manufacturing; Industrial Manufactur-
ing; Insurance; Leasing of Intangible Assets; Lodg-
ing; Machinery Manufacturing; Magnetic & Optical
Media; Manufacturing & Reproduction; Managed
Application & Network Services; Management of
Companies & Enterprises; Media; Membership
Organizations; Mining; Miscellaneous Manufactur-
ing; Natural Gas Distribution & Marketing; Non-
classifiable establishments; Nonmetallic Mineral
Product Manufacturing; Nonprofit Institutions; Oil
& Gas Exploration & Production; Oil & Gas Field
Services; Oil & Gas Well Drilling; Petroleum &
Coal Products Manufacturing; Pharmaceutical
Manufacturing; Primary Metals Manufacturing;
Private Households; Professional Services; Real
Estate; Religious Organizations; Rental & Leasing;
Restaurants, Bars & Food Services; Retail; Security
Products Manufacturing; Semiconductor & Other
Electronic Component Manufacturing; Telecom-
munications Equipment Manufacturing; Telecom-
munications Services; Transportation Equipment
Manufacturing; Transportation Services; Water
& Sewer Utilities; Wholesale; and Wood Product
Manufacturing.

Coverage can be brief, but generally includes a
fact sheet, overview, selected companies, industry
watch with video interviews, news from the last
90 days, and web resources for terminology, associations, and organizations, and online publications.
Hoover's print publications include (*Hoover's handbook of American business* (876), *Hoover's handbook of
private companies* (855)).

Pharmaceutical

Specialized Sources of Industry Data

1165 Freedonia focus reports. http://www
.freedoniagroup.com/FocusReports.aspx.
Freedonia Group. Cleveland, Ohio:
Freedonia Group. 2001–
                              HC106.82
Industry outlook information on a subscription basis.
More than 600 reports cover eighteen industry categories: automotive, chemicals, construction, consumer goods, electronics, energy, food and agriculture
(including tobacco), industrial components, life sciences (both medical and pharmaceutical), machinery,
metals and minerals, miscellaneous and service industries, packaging, paper and printing (including publishing), plastics, rubber, textiles and leather (including
apparel), and wood (including furniture and fixtures).
Provides market size, historical demand, forecasts of
demand, and profiles of leading companies. Browsable by major regions: Australia, Brazil, Canada, China,
France, Germany, India, Italy, Japan, Mexico, Russia,
South Korea, Spain, the U.K., and the U.S.

1166 Industry profile. http://www.phrma
.org/. Pharmaceutical Research and
Manufacturers of America. Washington:
Pharmaceutical Research and
Manufacturers of America. 1996–
ISSN 1934-8231
338.7616151
Formerly a print serial, this annual report can be downloaded from the PhRMA web site. Covers research and
development spending, information on incentives,
partnerships, Medicare and Medicaid, and industry
approaches to innovation. The Pharmaceutical Research
and Manufacturers of America website also has reports
on the U.S. health care system, the cost of prescription
drugs, and drug discovery and development.

**1167 Plunkett's biotech and genetics
industry almanac.** Jack W. Plunkett.
Houston, Tex.: Plunkett Research, 2001–
ISSN 1546-5756
338   HD9999.B44
Data on over 400 leading companies, both public
and private, in biotechnology, genetics, and pharmaceuticals. Company profiles include types of

business, brands and affiliates, contacts, employee
benefits and top salaries, sales and profit numbers,
growth plans, and competitive advantage. Especially
useful for the industry background and trends, statistics and rankings at the front of the volume (U.S.
biotech industry financing 1997–2005, U.S. health
expenditure amounts 1980–2015, global R&D
investments by research-based pharmaceutical companies 1970–2005, R&D spending by function,
U.S. FDA approval times for new drugs 1993–2005,
etc.), and information on the main associations and
organizations in the back of the volume. Most information is for the U.S., but some international coverage is provided. Available as an e-book.

1168 Standard and Poor's industry surveys.
Standard and Poor's. New York: Standard
and Poor's, 1973–2012 ISSN 0196-4666
332.67   HC106.6
Detailed analyses of 22 industry categories and the
major companies in each category. Contains a basic
analysis and a comprehensive source of information,
updated by a current analysis. The analysis includes
trends, information on how the industry operates,
key ratios and statistics (revenues, net income, profit
ratios, balance sheet ratios, equity ratios, per-share
data, company and product rankings), information
on how to analyze a company in that industry, and
a glossary. Company and industry indexes. Ceased
with edition of 2012.

Organizations and Associations

1169 Food and drug administration.
http://www.fda.gov/. Food and drug
administration. Washington: U.S.
Department of Health and Human
Services. 1996–
353.0077/8   RA395.A3
Home page for the FDA, with a wide range of information for the consumer and the researcher, including:
Enforcement Activities (clinical trials, enforcement
report, product recalls and alerts); Products Regulated by FDA (animal drugs and food, aquaculture,
bioengineered food, biologics, gene therapy, mobile
phones, sunlamps, tattoos, food, drugs, xenotransplantation); news; hot topics; publications; major
initiatives/activities (advisory committees, bar coding, buying medical products online, Data Council,

Facts@FDA) and Food Industry (Prior Notice of Imports, Registration of Food Facilities).

Internet Resources

1170 Drugs@FDA. http://www.accessdata.fda .gov/scripts/cder/drugsatfda. U.S. Food and Drug Administration, Center for Drug and Evaluation Research. Washington: U.S. Food and Drug Administration, Center for Drug and Evaluation Research. 2004?

RM300

Includes FDA-approved brand-name and generic drug products. Searchable by drug name, active ingredient, new drug application number (NDA), abbreviated new drug application (ANDA), and biologics license application (BLA). Provides a drug's FDA history and helps with finding labels for approved drug products. Also provides monthly drug approval reports. Further information and answers to questions relating to this website can be found at http://www.fda.gov/Drugs/InformationOnDrugs/ucm075234.htm.

Also from FDA, "Drug safety and availability" http://www.fda.gov/Drugs/DrugSafety/default.htm includes information for both consumers and health professionals on new drug warnings and other safety information. "Index to drug-specific information" (found under "Postmarket drug safety information for patients and providers") can be searched for drugs that have been the subject of some type of drug safety concern, with indication if a particular drug has an active FDA safety alert (cf. Website).

1171 WHO drug information. http://www. who.int/druginformation. World Health Organization. Geneva, Switzerland: World Health Organization ISSN 1010-9609

RS189.W47

Quarterly journal, available since 1987 in print and also online since 1996.

Provides an overview of topics relating to drug development and regulation that are of current relevance, with the latest international news, prescribing and access of medicines worldwide. Also introduces newly released guidance documents. Includes lists of proposed and recommended International Nonproprietary Names for Pharmaceutical Substances

(INN). For health professionals and policy makers. Further information and links to INNs, the current 16th ed. (Mar. 2009 and Mar. 2010 update) of the *WHO model list of essential medicines*, and other related WHO publications can be found at http://www. who.int/medicines/publications/en/.

Additional Reference Sources

1172 A dictionary of pharmacology and allied topics. 2nd ed. D. R. Laurence, John Carpenter. Amsterdam, The Netherlands; New York: Elsevier, 1998. xi, 373 p.
615.103   RS51.L38

First edition, 1994, had title *A dictionary of pharmacology and clinical drug evaluation*.

Includes currently accepted usage for pharmacological terms and relevant terminology from other disciplines (e.g., ethics, law, social policy, statistics), with etymology for most terms, as well as terms used by official regulatory authorities. Does not include individual drugs. Intended for basic and clinical pharmacologists and others involved in clinical drug evaluation.

1173 Burger's medicinal chemistry, drug discovery and development. 7th ed. Donald J. Abraham, David P. Rotella, Alfred Burger. Hoboken, N.J.: Wiley, 2010. 8 v., ill. (some col.) ISBN 9780470278154
615/.19   RS403.B8

First ed., 1951, to 4th ed., 1980–1, had title *Medicinal chemistry*. 5th ed., 1995–7; 6th ed., 2003.

Contents: v. 1 and 2, "Drug discovery"; v. 3, "Drug development"; v. 4, "Cardiovascular, endocrine and metabolic diseases"; v. 5, "Pulmonary, bone, vitamins and autocoid therapeutic agents"; v. 6, "Cancer"; v. 7, "Antiinfectives"; v. 8, "Central nervous systems disorders."

Updated and expanded edition. Comprehensive resource for information on drug studies and drug research, with the latest developments in medicinal drug research and drug development. Includes high priority areas and subjects, such as molecular modeling in drug design, virtual screening, bioinformatics, chemical information computing systems in drug discovery, structural biology of drug action, etc. Bibliographical references and index. For libraries serving medicinal chemists, pharmaceutical professionals, and other scientists. Also available as an e-book.

1174 Dictionary of pharmacy. Dennis B. Worthen, Julian H. Fincher. New York: Pharmaceutical Products Press, 2004. xiii, 528 p. ISBN 0789023288

615.103 RS51.D482

Comprehensive list of terms from pharmacy and also terminology relevant to pharmacy from several other disciplines. A–Z arrangement; cross-references (see, see also, contrast, and compare). In separate sections, includes abbreviations; Latin and Greek terms; weights and measures; practice standards; the code of ethics for pharmacists; and lists of professional associations, organizations, and colleges and schools of pharmacy in the United States and Canada. Resource for pharmacy students, faculty, and practicing pharmacists.

1175 Hoovers. http://www.hoovers.com/. Reference Press, Hoover's, Inc. Short Hills, N.J.: Dun & Bradstreet. 1996–

338.7 HG4057

More than 60 million records describe public and private companies primarily in the United States, but including Canada, United Kingdom, Europe, and Asia/Pacific. Profiles have an overview, history, family tree, industry information, products/operations, top competitors, competitive landscape, top executives with biographies, news, significant developments, and financial data. Financial summaries may include an income statement; balance sheet; cash flow; historical financials such as five years of P/E and per share; stock quotes; interactive stock charts; market data; earnings estimates; this year's ratios for the company, industry, and market; SEC filings; and industry watch for trends.

Content is tracked for 900 industries, organized into numerous larger categories: Agriculture & Forestry; Arts, Entertainment & Recreation; Beverage Manufacturing; Biotechnology Product Manufacturing; Business Services; Chemical Manufacturing; Commercial Equipment Repair & Maintenance; Commercial Printing; Computer Hardware Manufacturing; Computer Software; Construction; Consumer Products Manufacturing; Consumer Services; Contract Electronics Manufacturing; Education; Electric Power Generation; Electric Power Transmission, Distribution & Marketing; Electric Utilities; Electrical Products Manufacturing; Fabricated Metal Product Manufacturing; Financial Services; Food Manufacturing; Government; Health Care Products Manufacturing; Health Care; HVAC Equipment Manufacturing; Industrial Manufacturing; Insurance; Leasing of Intangible Assets; Lodging; Machinery Manufacturing; Magnetic & Optical Media; Manufacturing & Reproduction; Managed Application & Network Services; Management of Companies & Enterprises; Media; Membership Organizations; Mining; Miscellaneous Manufacturing; Natural Gas Distribution & Marketing; Nonclassifiable establishments; Nonmetallic Mineral Product Manufacturing; Nonprofit Institutions; Oil & Gas Exploration & Production; Oil & Gas Field Services; Oil & Gas Well Drilling; Petroleum & Coal Products Manufacturing; Pharmaceutical Manufacturing; Primary Metals Manufacturing; Private Households; Professional Services; Real Estate; Religious Organizations; Rental & Leasing; Restaurants, Bars & Food Services; Retail; Security Products Manufacturing; Semiconductor & Other Electronic Component Manufacturing; Telecommunications Equipment Manufacturing; Telecommunications Services; Transportation Equipment Manufacturing; Transportation Services; Water & Sewer Utilities; Wholesale; and Wood Product Manufacturing.

Coverage can be brief, but generally includes a fact sheet, overview, selected companies, industry watch with video interviews, news from the last 90 days, and web resources for terminology, associations, and organizations, and online publications. Hoover's print publications include (*Hoover's handbook of American business* (876), *Hoover's handbook of private companies* (855)).

1176 Red book: Pharmacy's fundamental reference. Thomson Healthcare. Montvale, N.J.: Thomson Healthcare, 2004–. ill. ISSN 1556-3391

338 HD9666.1.D75

Volumes in 1941/42–1943/44 had title *Drug topics price book* (continues the "Red book price list section" of the *Druggists' circular*, issues semiannually 1897–1940); 1944–92 had title *Drug topics red book*; 1993–94, *Red book*; 1995–2003, *Drug topics red book*.

Description based on 114th ed. 2010

Contents: 1. Emergency information; 2. Clinical reference guide; 3. Herbal medicine guide; 4. Practice management and professional development; 5. Pharmacy and healthcare organizations; 6. Drug reimbursement information; 7. Manufacturer/wholesaler information; 8. Product identification guide; 9. Rx product listings; 10. OTC non-drug product listings. Advertiser index.

Product, pricing, and clinical & pharmaceutical reference information for prescription and over-the-counter (OTC) drugs, many with full-color photographs. Provides nationally recognized average wholesale prices and direct and federal upper-limit prices for prescription drugs. Also includes prices for reimbursable medical supplies and, for example, a vitamin comparison table of popular multivitamin products, a guide to herbal/alternative medicines, a list of FDA-approved new drugs, generics, and OTC products, and also a list of "Web sites worth watching." Includes poison control centers and manufacturers, pharmaceutical wholesalers, and third-party administrator directories. Intended for pharmacists and other health care professionals. For electronic delivery options, see http://www.redbook.com/redbook/index.html.

Retail Trade

Specialized Sources of Industry Data

1177 Freedonia focus reports. http://www.freedoniagroup.com/FocusReports.aspx. Freedonia Group. Cleveland, Ohio: Freedonia Group. 2001–

HC106.82

Industry outlook information on a subscription basis. More than 600 reports cover eighteen industry categories: automotive, chemicals, construction, consumer goods, electronics, energy, food and agriculture (including tobacco), industrial components, life sciences (both medical and pharmaceutical), machinery, metals and minerals, miscellaneous and service industries, packaging, paper and printing (including publishing), plastics, rubber, textiles and leather (including apparel), and wood (including furniture and fixtures). Provides market size, historical demand, forecasts of demand, and profiles of leading companies. Browsable by major regions: Australia, Brazil, Canada, China, France, Germany, India, Italy, Japan, Mexico, Russia, South Korea, Spain, the U.K., and the U.S.

1178 IBISWorld United States. http://www.ibisworld.com/. IBISWorld. New York: IBISWorld. 1999–

HC103

700 reports on American industries. Industry reports can be located using NAICS numbers. Major categories include: Accommodation & Food Services; Administration, Business Support & Waste Management Services; Agriculture, Forestry, Fishing & Hunting; Arts, Entertainment & Recreation; Construction; Educational Services; Finance & Insurance; Healthcare & Social Assistance; Information; Manufacturing; Mining; Other Services (except Public Administration); Professional, Scientific & Technical Services; Real Estate & Rental and Leasing; Retail Trade; Transportation & Warehousing; Utilities; and Wholesale Trade.

Reports include industry definition; information about the supply chain; key statistics; segmentations (products and services segmentation, major market segments, industry concentration, geographic spread); market characteristics (market size, demand determinants, domestic and international markets, basis of competition, life cycle); industry conditions (barriers to entry, taxation, industry assistance, regulation and deregulation, cost structure, capital and labor intensity, technology and systems, industry volatility, globalization); key factors (sensitivities and success factors); key competitors; and industry performance (current and historical). Glossaries and guides to jargon. Setting this database apart are reports on small industries, such as parking lots and garages.

1179 Plunkett's retail industry almanac. Jack W. Plunkett. Houston, Tex.: Plunkett Research, 1997– ISSN 1532-5954

658   HF5429.3

Data on 500 leading companies, both public and private. Company profiles include types of business, brands and affiliates, contacts, employee benefits and top salaries, sales and profit numbers, growth plans, and competitive advantage. Especially useful for the industry background, trends, statistics and rankings at the front of the volume (U.S. retail and food services sales by kinds of businesses: 2001–2005; U.S. shopping centers at a glance: 1980–2005; ten largest shopping centers, U.S.; selected shopping patterns, 1996–2005; monthly distribution of non-anchor tenant sales; U.S. malls; store closing announcements;

U.S. retail industry; estimated quarterly U.S. retail sales: total and e-commerce), and information on the main associations and organizations in the back of the volume. Information is for the U.S. Available as an e-book.

1180 Standard and Poor's industry surveys.
Standard and Poor's. New York: Standard and Poor's, 1973–2012 ISSN 0196-4666
332.67   HC106.6

Detailed analyses of 22 industry categories and the major companies in each category. Contains a basic analysis and a comprehensive source of information, updated by a current analysis. The analysis includes trends, information on how the industry operates, key ratios and statistics (revenues, net income, profit ratios, balance sheet ratios, equity ratios, per-share data, company and product rankings), information on how to analyze a company in that industry, and a glossary. Company and industry indexes. Ceased with edition of 2012.

Additional Reference Sources

1181 Directory of apparel specialty stores.
Chain Store Guide Information Services, CSG Information Services. Tampa, Fla.: Business Guides, 1997– ISSN 1092-4442
381.45687029473   HD9940.U3

Entries for retailers with a minimum of $500,000 in annual sales. Arranged by category (women's, men's, children's, and family apparel, accessory retailers, sporting goods retailers, and resident buyers). Provides contact information, year founded, total sales, product sales, number of units, trade names, total selling square feet, average check-outs, product lines carried, apparel price lines, key personnel, and geographic areas of operation. Indexed by product, name of company, and exclusion. Also available in online form.

1182 Directory of department stores. Chain Store Guide Information Services. Tampa, Fla.: Business Guides, 1998–. ill.
ISSN 1097-7023
381/.142/02573   HF5465.U3

Lists companies with a minimum $250,000 sales volume, including department stores, shoe stores, jewelry stores, leather/luggage stores, and optical stores.

Listings give contact information, year founded, total sales, breakdown of type of sales (footwear, apparel, etc.), customer sales (breakdown of sales channels, internet, catalog, retail), private label, internet orders, mail order, catalog names, total units, trade names, total selling square feet, average check outs, product lines, price lines, areas of operation, and key personnel. Also lists resident buyers, with contact information, stores served, and key personnel representing those stores. Available in online form.

1183 The Fairchild dictionary of retailing.
2nd ed. Rona Ostrow. New York: Fairchild Publications, 2009. viii, 471 p.
ISBN 9781563673443
658.87003   HF5415

Defines some 10,000 terms in alphabetical order, updating the 1st edition of 1985 (as *Dictionary of Retailing*). Reflects innovations in online e-commerce, consumer and market research, distribution, and marketing. Bibliography includes Web resources.

1184 Feet and footwear: a cultural encyclopedia. Margo DeMello. Santa Barbara, Calif.: Greenwood Press/ ABC-CLIO, 2009. xxii, 360 p., ill.
ISBN 9780313357145
391.4/1303   GT2130

Contains 165 entries in alphabetical order, with cross-references and suggestions for further reading. Provides historical and cultural context, with coverage of local customs, mythology, health issues, marketing and shoe brands, and shoes in the media. Bibliography and resource guide. Index. Available as an e-book.

1185 Hoovers. http://www.hoovers.com/.
Reference Press, Hoover's, Inc. Short Hills, N.J.: Dun & Bradstreet. 1996–
338.7   HG4057

More than 60 million records describe public and private companies primarily in the United States, but including Canada, United Kingdom, Europe, and Asia/Pacific. Profiles have an overview, history, family tree, industry information, products/operations, top competitors, competitive landscape, top executives with biographies, news, significant developments, and financial data. Financial summaries may include an income statement; balance sheet; cash flow; historical financials such as five years of P/E and per share; stock quotes; interactive stock charts; market data; earnings estimates; this year's ratios for the company, industry, and market; SEC filings; and industry watch for trends.

Content is tracked for 900 industries, organized into numerous larger categories: Agriculture & Forestry; Arts, Entertainment & Recreation; Beverage Manufacturing; Biotechnology Product Manufacturing; Business Services; Chemical Manufacturing; Commercial Equipment Repair & Maintenance; Commercial Printing; Computer Hardware Manufacturing; Computer Software; Construction; Consumer Products Manufacturing; Consumer Services; Contract Electronics Manufacturing; Education; Electric Power Generation; Electric Power Transmission, Distribution & Marketing; Electric Utilities; Electrical Products Manufacturing; Fabricated Metal Product Manufacturing; Financial Services; Food Manufacturing; Government; Health Care Products Manufacturing; Health Care; HVAC Equipment Manufacturing; Industrial Manufacturing; Insurance; Leasing of Intangible Assets; Lodging; Machinery Manufacturing; Magnetic & Optical Media; Manufacturing & Reproduction; Managed Application & Network Services; Management of Companies & Enterprises; Media; Membership Organizations; Mining; Miscellaneous Manufacturing; Natural Gas Distribution & Marketing; Nonclassifiable establishments; Nonmetallic Mineral Product Manufacturing; Nonprofit Institutions; Oil & Gas Exploration & Production; Oil & Gas Field Services; Oil & Gas Well Drilling; Petroleum & Coal Products Manufacturing; Pharmaceutical Manufacturing; Primary Metals Manufacturing; Private Households; Professional Services; Real Estate; Religious Organizations; Rental & Leasing; Restaurants, Bars & Food Services; Retail; Security Products Manufacturing; Semiconductor & Other Electronic Component Manufacturing; Telecommunications Equipment Manufacturing; Telecommunications Services; Transportation Equipment Manufacturing; Transportation Services; Water & Sewer Utilities; Wholesale; and Wood Product Manufacturing.

Coverage can be brief, but generally includes a fact sheet, overview, selected companies, industry watch with video interviews, news from the last 90 days, and web resources for terminology, associations, and organizations, and online publications. Hoover's print publications include (*Hoover's handbook of American business* (876), *Hoover's handbook of private companies* (855)).

1186 The retail market research yearbook. Richard K. Miller and Associates. Loganville, Ga.: Richard K. Miller and Associates, 2005– 381 p. ISSN 1930-966X

An overview of the retail market, with information on companies, consumers, and resources for each retail industry segment. Chapters include: Market summary; Current and future trends; Industry profile; Department stores; Discount stores and supercenters; Warehouse clubs; Supermarkets; Variety and dollar stores; Drug stores; Apparel; Footwear; Jewelry; Health, beauty, and cosmetics; Consumer electronics; Home decor and furnishings; Home centers and hardware; Housewares and home textiles; Book stores; Music and video; Office products; Sporting goods; Toys and video games; Pet supplies; Crafts and fabrics; Photography; Closeout and off-price chains; Convenience stores; Military post exchanges; Resale and thrift stores; E-commerce; Catalog and mail-order retail; Television home shopping; Christmas holiday shopping; Back-to-school; Holiday markets; and The bridal and wedding market.

1187 RN and WPL encyclopedia. Salesman's Guide, Inc. New York: Salesman's Guide, 1984– ISSN 1526-3851

338.768702573   HD9940.U3

Over 121,500 entries for registered numbers (RN's) and wool product labels (WPL's) for over 31,500 U.S. textile manufacturers. Gives name of manufacturer and contact information.

Telecommunications

Specialized Sources of Industry Data

1188 Hoovers. http://www.hoovers.com/. Reference Press, Hoover's, Inc. Short Hills, N.J.: Dun & Bradstreet. 1996–

338.7   HG4057

More than 60 million records describe public and private companies primarily in the United States, but including Canada, United Kingdom, Europe, and Asia/Pacific. Profiles have an overview, history, family tree, industry information, products/operations, top competitors, competitive landscape, top executives with biographies, news, significant developments, and financial data. Financial summaries may include an income statement; balance sheet; cash flow; historical financials such as five years of P/E and per share; stock quotes; interactive stock charts; market data; earnings estimates; this year's ratios for the company, industry, and market; SEC filings; and industry watch for trends.

Content is tracked for 900 industries, organized into numerous larger categories: Agriculture & Forestry; Arts, Entertainment & Recreation; Beverage Manufacturing; Biotechnology Product Manufacturing; Business Services; Chemical Manufacturing; Commercial Equipment Repair & Maintenance; Commercial Printing; Computer Hardware Manufacturing; Computer Software; Construction; Consumer Products Manufacturing; Consumer Services; Contract Electronics Manufacturing; Education; Electric Power Generation; Electric Power Transmission, Distribution & Marketing; Electric Utilities; Electrical Products Manufacturing; Fabricated Metal Product Manufacturing; Financial Services; Food Manufacturing; Government; Health Care Products Manufacturing; Health Care; HVAC Equipment Manufacturing; Industrial Manufacturing; Insurance; Leasing of Intangible Assets; Lodging; Machinery Manufacturing; Magnetic & Optical Media; Manufacturing & Reproduction; Managed Application & Network Services; Management of Companies & Enterprises; Media; Membership Organizations; Mining; Miscellaneous Manufacturing; Natural Gas Distribution & Marketing; Nonclassifiable establishments; Nonmetallic Mineral Product Manufacturing; Nonprofit Institutions; Oil & Gas Exploration & Production; Oil & Gas Field Services; Oil & Gas Well Drilling; Petroleum & Coal Products Manufacturing; Pharmaceutical Manufacturing; Primary Metals Manufacturing; Private Households; Professional Services; Real Estate; Religious Organizations; Rental & Leasing; Restaurants, Bars & Food Services; Retail; Security Products Manufacturing; Semiconductor & Other Electronic Component Manufacturing; Telecommunications Equipment Manufacturing; Telecommunications Services; Transportation Equipment Manufacturing; Transportation Services; Water & Sewer Utilities; Wholesale; and Wood Product Manufacturing.

Coverage can be brief, but generally includes a fact sheet, overview, selected companies, industry watch with video interviews, news from the last 90 days, and web resources for terminology, associations, and organizations, and online publications. Hoover's print publications include (*Hoover's*

handbook of American business (876), *Hoover's handbook of private companies* (855)).

1189 Plunkett's telecommunications industry almanac. Jack W. Plunkett. Houston, Tex.: Plunkett Research, 2000–
ISSN 1550-4514
384.025   HE7621

Data on nearly 500 leading companies, from large international corporations like Siemens AG to small private companies like Go Daddy Group. Company profiles include types of business, brands and affiliates, contacts, employee benefits and top salaries, sales and profit numbers, growth plans, and competitive advantage. Especially useful for the industry trends, statistics and rankings at the front of the volume (the baby bells: then and now, U.S. telecommunications firms-estimated revenue and expenses 2001–2004, U.S. telecommunications equipment export and import 2000–2005, U.S. telecommunications industry employment 1996–2005, average annual household telecommunications expenditures by type of provider: 1995–2005, cellular wireless speeds compared by standard, CTIA 12-month U.S. wireless industry survey results: 1985–2005, U.S. wireless telecom carriers except satellite, estimated revenue and expenses: 2001–2004, North American cable internet subscribers, U.S. cable networks-estimated revenues and expenses: 2001–2004, number of high speed internet lines, U.S.: 2000–2006, internet access technologies compared), and information on the main associations and organizations in the back of the volume. Most information is for the U.S., but some international coverage is provided. Available as an e-book.

1190 Standard and Poor's industry surveys. Standard and Poor's. New York: Standard and Poor's, 1973–2012 ISSN 0196-4666
332.67   HC106.6

Detailed analyses of 22 industry categories and the major companies in each category. Contains a basic analysis and a comprehensive source of information, updated by a current analysis. The analysis includes trends, information on how the industry operates, key ratios and statistics (revenues, net income, profit ratios, balance sheet ratios, equity ratios, per-share data, company and product rankings), information on how to analyze a company in that industry, and a glossary. Company and industry indexes. Ceased with edition of 2012.

1191   SPECIALIZED INDUSTRY INFORMATION

Organizations and Associations

1191 CTIA. http://www.ctia.org/. Cellular Telecommunications Industry Association. Washington: CTIA.org. 2007–

Home page of the Cellular Telecommunications Industry Association, founded in 1984 to represent "all sectors of wireless communications—cellular, personal communication services and enhanced specialized mobile radio." —*About us*. The website is divided into six sections: Media (press releases, industry info, publications, multimedia library), Advocacy (policy topics, position papers, FCC filings, research, federal and state affairs), Consumer Info, Membership, Conventions and Events, and Business Resources (Wireless Internet Caucus, certification, common short code, industry directory, career center). Most useful for the industry statistics (total number of wireless subscribers, roaming revenues, average monthly bill, number of U.S. cell sites) and glossary.

1192 FCC.gov. http://www.fcc.gov/. Federal Communications Commission. Washington: Federal Communications Commission. 2007

Home page for the Federal Communications Commission, founded in 1923 to regulate interstate and international communications, now including radio, television, wire, satellite and cable. The website contains a treasure trove of information, including reports, statistics, trends, rules and regulations, and more. Examples include annual reports on cable industry prices, periodic reviews of the radio industry, the statistics of communications common carriers, statistical trends in telephony, local and long distance telephone industries, local telephone competition and broadband deployment, telephone industry infrastructure and service quality, federal-state joint board monitoring reports, telephone numbering facts, and international traffic data. The "FCC Consumer Publications Library" on the Web site provides printable articles about broadcasting, telephone service, privacy issues and other consumer-oriented topics.

1193 International telecommunication union. http://www.itu.int/. International Telecommunication Union, Répertoire des fréquences. Genève [Geneva, Switzerland]: International Telecommunication Union. 1997–

HE7601

Home page of ITU, a trade association focusing on radio communications, standardization, and development in the information and communication technology industry. Their website has news, events, and publications. Recent publications include: *ITU internet reports 2006: digital.life*; *World information society report*; *World telecommunication standardization assembly*; *Measuring the information society ICT opportunity index and world telecommunication/ICT indicators*; *Radio regulations*; and *Telecommunications industry at a glance*. Most publications are available for a fee, but often a free executive summary is provided online.

1194 Telecommunications industry association. http://www.tiaonline.org/. Telecommunications Industry Association. Arlington, Va.: Telecommunications Industry Association. 1997–
384/.041   HD9696.T443

Home page for advocacy organization, founded in 1924, to promote the information, communications, and entertainment technology industries. Website has information on standards, numbering resources (Electronic Serial Number Assignment, Mobile Equipment IDentifier, System Operator Code), publications (*Industry Playbook* and *Technology and Policy Primer*, letters, filings, policy trackers, legislative-regulatory call agendas), Market Review and Forecast (available for a fee), news, events, and a section for members only.

Additional Reference Sources

1195 Desktop encyclopedia of telecommunications. 3rd ed. Nathan J. Muller. New York: McGraw-Hill, 2002. xx, 1250 p., ill. ISBN 0071381481
621.38203   TK5102.M85

Written for nontechnical professionals, the *Encyclopedia* explains local and wide-area networking, equipment and services, network applications, regulations, standards, industry trends, and covers industry organizations. Articles can be thorough, with information on the evolution of a technology or a regulation. The second edition is available as an e-book through NetLibrary.

236

1196 Encyclopedia of wireless telecommunications. Francis Botto. Boston: McGraw-Hill, 2002. 1 v. (various pagings), ill. ISBN 9780071390255

621.38203   TK5103.2

While no print source can keep up with the pace of technological advances, this source provides a solid background on architectures, devices and handsets, free space communications technology, globalization, infrastructure, LAN technologies, local communication technologies (Bluetooth, Piano, IrDA, etc.), principles of radio and light, services and products, e-business, and standards and protocols.

1197 FACCTS. http://www.faulkner.com/ showcase/faccts.htm. Faulkner Information Services. Pennsauken, N.J.: Faulkner Information Services. 1995– ISSN 1082-7471

005   QA76.753

Over 1,200 reports on trends, issues, market conditions, implementation guides, companies, products, and services in information technology. Arranged into 14 categories: enterprise data networking, broadband, information security, electronic government, electronic business, content management, IT asset management, application development, Web site management, converging communications, telecom and global network services, mobile business strategies, wireless communications, and Internet strategies. Especially useful for the up-to-date technology trend reports. Also from this publisher: *Faulkner's advisory for IT studies (FAITS)*.

1198 The Irwin handbook of telecommunications. 5th ed. James H. Green. New York: McGraw-Hill, 2006. xxxviii, 770 p., ill. ISBN 9780071452229

621.382   TK5102.3.U6

Serves almost as a textbook for telecommunications, with background information, trends, definitions, and applications for telecommunications. Parts of the book include: Principles of telecommunications, Switching systems, Transmission technologies, Customer premise systems, Telecommunications networks. Appendix A: Telecommunications acronym dictionary; Appendix B: Glossary. Bibliography. Available as an e-book.

1199 Major telecommunications companies of the world. Graham & Whiteside Ltd. Farmington Hills, Mich.: Gale Cengage, 1998– ISSN 1369-5460

384.043025   HE7621

Annual. Entries for 3,500 companies from around the world, giving contact information, executives' names, principal activities, parent company, subsidiaries, status (public/private), number of employees, and principal shareholders. Includes companies in the cellular and internet markets. Useful for libraries that do not have good international business directories.

1200 Passport GMID. http://www.euromonitor .com/. Euromonitor International. London, U.K.: Euromonitor International. [1999–]

658.8   HF5415.2

Also known under previous product names as *Global market information database, GMID*, or *Euromonitor GMID*. Market reports, company profiles, and demographic, economic, and marketing statistics for 205 countries. Market reports are for 16 consumer markets (food and drink, tobacco, toys, etc.) and 14 industrial and service markets (accountancy, broadcasting, chemicals, property services, etc.).

Reports have market size, market sectors, share of market, marketing activity, research and development, corporate overview, distribution, consumer profiles, market forecasts, sector forecasts, sources, and definitions. Additional reports are available for market segments, such as baby food. Company profiles have background, recent news, competitve environment, and outlook. Consumer lifestyle reports and very useful marketing background analyze the consumer by country, gender, age, marital status, educational attainment, ethnicity, religion, home ownership, household profile, employment, income, health, eating and personal grooming habits, leisure activities, personal finance, communication, transport, and travel.

Search for data, which can be exported into Excel or browse for reports. Data are available since 1977 and include inflation, exchange rates, GDP, GNI, government expenditures, government finance, income, labor, and money supply.

Similar information on a smaller scale is available in Research monitor (783) from the same publisher.

Transportation

Specialized Sources of Industry Data

1201 Aerospace facts and figures. Aerospace Industries Association of America, Aerospace Research Center. Los Angeles: Aero Publishers, 1945–2009. ill.
ISSN 0898-4425
629.105   TL501
Includes sections for aerospace summary, aircraft production (sales, orders, production), missile programs (orders, sales, outlays), space programs (orders, sales, outlays), air transportation (operating expenses, revenues, traffic and passenger statistics, jet fuels costs and consumption, air cargo statistics), research and development (federal outlays, Department of Defense outlays), foreign trade (U.S. imports and exports), employment and finance (income statement, balance sheet, operating ratios, capital expenditures). Data are drawn from both government and commercial sources. Ceased with edition of 2009. Succeeded by *Aerospace industry report*.

1202 The airline encyclopedia, 1909–2000. Myron J. Smith. Lanham, Md.: Scarecrow Press, 2002. 3 v., ill.
ISBN 9780810837904
387.703   HEISBN 9780
Provides operational and statistical information for global airlines companies. More than 6,000 company profiles in alphabetical order, ranging in length from a few lines to several pages. Indicates contact information, ownership, aircraft flown and historical developments. Useful for finding historic information on international companies, details about terrorist episodes and in-flight crime, accidents and incidents, natural disasters, and literary or film references. Appendices include a list of acronyms and abbreviations, and a list of sources. Regional index of carriers by continent and nation, showing years of operation. Name and subject index, including detailed entries for incidents, skyjackings and crashes by exact date and carrier, lists of firsts, and a list of major strikes.

1203 Census of transportation. United States Dept. of Commerce, Bureau of the Census. Washington: U.S. Dept. of Commerce, Bureau of the Census, 1963–2003. 54 v.
380.50973   HE203.C44
Includes the results of the truck inventory and use survey, commodity transportation survey, vehicle inventory and use survey, and national travel survey. Begun in 1963 and continued through data of 1997 (published in 2003). Information is now part of the *Economic Census*). The Economic Census from 1977 to 2007 is available online at http://www.census.gov/prod/www/economic_census.html.

1204 Data and statistics: Bureau of Transportation Statistics. http://www.rita.dot.gov/bts/data_and_statistics/index.html. Research and Innovative Technology Administration (RITA). Washington: U.S. Department of Transportation. 2013–
380   HE202.5
Portal to extensive series of websites covering transportation statistics by mode (such as airline, highway, maritime and rail), region (international, U. S. national, state and local), and subject (such as energy and environment, traffic congestion, freight and passenger, safety, and infrastructure). Points to resources on websites of other U.S. government agencies.

1205 IBISWorld United States. http://www.ibisworld.com/. IBISWorld. New York: IBISWorld. 1999–
                                HC103
700 reports on American industries. Industry reports can be located using NAICS numbers. Major categories include: Accommodation & Food Services; Administration, Business Support & Waste Management Services; Agriculture, Forestry, Fishing & Hunting; Arts, Entertainment & Recreation; Construction; Educational Services; Finance & Insurance; Healthcare & Social Assistance; Information; Manufacturing; Mining; Other Services (except Public Administration); Professional, Scientific & Technical Services; Real Estate & Rental and Leasing; Retail Trade; Transportation & Warehousing; Utilities; and Wholesale Trade.

Reports include industry definition; information about the supply chain; key statistics; segmentations (products and services segmentation, major market segments, industry concentration, geographic spread); market characteristics (market size, demand determinants, domestic and international markets, basis of competition, life cycle); industry conditions (barriers to entry, taxation, industry assistance, regulation and deregulation, cost structure, capital and labor intensity, technology and systems, industry volatility, globalization); key factors (sensitivities and success factors); key competitors; and industry performance (current and historical). Glossaries and guides to jargon. Setting this database apart are reports on small industries, such as parking lots and garages.

1206 National transportation library. http:// ntl.bts.gov/. Research and Innovative Technology Administration (RITA). Washington: U.S. Dept. of Transportation. 1998–

Provides links to many government transportation resources, including a State Department of Transportation (DOT) Google search, TRB Research in Progress (RIP) Database, International Transport Research Documentation (ITRD) Database, National Technical Information Service Database (indexes government-funded documents published since 1990), TranStats (statistical data), Rural and Agricultural Transportation: Data & Information Resources, as well as resources the library created (bibliographies, Transportation Libraries Directory, and information about their reference service).

1207 National transportation safety board. http://www.ntsb.gov/. U.S. National Transportation Safety Board. Washington: National Transportation Safety Board. 2007

TE153.N364

The NTSB examines the safety of aviation, highways, marine, pipeline and hazardous materials, railroad, and transportation disaster assistance, and issues reports and recommendations. Reports include Accident Reports, Annual Review of Aircraft Accident Data, reports in the Aviation Accident Database, Legal Matters, and Opinions & Orders. Some online reports date back to the early 1970s.

1208 Plunkett's airline, hotel, and travel industry almanac. Jack W. Plunkett. Houston, Tex.: Plunkett Research, 2002–. ill. ISSN 1554-1215

387.7   HE9803.A2

Data on more than 300 major companies, both public and private: airlines, bus companies, resort chains,

car rentals and more. Company profiles include types of business, brands and affiliates, contacts, employee benefits and top salaries, sales and profit numbers, growth plans, and competitive advantage. Especially useful for the industry trends, statistics and rankings (forecasts to 2032, top destinations worldwide, top airlines, top tourism nations, etc.) at the front of the volume and information on the main associations and organizations in the back of the volume. Most information is for the U.S., but some international coverage is provided. Available as an e-book.

1209 Plunkett's transportation, supply chain, and logistics industry almanac. Jack W. Plunkett. Houston, Tex.: Plunkett Research, 2004–. ill.

HE9.U5

Data on nearly 500 leading companies, from large international corporations like DaimlerChrysler AG to privately held companies like Amtrak. Company profiles include types of business, brands and affiliates, contacts, employee benefits and top salaries, sales and profit numbers, growth plans, and competitive advantage. Especially useful for the industry trends, statistics and rankings at the front of the volume (Transportation services index: 1992–2005, Top countries for U.S. exports and imports: 2000–2005, U.S. surface trade with Canada and Mexico, U.S. aviation forecasts: 2004–2015, U.S. airline passenger activity: 1998–2015, U.S. airline yearly operating financials: 1999–Q1 2005, Domestic air freight capacity utilization: 1992–2005, U.S. foreign waterborne freight: 1998–2005, Amtrak ridership: 1992–2005, Rail freight revenue ton miles: 1992–2005), and information on the main associations and organizations in the back of the volume. Most information is for the U.S., but some international coverage is provided. Available as an e-book.

1210 Public transportation fact book. American Public Transit Association. Washington: American Public Transit Association, 1950–. ill., charts, diagrs., tables ISSN 0149-3132

388.40973   HE4441

Includes aggregate data for all transit systems in the U.S. and summary data for Canadian transit. Includes an overview of transit facts and issues, a profile of U.S. transit, financial information (capital expenses and funds, operating expenses and funds), employees, ridership and transit usage, and a section on energy and the environment. Glossary and index. Current year's edition is available online from APTA at http://www .apta.com/resources/statistics/Documents/FactBook.

1211 Railroad facts. Association of American Railroads. Washington: Office of Information and Public Affairs, Association of American Railroads, 1983–. ill. ISSN 0742-1850

385.0973   HE2713

Annual. Continues *Yearbook of railroad facts* (1965–82). Summary of railroad operations throughout the year. Includes statistics on finance, operations, plant and equipment, employment and compensation, fuel consumption and costs. Also profiles major U.S. railroads, Amtrak, the two largest railroads in Canada, and the two largest railways in Mexico.

1212 Shipping statistics and market review. Institut für Seeverkehrswirtschaft und -Logistik. Bremen, Germany: Institute of Shipping Economics and Logistics, 1957– ISSN 0947-0220

387.544021   HE561

Provides an overview of the shipping and shipbuilding industry, with information on supply and demand, freight rates, ports, and traffic. Organized into three sections: market review, statistical topics, and market analysis. Also available in online format.

1213 Standard and Poor's industry surveys. Standard and Poor's. New York: Standard and Poor's, 1973–2012 ISSN 0196-4666

332.67   HC106.6

Detailed analyses of 22 industry categories and the major companies in each category. Contains a basic analysis and a comprehensive source of information, updated by a current analysis. The analysis includes trends, information on how the industry operates, key ratios and statistics (revenues, net income, profit ratios, balance sheet ratios, equity ratios, per-share data, company and product rankings), information on how to analyze a company in that industry, and a glossary. Company and industry indexes. Ceased with edition of 2012.

1214 Transportation statistics annual report. http://www.bts.gov/publications/ transportation_statistics_annual_report/.

Bureau of Transportation Statistics. Washington: Bureau of Transportation Statistics, U.S. Dept. of Transportation. 1994– ISSN 1932-3700

380   HE202.5

Presents transportation indicators and statistics. Covers traffic flows (passenger border crossings, Amtrak station boardings, domestic freight ton-miles, etc.), condition of the transportation system (highways, bridges, airport runways, transit fleet vehicles, and rail, aircraft, and maritime vessel fleets), accidents (fatalities and injuries by means of transportation), variables influencing traveling behavior (travel time, vehicle availability, distance, income, ethnicity), travel times, availability of mass transit and number of passengers served, travel costs of intracity commuting and intercity trips, productivity in the transportation sector, transportation and economic growth, government transportation finance (revenues, expenditures, investment, subsidies), transportation-related variables that influence global competitiveness, frequency of vehicle and transportation facility repairs, vehicle weights, transportation energy, and collateral damage to the human and natural environment. Data is normally for one year or ten years. All reports since 1994 are available online.

Organizations and Associations

1215 International air transport association. http://www.iata.org/. International Air Transport Association. Geneva, Switzerland: International Air Transport Association. 1996–

387.70601   HE9761.1

Home page of the international trade group representing some 240 airlines carrying passengers and cargo. Recent editions of *IATA's annual review* are posted online in PDF, with statistics about the previous year, a chapter on the state of the industry, and indication of trends and issues. A primary focus for IATA is safety procedures, now including security, and associated regulations.

1216 National transportation safety board. http://www.ntsb.gov/. U.S. National Transportation Safety Board. Washington: National Transportation Safety Board. 2007

TE153.N364

The NTSB examines the safety of aviation, highways, marine, pipeline and hazardous materials, railroad, and transportation disaster assistance, and issues reports and recommendations. Reports include Accident Reports, Annual Review of Aircraft Accident Data, reports in the Aviation Accident Database, Legal Matters, and Opinions & Orders. Some online reports date back to the early 1970s.

Internet Resources

1217 Data and statistics: Bureau of Transportation Statistics. http://www .rita.dot.gov/bts/data_and_statistics/index .html. Research and Innovative Technology Administration (RITA). Washington: U.S. Department of Transportation. 2013–
380   HE202.5
Portal to extensive series of websites covering transportation statistics by mode (such as airline, highway, maritime and rail), region (international, U. S. national, state and local), and subject (such as energy and environment, traffic congestion, freight and passenger, safety, and infrastructure). Points to resources on websites of other U.S. government agencies.

1218 National transportation library. http:// ntl.bts.gov/. Research and Innovative Technology Administration (RITA). Washington: U.S. Dept. of Transportation. 1998–
Provides links to many government transportation resources, including a State Department of Transportation (DOT) Google search, TRB Research in Progress (RIP) Database, International Transport Research Documentation (ITRD) Database, National Technical Information Service Database (indexes government-funded documents published since 1990), TranStats (statistical data), Rural and Agricultural Transportation: Data & Information Resources, as well as resources the library created (bibliographies, Transportation Libraries Directory, and information about their reference service).

1219 Transport research international documentation: TRID. http://trid.trb .org/. Tranportation Research Board. Washington: National Academy of Sciences. 2011–
                                       HE151

Bibliographic database covering more than one million worldwide publications about transportation research, with indexing, abstracts, and some URLs for full text. Formed in 2011 by merger of the Transportation Research Board's *Transportation research information services* (TRIS) database with OECD's Joint Transport Research Centre's *International transport research documentation* (ITRD) database. Sponsored by the National Academy of Sciences, the National Academy of Engineering, the Institute of Medicine, and the National Research Council.

1220 TRIS online. http://www.trb.org/ InformationServices/InformationServices .aspx. National Transportation Library (U.S.), National Research Council (U.S.). Washington: National Transport Library, Bureau of Transportation Statistics and Transportation Research Board. [1999?–]
                                       HE151
Index of over half a million technical reports, books, websites, and articles on transportation. Covers aviation, economics and finance, energy and environment, freight, geographic information services, highway/road transportation, intelligent transportation systems, laws and regulations, maritime/waterways, operations and traffic control, pedestrians and bicycles, planning and policy, public transportation, rail transportation, references and directories, and safety and security.

Additional Reference Sources

1221 Directory of United States exporters. New York: Journal of Commerce, 1990–2010 ISSN 1057-6878
                                   HF3011.D63
Describes U.S. cargo shippers and the products they export. Gives contact information, SIC code, top executives, TEU's (twenty-foot equivalent unit container size) and metric tonnage, estimated value, ports of exit, and products. Arranged by state and indexed by company and product (uses Harmonized Commodity Codes). Also provides contact information for: export assistance centers, U.S. and foreign commercial service international posts, trade commissions, foreign embassies and consulates, U.S. foreign trade zones, world ports, and banks and other financial services. Companion to *Directory of United States importers* (852). Ceased with edition of 2010.

1222 Directory of United States importers.
Journal of Commerce, Inc. New York:
Journal of Commerce, 1991–2010. ill.
ISSN 1057-5111
382.502573   HF3012.D53
A geographical listing of importers to the U.S., indexed
by products (Harmonized Commodity Codes) and
industry [Standard Industrial Classification (SIC)
codes]. Gives contact information, SIC code, top
executives, TEU's (Twenty-foot Equivalent Unit container size) and metric tonnage, estimated value, ports
of exit, and products. Also provides contact information for: trade commissions, foreign embassies and
consulates in the U.S., U.S. foreign trade zones, world
ports, and banks and other financial services. Companion to the *Directory of United States exporters* (851).
Ceased with the edition of 2010.

1223 Glossary of transport: English,
French, Italian, Dutch, German,
Swedish. Gordon Logie. Amsterdam, The
Netherlands; New York: Elsevier Scientific,
1980. xxvii, 296 p. ISBN 9780444417312
380.503   HE141
Gives equivalent terms in the broad subject areas
of transport and transportation studies, roads and
road traffic, parking and road vehicles, railways,
waterborne transport, and aviation. Indexes in all six
languages.

1224 Handbook of transportation science.
2nd ed. Randolph W. Hall. Boston:
Kluwer Academic Publishers, 2003. vi,
741 p., ill. ISBN 9781402072468
388   HE192.5
Provides information on transportation fundamen-
tals. Includes: human elements in transportation,
flows and congestion, spatial models, routing and
network models, and economic models. Each chapter contains a lengthy list of references. Available as
an e-book.

1225 Harris U.S. manufacturers directory.
National ed. Harris InfoSource, National
Association of Manufacturers (U.S.).
Twinsburg, Ohio: Harris InfoSource,
2000– ISSN 1531-8273
338   HF5035
Entries for U.S. companies include location, contact
information, industry descriptions, Standard Industrial

Classification (SIC) or NAICS codes, executive names,
and size. Indexed by company name, geography,
product or service category, and SIC code. Libraries
receiving questions about local companies may want
to invest in the regional and state directories also published by Harris. Regional editions are published for
the Northeast, Southeast, Midwest, and West. Available in an online version.

1226 Hoovers. http://www.hoovers.com/.
Reference Press, Hoover's, Inc. Short Hills,
N.J.: Dun & Bradstreet. 1996–
338.7   HG4057
More than 60 million records describe public and
private companies primarily in the United States, but
including Canada, United Kingdom, Europe, and
Asia/Pacific. Profiles have an overview, history, family tree, industry information, products/operations,
top competitors, competitive landscape, top executives with biographies, news, significant developments, and financial data. Financial summaries may
include an income statement; balance sheet; cash
flow; historical financials such as five years of P/E
and per share; stock quotes; interactive stock charts;
market data; earnings estimates; this year's ratios for
the company, industry, and market; SEC filings; and
industry watch for trends.

Content is tracked for 900 industries, organized
into numerous larger categories: Agriculture & Forestry; Arts, Entertainment & Recreation; Beverage
Manufacturing; Biotechnology Product Manufac-
turing; Business Services; Chemical Manufacturing;
Commercial Equipment Repair & Maintenance;
Commercial Printing; Computer Hardware Manufacturing; Computer Software; Construction; Consumer
Products Manufacturing; Consumer Services; Contract Electronics Manufacturing; Education; Electric
Power Generation; Electric Power Transmission, Dis-
tribution & Marketing; Electric Utilities; Electrical
Products Manufacturing; Fabricated Metal Product
Manufacturing; Financial Services; Food Manufactur-
ing; Government; Health Care Products Manufactur-
ing; Health Care; HVAC Equipment Manufacturing;
Industrial Manufacturing; Insurance; Leasing of
Intangible Assets; Lodging; Machinery Manufactur-
ing; Magnetic & Optical Media; Manufacturing &
Reproduction; Managed Application & Network
Services; Management of Companies & Enterprises;
Media; Membership Organizations; Mining; Miscel-
laneous Manufacturing; Natural Gas Distribution

& Marketing; Nonclassifiable establishments; Non-metallic Mineral Product Manufacturing; Nonprofit Institutions; Oil & Gas Exploration & Production; Oil & Gas Field Services; Oil & Gas Well Drilling; Petroleum & Coal Products Manufacturing; Pharmaceutical Manufacturing; Primary Metals Manufacturing; Private Households; Professional Services; Real Estate; Religious Organizations; Rental & Leasing; Restaurants, Bars & Food Services; Retail; Security Products Manufacturing; Semiconductor & Other Electronic Component Manufacturing; Telecommunications Equipment Manufacturing; Telecommunications Services; Transportation Equipment Manufacturing; Transportation Services; Water & Sewer Utilities; Wholesale; and Wood Product Manufacturing.

Coverage can be brief, but generally includes a fact sheet, overview, selected companies, industry watch with video interviews, news from the last 90 days, and web resources for terminology, associations, and organizations, and online publications. Hoover's print publications include (*Hoover's handbook of American business* (876), *Hoover's handbook of private companies* (855)).

1227 Lloyd's maritime directory. Lloyd's of
London Press. Colchester, Essex, U.K.:
Lloyd's of London Press, 1982–. ill.
ISSN 0268-327X
387.2025   HE951

Annual. Lists shippers, shipowners, towage, salvage, ship management services, builders, and repairers worldwide. Gives contact information, main personnel, services, and repair facilities.

1228 Register of ships. IHS Fairplay.
Redhill, Surrey, [U.K.]: IHS Fairplay,
2011–. 4 v.
                            HE565.A3

Successor to the Lloyd's publication, Register of ships (1229). Covers all sea-going, self-propelled merchant ships of 100 gross tons and above. For 100,000 vessels, provides current name and former names, ship identification numbers including LR/IMO number, ship types, cargo facilities, builder and date of build, owner and manager, registration, flag and classification, tonnage and dimensions, main and auxiliary machinery details, and call sign and official number. Supplemented by *Shipfinder online*.

1229 Register of ships. Lloyd's Register
of Shipping. London: Lloyd's Register
of Shipping, 1966–2010
ISSN 0141-4909
623.82405   HE565.A3

Published under varying titles since 1760 and by Lloyd's since 1834. Merged with *Underwriters' registry for iron vessels* in 1885. Ceased with edition of 2009/2010, and succeeded by Register of ships (1228) from IHS Fairplay. Recent issues in four or more volumes, with some variation in contents. The "Register of ships" gives the names, classes, and general information concerning the ships classed by Lloyd's register, together with particulars of all known ocean-going merchant ships in the world of 100 tons gross and upwards. It also lists lighters carried on board ship, floating docks, liquefied gas carriers, ships carrying refrigerated cargo, refrigerated cargo containers, refrigerated stores and container terminals, and offshore drilling rigs. The "Register" is updated by means of cumulative monthly supplements containing the latest survey records for all classed ships, and changes of name, ownership, flag, tonnage, etc., for all ships, whether classed or not. The "Shipowners" section gives a list of owners and managers of the ships recorded in the "Register" with their fleets, as well as lists of former and compound names of ships. An appendix contains a list of shipbuilders with existing ships they have built, marine engine builders and boilermakers, dry and wet docks, telegraphic addresses and codes used by shipping firms, marine insurance companies and marine associations.

**1230 Supply chain and transportation
dictionary. 4th ed.** Joseph L.
Cavinato. Norwell, Mass.: Kluwer
Academic, 2000. vii, 398 p.
ISBN 9780792384441
388.04403   HF5761

Over 5,000 short definitions on supply chain management, transportation, distribution, logistics, material, and purchasing. Appendixes for transportation rates; standard abbreviations; key word translations; 1990 INCO terms; official two letter postal codes, U.S. and Canada; official internet codes; world times; and metric conversion factors.

Utilities and Energy

Specialized Sources of Industry Data

1231 Basic petroleum data book. American
Petroleum Institute (API). Washington:
American Petroleum Institute, 1981–
ISSN 0730-5621
338.2728021   HD9564

Worldwide petroleum statistics since 1947. No published twice a year. Provides "historical data on energy, reserves, exploration and drilling, production, finance, prices, demand, refining, imports, exports, offshore transportation, natural gas and the Organization of Petroleum Exporting Countries (OPEC)." Includes a glossary and source list.

1232 BP statistical review of world energy.
http://www.bp.com/statisticalreview.
British Petroleum. London: BP. 1999–
333.79   HD9560.4

Successor to the annual print series. Web site with graphics and a link to download the current edition in PDF. Information, analysis, and historical data on energy markets worldwide. Organized into five parts: group chief executives introduction; 2005 in review; review by energy type (oil, natural gas, coal, nuclear energy, hydroelectricity, primary energy, renewable energy, and electricity); downloads; using the review; and energy charting tool.

Historical data include oil: proved reserves; oil: proved reserves—barrels (from 1980); oil: production—barrels (from 1965); oil: production—tonnes (from 1965); oil: consumption—barrels (from 1965); oil: consumption—tonnes (from 1965); oil: regional consumption—by product group (from 1965); oil: spot crude prices; oil: crude prices since 1861; oil: refinery capacities (from 1965); oil: refinery throughputs (from 1980); oil: regional refining margins (from 1992); oil: trade movements (from 1980); oil: inter-area movements; oil: imports and exports; gas: proved reserves—bcm (from 1980); gas: production—bcm (from 1970); gas: production—bcf (from 1970); gas: production—Mtoe (from 1970); gas: consumption—bcm (from 1965); gas: consumption—bcf (from 1965); gas: consumption—Mtoe (from 1965); gas: trade movements pipeline; gas: trade movements LNG; gas: prices; coal: reserves; coal: production—tonnes

(from 1981); coal: production—Mtoe (from 1981); coal: consumption—Mtoe (from 1965); coal: prices; nuclear energy: consumption—TWh (from 1965); nuclear energy: consumption—Mtoe (from 1965); hydroelectricity: consumption—TWh (from 1965); hydroelectricity: consumption—Mtoe (from 1965); primary energy: consumption—Mtoe (from 1965); primary energy: consumption by fuel type—Mtoe; electricity generation—TWh (from 1990); and approximate conversion factors.

**1233 Energy information administration
EIA.** http://www.eia.gov/. Energy
Information Administration. Washington:
Energy Information Administration. 2007–
HD9502.U6

The EIA is the statistical agency of the U.S. Department of Energy. The website has energy statistics for petroleum, natural gas, electricity, coal, nuclear energy, and renewable and alternative fuels. Also has detailed international country energy information, forecasts and analyses, state and national historical data, households, buildings and industry, information about environmental issues, and an Energy Kid's Page.

1234 Freedonia focus reports. http://www
.freedoniagroup.com/FocusReports.aspx.
Freedonia Group. Cleveland, Ohio:
Freedonia Group. 2001–
HC106.82

Industry outlook information on a subscription basis. More than 600 reports cover eighteen industry categories: automotive, chemicals, construction, consumer goods, electronics, energy, food and agriculture (including tobacco), industrial components, life sciences (both medical and pharmaceutical), machinery, metals and minerals, miscellaneous and service industries, packaging, paper and printing (including publishing), plastics, rubber, textiles and leather (including apparel), and wood (including furniture and fixtures). Provides market size, historical demand, forecasts of demand, and profiles of leading companies. Browsable by major regions: Australia, Brazil, Canada, China, France, Germany, India, Italy, Japan, Mexico, Russia, South Korea, Spain, the U.K., and the U.S.

1235 IBISWorld United States. http://www
.ibisworld.com/. IBISWorld. New York:
IBISWorld. 1999–
HC103

700 reports on American industries. Industry reports can be located using NAICS numbers. Major categories include: Accommodation & Food Services; Administration, Business Support & Waste Management Services; Agriculture, Forestry, Fishing & Hunting; Arts, Entertainment & Recreation; Construction; Educational Services; Finance & Insurance; Healthcare & Social Assistance; Information; Manufacturing; Mining; Other Services (except Public Administration); Professional, Scientific & Technical Services; Real Estate & Rental and Leasing; Retail Trade; Transportation & Warehousing; Utilities; and Wholesale Trade.

Reports include industry definition; information about the supply chain; key statistics; segmentations (products and services segmentation, major market segments, industry concentration, geographic spread); market characteristics (market size, demand determinants, domestic and international markets, basis of competition, life cycle); industry conditions (barriers to entry, taxation, industry assistance, regulation and deregulation, cost structure, capital and labor intensity, technology and systems, industry volatility, globalization); key factors (sensitivities and success factors); key competitors; and industry performance (current and historical). Glossaries and guides to jargon. Setting this database apart are reports on small industries, such as parking lots and garages.

1236 Plunkett's energy industry almanac.
Jack W. Plunkett. Houston, Tex.: Plunkett Research, 1999–. ill. ISSN 1542-5061
338   HD9502.U5
Annual. Data on nearly 500 leading companies, both public and private. Company profiles include types of business, brands and affiliates, contacts, employee benefits and top salaries, sales and profit numbers, growth plans, and competitive advantage. Especially useful for the industry background (definition of the industry, deregulation, technology's impact on the industry), trends, statistics and rankings at the front of the volume (U.S. energy imports and exports: selected years since 1950, U.S. energy consumption and expenditures indicators: selected years since 1950, Renewable energy consumption in the transportation and electric power sectors: since 2000, U.S. energy production, Total and by renewable energy power sources: since 1950), and information on the main associations and organizations

in the back of the volume. Figures in the 2013 edition are current to 2011. Most information is for the U.S., but some international coverage is provided. Available as an e-book. Since 2004, complemented by *Plunkett's renewable, alternative & hydrogen energy industry almanac*.

1237 Standard and Poor's industry surveys.
Standard and Poor's. New York: Standard and Poor's, 1973–2012 ISSN 0196-4666
332.67   HC106.6
Detailed analyses of 22 industry categories and the major companies in each category. Contains a basic analysis and a comprehensive source of information, updated by a current analysis. The analysis includes trends, information on how the industry operates, key ratios and statistics (revenues, net income, profit ratios, balance sheet ratios, equity ratios, per-share data, company and product rankings), information on how to analyze a company in that industry, and a glossary. Company and industry indexes. Ceased with edition of 2012.

Organizations and Associations

1238 Edison electric institute. http://www.eei.org/. Edison Electric Institute. Washington: Edison Electric Institute. 2003–
HD9685.U5
Home page for institute representing shareholder-owned electric companies. Its website has industry information (electricity policy, energy infrastructure, environmental issues, retail services and delivery, reliability issues, and accounting issues), industry overview and statistics, meetings, news, and their magazine *ElectricPerspectives*.

Additional Reference Sources

1239 Hoovers. http://www.hoovers.com/. Reference Press, Hoover's, Inc. Short Hills, N.J.: Dun & Bradstreet. 1996–
338.7   HG4057
More than 60 million records describe public and private companies primarily in the United States, but including Canada, United Kingdom, Europe, and Asia/Pacific. Profiles have an overview, history,

family tree, industry information, products/operations, top competitors, competitive landscape, top executives with biographies, news, significant developments, and financial data. Financial summaries may include an income statement; balance sheet; cash flow; historical financials such as five years of P/E and per share; stock quotes; interactive stock charts; market data; earnings estimates; this year's ratios for the company, industry, and market; SEC filings; and industry watch for trends.

Content is tracked for 900 industries, organized into numerous larger categories: Agriculture & Forestry; Arts, Entertainment & Recreation; Beverage Manufacturing; Biotechnology Product Manufacturing; Business Services; Chemical Manufacturing; Commercial Equipment Repair & Maintenance; Commercial Printing; Computer Hardware Manufacturing; Computer Software; Construction; Consumer Products Manufacturing; Consumer Services; Contract Electronics Manufacturing; Education; Electric Power Generation; Electric Power Transmission, Distribution & Marketing; Electric Utilities; Electrical Products Manufacturing; Fabricated Metal Product Manufacturing; Financial Services; Food Manufacturing; Government; Health Care Products Manufacturing; Health Care; HVAC Equipment Manufacturing; Industrial Manufacturing; Insurance; Leasing of Intangible Assets; Lodging; Machinery Manufacturing; Magnetic & Optical Media; Manufacturing & Reproduction; Managed Application & Network Services; Management of Companies & Enterprises; Media; Membership Organizations; Mining; Miscellaneous Manufacturing; Natural Gas Distribution & Marketing; Nonclassifiable establishments; Nonmetallic Mineral Product Manufacturing; Nonprofit Institutions; Oil & Gas Exploration & Production; Oil & Gas Field Services; Oil & Gas Well Drilling; Petroleum & Coal Products Manufacturing; Pharmaceutical Manufacturing; Primary Metals Manufacturing; Private Households; Professional Services; Real Estate; Religious Organizations; Rental & Leasing; Restaurants, Bars & Food Services; Retail; Security Products Manufacturing; Semiconductor & Other Electronic Component Manufacturing; Telecommunications Equipment Manufacturing; Telecommunications Services; Transportation Equipment Manufacturing; Transportation Services; Water & Sewer Utilities; Wholesale; and Wood Product Manufacturing.

Coverage can be brief, but generally includes a fact sheet, overview, selected companies, industry watch with video interviews, news from the last 90 days, and web resources for terminology, associations, and organizations, and online publications. Hoover's print publications include (*Hoover's handbook of American business* (876), *Hoover's handbook of private companies* (855)).

1240 Macmillan encyclopedia of energy.
John Zumerchik. New York: Macmillan Reference USA, 2001. 3 v., ill.
ISBN 0028650212
621.04203   TJ163.28.M33
Three-volume set contains 253 alphabetically arranged entries. Includes more than 600 photographs, illustrations, sidebars, and maps. Interdisciplinary approach includes all aspects of energy consumption. Alternative energy sources addressed in depth. Entries include cross-references and bibliographies. Appropriate for high-school students and up. Vol. 1 includes list of articles, list of contributors, and list of commonly used abbreviations and mathematical symbols. Vol. 3 includes "Energy timeline" and index.

Occupations and Careers

Guides and Handbooks

1241 The almanac of American employers: market research, statistics and trends pertaining to the leading corporate employers in America. Jack W. Plunkett. Houston, Tex.: Plunkett Research, 1985–
ISSN 1088-3150
338.7/4/02573   HF5382.75.U6
A comprehensive guide to the labor market in the U.S., with profiles of more than 500 major companies, both private and public. Unique features include information on companies most likely to hire women and minorities, company hiring patterns (will hire MBA's, engineers, liberal arts majors, etc.), and company profiles that give textual information including corporate culture and plans for growth. Historical and projected statistics are updated in each edition, and include a U.S. Employment Overview; Total Employees, All Nonfarm Payrolls, Private Industry & Government; U.S. Civilian Labor Force; Number of People Employed and Unemployed, U.S.; Unemployed Jobseekers by Sex, Reason for Unemployment & Active Job Search Methods Used; U.S. Labor Force Ages 16 to 24 Years Old by School Enrollment, Educational Attainment, Sex, Race & Ethnicity; Medical Care Benefits in the U.S.: Access, Participation and Take-Up Rates; Retirement Benefits in the U.S.: Access, Participation and Take-Up Rates; Top 30 U.S. Occupations by Numerical Change in Job Growth; Top 30 U.S. Occupations by Percent Change in Job Growth; Occupations with the Largest Expected Employment Increases, U.S.; and Occupations with the Fastest Expected Decline. For the top "American Employers 500" list of firms, shows lists by Number of Employees, By Revenues, and By Profits; and organized by Industry List With Codes, Index of Companies Within Industry Groups, Alphabetical Index, Index of U.S. Headquarters Location by State, Index by Regions of the U.S. Where the Firms Have Locations, Index of Firms with International Operations, and Index of Firms Noted as Hot Spots for Advancement for Women & Minorities. Suggests Seven Keys for Job Seekers (Financial Stability, Growth Plan, Research and Development Programs, Product Launch and Production, Marketing and Distribution Methods, Employee Benefits, Quality of Work Factors, Other Considerations).

1242 Best career and education Web sites: a quick guide to online job search.
5th ed. Anne Wolfinger, Rachel Singer Gordon. Indianapolis, Ind.: JIST Works, 2007. viii, 198 p., ill. ISBN 159357312X
025.06331702   HF5382.75.U6W65
Contains 340 annotated entries for web sites on mentoring, training, certification, and job searching. Includes professional associations and megasites, as well as sites for jobs within specific states. Available as an e-book.

1243 Career information center. MacMillan Reference. Farmington Hills, Mich.: Gale, 1979–. 16 v., ill. ISSN 1082-703X

331.7   HF5382.5.U5

Career options in agribusiness, environment & natural resources; communications & the arts; computers, business & office; construction; consumer, homemaking & personal services; engineering, science & technology; health; hospitality & recreation; manufacturing; marketing & distribution; public & community services; and transportation. Includes an overview of employment trends. Over 700 job profiles, each with a job summary chart, a job description, and salary information. Index. The 10th ed. appeared in 2014. Available as an e-book.

1244 Encyclopedia of careers and vocational guidance. 15th ed. Ferguson Publ. New York: Ferguson Publ., 2011. 5 v., ill. ISBN 9780816083138

331.702   HF5381

Overviews careers, with advice on preparing for and searching for a position. Describes educational and training requirements, duties, salaries, and prospects. Each volume contains a complete index of the job titles. Vol. 1 (Career guidance and career field profiles) describes 90 industries, their historical backgrounds, employment statistics, products, structure, and career patterns and outlooks. Vols. 2–5 discuss some 750 careers in 14 broad categories (e.g., professional, clerical, machine trades). Appendixes list organizations that assist in training and job placement for disabled and other special groups and provide information on internships, apprenticeships, and training programs. The 16th ed. has been announced for 2014 publication.

1245 Ferguson's career guidance center. http://www.infobasepublishing.com/Bookdetail.aspx?ISBN=0816043809&Ebooks=0. J.G. Ferguson Publishing Company (Firm). New York: Facts on File, Inc.; Infobase Learning. 2003–

HF5382.5.U5

Searchable resource for job seekers and those making educational choices on the basis of career planning. Covers 94 industries and 3,400 job profiles. Information on job hunting skills. Both text and video formats. Includes a database of scholarship and internship opportunities.

1246 GMAT: strategies, practice, and review. Kaplan Test Prep and Admissions. New York: Kaplan Publ., 2010–. ill.

650./076   HF1118

Practice tests and questions for preparation to take the Graduate Management Admissions Test of skills such as critical reasoning, reading comprehension, mathematics, problem-solving, and analytical writing. Advice, strategies and explanations for test-taking and the graduate business school admissions process. One of many competing guides.

1247 Job choices for business and liberal arts students. National Association of Colleges and Employers. Bethlehem, Pa.: National Association of Colleges and Employers, 2003–2012. ill. ISSN 0069-5734

331.7   HF5382.5.U5

Lists employers, with information on desired qualifications and benefits offered, and contact information. Also has articles on resume writing, interviewing, and networking. Other similar titles from this publisher are *Job Choices for Science, Engineering, and Technology Students* and *Job Choices: Diversity Edition*. Ceased with edition of 2012.

1248 Jobs and careers abroad. Deborah Penrith. Oxford, U.K.: Vacation Work Publications, 1971–. ill. ISSN 0143-3482

331.12/5   HF5549.5.E45

Information on finding international jobs. Contains chapters on finding jobs, rules and regulations for working abroad, learning the language, chapters on specific careers, and a section on employment in different regions (Western Europe, Eastern and Central Europe, the Americas, Australasia, Asia, Middle East and North Africa, and Africa). Formerly called *Directory of jobs and careers abroad*. Appendixes for further reading, worldwide living standards, and company classifications. The same company publishes related titles such as *Live & work in Germany* or *Live & work in Japan*.

1249 Occupational outlook handbook. http://www.bls.gov/ooh/. United States Bureau of Labor Statistics. Washington: U.S. Department of Labor. 1998–

331   HD8051

Biennial official government estimate of trends and potential employment in 800 occupations. Browsable by major Occupation Groups (such as Healthcare or Media & Communication), by rate of pay, by projected rate of job growth, by projected absolute number of new jobs, or alphabetically. Searchable by rate of pay, level of required education, and anticipated numbers of new openings. Entries for each occupation indicate median pay, required education or credentials, number of jobs nationally, and anticipated growth. Launched in print in 1949, and available on the Web since 1998. Reprints (932) are sold by private publishers as well.

1250 Occupational outlook handbook.
JIST Works, Inc. Indianapolis, Ind.: JIST Works, 1987–. ill. ISSN 0082-9072
331   HF5381.U62
Reprint of the original U.S. government publication: current information is freely available online (629). Gives information on employment trends and outlook in more than 800 occupations. Indicates nature of work, qualifications, earnings and working conditions, entry level jobs, information on the job market in each state, where to go for more information, etc. The similar *Career guide to industries* ceased in 2012.

1251 The official guide for GMAT review.
Graduate Management Admission Council (GMAC), Educational Testing Service (ETS). Princeton, N.J.; Hoboken, N.J.: ETS; Wiley Pub., 1986–. ill.
650/.076   HF1118
Tips for applying to graduate business schools, and sample questions for study in advance of taking the Graduate Management Admission Test. One of several similar titles, such as *Barron's GMAT*; there are also many test preparation products in electronic formats.

1252 What color is your parachute?. Richard Nelson Bolles. Berkeley, Calif.: Ten Speed Press, 1971–. ill. ISSN 8755-4658
650.1405   HF5382.7
Perhaps the best-known guide to discovering the career that is right for you, with tips on finding a job and on interviewing. Updated annually to reflect current trends and conditions. There are additional versions for teens and retired persons. Supplemented by a web site at http://www.jobhuntersbible.com/ with information about job search web sites, the use

of social media for job leads, online career aptitude tests, salary information sources, and links to sample resumes.

Directories

1253 The best . . . business schools.
Princeton Review (Firm). New York: Random House, 2004– ISSN 2168-9334
650/.071/173   HF1131
For each school, a two-page entry provides address, URL, telephone number, tuition figures, admissions criteria, and deadlines. Indicates areas of specialization, student body profile, and recent job placement information. Includes survey results from students. Essays on the application process and costs. Title varies slightly with number of recommended schools, for example, *The Best 295 Business Schools (2014 Edition)*. Indexes by name, location, cost, and MBA concentration.

1254 The Directory of executive recruiters.
Kennedy & Kennedy (Firm). Fitzwilliam, N.H.: Kennedy Information, 1971–2008 ISSN 0090-6484
658.3111   HF5549.5.R44
Lists over 16,000 recruiters, with contact information, summary of the firm's specialty, key contacts, salary minimum, and targeted functions and industries. Indexed by function, industry, and specialty. Ceased with edition of 2008.

1255 Job hunter's sourcebook: where to find employment leads and other job search resources. Gale Research Inc., Detroit Public Library. Detroit: Gale Cengage, 1991– ISSN 1053-1874
331.128097305   HF5382.75.U6
Guide to sources useful for more than 200 occupations. Organized into two parts: Pt. 1, Sources of job-hunting information by professions and occupations; pt. 2, Sources of essential job-hunting information. Sources include help-wanted ads in various periodicals (including trade and professional journals, as well as sources like *National Business Employment Weekly*), placement and referral services, employer directories and networking lists, handbooks and manuals, employment agencies, web sites, and trade shows. Now annual: 13th ed. appeared in 2013.

1256 The National job bank. B. Adams
(Firm). Brighton, Mass.: B. Adams, 1983–
ISSN 1051-4872
331.12802573   HF5382.5.U5
Arranged by state; within state listings, public and
private firms are listed by industry. Entries give directory information, contact persons, and brief business
descriptions. Entries may indicate typical job classifications, projected hiring activity, and training
programs. Regional directories that follow the same
format are also available.

**1257 Peterson's graduate programs
in business, education, health,
information studies, law and social
work.** Peterson's (Firm). Princeton, N.J.:
Peterson's, 1997–2012. ill.
ISSN 1088-9442
378.15530257   L901
The standard guide to graduate schools, with information on programs offered; degree requirements;
number and gender of faculty; number, gender, and
ethnicity of students; average student age; percentage of students accepted; entrance requirements;
application deadlines; application fee; costs; and
financial aid. Ceased in print format with 2012, but
similar content is available online at http://www
.petersons.com/graduate-schools.aspx.

1258 Riley guide. http://www.rileyguide.com/.
Margaret F. Dikel. [Rockville, Md.]:
[Margaret F. Dikel]. 1998–
Links to various websites with information on
how to job search; before you search; where to
search; resumes and cover letters; research and target employers and locations; network, interview,
and negotiate; and salary guides and guidance. It
includes an A–Z index and an area for recruiters and
employers. Most of the sites listed are free, but fee-
based resources are also included.

**1259 The Wall Street Journal guide to
the top business schools.** Wall Street
Journal, Harris Interactive (Firm). New
York: Simon and Schuster, 2003–
ISSN 1544-2977
650   HF1101
Annual. Ranks business schools using recruiter surveys. Lists include top-ranked national, regional,
and international programs, top schools for major

industries, by academic discipline, for recruiting
women, for recruiting minorities, and for recruiting
MBAs with high ethical standards. Detailed profiles
of full-time programs are included, with the school's
ranking, admissions process, test scores, the industries and companies most likely to hire graduates,
and expected first-year salaries.

Statistics

**1260 American salaries and wages survey:
statistical data derived from more
than 410 government, business and
news sources.** Gale Research Inc. Detroit:
Gale Research, 1991– ISSN 1055-7628
331.2973021   HD4973.A67
Data on some 4,000 occupations, with information
on salaries by state and major metropolitan area.
Gives a low, mid, and high wage offered. Useful for
salary negotiations.

1261 National compensation survey. http://
www.bls.gov/ncs/home.htm. U.S. Dept.
of Labor, Bureau of Labor Statistics.
Washington: Bureau of Labor Statistics.
1998–
                          HD4976.A735N38
Summarizes wages, earnings, and hours for cities,
regions, and the nation. "Wage data are shown by
industry, occupational group, full-time and part-
time status, union and nonunion status, establishment size, time and incentive status, and job
level." —*Summary.* Also includes benefits and
the Employment Cost Index, which is released
quarterly.

Internet Resources

1262 Aboutjobs.com. http://www.aboutjobs
.com/. AboutJobs.com, Inc. [Sagamore
Beach, Mass.]: AboutJobs.com, Inc. 1996–
331.124   HF5382.7
Allows employers and jobseekers to share and
review information online. Searchable by place
and employer. Links to related web sites such as
InternJobs.com, OverseasJobs.com, ResortJobs.com,
and SummerJobs.com. Sections for career and job-
hunting advice.

1263 CareerBuilder.com: jobs and job search advice, employment and careers. http://www.careerbuilder.com/. CareerBuilder (Firm). Chicago: CareerBuilder, LLC. 1995–
331.124   HD5710.5

Allows employers and job seekers to post and review job ads and resumes. Job postings can be searched by keyword, place, industry, category, full- or part-time, education level, and salary range. Salary calculator shows typical rates of pay by place. Advice on job seeking, resumes and cover letters, interviews, and career strategy.

1264 CareerOneStop: pathways to career success. http://www.careeronestop.org/. United States. Department of Labor. Employment and Training Administration. Washington: U.S. Dept. of Labor. 2002–
331.25   HF5382.7

U.S. government-sponsored resource portal with advice for students, veterans and other job-seekers. Includes career exploration tools, comparative salary information by job category and location, information about training programs, a searchable job bank, advice about resumes/cover letters and interviews, and a service locator to identify agencies and career centers by place.

1265 Indeed.com job search: one search, all jobs. http://www.indeed.com/. Indeed.com (Firm). Austin, Tex.; Stamford, Conn.: Indeed.com. 2004–
331.124   HF5382.7

Currently the online job search site with the most heavy traffic. Like competitor *SimplyHired*, Indeed aggregates job listings from other sources. Job seekers and employers can post and search job postings and resumes. Covers some 50 companies with content in 28 languages. A salary search feature tracks recent figures by job title and location. Reports on trends compare keywords in job ads, hiring in the largest 50 U.S. metropolitan areas, ratios of jobs versus job seekers by place, and monthly, quarterly and annual changes within 13 industries. A list of best places to work, based on user reviews, can be sorted by place.

1266 Internships.com: educators, help students find internships. http://www.internships.com/. Internships.com. Burbank, Calif.: CareerArc Group, LLC. 2010–
331.25   LC1072

Allows students and universities to match with internship positions at companies, non-profits, and government agencies. Listings can be searched by city, employer name, and job category. Covers paid or unpaid, and full- or part-time opportunities. Tips for finding suitable positions and interviewing. Sample resumes and cover letters. An "Internship Predictor" helps students seek the right placements. Advice to companies establishing internship programs.

1267 Monster.com. http://www.monster.com/. Monster (Firm). New York: Monster Worldwide, Inc. 1994–
331.124   HF5382.7

Monster pioneered the idea of web sites for job seeking and hiring. Job seekers and employers can post and browse resumes and job ads. Listings can be searched by place, company name, job type, education level, years of experience, and more. Also offers a resume checklist, interviewing tips, an FAQ for job seekers, sample cover letters, and career advice.

1268 Riley guide. http://www.rileyguide.com/. Margaret F. Dikel. [Rockville, Md.]: [Margaret F. Dikel]. 1998–

Links to various websites with information on how to job search; before you search; where to search; resumes and cover letters; research and target employers and locations; network, interview, and negotiate; and salary guides and guidance. It includes an A–Z index and an area for recruiters and employers. Most of the sites listed are free, but fee-based resources are also included.

1269 Salary.com. http://salary.com/. Salary.com. Wellesley, Mass.: Salary.com. 2000–
                                                HD4961

Useful for the various tools: salary report, college tuition planner, benefits calculator, job listings, cost-of-living wizard, performance self-test, and job assessor.

1270 USAJobs.gov: the federal government's official jobs site. https://www.usajobs.gov/. United States Office of Personnel Management. Washington: United States Office of Personnel Management. 1996–
351.73023   JK692

Official U.S. government website for available federal jobs. Listed positions can be searched by job titles or skills, and by place. Job postings indicate salary range, pay grade, location, application deadline, hiring agency, and eligibility or requirements. It is possible to apply online directly from the site.

1271 Vault: career intelligence. http://www
.vault.com/. Vault (Firm). New York: Vault,
Inc. 1996–
331.124   HF5382.7

Offers job postings, ranked lists of the best firms to work for, ratings of employers, overviews of industries and professions, company profiles, summaries of job qualifications and salaries for specific jobs, and sample resumes and cover letters. Provides some information without charge, with greater resources for subscribers. Formerly VaultReports.com and *Vault online career library*. Also publishes a range of guides about specific careers and the process of job-seeking.

INDEX

Note: Numbers in bold refer to entry numbers. Numbers in roman type refer to mentions in annotations of other works.

O